VWEEEEEN

岸本斉史

I recently bought an air purifier.
My assistants are overjoyed, and
I kinda feel good too.

—*Masashi Kishimoto, 2006*

Author/artist Masashi Kishimoto was born in 1974 in rural
Okayama Prefecture, Japan. After spending time in art college,
he won the Hop Step Award for new manga artists with his
manga **Karakuri** (Mechanism). Kishimoto decided to base his
next story on traditional Japanese culture. His first version of
Naruto, drawn in 1997, was a one-shot story about fox spirits;
his final version, which debuted in **Weekly Shonen Jump** in
1999, quickly became the most popular ninja manga in Japan.

NARUTO VOL. 36
The SHONEN JUMP Manga Edition

STORY AND ART BY MASASHI KISHIMOTO

Translation/Mari Morimoto
English Adaptation/Deric A. Hughes & Benjamin Raab
Touch-up Art & Lettering/Inori Fukuda Trant
Design/Sean Lee
Editor/Joel Enos

Editor in Chief, Books/Alvin Lu
Editor in Chief, Magazines/Marc Weidenbaum
VP, Publishing Licensing/Rika Inouye
VP, Sales & Product Marketing/Gonzalo Ferreyra
VP, Creative/Linda Espinosa
Publisher/Hyoe Narita

Printed in the U.S.A.

Published by VIZ Media, LLC
P.O. Box 77010
San Francisco, CA 94107

SHONEN JUMP Manga Edition
10 9 8 7 6 5 4 3 2 1
First printing, February 2009

www.viz.com

THE WORLD'S
MOST POPULAR MANGA

SHONEN JUMP

www.shonenjump.com

SHONEN JUMP MANGA EDITION

NARUTO

VOL. 36
CELL NUMBER 10

STORY AND ART BY
MASASHI KISHIMOTO

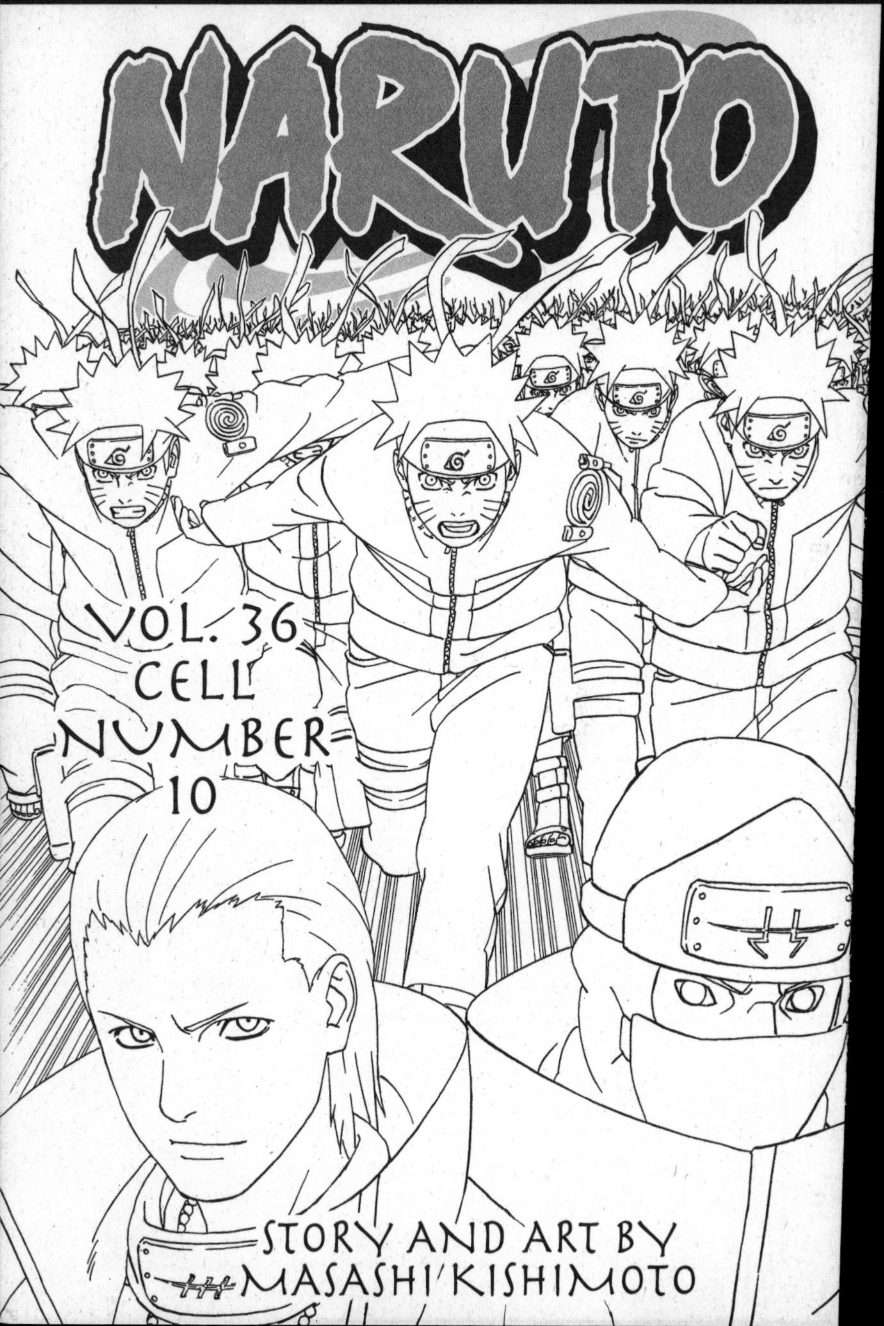

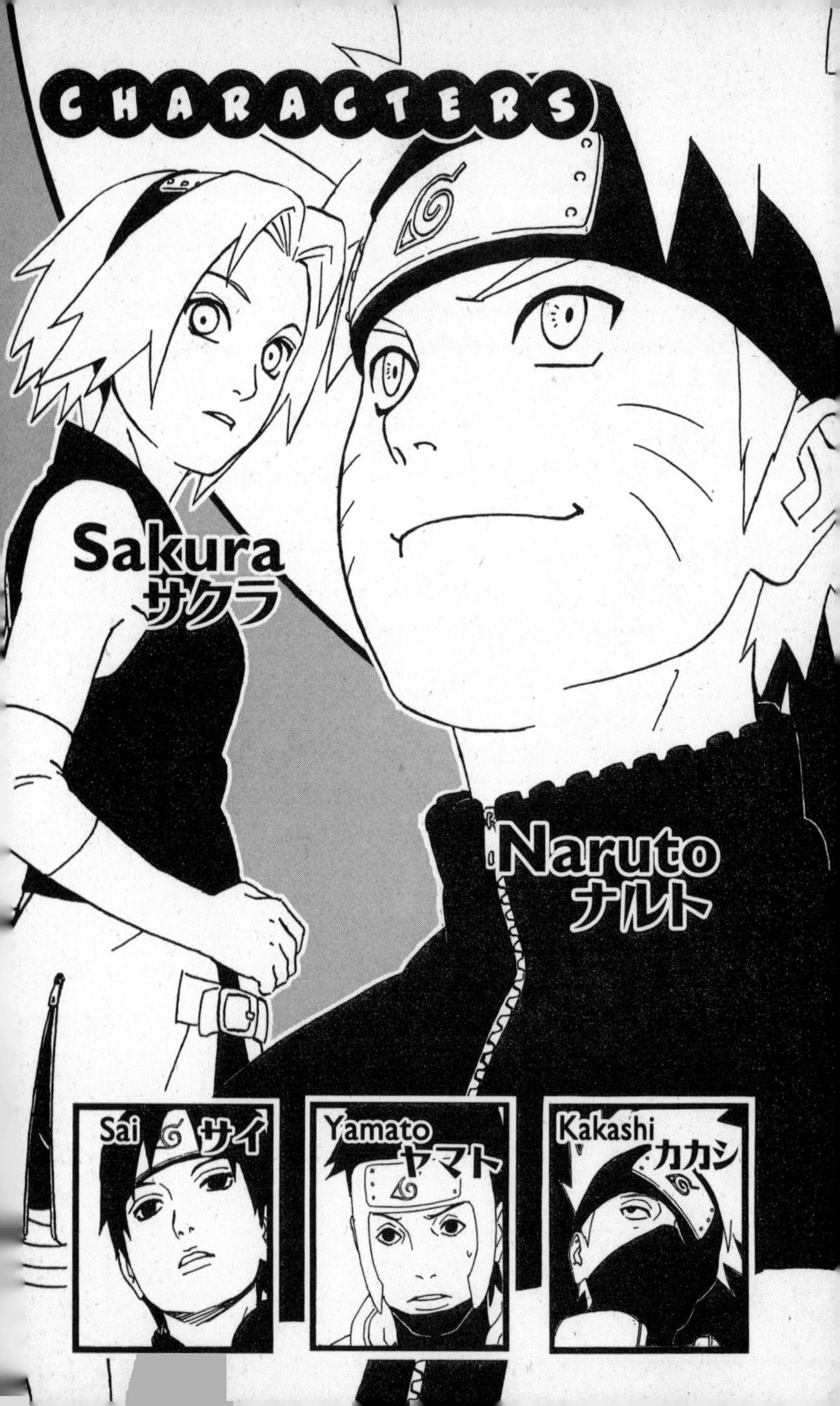
CHARACTERS
Naruto
ナルト
Sakura
サクラ
Kakashi
カカシ
Yamato
ヤマト
Sai
サイ

Hidan 飛段
Sasuke サスケ
Tsunade 綱手
Kakuzu 角都
Asuma アスマ
Shikamaru シカマル

The Story So Far...

Naruto, the biggest troublemaker at the Ninja Academy in Konohagakure, finally becomes a ninja along with his classmates Sasuke and Sakura. During the Chûnin Selection Exams, Orochimaru and his henchmen launch *Operation Destroy Konoha*. Naruto's mentor, the Third Hokage, sacrifices his own life to stop the attack, and Tsunade becomes Fifth Hokage. Lured by Orochimaru's promise of power, Sasuke leaves Konohagakure after defeating Naruto, who fights valiantly to stop his friend...

Two years pass and Naruto and his comrades grow up and track down Sasuke. However, they are left in the dust by Sasuke's immense power, and he escapes once more.

Meanwhile, Hidan and Kakuzu—members of the Akatsuki—seek to fulfill their organization's goal to possess all the jinchûriki hosts by confronting and capturing Yugito, the Two-Tailed Cat Demon. Though their plans for these immensely powerful beasts remain a mystery, it's a threat Konoha can ill afford to take lightly, especially after this deadly duo lays siege to a monastery in the Land of Fire and slaughters all the monks. Among them, Lord Chiriku—formerly of the Guardian Shinobi Twelve—whose body it now falls to Captain Asuma and Cell 10 to locate and retrieve...

NARUTO

VOL. 36
CELL NUMBER 10

CONTENTS

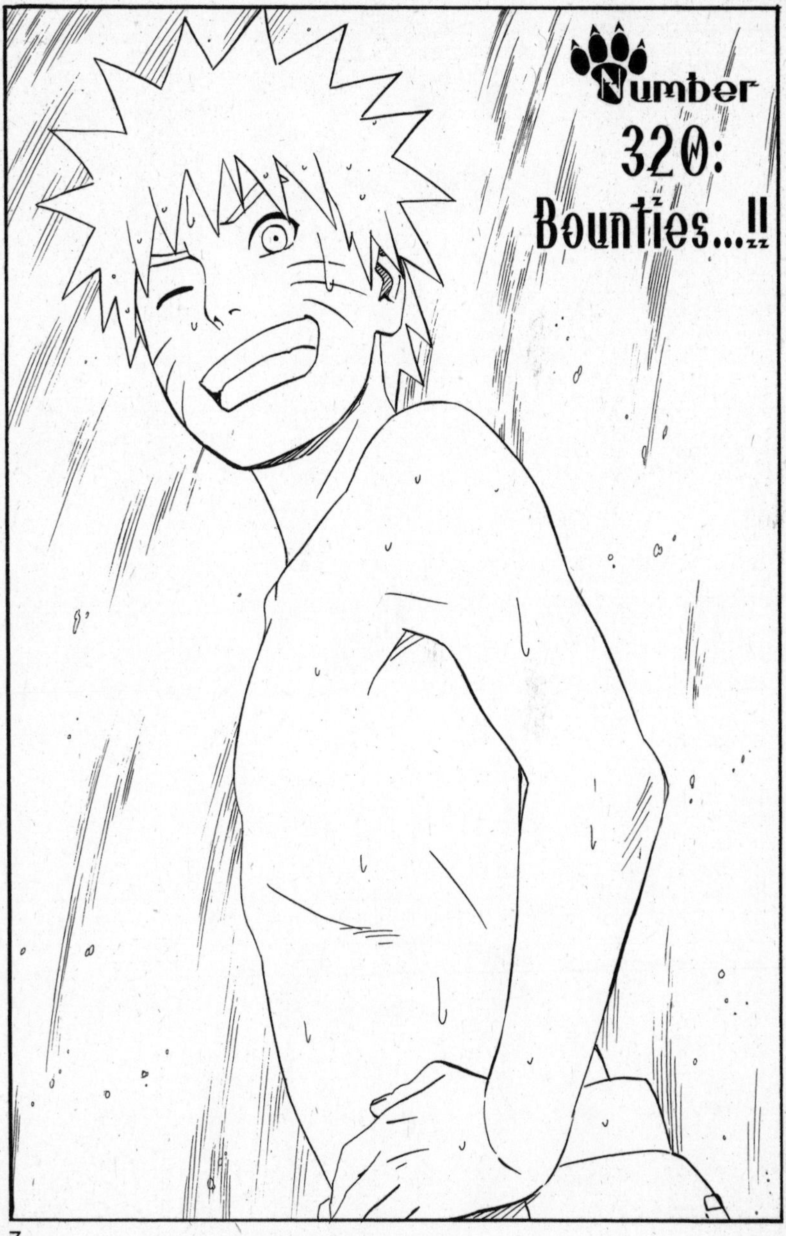
Number
320:
Bounties...!!

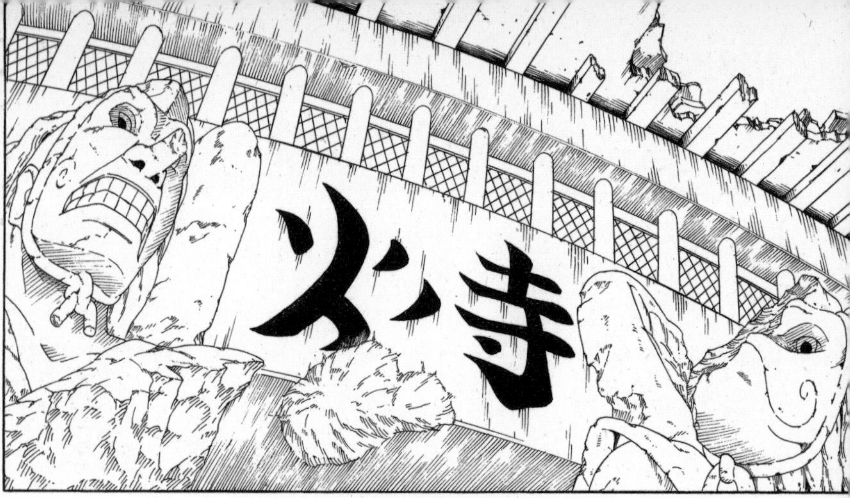
火寺

(FIRE TEMPLE)

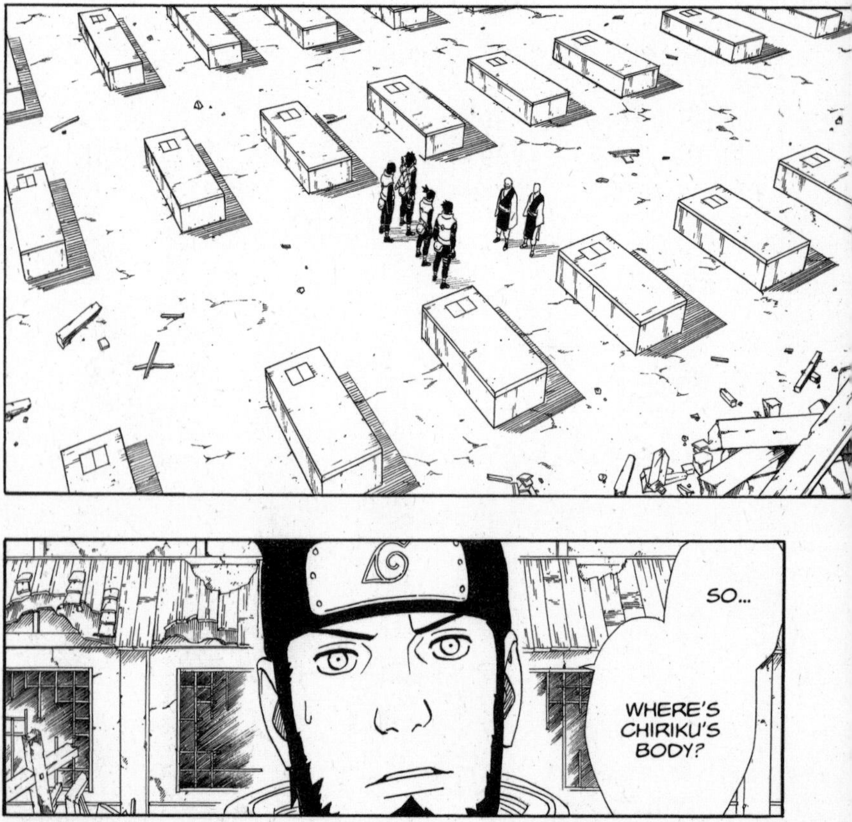
SO...
WHERE'S CHIRIKU'S BODY?

READ THIS WAY

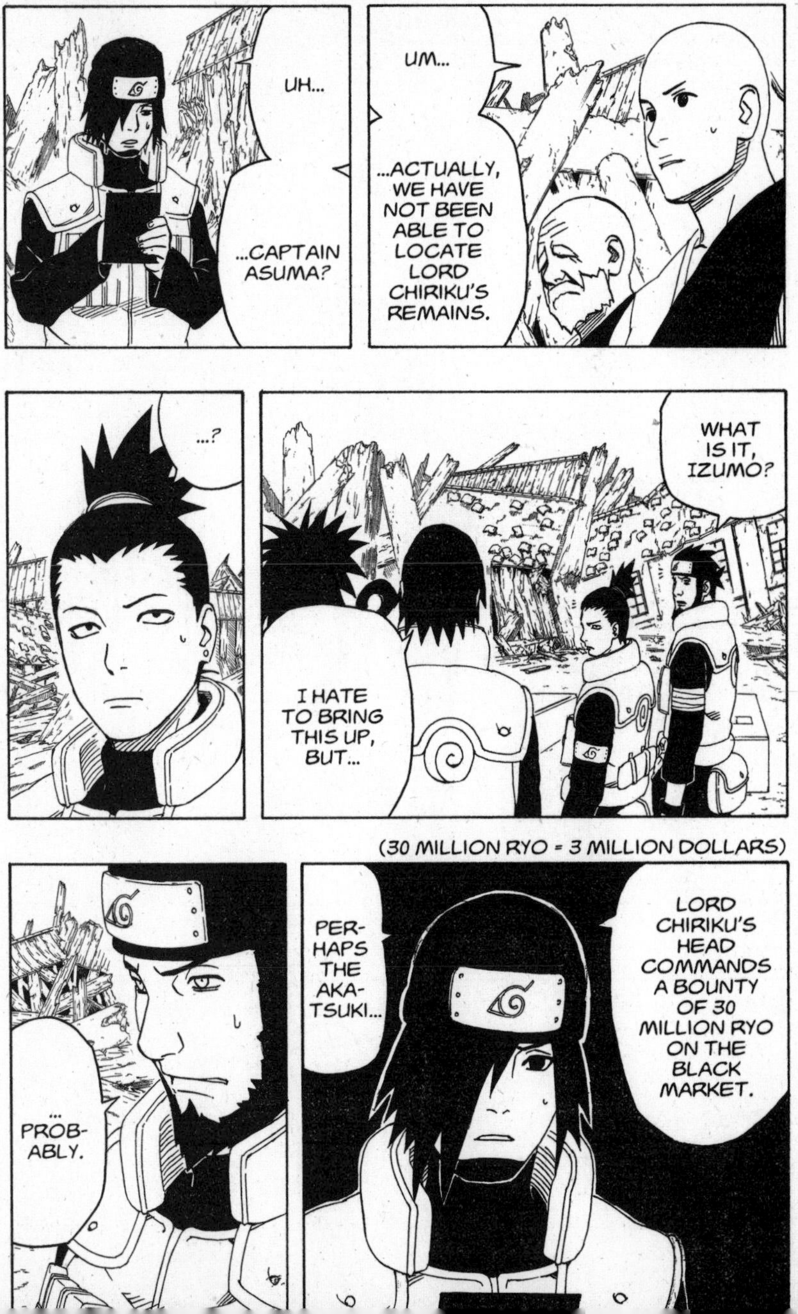
UM...
...ACTUALLY, WE HAVE NOT BEEN ABLE TO LOCATE LORD CHIRIKU'S REMAINS.
UH...
...CAPTAIN ASUMA?
WHAT IS IT, IZUMO?
I HATE TO BRING THIS UP, BUT...
...?
(30 MILLION RYO = 3 MILLION DOLLARS)
LORD CHIRIKU'S HEAD COMMANDS A BOUNTY OF 30 MILLION RYO ON THE BLACK MARKET.
PER-HAPS THE AKA-TSUKI...
... PROB-ABLY.

COLLEC-
TION
OFFICE,
HUH...

...WHICH
MEANS THE
ENEMY IS
LUGGING
AROUND A
BODY,
RIGHT?

FLIP
FLIP

IZUMO...
WHERE'S
THAT
COLLEC-
TION
OFFICE?

...

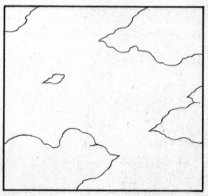

WHICH
ONE?
THERE
ARE FIVE
IN THIS
VICINITY
ALONE.

READ THIS WAY

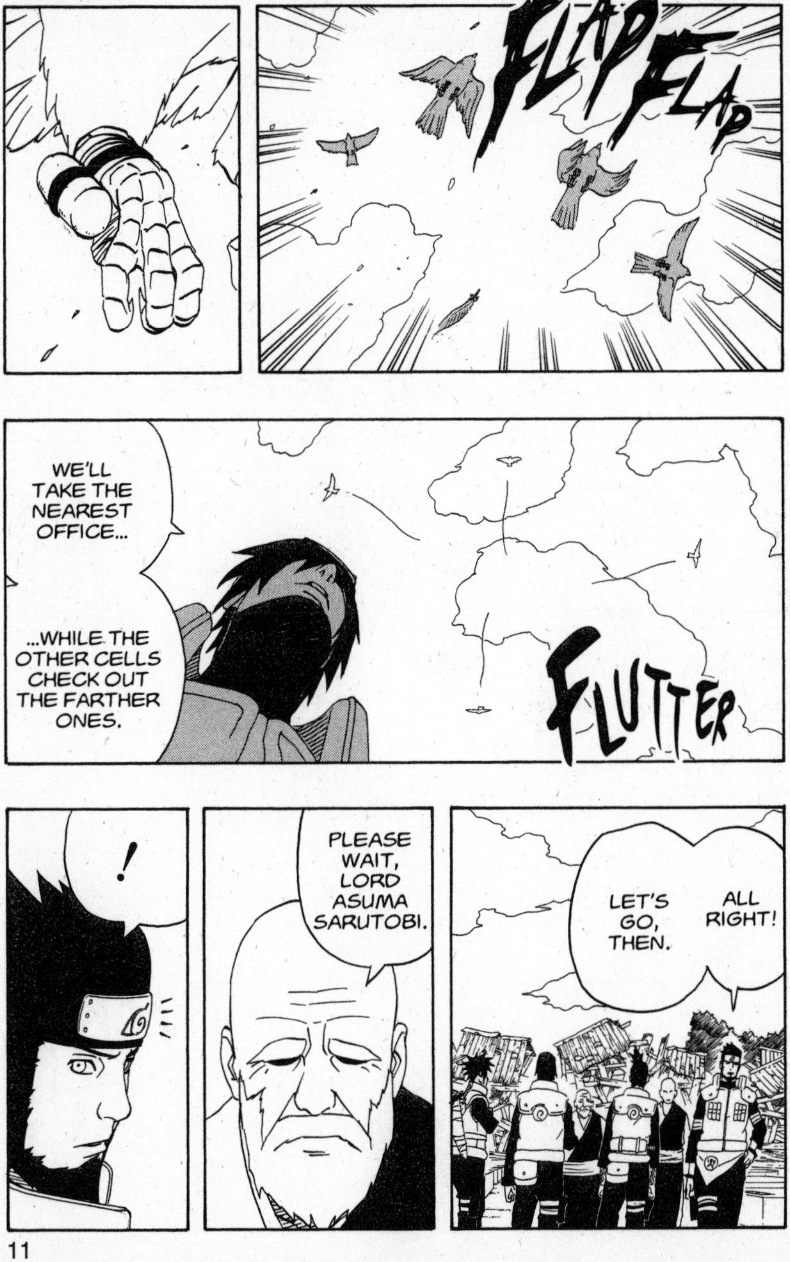
FLAP FLAP
WE'LL TAKE THE NEAREST OFFICE...
...WHILE THE OTHER CELLS CHECK OUT THE FARTHER ONES.
FLUTTER
LET'S GO, THEN.
ALL RIGHT!
PLEASE WAIT, LORD ASUMA SARUTOBI.
!

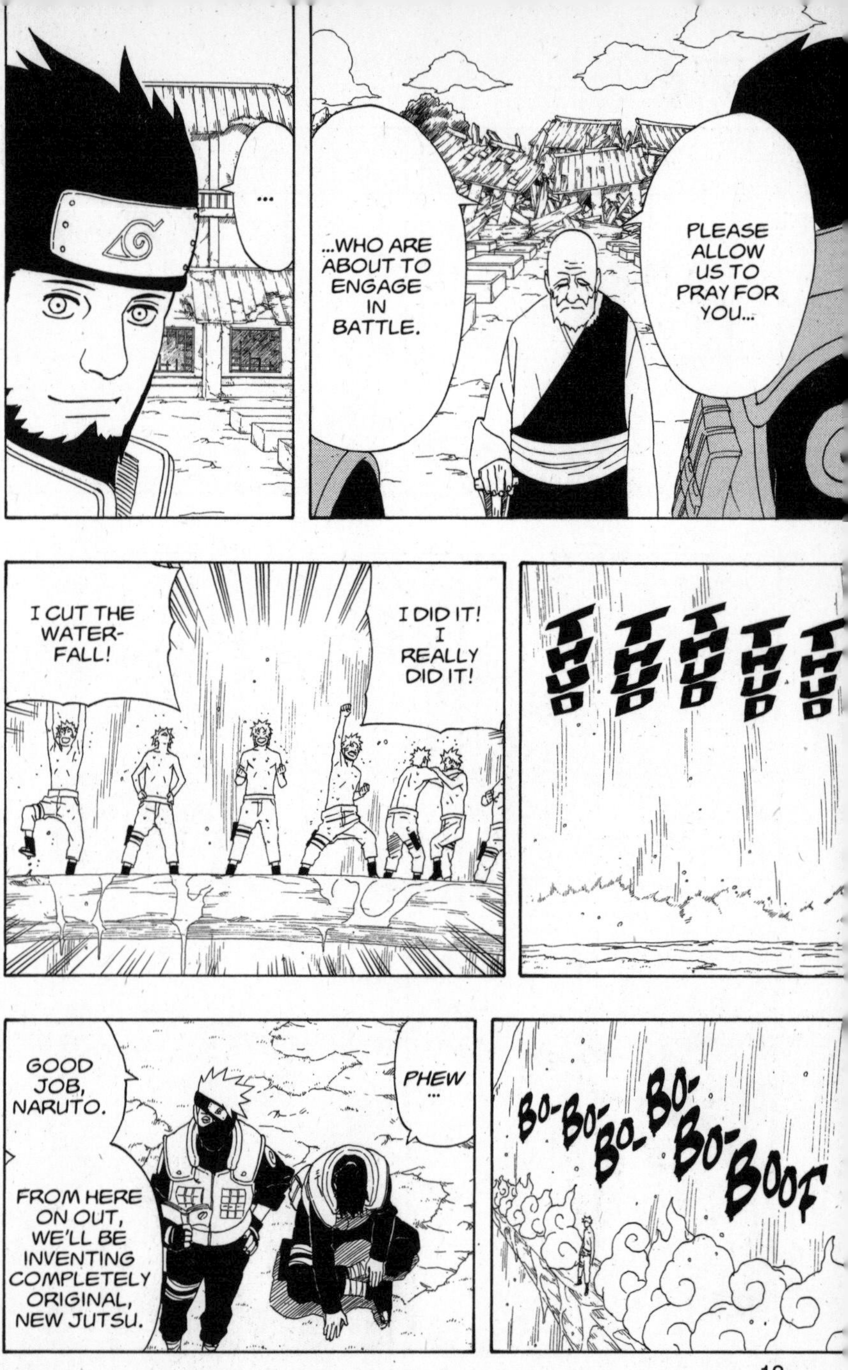
PLEASE ALLOW US TO PRAY FOR YOU...
...WHO ARE ABOUT TO ENGAGE IN BATTLE.
...
THUD THUD THUD THUD THUD
I DID IT! I REALLY DID IT!
I CUT THE WATER-FALL!
BO-BO-BO-BO-BO-BOOF
PHEW...
GOOD JOB, NARUTO.
FROM HERE ON OUT, WE'LL BE INVENTING COMPLETELY ORIGINAL, NEW JUTSU.

READ THIS WAY

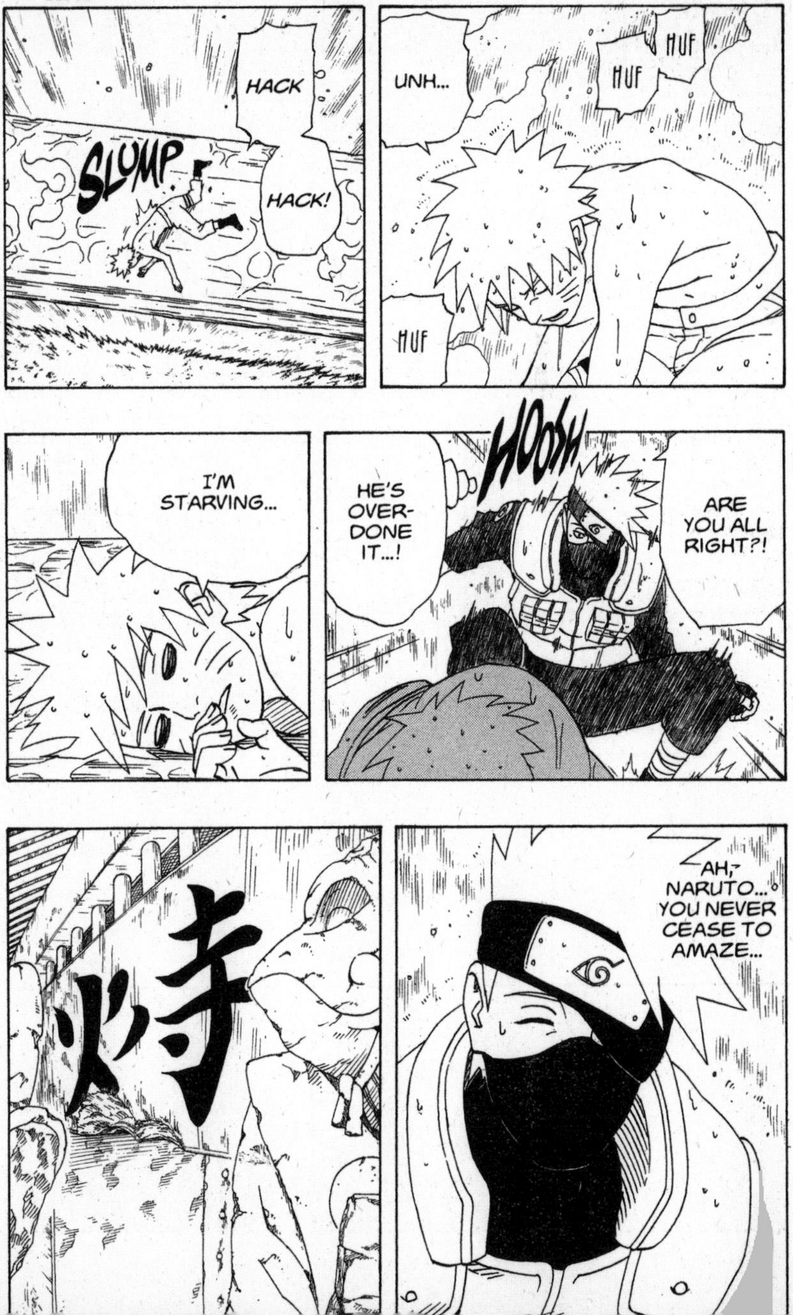

HUF
HUF
UNH...
HUF
HACK
HACK!
SLUMP
HOOSH
ARE YOU ALL RIGHT?!
HE'S OVER-DONE IT...!
I'M STARVING...
AH, NARUTO... YOU NEVER CEASE TO AMAZE...

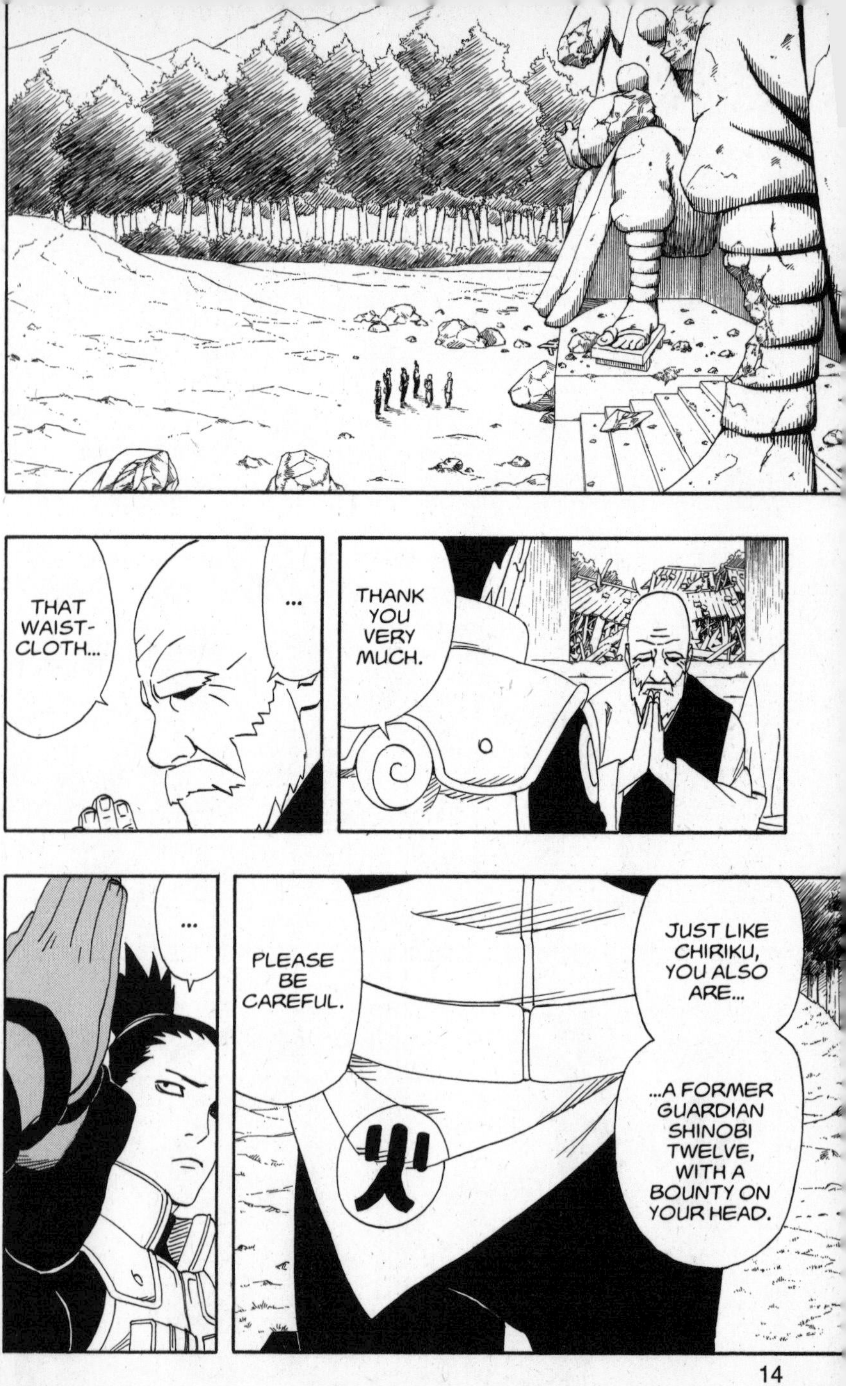
THANK YOU VERY MUCH.
...
THAT WAIST-CLOTH...
JUST LIKE CHIRIKU, YOU ALSO ARE...
...A FORMER GUARDIAN SHINOBI TWELVE, WITH A BOUNTY ON YOUR HEAD.
PLEASE BE CAREFUL.
...

READ THIS WAY

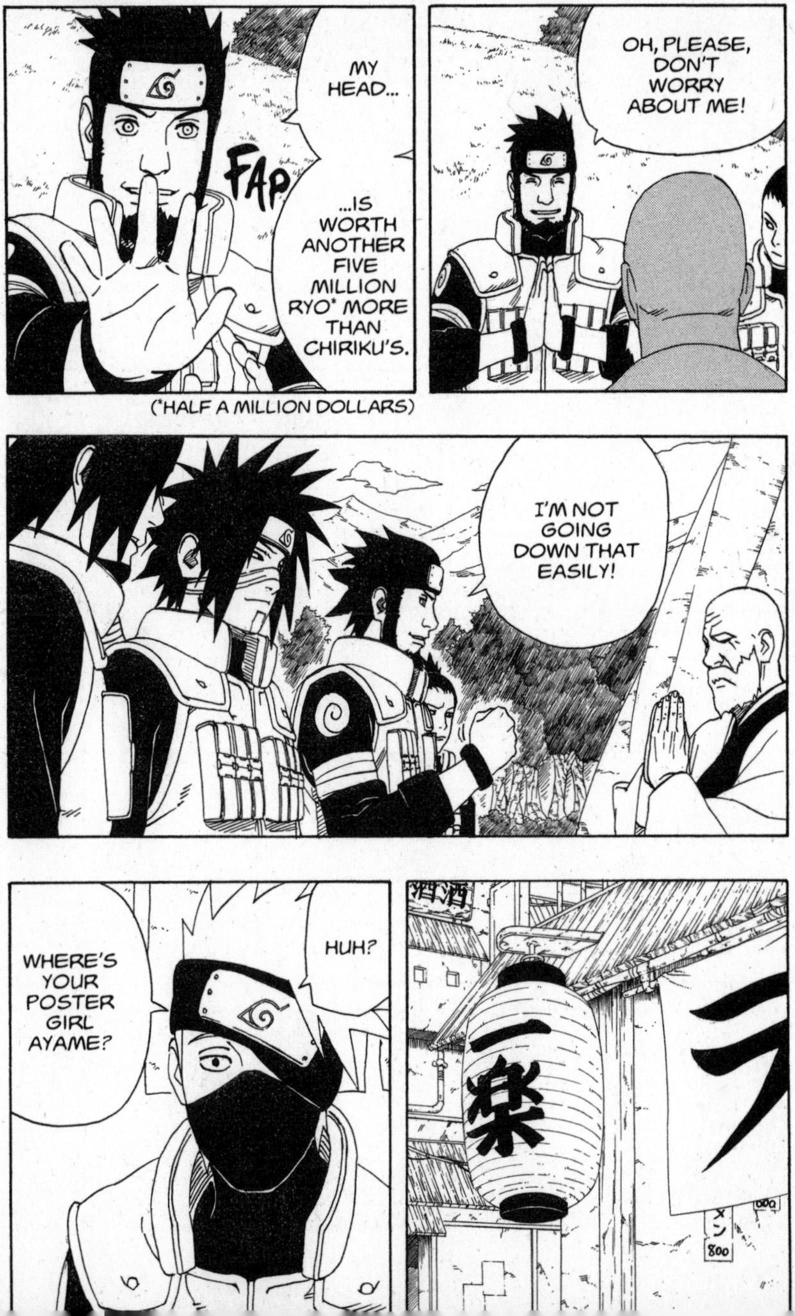
OH, PLEASE, DON'T WORRY ABOUT ME!
MY HEAD...
FAP
...IS WORTH ANOTHER FIVE MILLION RYO* MORE THAN CHIRIKU'S.
(*HALF A MILLION DOLLARS)
I'M NOT GOING DOWN THAT EASILY!
一楽
800
HUH?
WHERE'S YOUR POSTER GIRL AYAME?

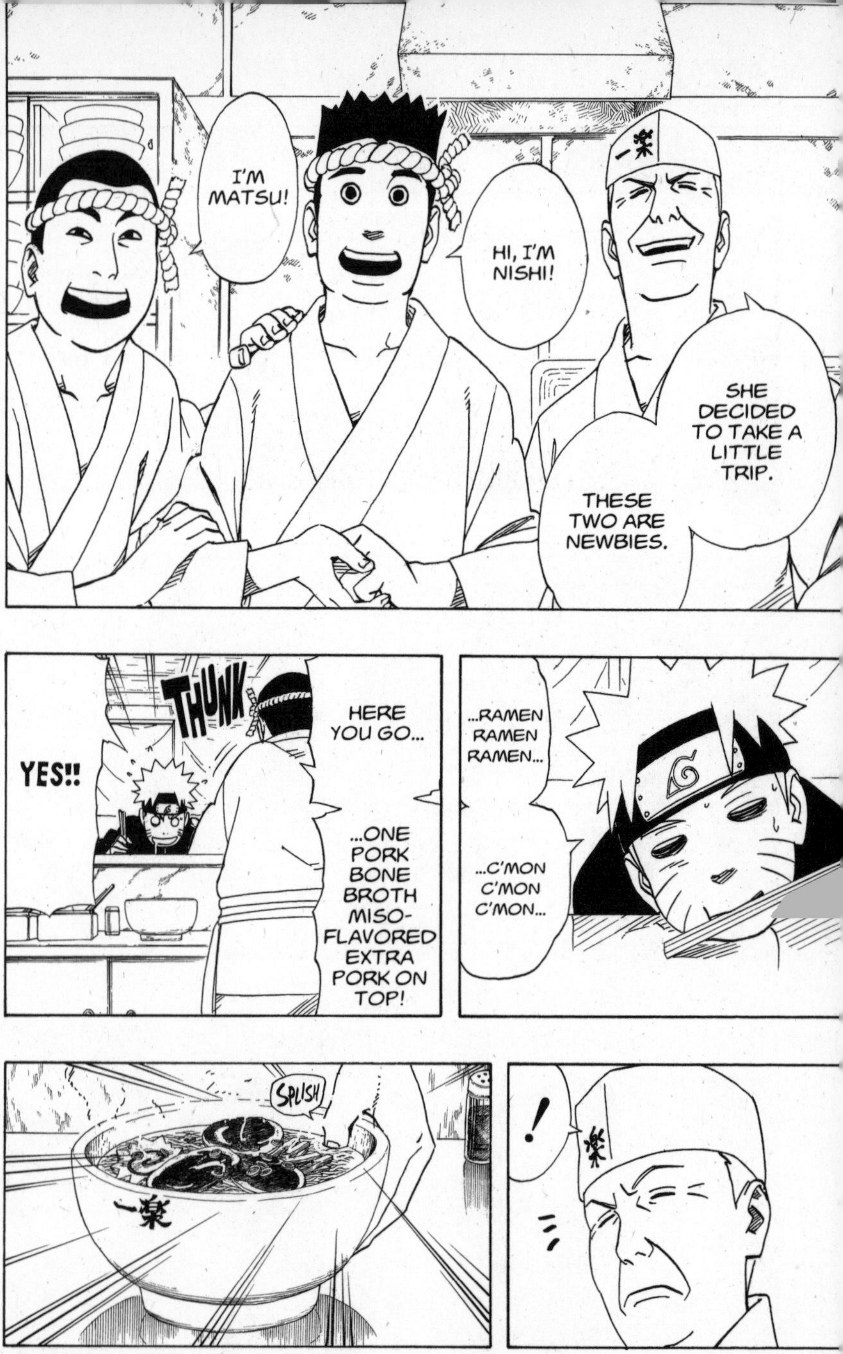
SHE DECIDED TO TAKE A LITTLE TRIP.
THESE TWO ARE NEWBIES.
HI, I'M NISHI!
I'M MATSU!
...RAMEN RAMEN RAMEN...
...C'MON C'MON C'MON...
HERE YOU GO...
...ONE PORK BONE BROTH MISO-FLAVORED EXTRA PORK ON TOP!
THUNK
YES!!
!
SPLISH

READ THIS WAY

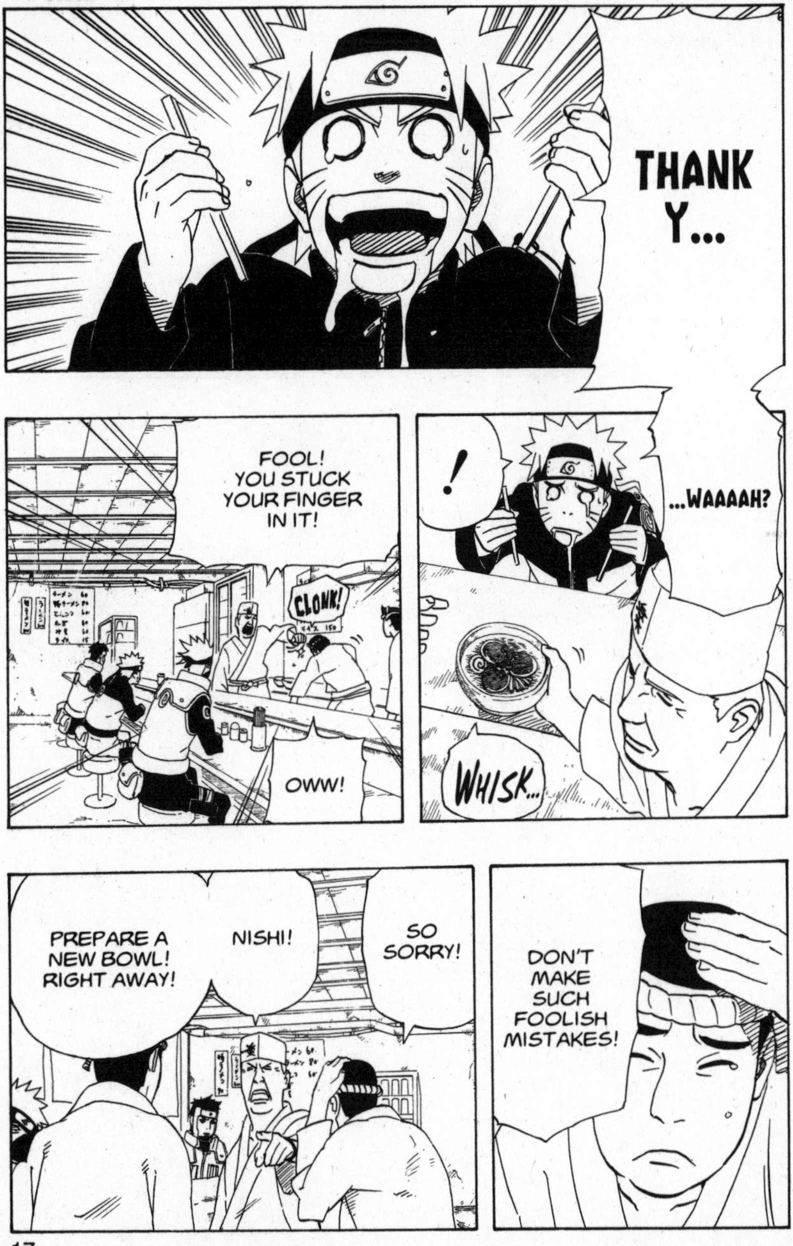
THANK Y...
!
...WAAAAH?
WHISK...
FOOL! YOU STUCK YOUR FINGER IN IT!
CLONK!
OWW!
DON'T MAKE SUCH FOOLISH MISTAKES!
SO SORRY!
NISHI!
PREPARE A NEW BOWL! RIGHT AWAY!

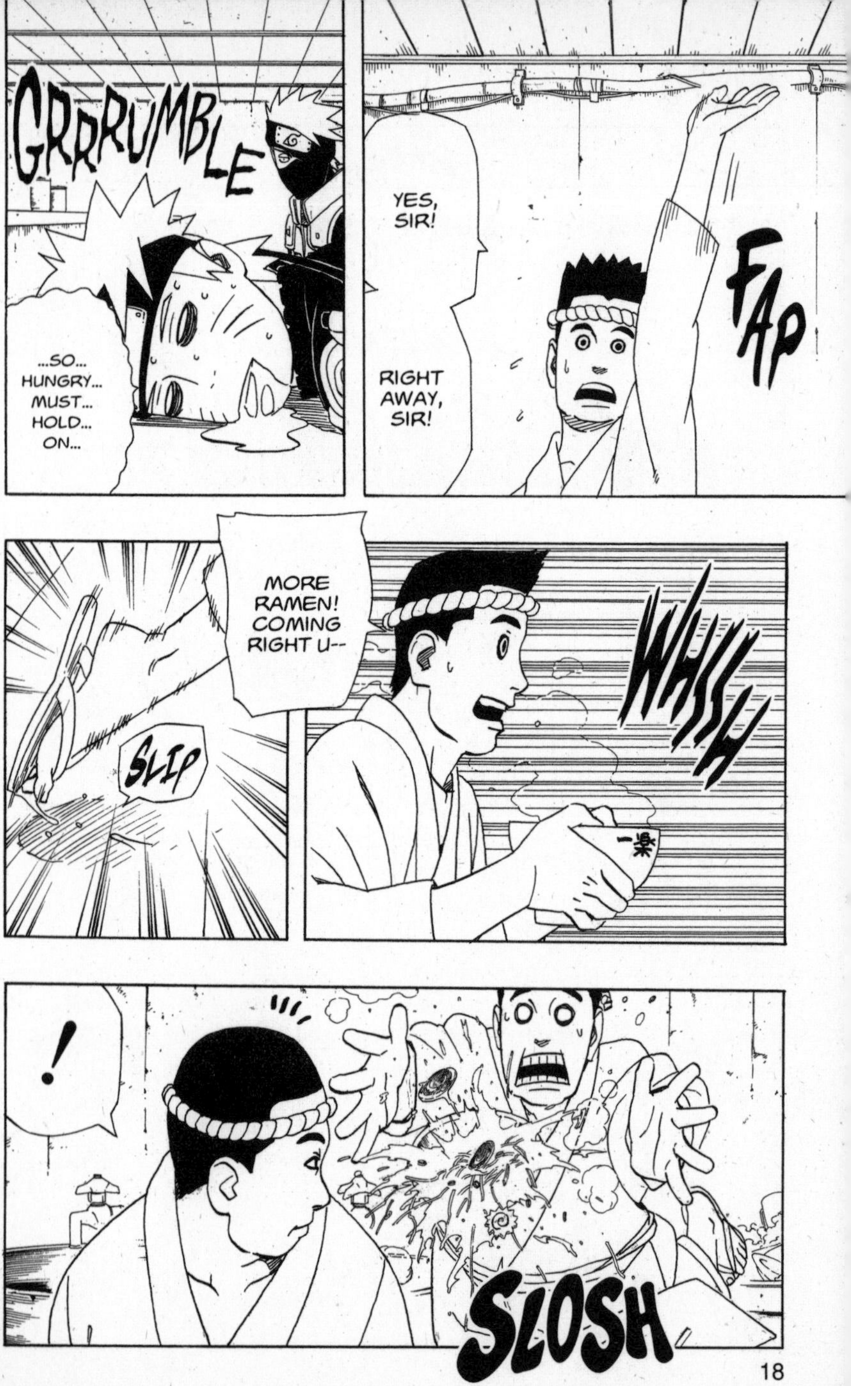
YES, SIR!
FAP
RIGHT AWAY, SIR!
GRRRUMBLE
...SO... HUNGRY... MUST... HOLD... ON...
MORE RAMEN! COMING RIGHT U--
WHSSH
SLIP
!
SLOSH

READ THIS WAY

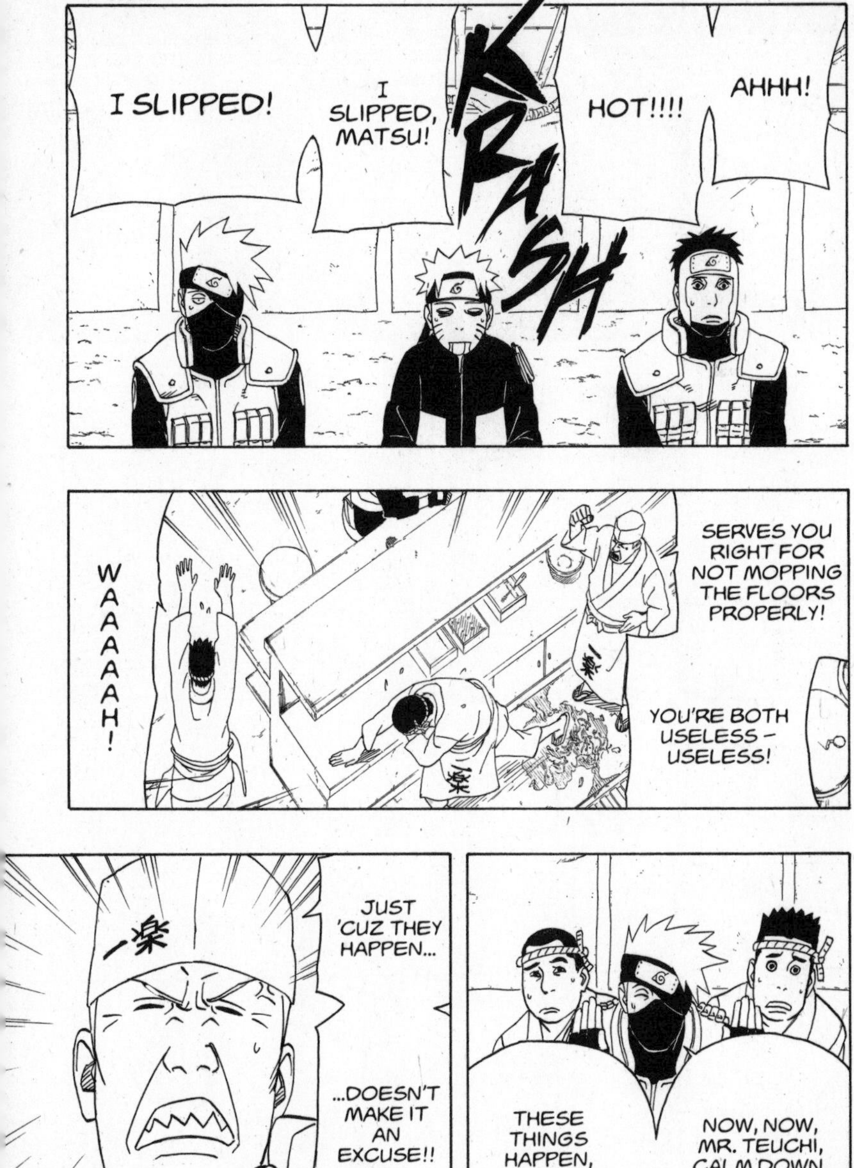
AHHH!
HOT!!!!
KRASH
I SLIPPED, MATSU!
I SLIPPED!
SERVES YOU RIGHT FOR NOT MOPPING THE FLOORS PROPERLY!
YOU'RE BOTH USELESS – USELESS!
WAAAAAAAH!
NOW, NOW, MR. TEUCHI, CALM DOWN.
THESE THINGS HAPPEN, A-HA HA.
JUST 'CUZ THEY HAPPEN...
...DOESN'T MAKE IT AN EXCUSE!!

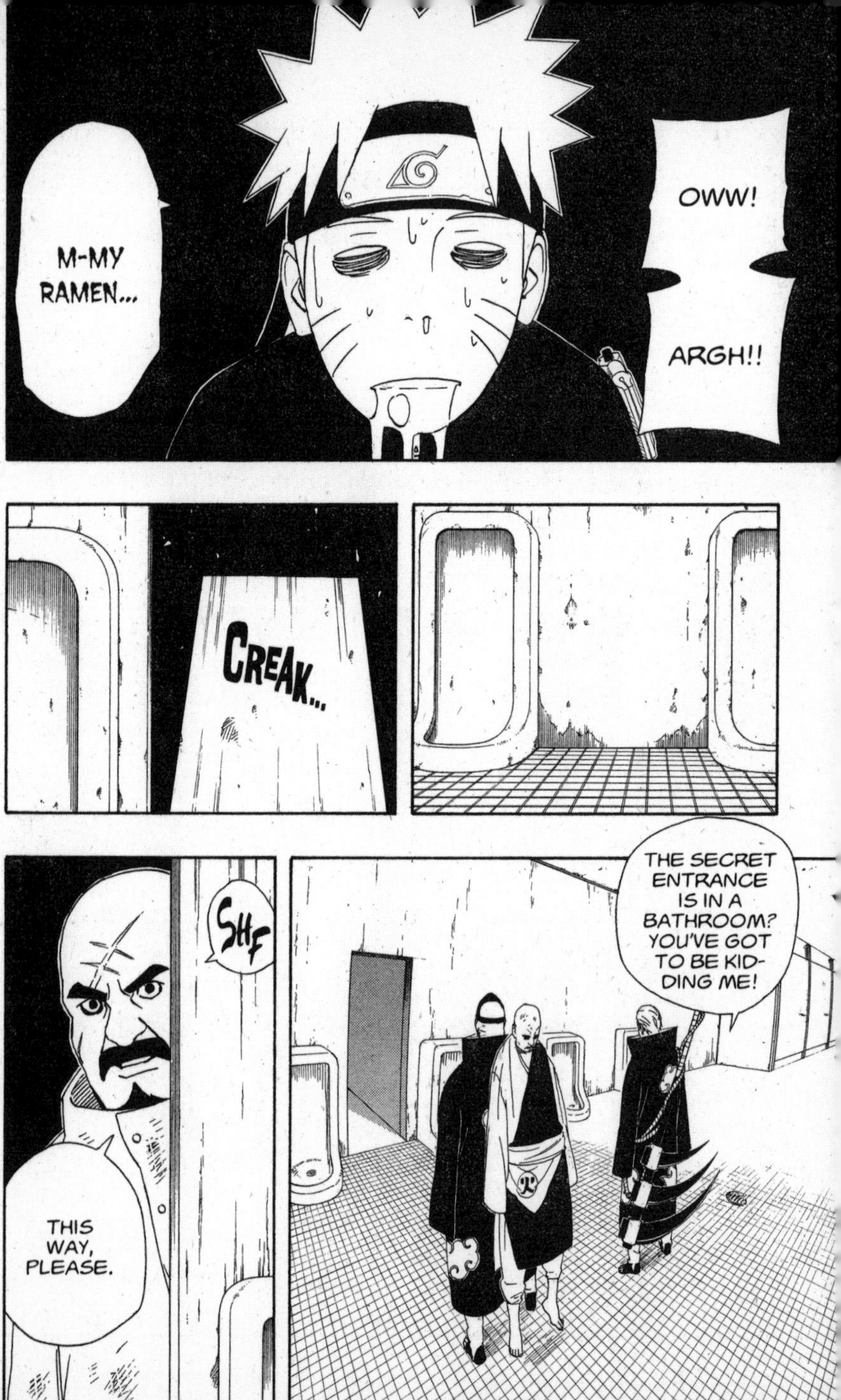
OWW!
ARGH!!
M-MY RAMEN...
CREAK...
THE SECRET ENTRANCE IS IN A BATHROOM? YOU'VE GOT TO BE KID-DING ME!
SHF
THIS WAY, PLEASE.

THAT'S CHIRIKU, ALL RIGHT...

SURE CAUGHT YOURSELF A BIG FISH THIS TIME, MR. KAKUZU.

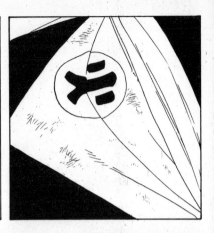

YEAH...

SCRAPE...

IT STINKS IN HERE, EH.

21

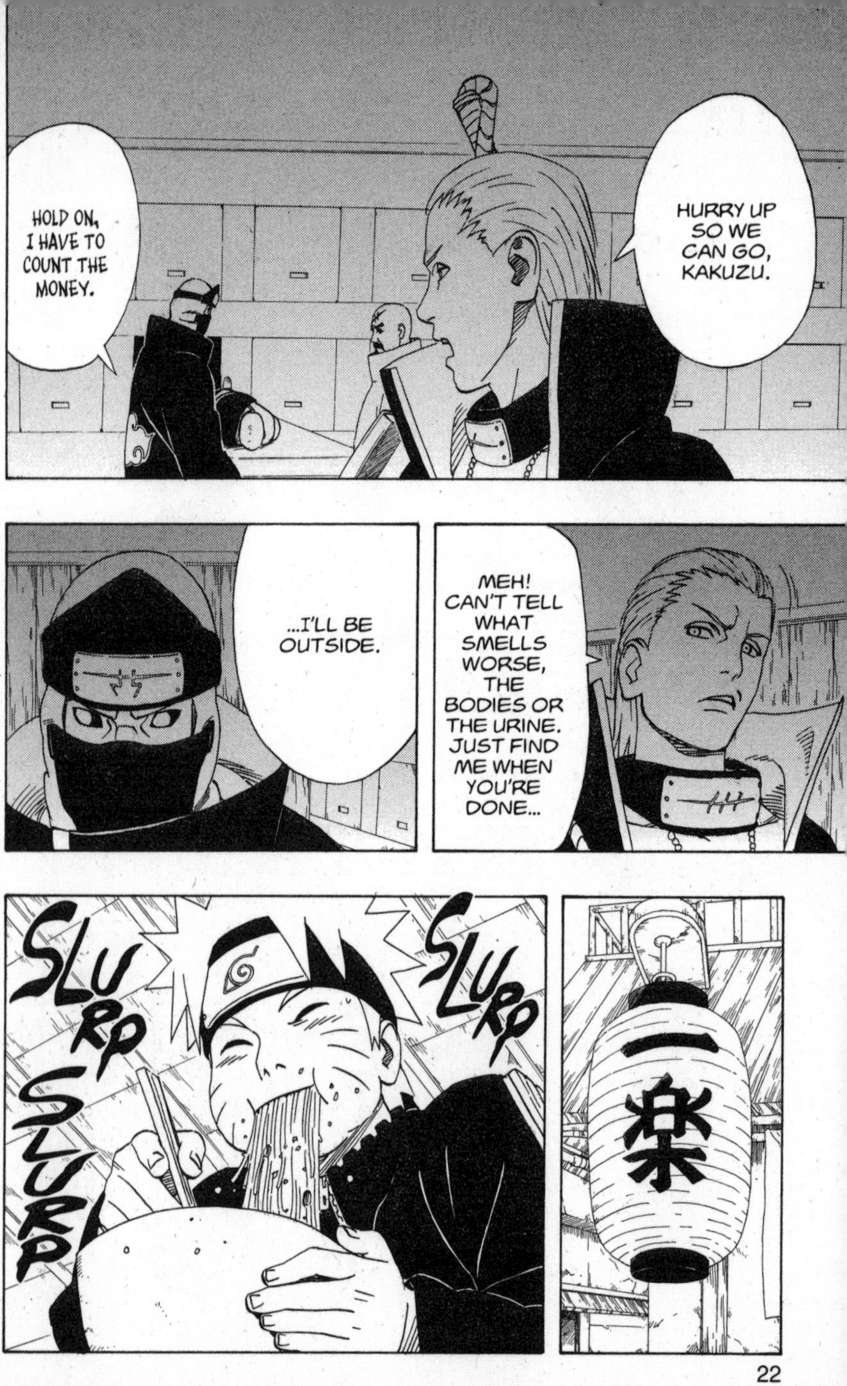
HURRY UP SO WE CAN GO, KAKUZU.
HOLD ON, I HAVE TO COUNT THE MONEY.
MEH! CAN'T TELL WHAT SMELLS WORSE, THE BODIES OR THE URINE. JUST FIND ME WHEN YOU'RE DONE...
...I'LL BE OUTSIDE.
一楽
SLURP
SLURP
SLURP
SLURP

READ THIS WAY

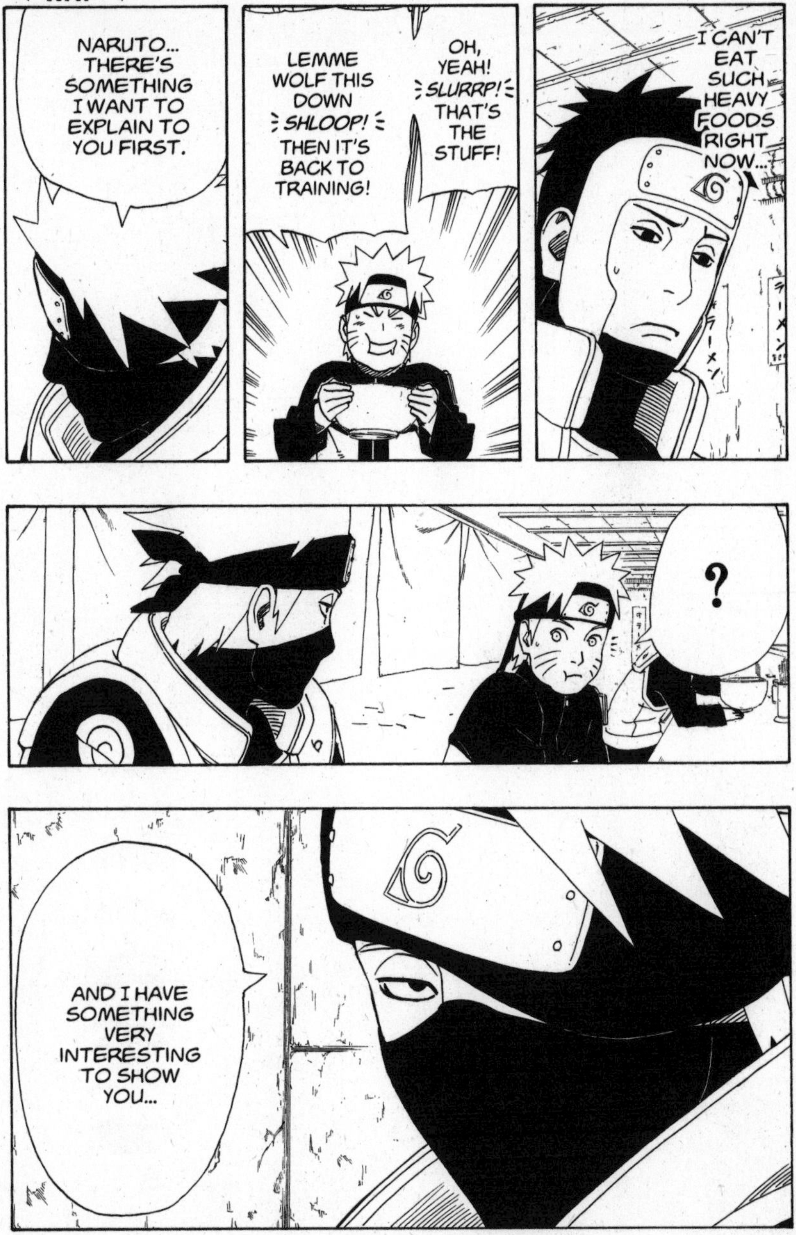

I CAN'T EAT SUCH HEAVY FOODS RIGHT NOW...
OH, YEAH! SLURRP! THAT'S THE STUFF!
LEMME WOLF THIS DOWN SHLOOP! THEN IT'S BACK TO TRAINING!
NARUTO... THERE'S SOMETHING I WANT TO EXPLAIN TO YOU FIRST.
?
AND I HAVE SOMETHING VERY INTERESTING TO SHOW YOU...

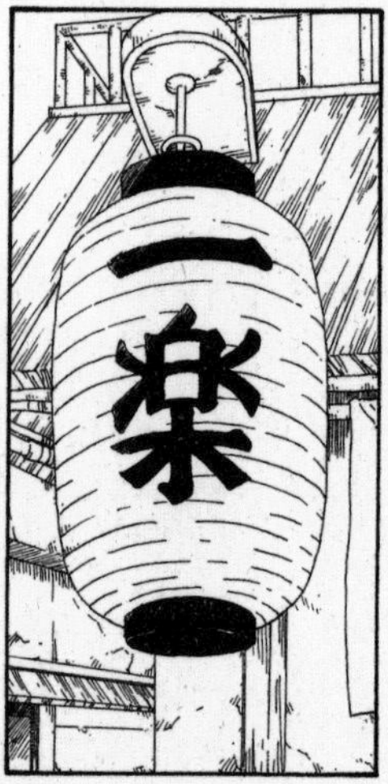
一楽

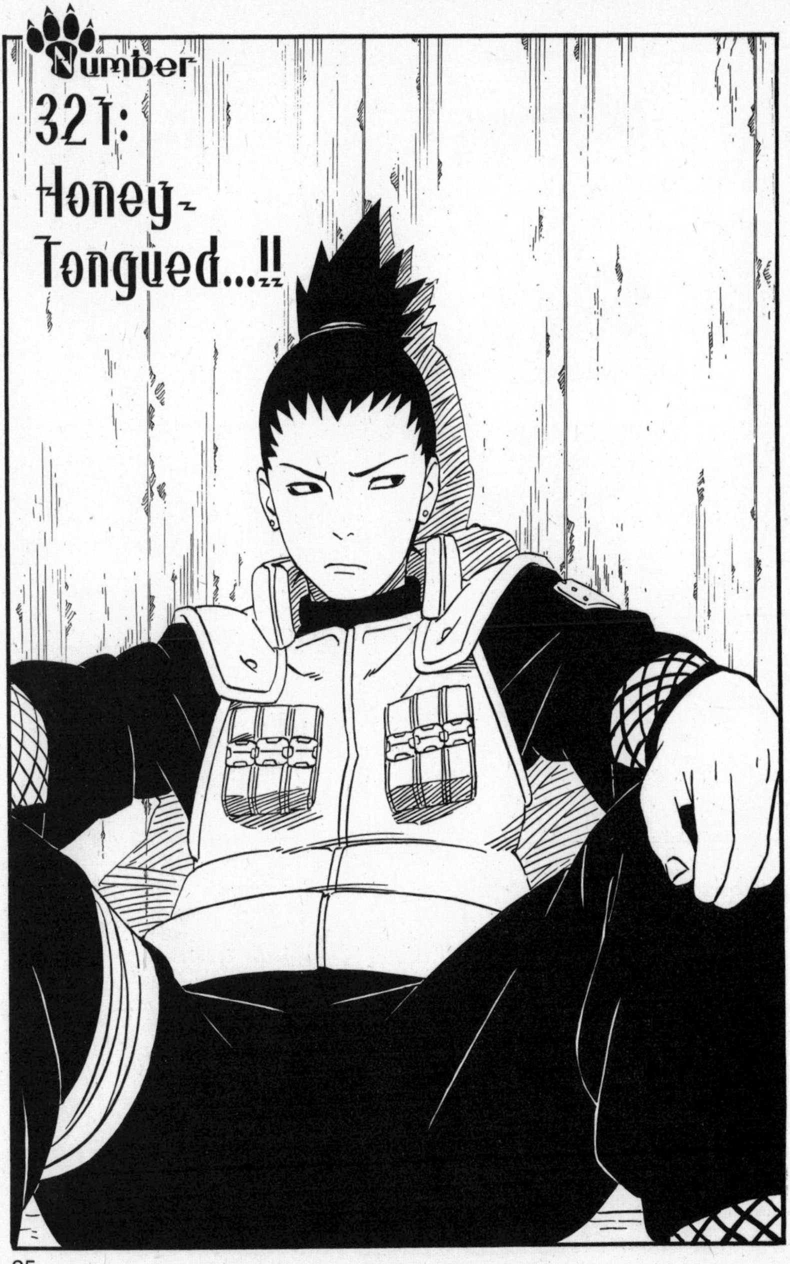
Number
321:
Honey-
Tongued...!!

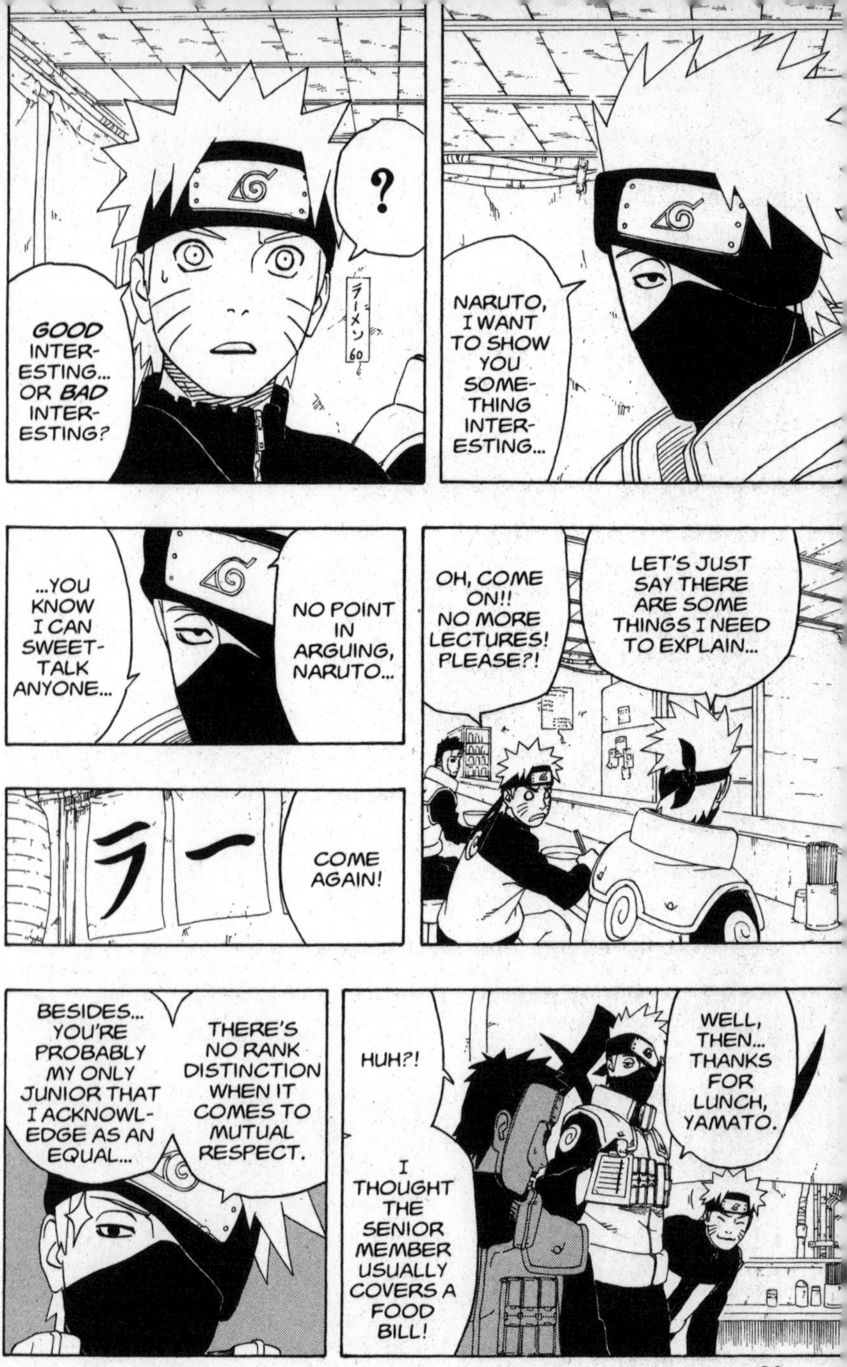
NARUTO, I WANT TO SHOW YOU SOMETHING INTERESTING...
?
ラーメン 60
GOOD INTERESTING... OR *BAD* INTERESTING?
LET'S JUST SAY THERE ARE SOME THINGS I NEED TO EXPLAIN...
OH, COME ON!! NO MORE LECTURES! PLEASE?!
NO POINT IN ARGUING, NARUTO...
...YOU KNOW I CAN SWEET-TALK ANYONE...
COME AGAIN!
ラー
WELL, THEN... THANKS FOR LUNCH, YAMATO.
HUH?!
I THOUGHT THE SENIOR MEMBER USUALLY COVERS A FOOD BILL!
THERE'S NO RANK DISTINCTION WHEN IT COMES TO MUTUAL RESPECT.
BESIDES... YOU'RE PROBABLY MY ONLY JUNIOR THAT I ACKNOWLEDGE AS AN EQUAL...

READ THIS WAY

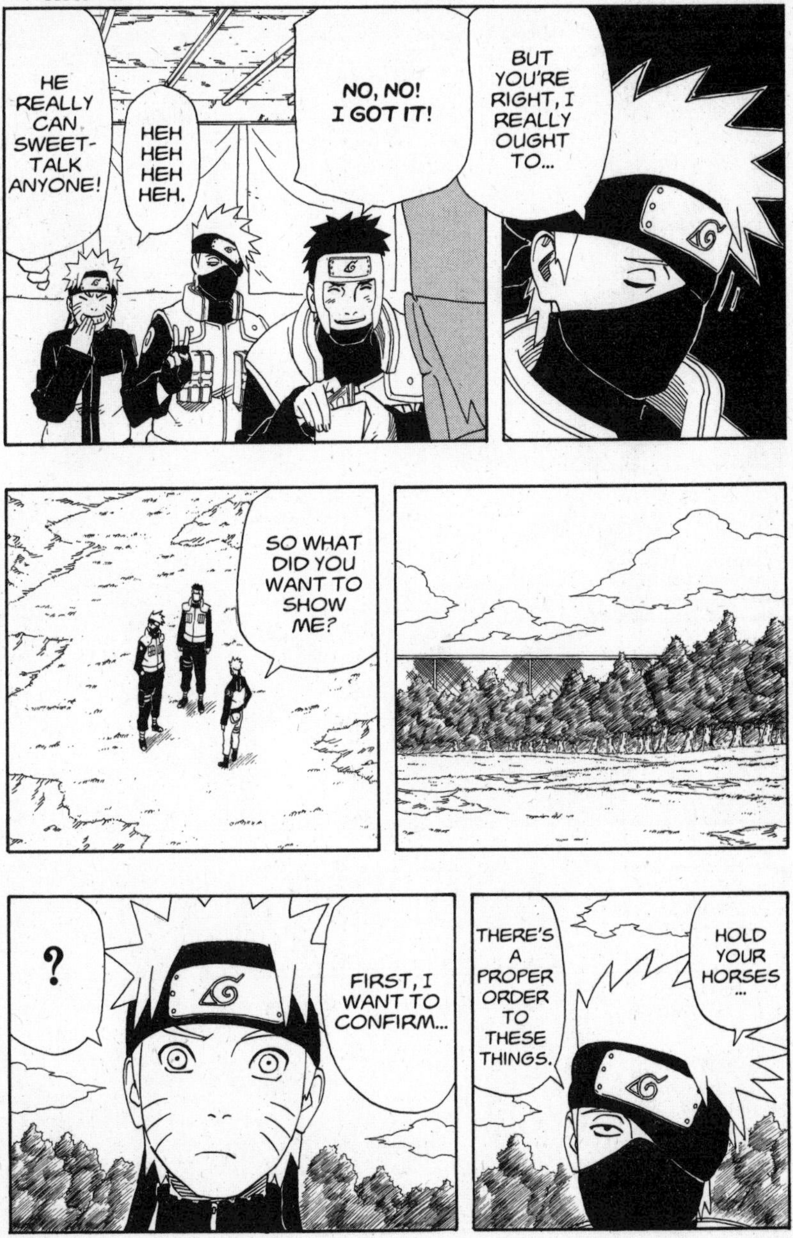
BUT YOU'RE RIGHT, I REALLY OUGHT TO...
NO, NO! I GOT IT!
HEH HEH HEH HEH.
HE REALLY CAN SWEET-TALK ANYONE!
SO WHAT DID YOU WANT TO SHOW ME?
HOLD YOUR HORSES ...
THERE'S A PROPER ORDER TO THESE THINGS.
FIRST, I WANT TO CONFIRM...
?

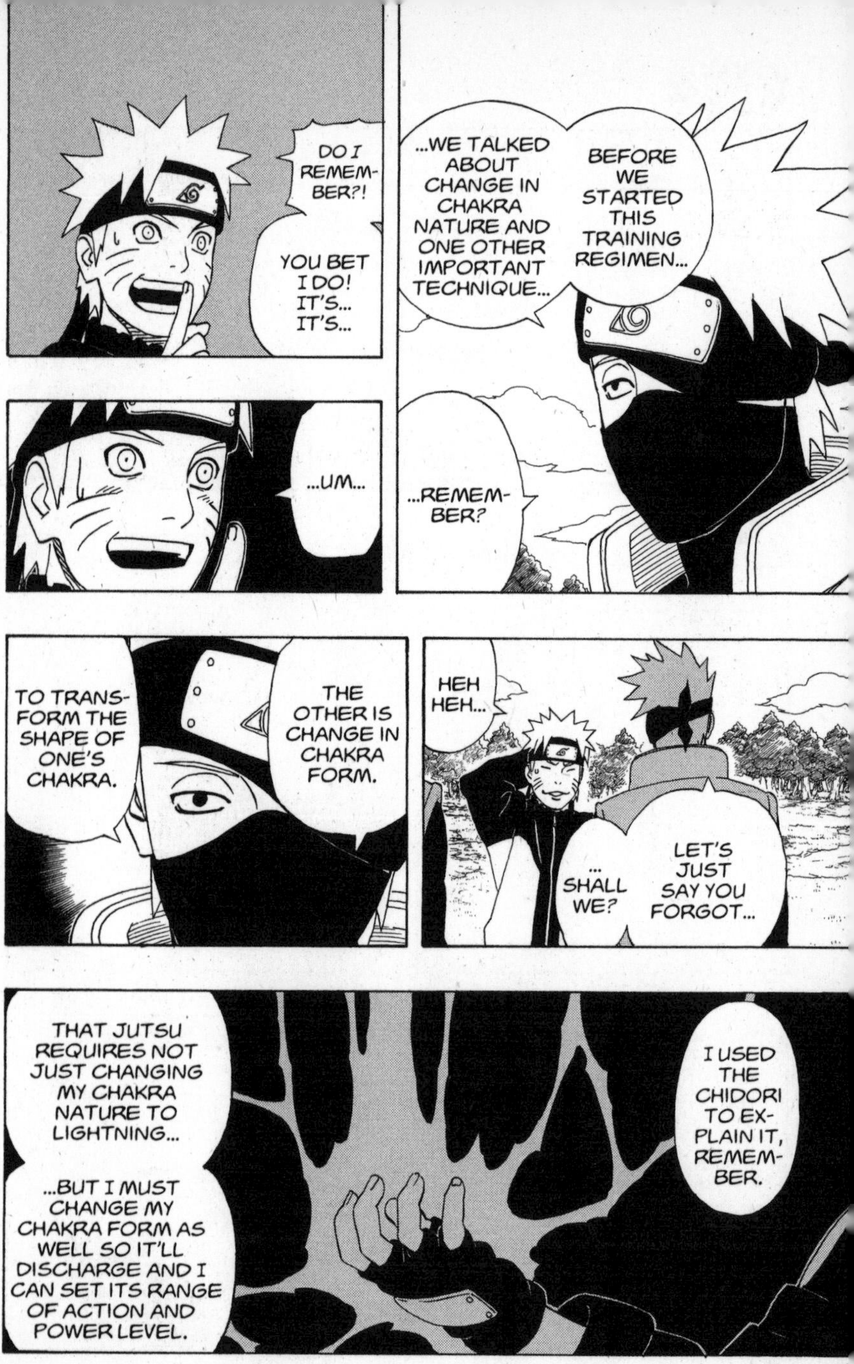
BEFORE WE STARTED THIS TRAINING REGIMEN...
...WE TALKED ABOUT CHANGE IN CHAKRA NATURE AND ONE OTHER IMPORTANT TECHNIQUE...
...REMEMBER?
DO I REMEMBER?!
YOU BET I DO! IT'S... IT'S...
...UM...
HEH HEH...
LET'S JUST SAY YOU FORGOT...
...SHALL WE?
THE OTHER IS CHANGE IN CHAKRA FORM.
TO TRANSFORM THE SHAPE OF ONE'S CHAKRA.
I USED THE CHIDORI TO EXPLAIN IT, REMEMBER.
THAT JUTSU REQUIRES NOT JUST CHANGING MY CHAKRA NATURE TO LIGHTNING...
...BUT I MUST CHANGE MY CHAKRA FORM AS WELL SO IT'LL DISCHARGE AND I CAN SET ITS RANGE OF ACTION AND POWER LEVEL.

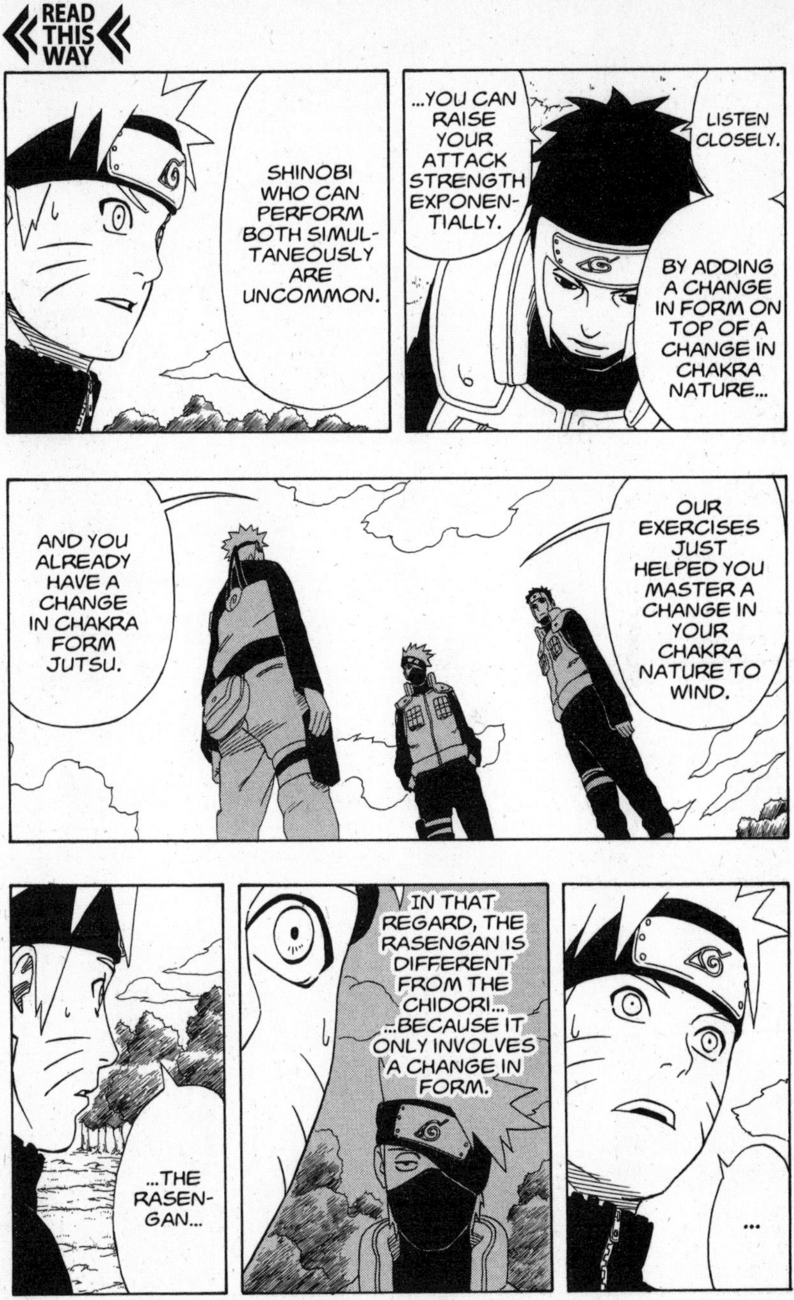
READ THIS WAY
LISTEN CLOSELY.
BY ADDING A CHANGE IN FORM ON TOP OF A CHANGE IN CHAKRA NATURE...
...YOU CAN RAISE YOUR ATTACK STRENGTH EXPONENTIALLY.
SHINOBI WHO CAN PERFORM BOTH SIMULTANEOUSLY ARE UNCOMMON.
OUR EXERCISES JUST HELPED YOU MASTER A CHANGE IN YOUR CHAKRA NATURE TO WIND.
AND YOU ALREADY HAVE A CHANGE IN CHAKRA FORM JUTSU.
...
IN THAT REGARD, THE RASENGAN IS DIFFERENT FROM THE CHIDORI...
...BECAUSE IT ONLY INVOLVES A CHANGE IN FORM.
...THE RASENGAN...

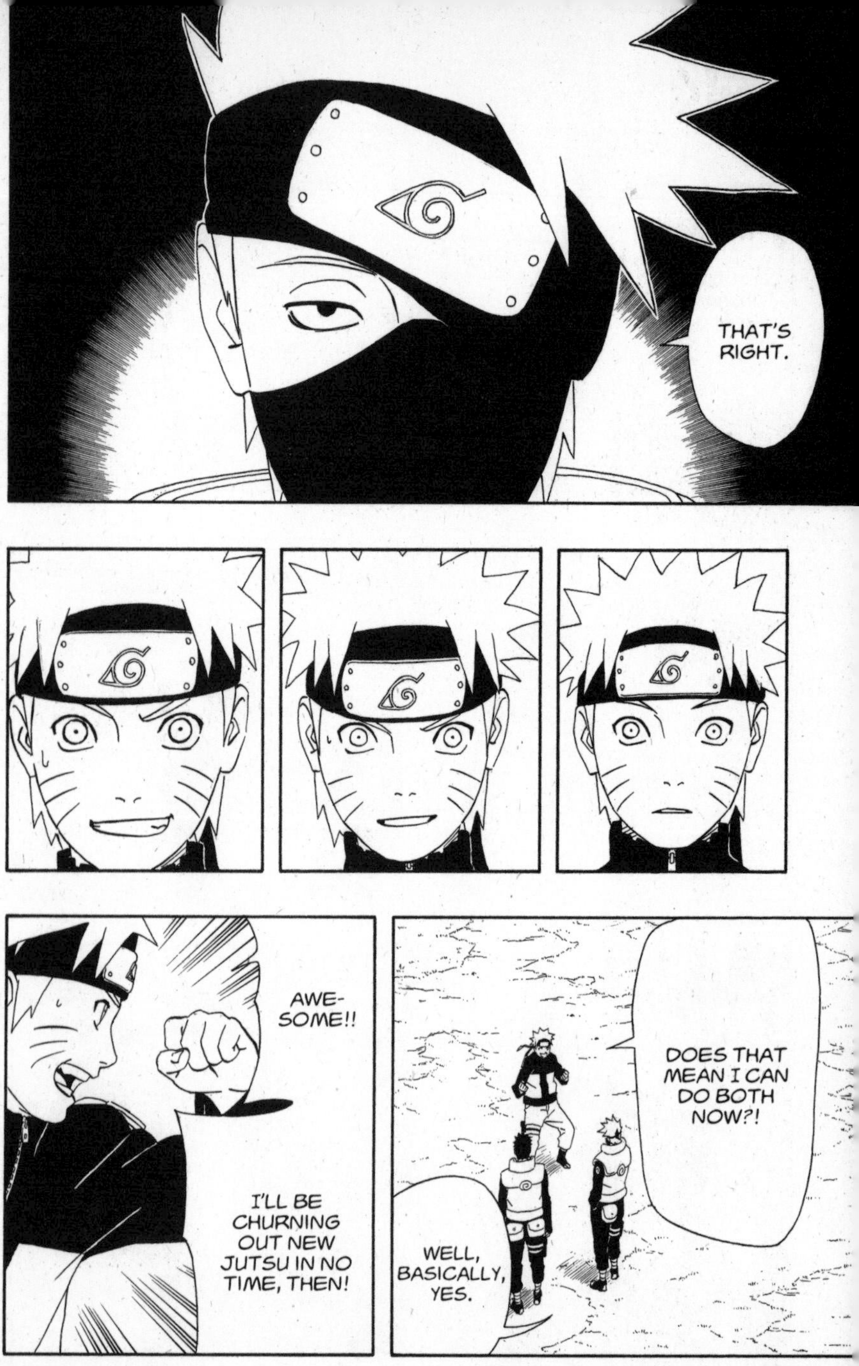
THAT'S RIGHT.
DOES THAT MEAN I CAN DO BOTH NOW?!
WELL, BASICALLY, YES.
AWE-SOME!!
I'LL BE CHURNING OUT NEW JUTSU IN NO TIME, THEN!

READ THIS WAY

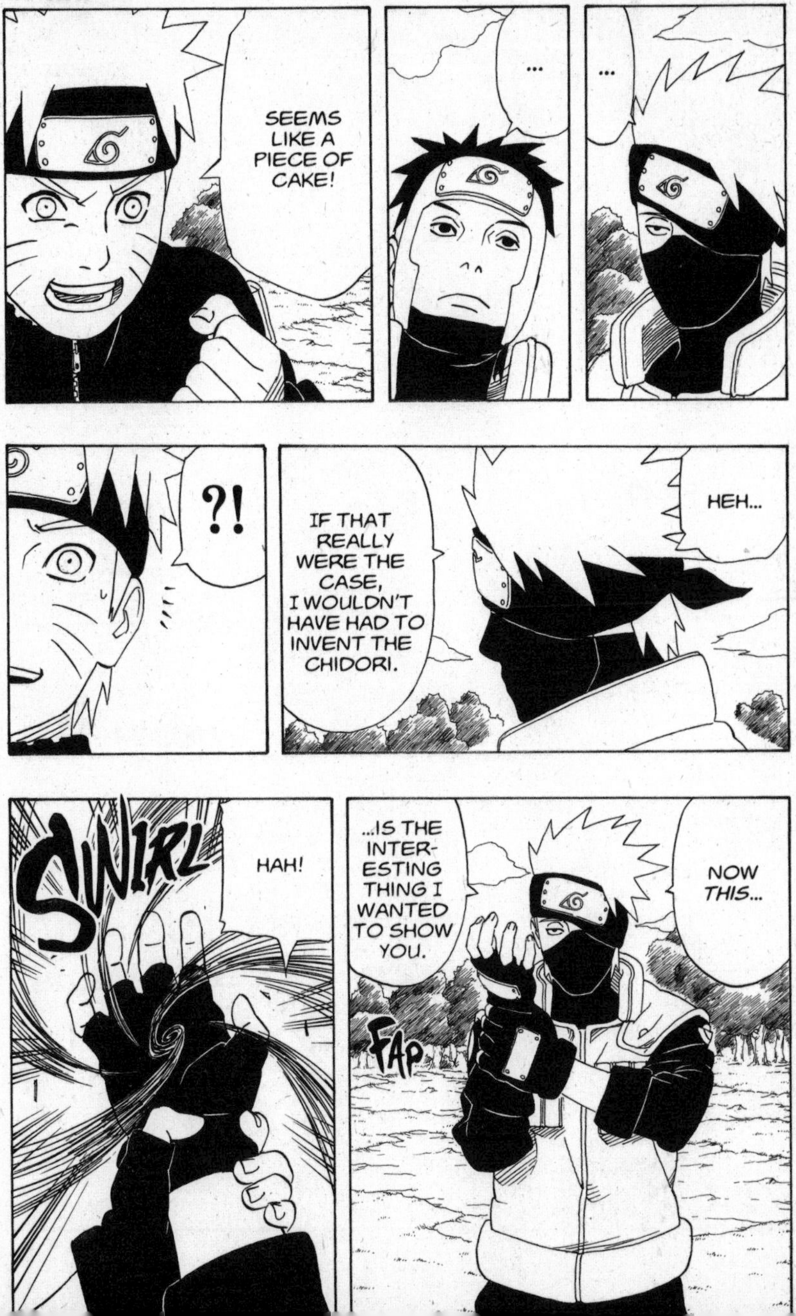
...
...
SEEMS LIKE A PIECE OF CAKE!
HEH...
IF THAT REALLY WERE THE CASE, I WOULDN'T HAVE HAD TO INVENT THE CHIDORI.
?!
NOW THIS...
...IS THE INTER-ESTING THING I WANTED TO SHOW YOU.
FAP
HAH!
SWIRL

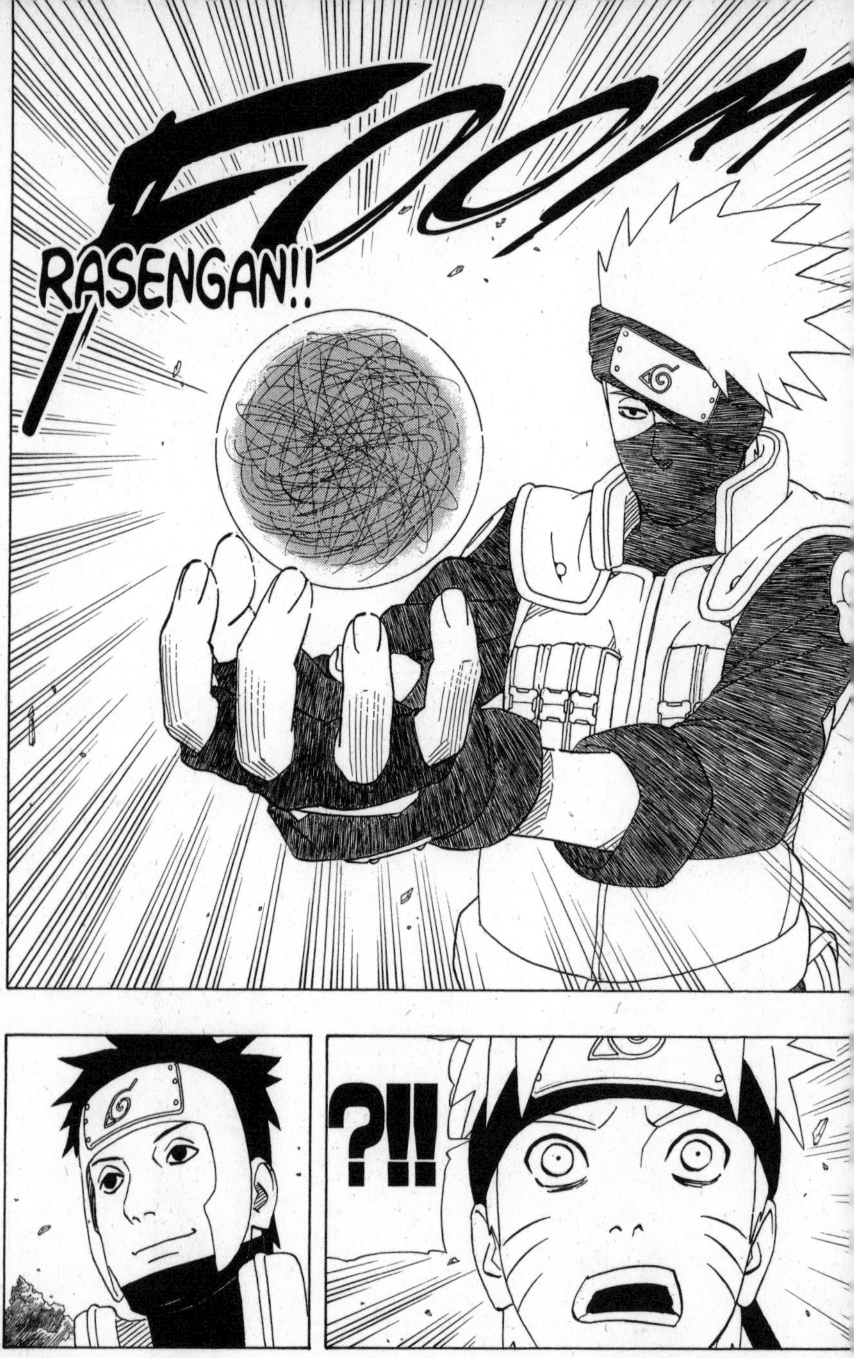
RASENGAN!!
?!!

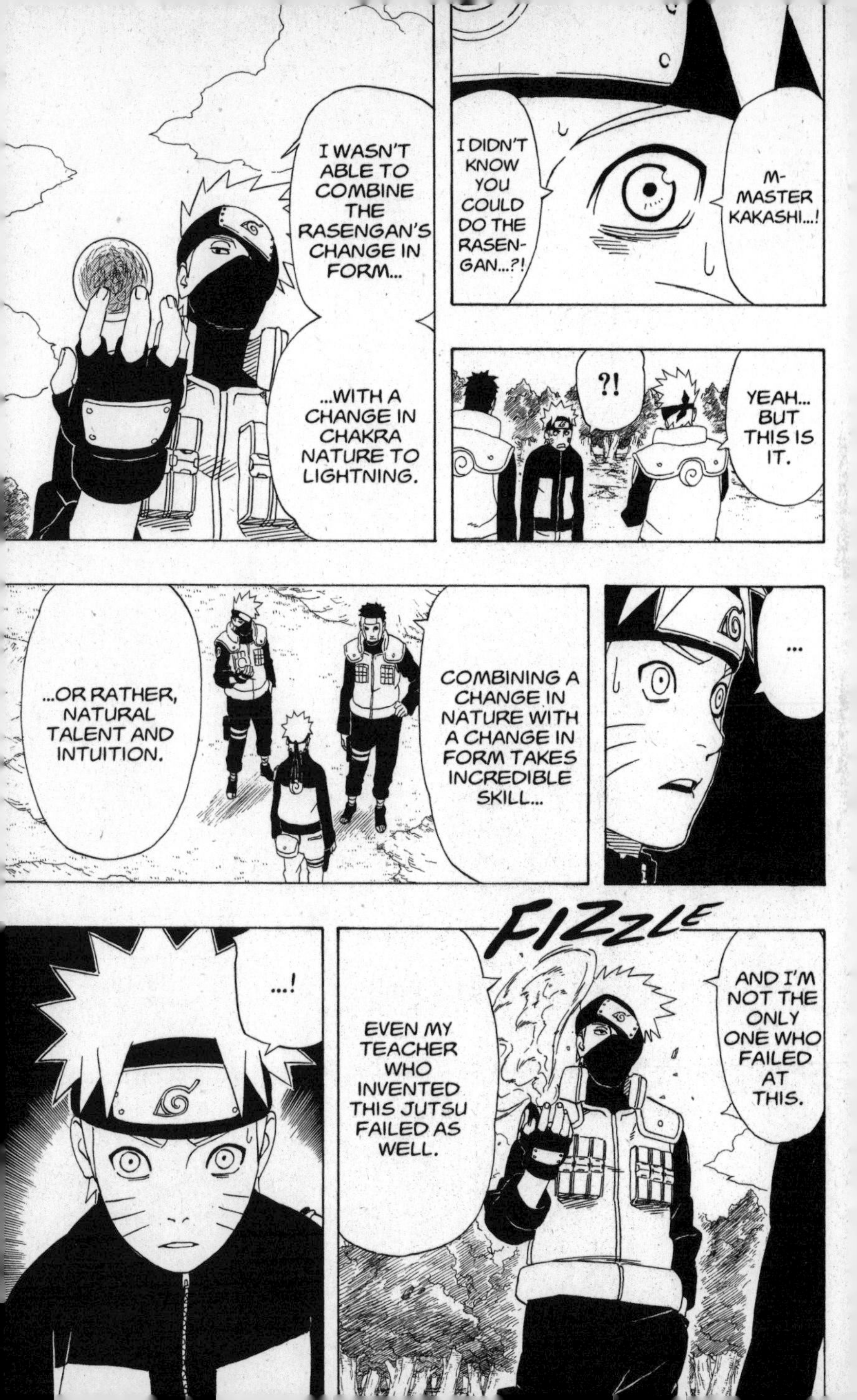
M-MASTER KAKASHI...!
I DIDN'T KNOW YOU COULD DO THE RASEN-GAN...?!
YEAH... BUT THIS IS IT.
?!
I WASN'T ABLE TO COMBINE THE RASENGAN'S CHANGE IN FORM...
...WITH A CHANGE IN CHAKRA NATURE TO LIGHTNING.
...
COMBINING A CHANGE IN NATURE WITH A CHANGE IN FORM TAKES INCREDIBLE SKILL...
...OR RATHER, NATURAL TALENT AND INTUITION.
FIZZLE
AND I'M NOT THE ONLY ONE WHO FAILED AT THIS.
EVEN MY TEACHER WHO INVENTED THIS JUTSU FAILED AS WELL.
...!

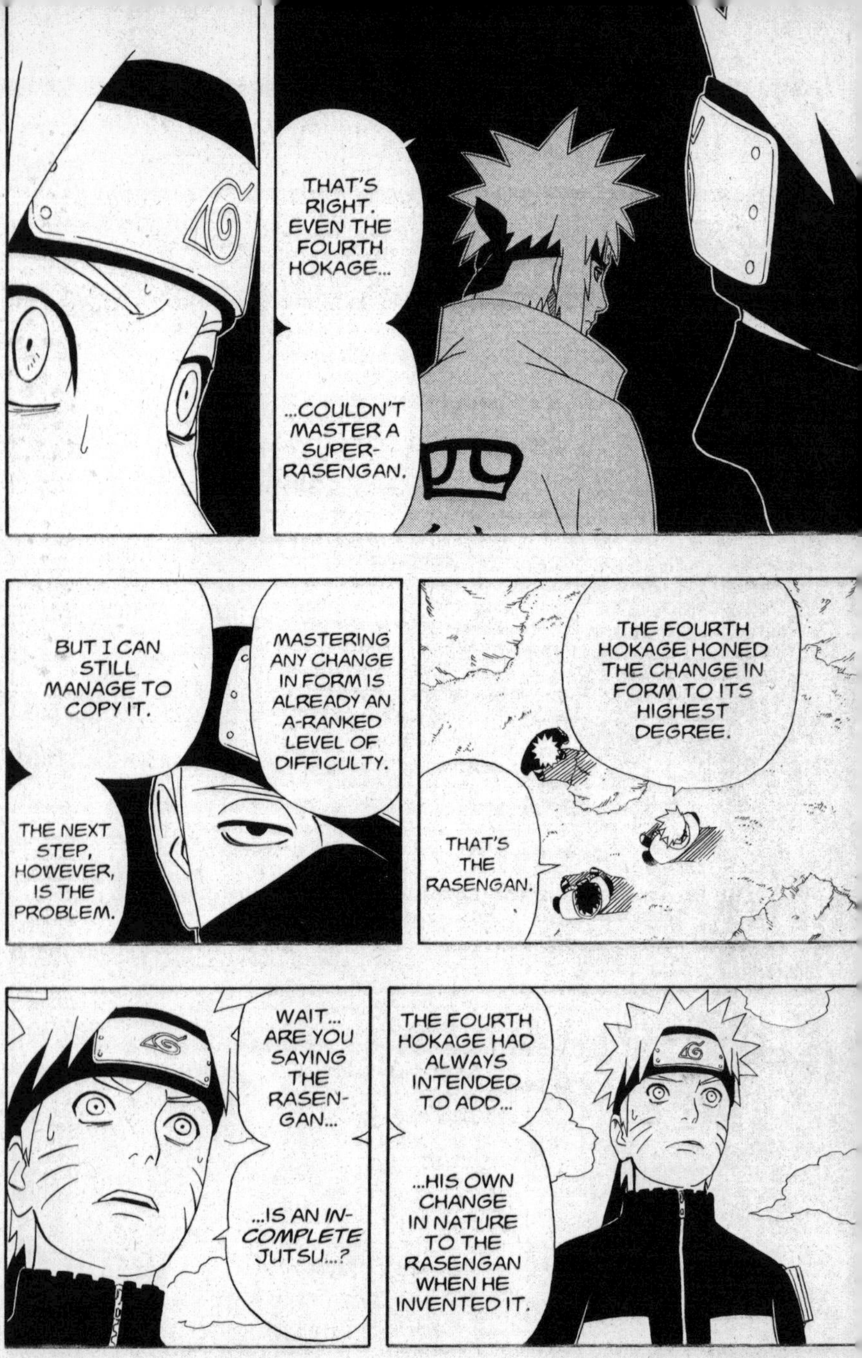
THAT'S RIGHT. EVEN THE FOURTH HOKAGE...
...COULDN'T MASTER A SUPER-RASENGAN.
THE FOURTH HOKAGE HONED THE CHANGE IN FORM TO ITS HIGHEST DEGREE.
THAT'S THE RASENGAN.
MASTERING ANY CHANGE IN FORM IS ALREADY AN A-RANKED LEVEL OF DIFFICULTY.
BUT I CAN STILL MANAGE TO COPY IT.
THE NEXT STEP, HOWEVER, IS THE PROBLEM.
THE FOURTH HOKAGE HAD ALWAYS INTENDED TO ADD...
...HIS OWN CHANGE IN NATURE TO THE RASENGAN WHEN HE INVENTED IT.
WAIT... ARE YOU SAYING THE RASEN-GAN...
...IS AN *IN-COMPLETE* JUTSU...?

READ THIS WAY

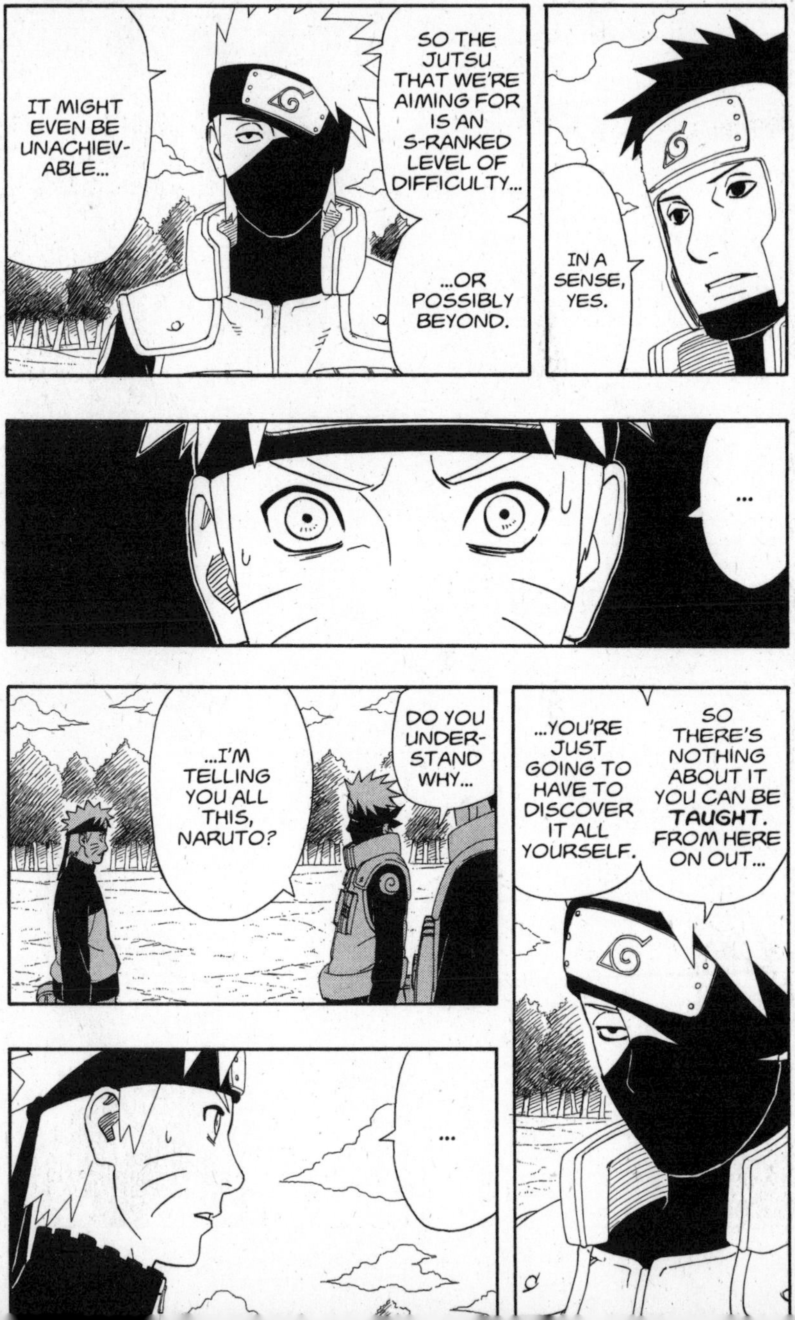
IN A SENSE, YES.
SO THE JUTSU THAT WE'RE AIMING FOR IS AN S-RANKED LEVEL OF DIFFICULTY...
...OR POSSIBLY BEYOND.
IT MIGHT EVEN BE UNACHIEV-ABLE...
...
SO THERE'S NOTHING ABOUT IT YOU CAN BE **TAUGHT**. FROM HERE ON OUT...
...YOU'RE JUST GOING TO HAVE TO DISCOVER IT ALL YOURSELF.
DO YOU UNDER-STAND WHY...
...I'M TELLING YOU ALL THIS, NARUTO?
...

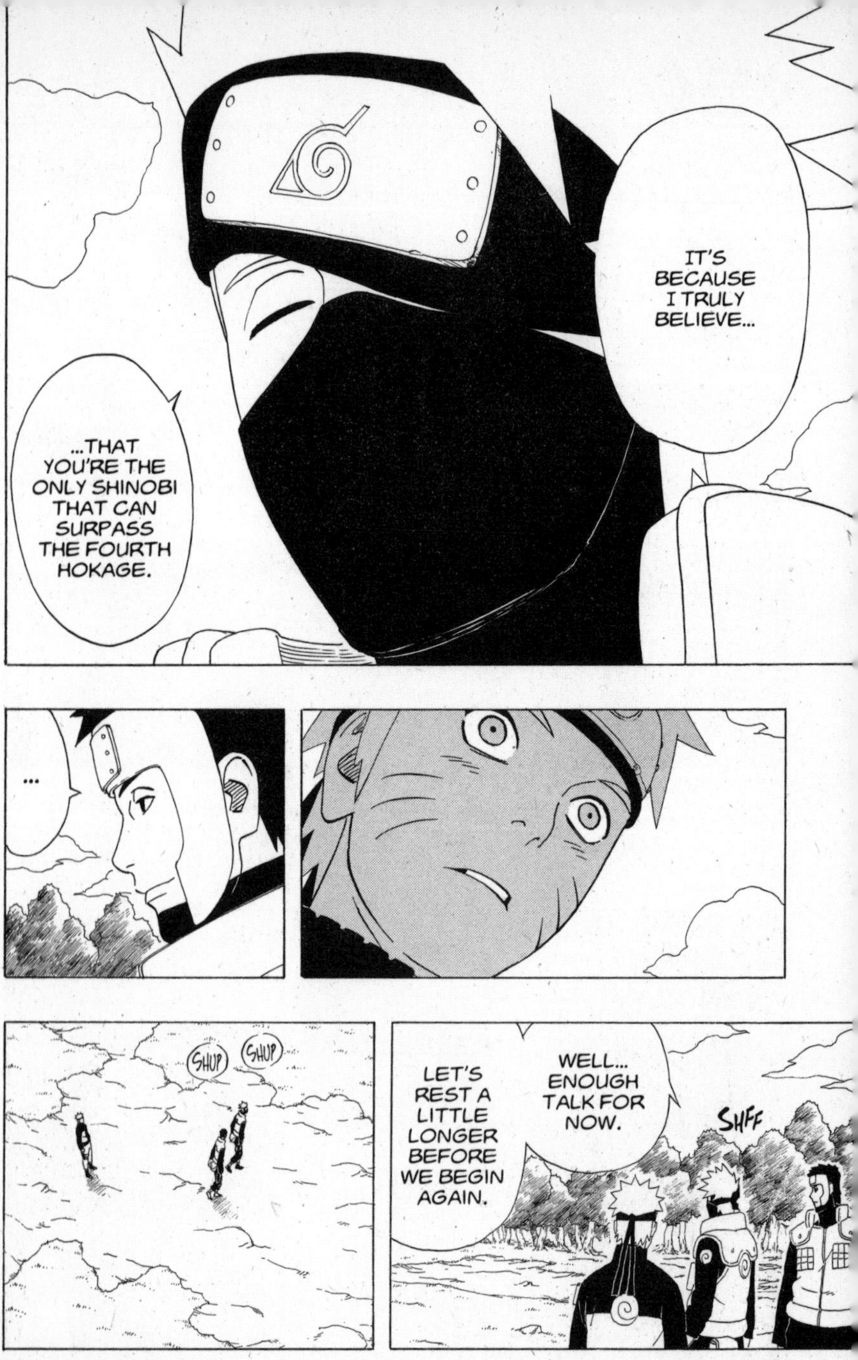
IT'S BECAUSE I TRULY BELIEVE...
...THAT YOU'RE THE ONLY SHINOBI THAT CAN SURPASS THE FOURTH HOKAGE.
...
WELL... ENOUGH TALK FOR NOW.
LET'S REST A LITTLE LONGER BEFORE WE BEGIN AGAIN.
SHFF
SHUP
SHUP

READ THIS WAY

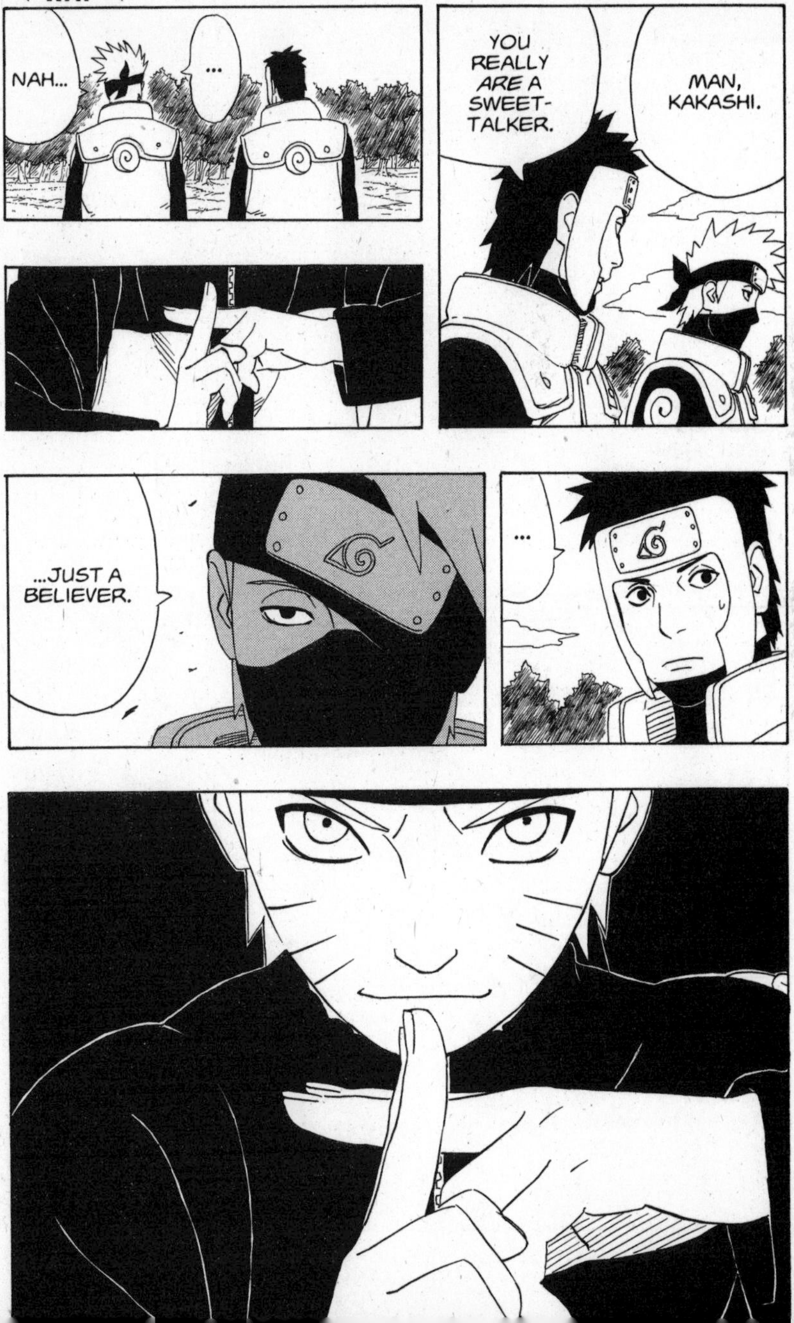
MAN, KAKASHI.
YOU REALLY ARE A SWEET-TALKER.
...
NAH...
...
...JUST A BELIEVER.

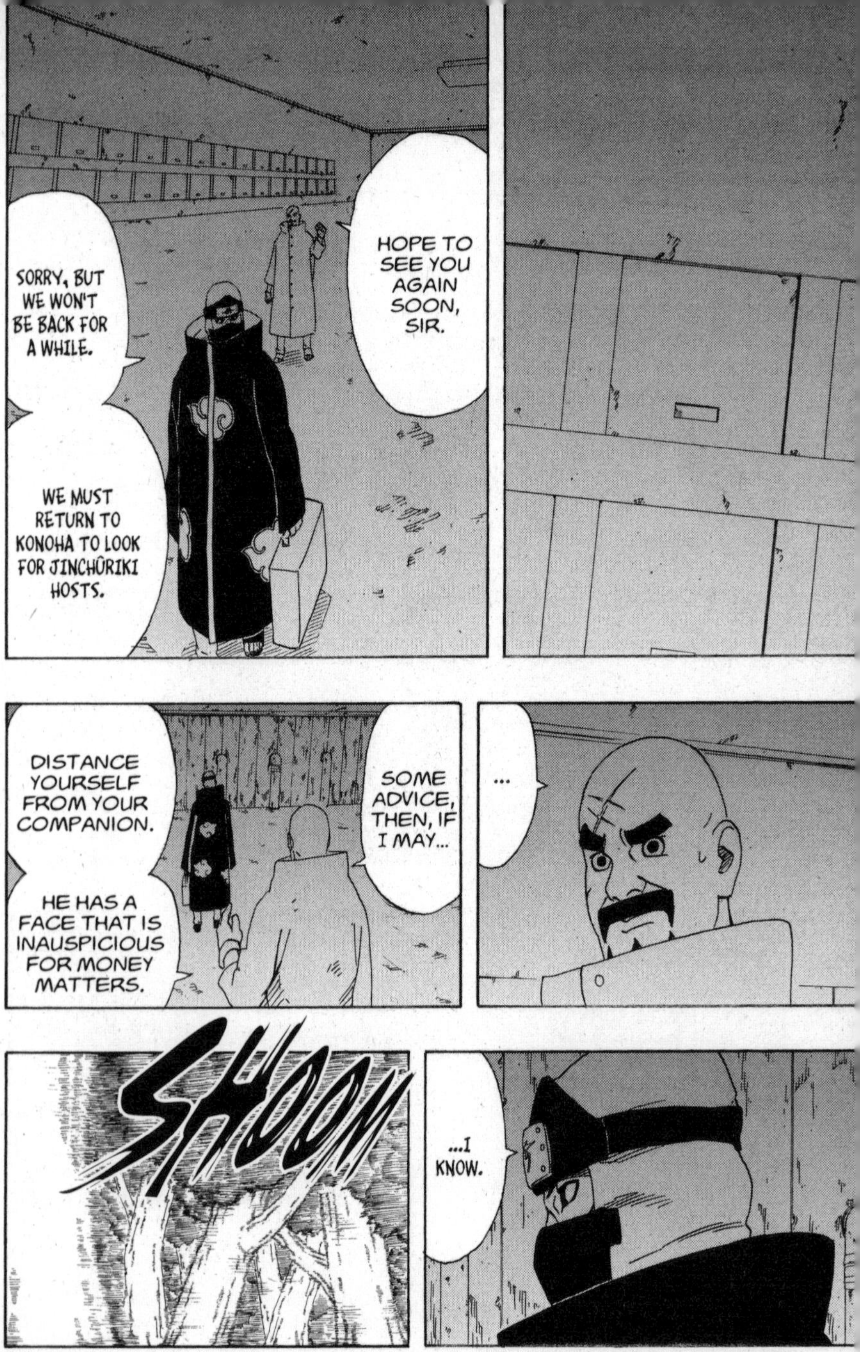
HOPE TO SEE YOU AGAIN SOON, SIR.
SORRY, BUT WE WON'T BE BACK FOR A WHILE.
WE MUST RETURN TO KONOHA TO LOOK FOR JINCHÛRIKI HOSTS.
...
SOME ADVICE, THEN, IF I MAY...
DISTANCE YOURSELF FROM YOUR COMPANION.
HE HAS A FACE THAT IS INAUSPICIOUS FOR MONEY MATTERS.
...I KNOW.
SHOOM

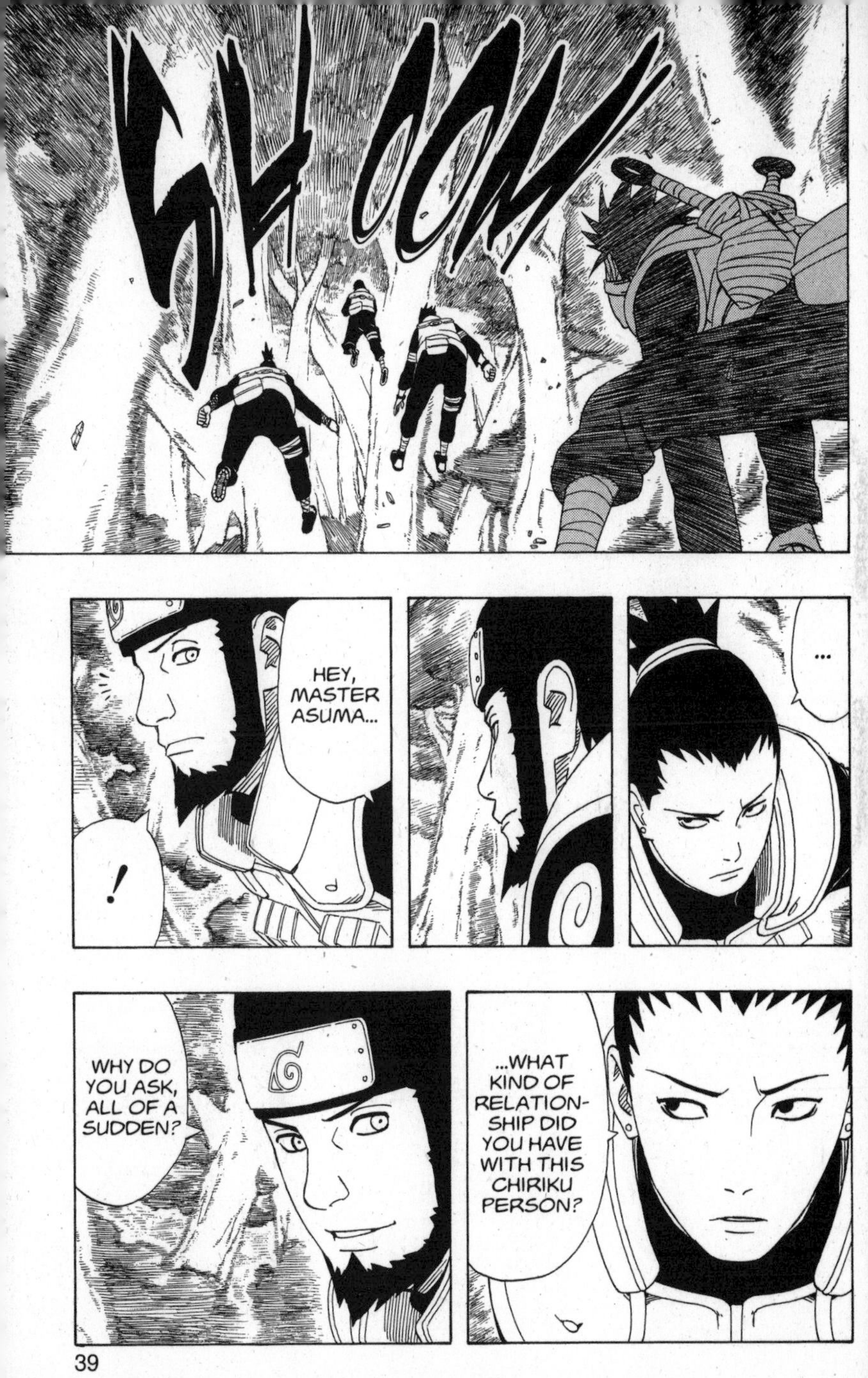
SHOOM
...
HEY, MASTER ASUMA...
!
...WHAT KIND OF RELATION-SHIP DID YOU HAVE WITH THIS CHIRIKU PERSON?
WHY DO YOU ASK, ALL OF A SUDDEN?

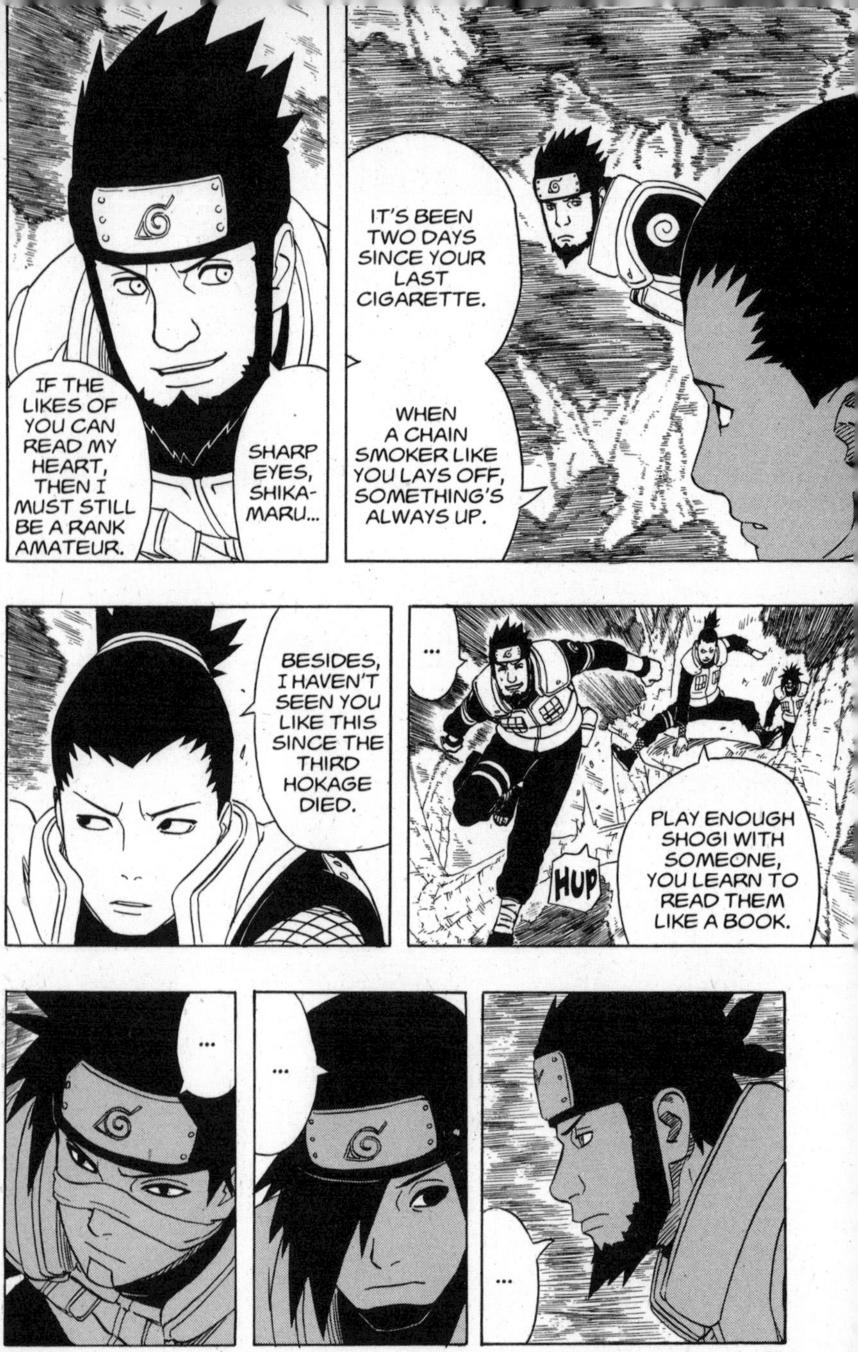
IT'S BEEN TWO DAYS SINCE YOUR LAST CIGARETTE.
WHEN A CHAIN SMOKER LIKE YOU LAYS OFF, SOMETHING'S ALWAYS UP.
SHARP EYES, SHIKA-MARU...
IF THE LIKES OF YOU CAN READ MY HEART, THEN I MUST STILL BE A RANK AMATEUR.
...
PLAY ENOUGH SHOGI WITH SOMEONE, YOU LEARN TO READ THEM LIKE A BOOK.
HUP
BESIDES, I HAVEN'T SEEN YOU LIKE THIS SINCE THE THIRD HOKAGE DIED.
...
...
...

READ THIS WAY

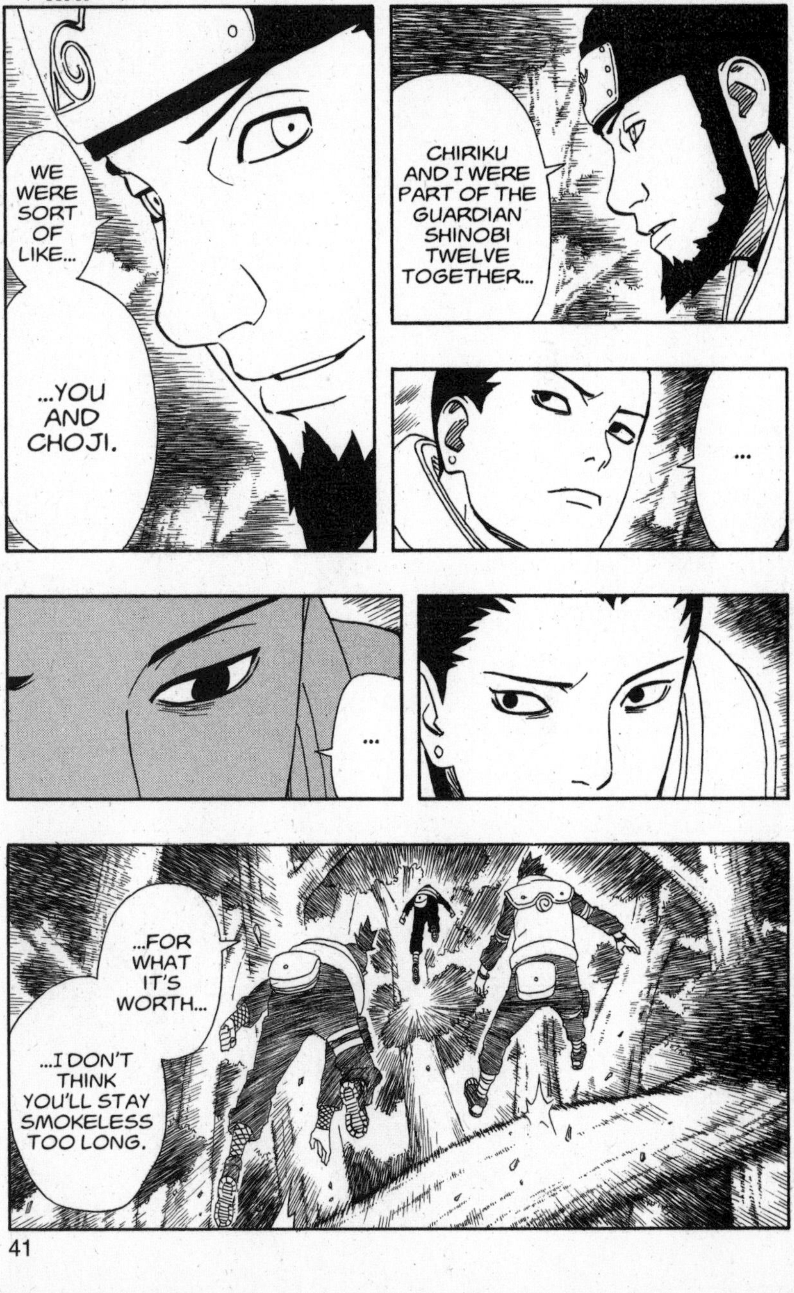

CHIRIKU AND I WERE PART OF THE GUARDIAN SHINOBI TWELVE TOGETHER...
WE WERE SORT OF LIKE...
...YOU AND CHOJI.
...
...
...FOR WHAT IT'S WORTH...
...I DON'T THINK YOU'LL STAY SMOKELESS TOO LONG.

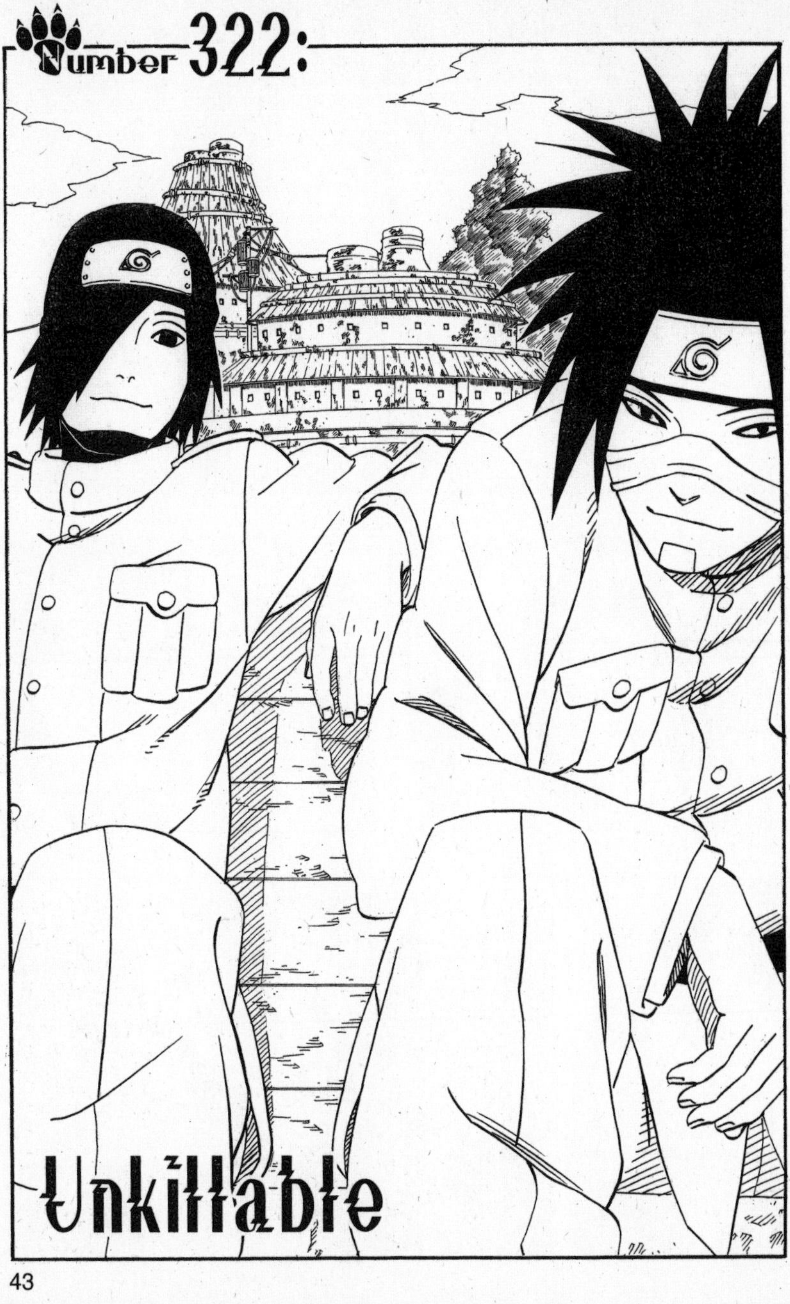
Number 322:
Unkillable

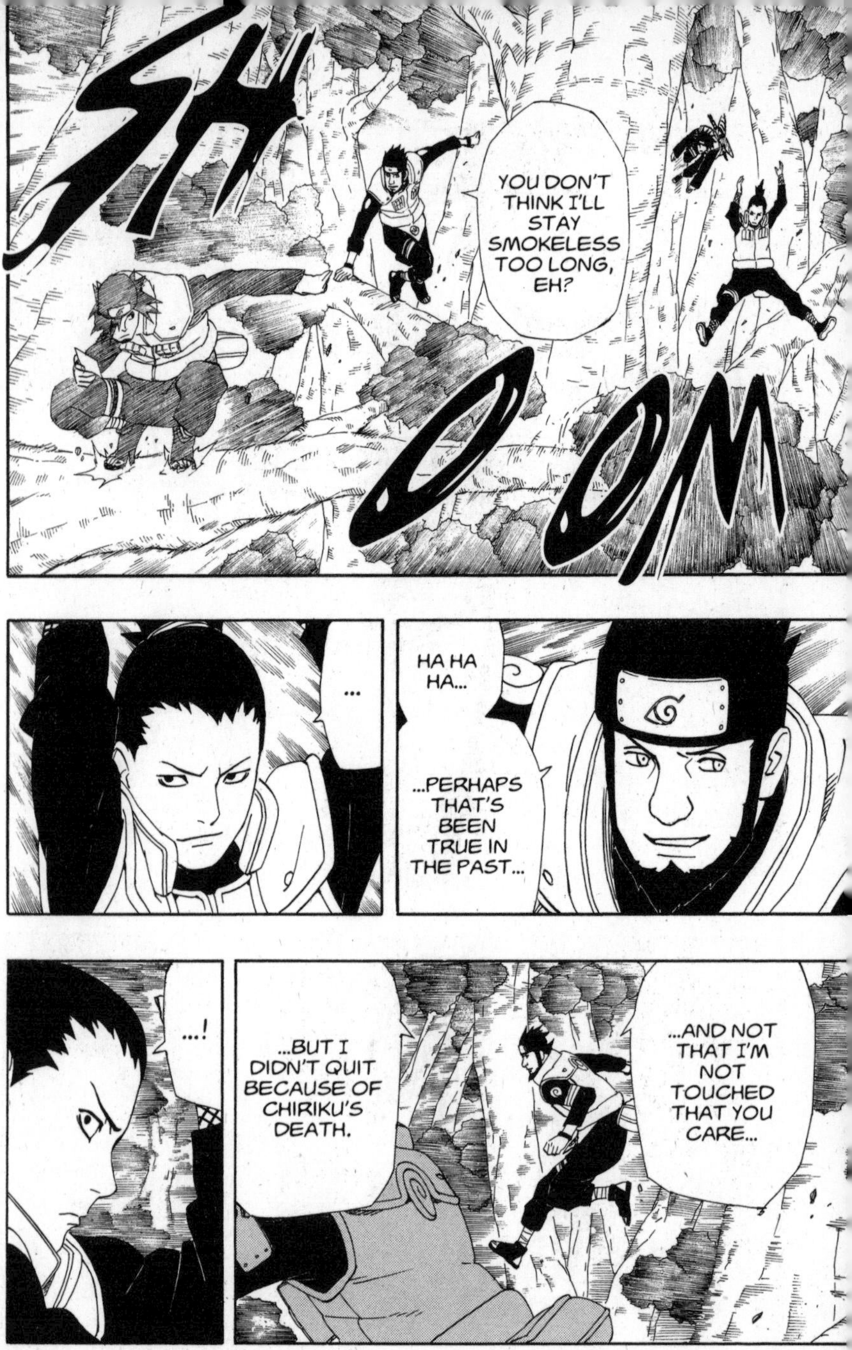
YOU DON'T THINK I'LL STAY SMOKELESS TOO LONG, EH?
SHOOM
HA HA HA...
...PERHAPS THAT'S BEEN TRUE IN THE PAST...
...
...AND NOT THAT I'M NOT TOUCHED THAT YOU CARE...
...BUT I DIDN'T QUIT BECAUSE OF CHIRIKU'S DEATH.
...!

READ THIS WAY

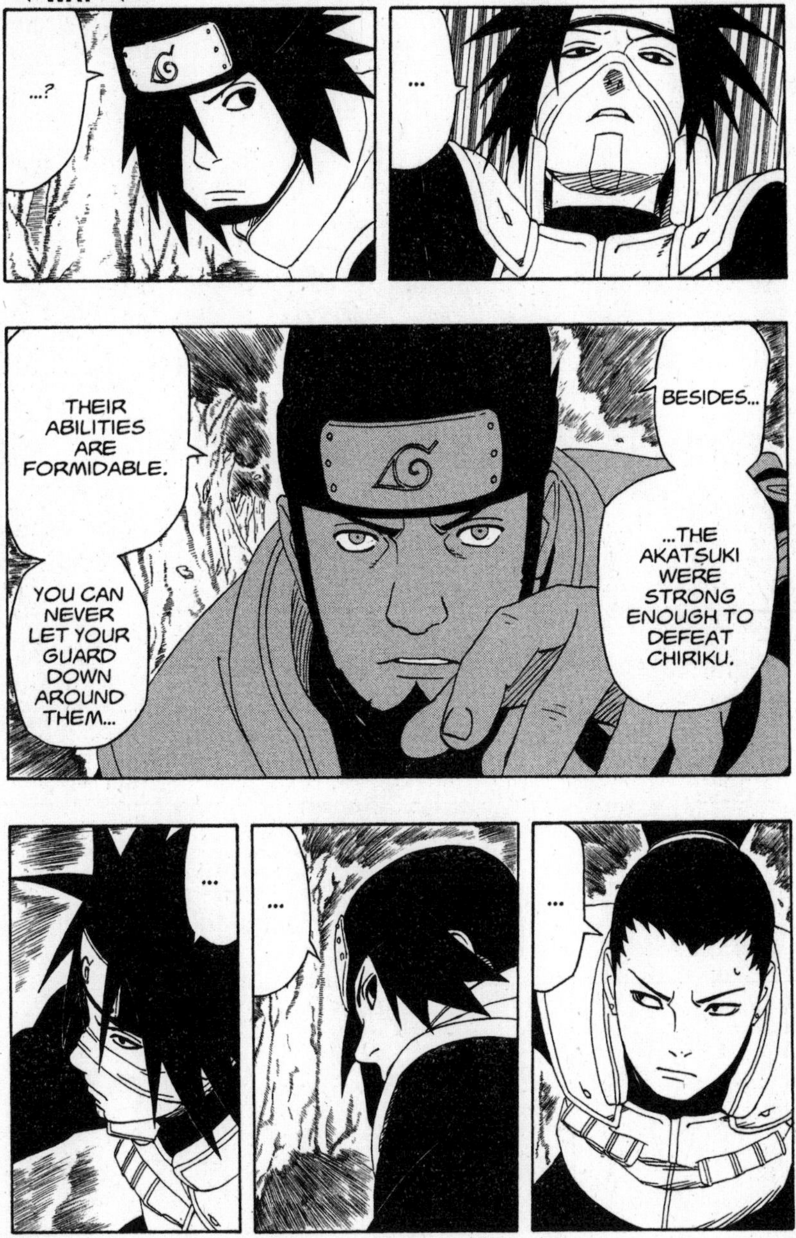
...
...?
BESIDES...
...THE AKATSUKI WERE STRONG ENOUGH TO DEFEAT CHIRIKU.
THEIR ABILITIES ARE FORMIDABLE.
YOU CAN NEVER LET YOUR GUARD DOWN AROUND THEM...
...
...
...

YOU ARE RIGHT... HIDAN IS INAUSPICIOUS IN MONEY MATTERS.

BUT I CAN HAVE NO OTHER COMPANION.

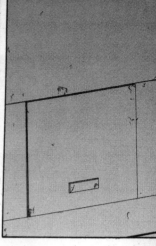

THERE'S A REASON FOR THAT.

...?

CREAK

ALL THOSE WHO HAVE PAIRED WITH ME IN THE PAST HAVE DIED.

?

REASON ...?

46

READ THIS WAY

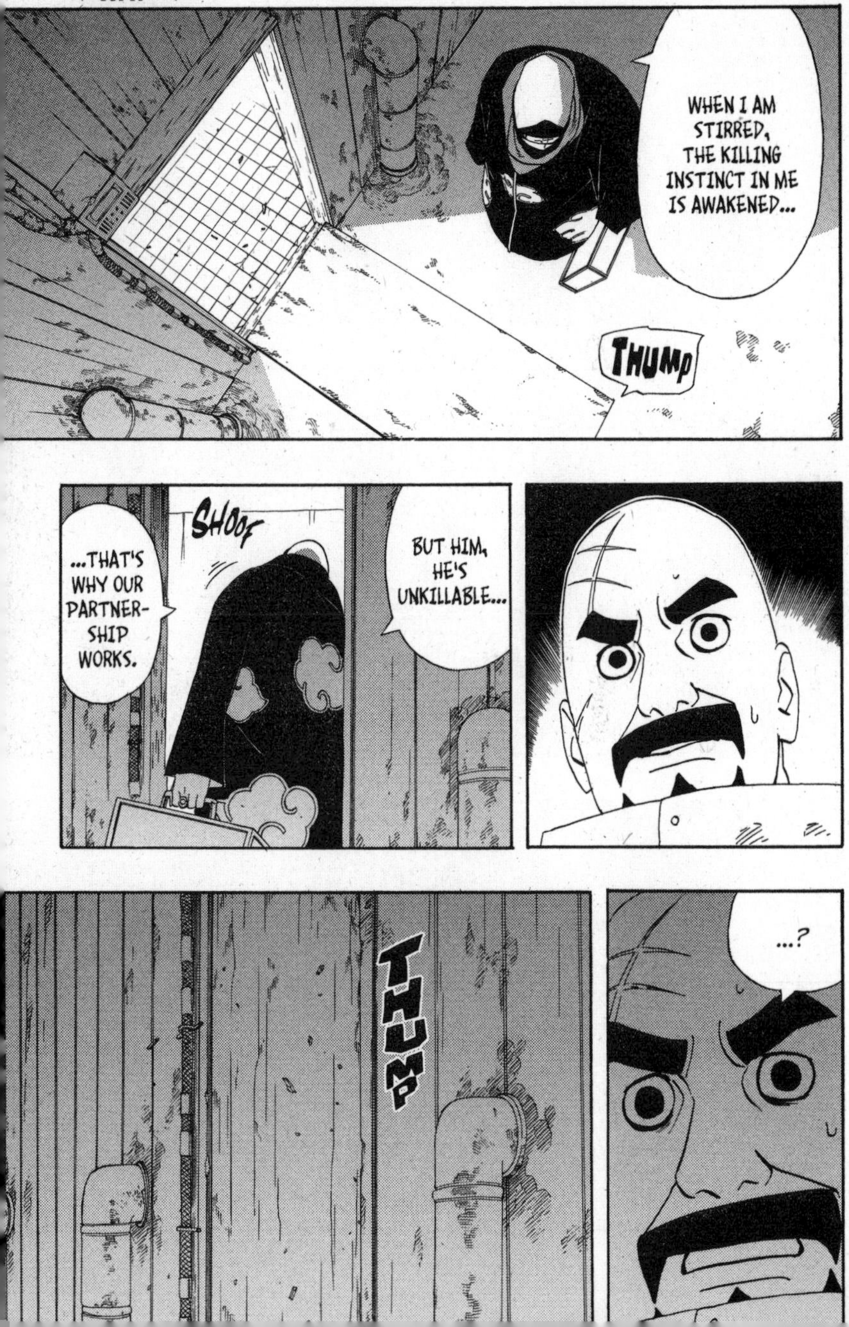
WHEN I AM STIRRED, THE KILLING INSTINCT IN ME IS AWAKENED...
THUMP
BUT HIM, HE'S UNKILLABLE...
SHOOF
...THAT'S WHY OUR PARTNER-SHIP WORKS.
...?
THUMP

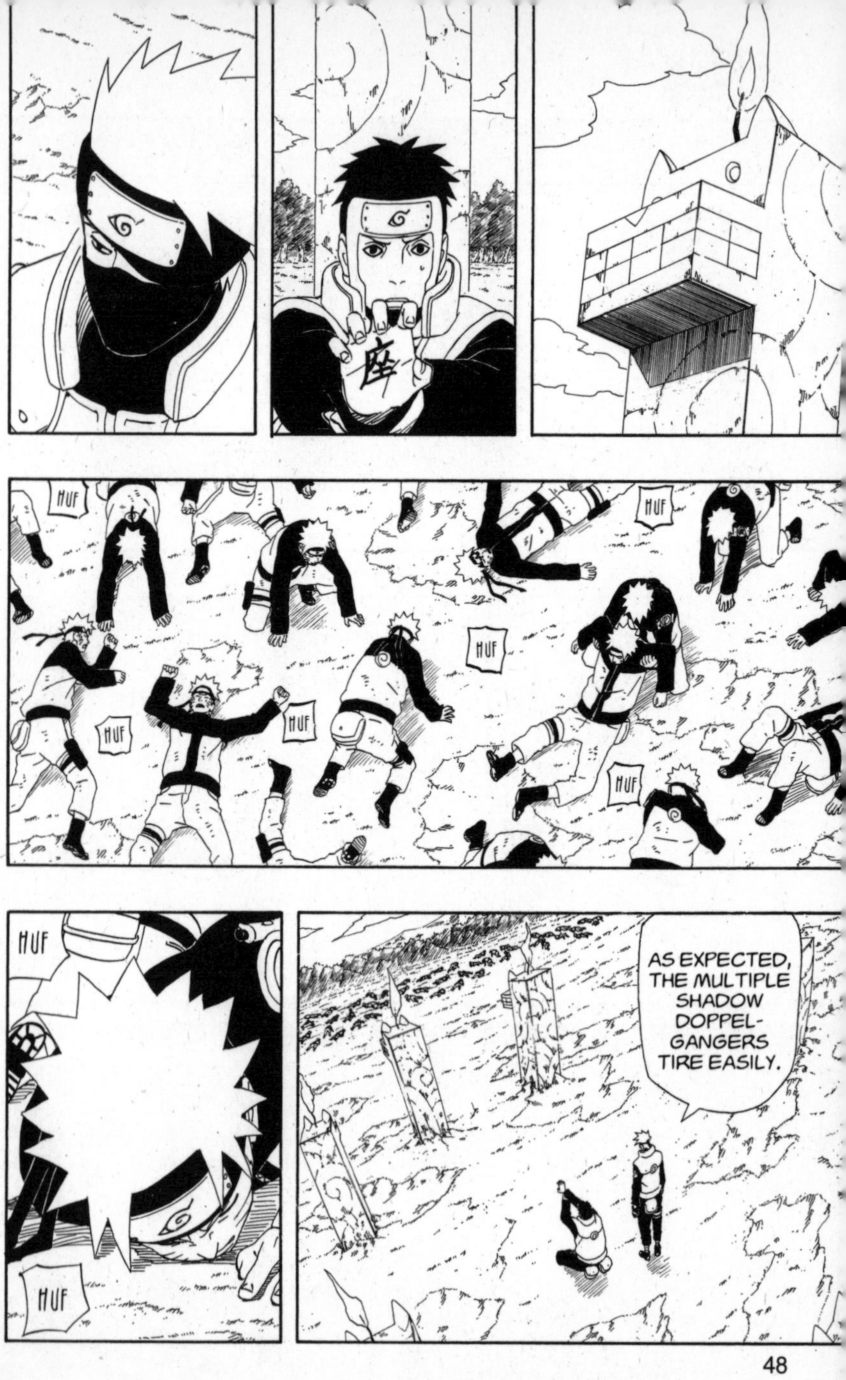
HUF
HUF
HUF
HUF
HUF
HUF
AS EXPECTED, THE MULTIPLE SHADOW DOPPEL-GANGERS TIRE EASILY.
HUF
HUF

READ THIS WAY

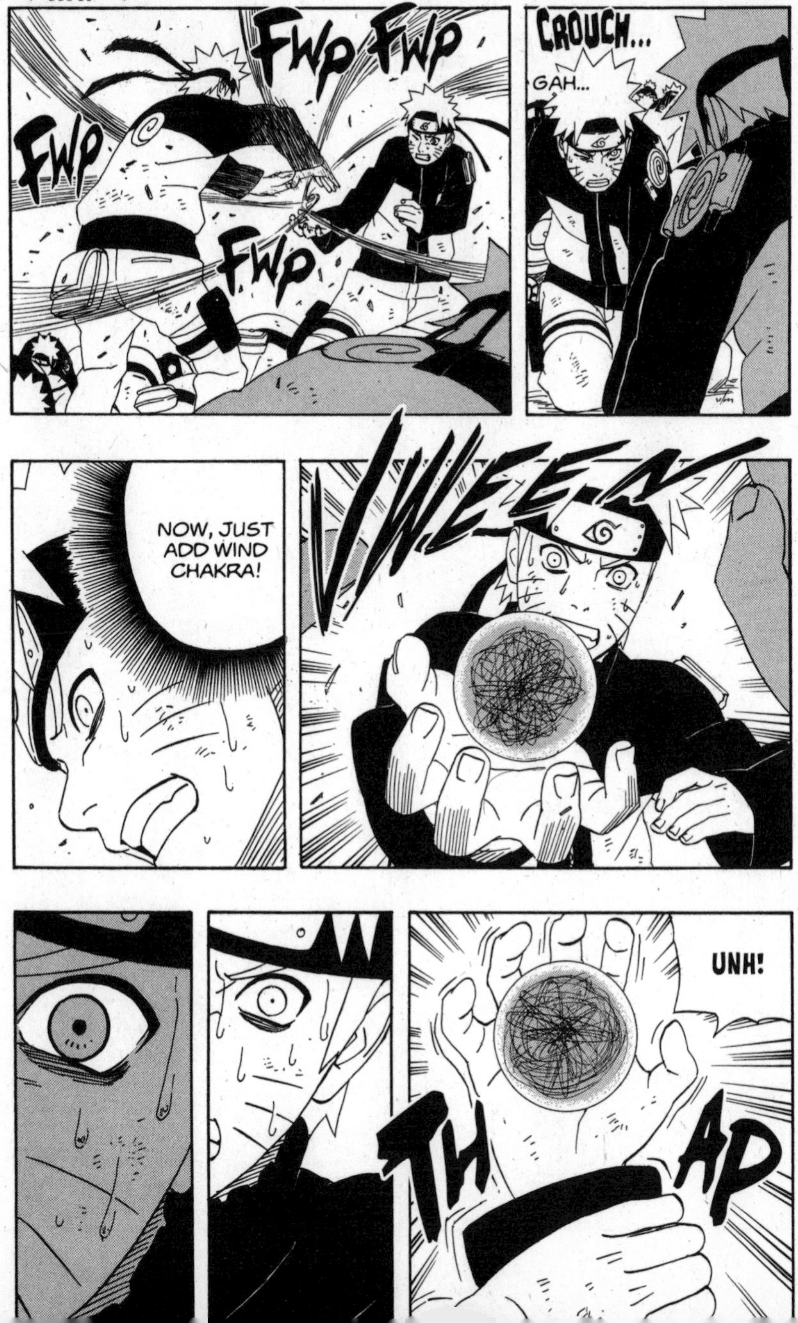
CROUCH...
GAH...
FWP FWP
FWP
FWP
VWEEN
NOW, JUST ADD WIND CHAKRA!
UNH!
THAP

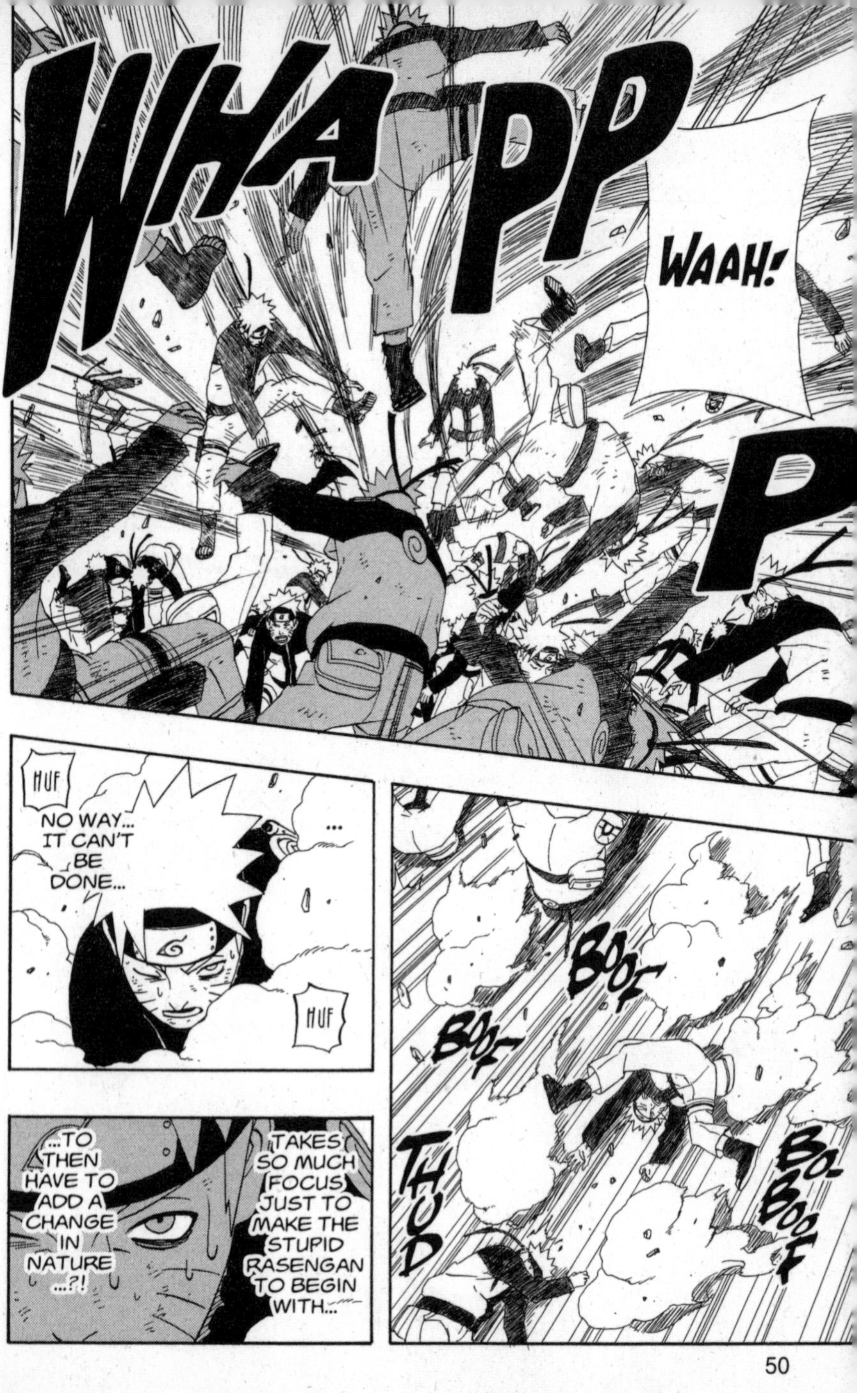
WHAPP
WAAH!
P
BOOF
BOOF
THUD
BA-BOOOF
HUF
NO WAY... IT CAN'T BE DONE...
...
HUF
TAKES SO MUCH FOCUS JUST TO MAKE THE STUPID RASENGAN TO BEGIN WITH...
...TO THEN HAVE TO ADD A CHANGE IN NATURE ...?!

READ THIS WAY

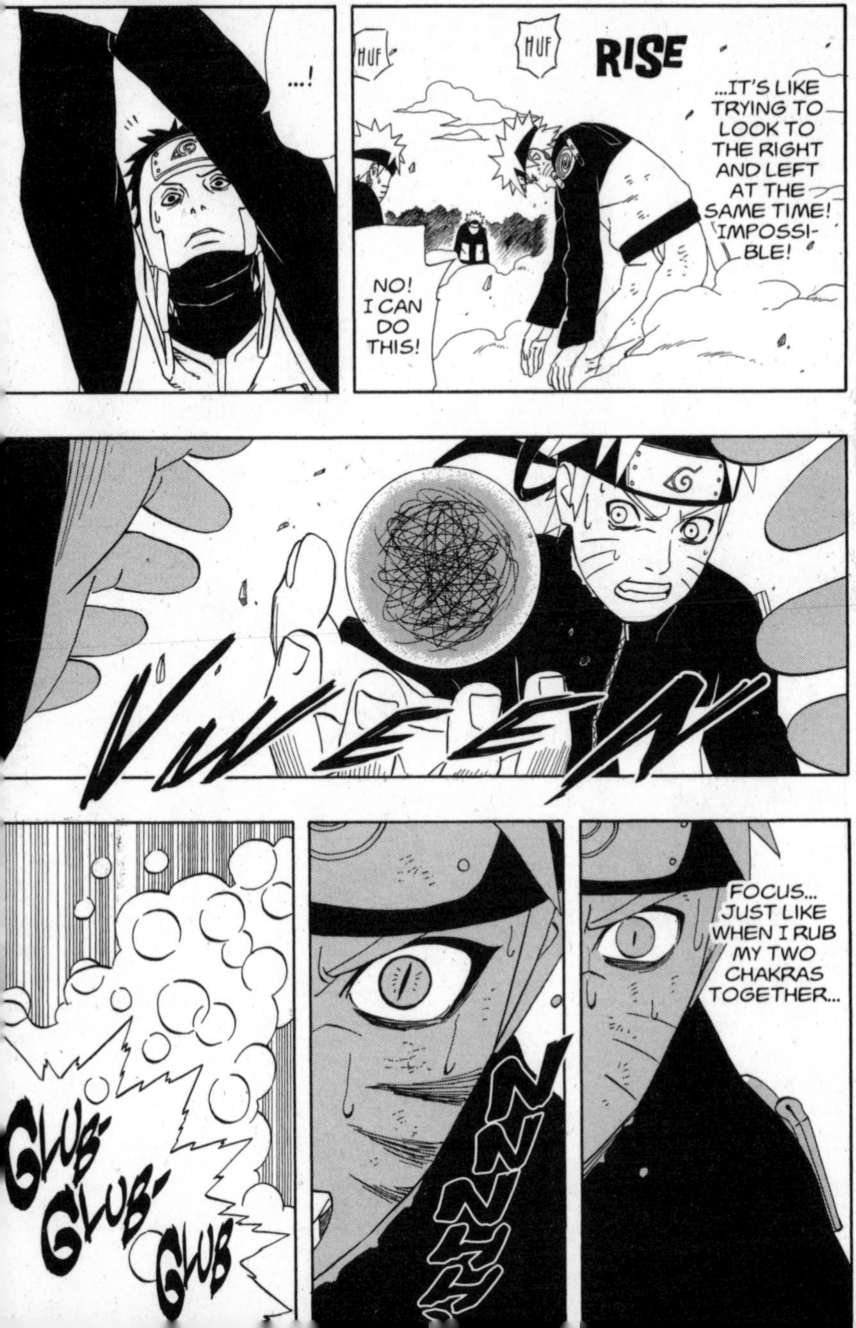

HUF
HUF
RISE
...IT'S LIKE TRYING TO LOOK TO THE RIGHT AND LEFT AT THE SAME TIME! IMPOSSIBLE!
NO! I CAN DO THIS!
...!
VWEEEN
FOCUS... JUST LIKE WHEN I RUB MY TWO CHAKRAS TOGETHER...
GLUB-GLUB-GLUB

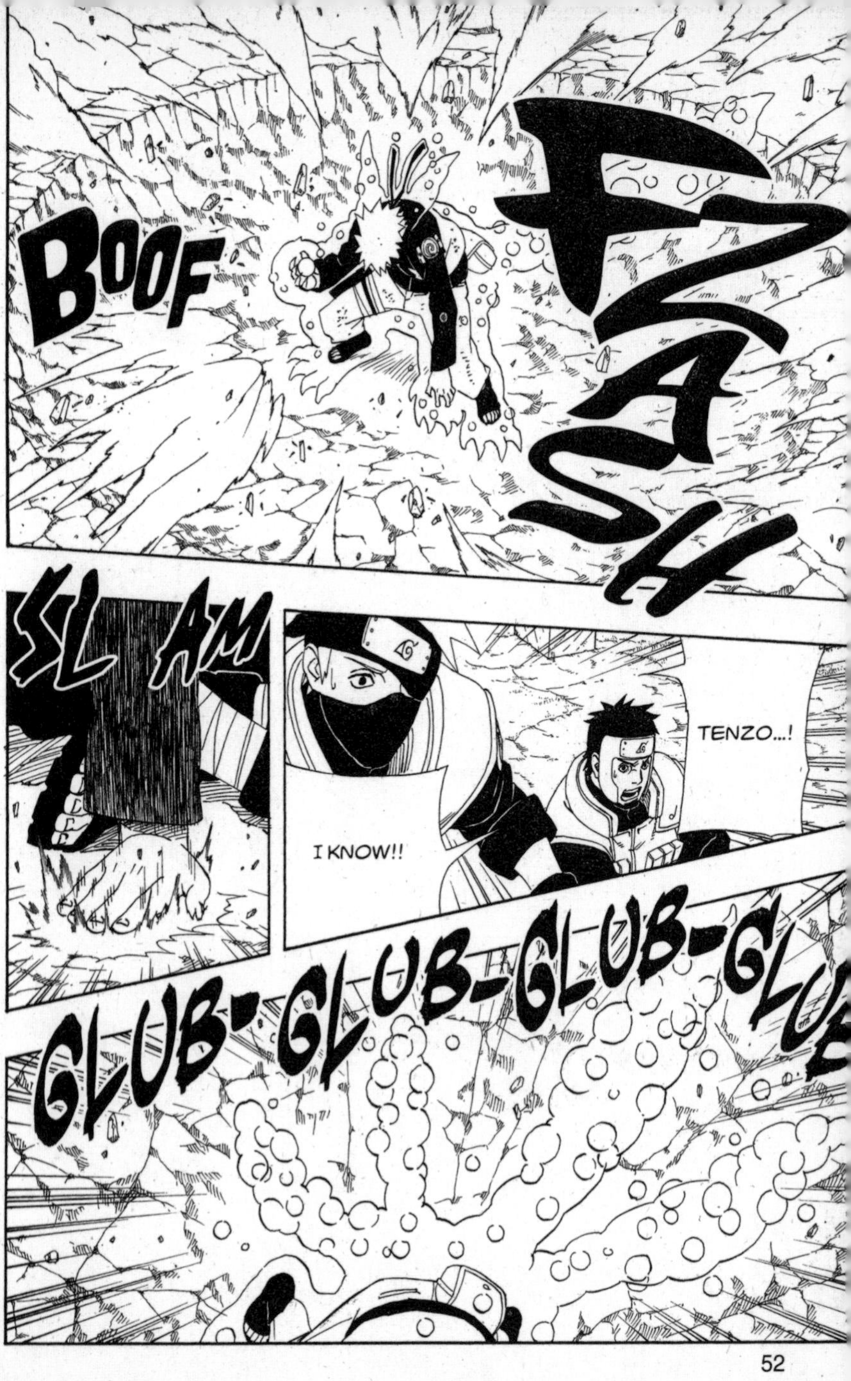
FZASH
BOOF
TENZO...!
I KNOW!!
SLAM
GLUB-GLUB-GLUB-GLUB-GLU

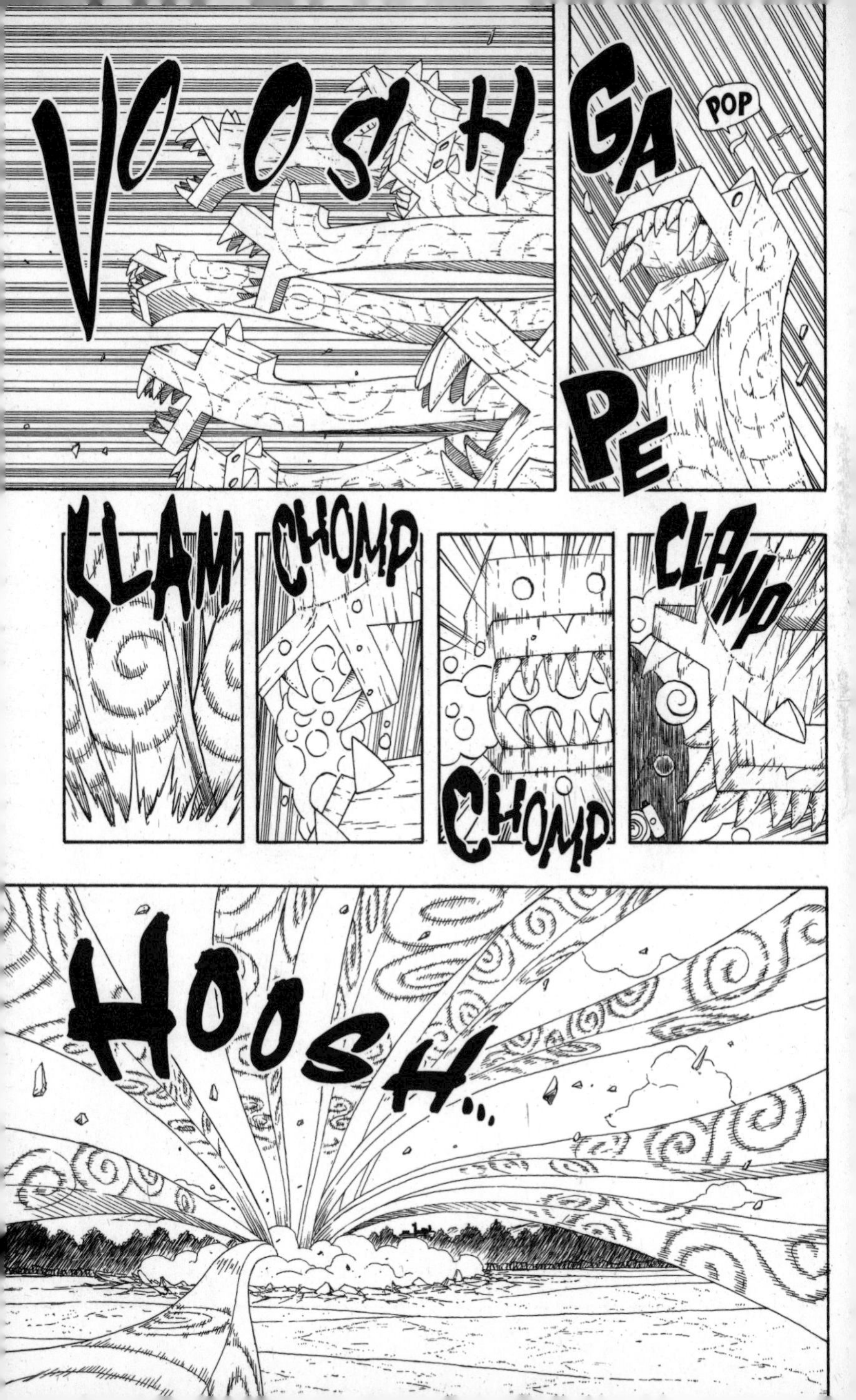
POP
GA
PE
VOOSH
CLAMP
CHOMP
CHOMP
SLAM
HOOSH...

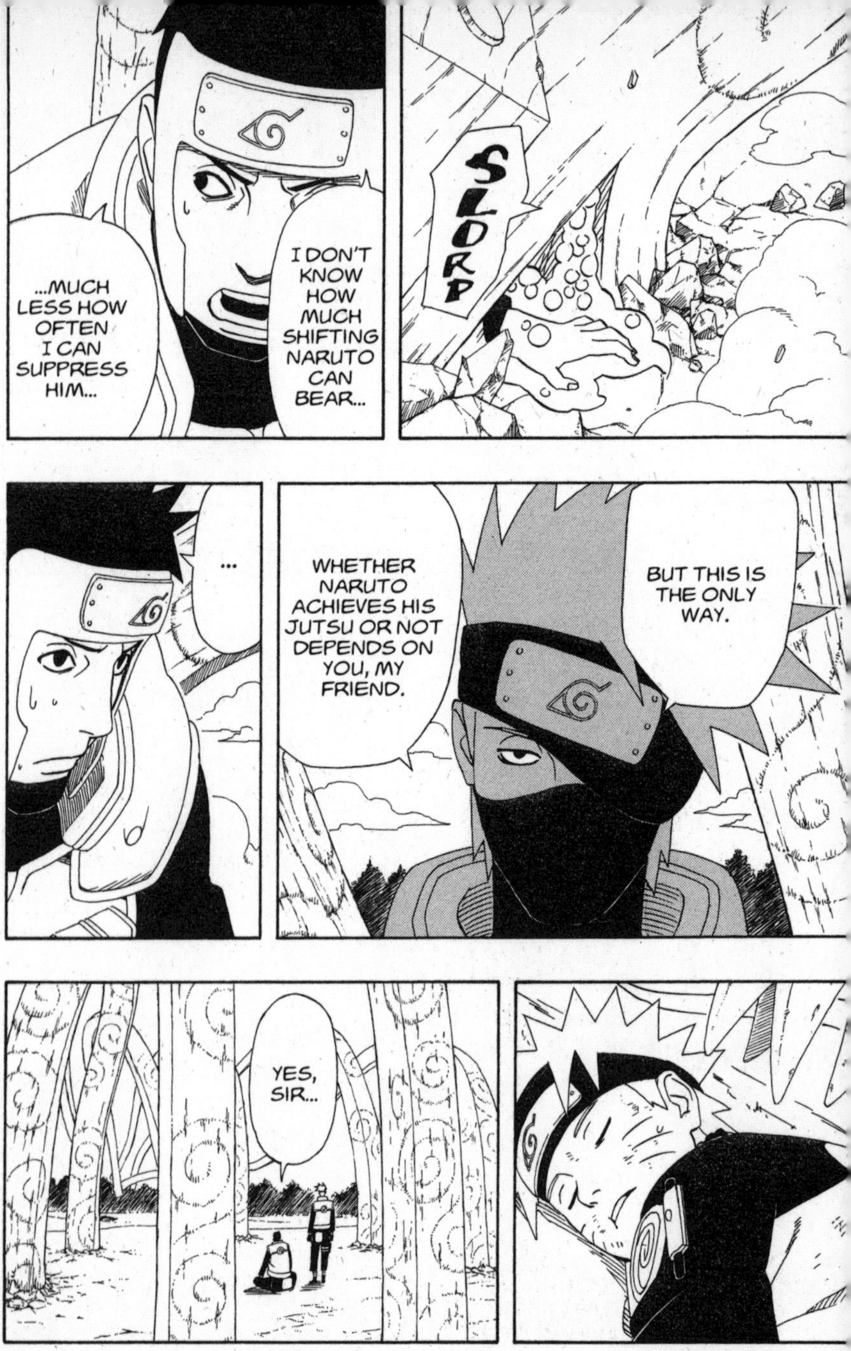
I DON'T KNOW HOW MUCH SHIFTING NARUTO CAN BEAR...
...MUCH LESS HOW OFTEN I CAN SUPPRESS HIM...
SLORP
...
WHETHER NARUTO ACHIEVES HIS JUTSU OR NOT DEPENDS ON YOU, MY FRIEND.
BUT THIS IS THE ONLY WAY.
YES, SIR...

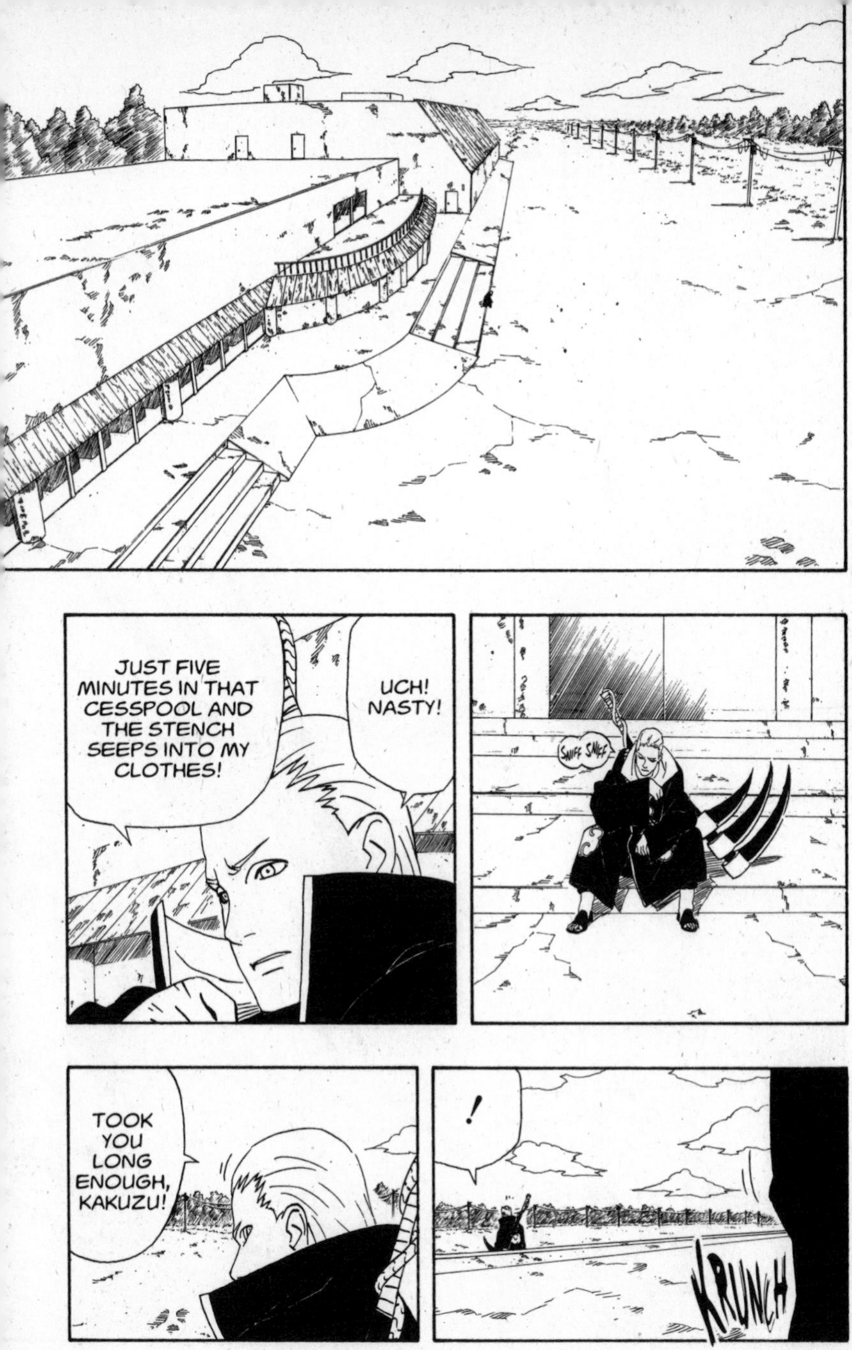
SNIFF SNIFF
UCH! NASTY!
JUST FIVE MINUTES IN THAT CESSPOOL AND THE STENCH SEEPS INTO MY CLOTHES!
!
KRUNCH
TOOK YOU LONG ENOUGH, KAKUZU!

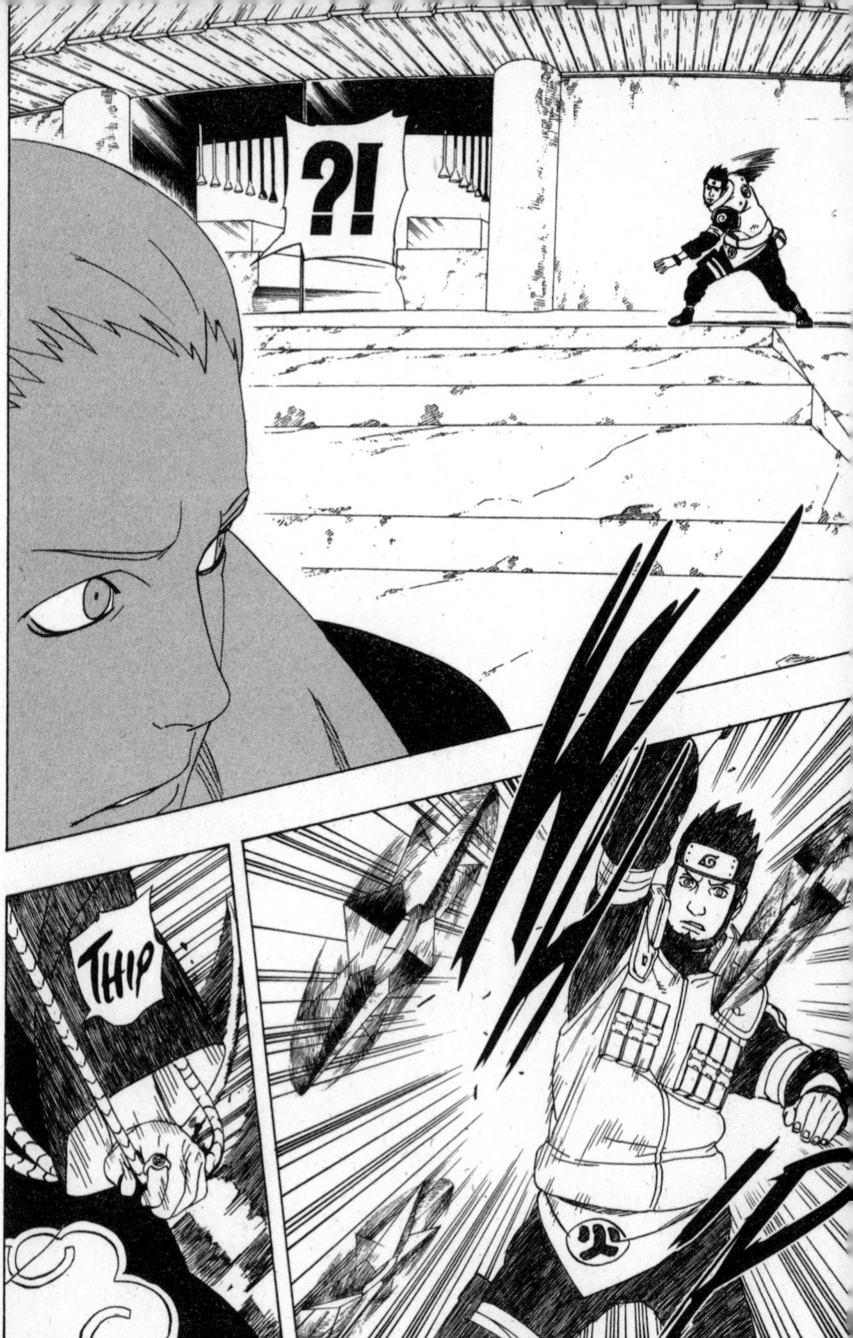
?!
THIP

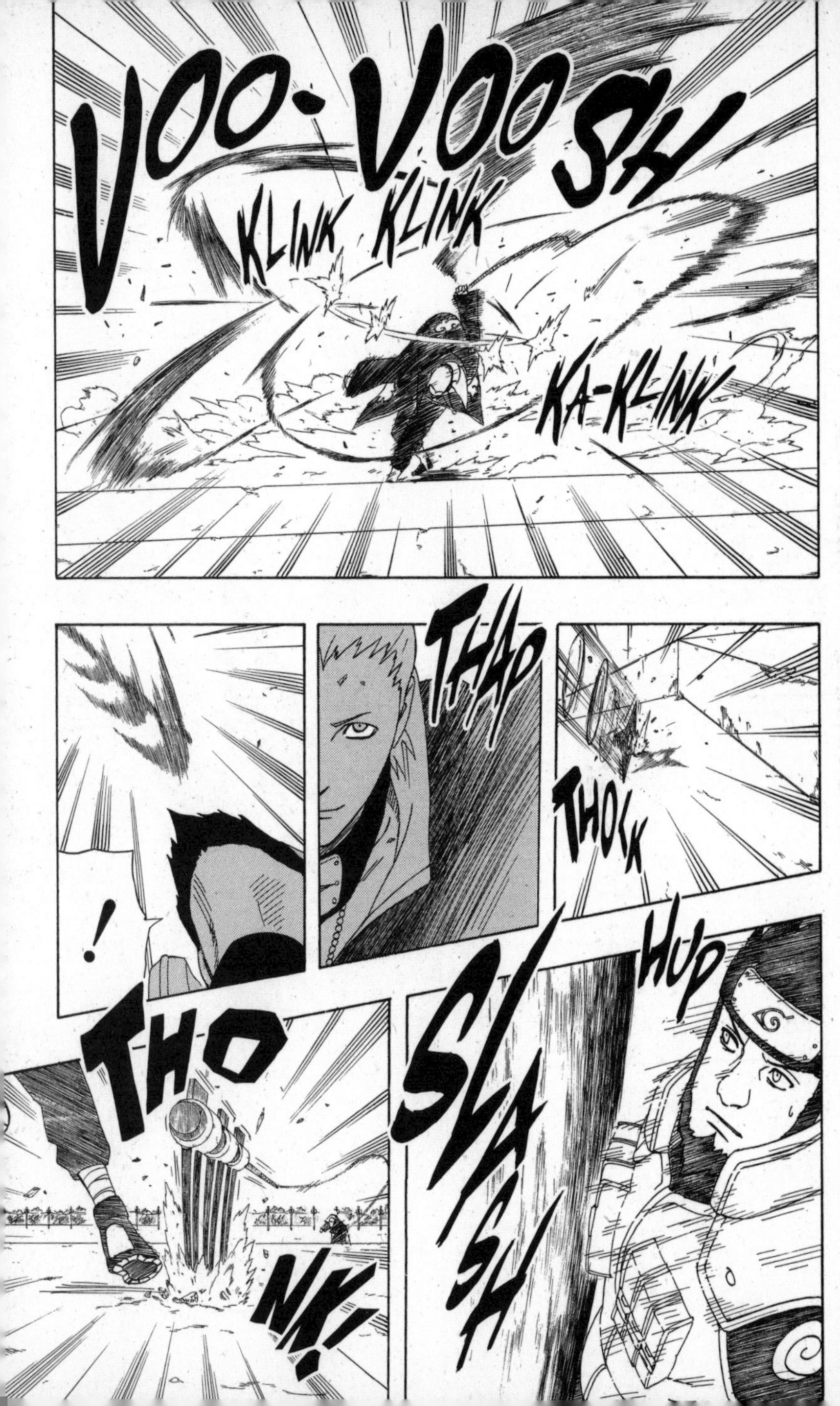
VOO-VOOSH
KLINK KLINK
KA-KLINK
THOLK
THAP
!
HUP
SLASH
THO
NK!

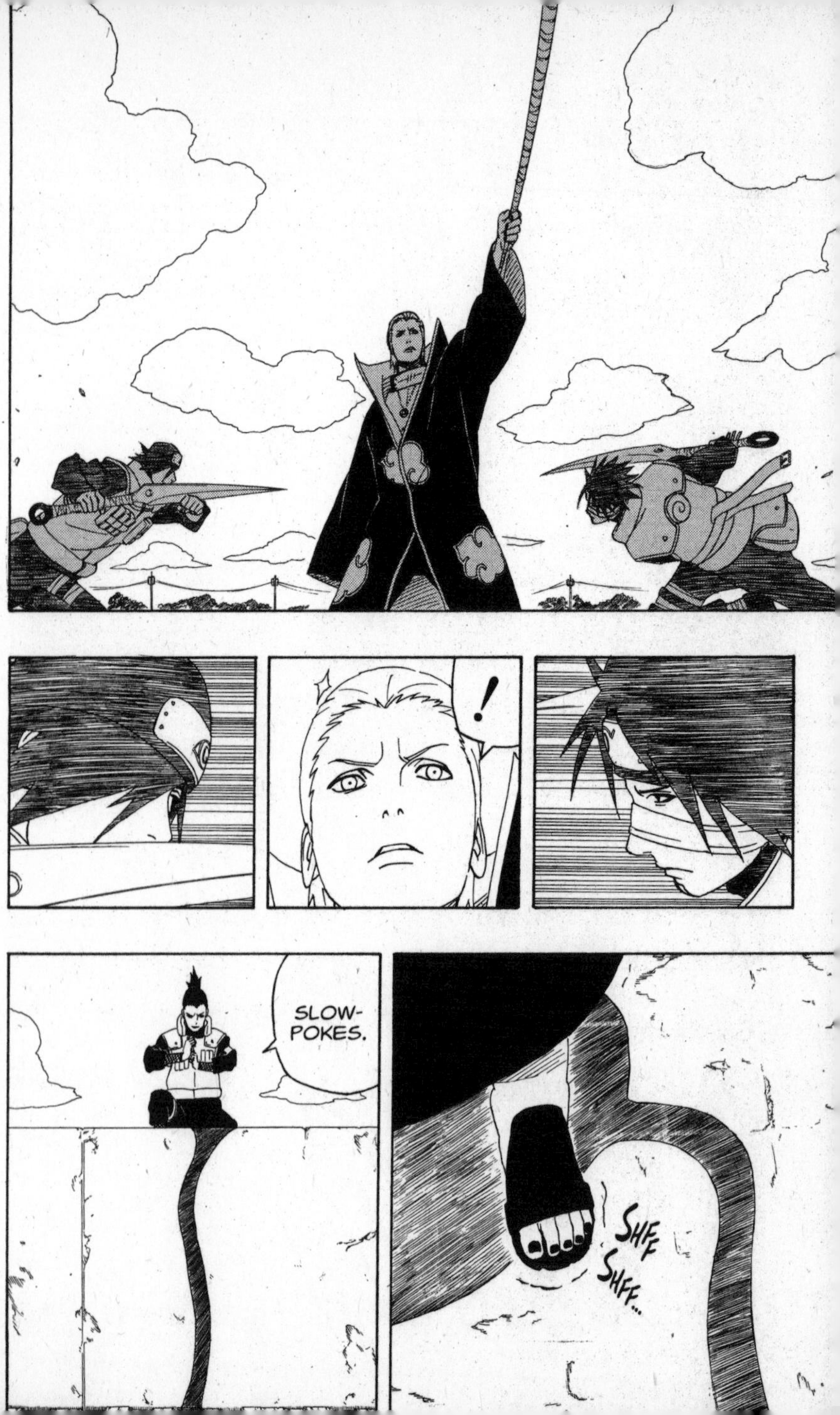
!
SHFF
SHFF...
SLOW-POKES.

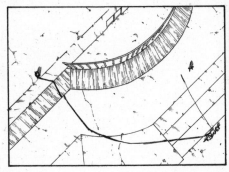

ONE DOWN.

...WHO ARE YOU PEOPLE, ANYWAY?

YEESH, OWW...

NARUTO

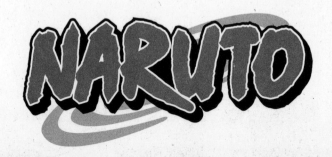

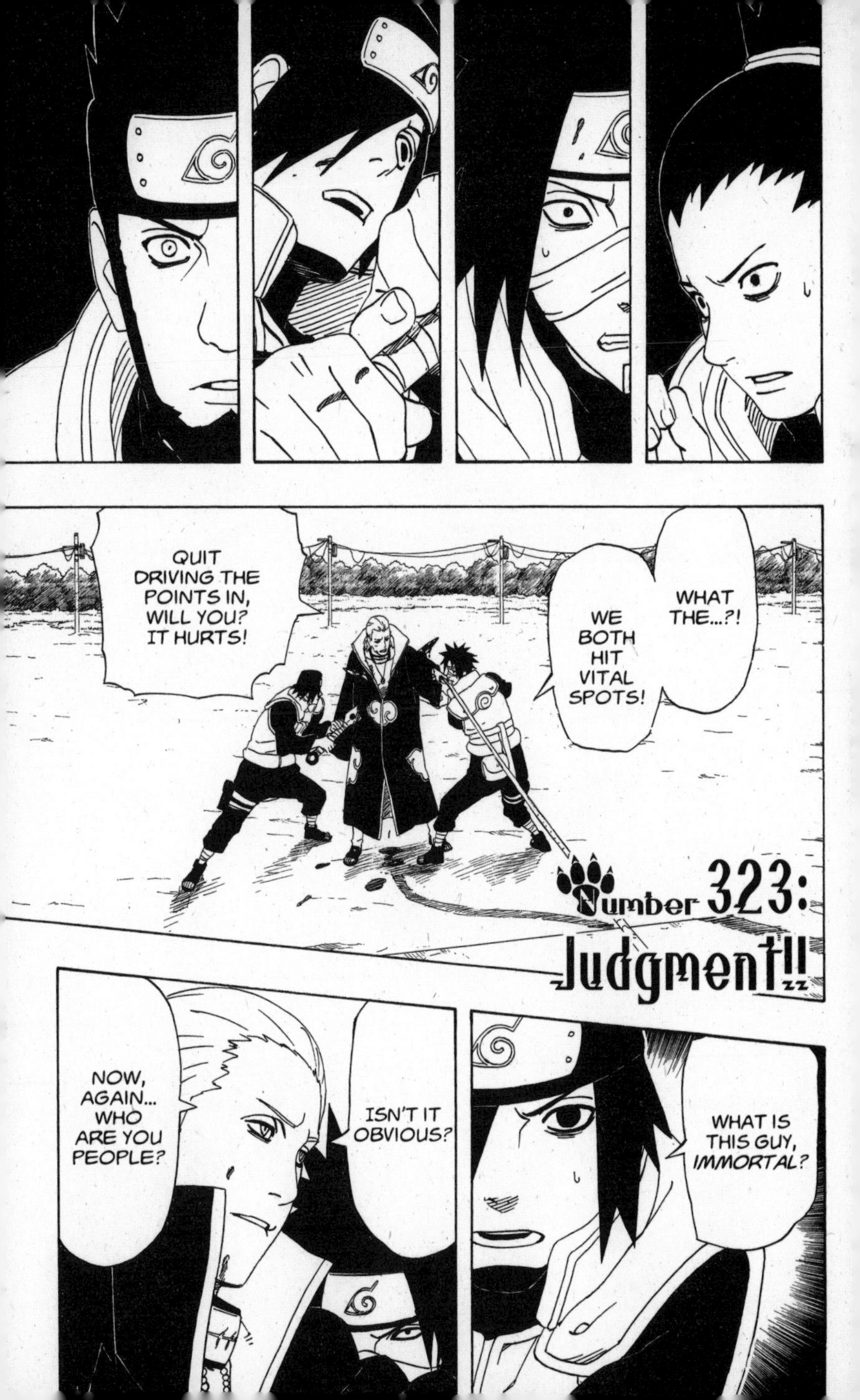
WHAT THE...?!
WE BOTH HIT VITAL SPOTS!
QUIT DRIVING THE POINTS IN, WILL YOU? IT HURTS!
Number 323: Judgment!!
WHAT IS THIS GUY, IMMORTAL?
NOW, AGAIN... WHO ARE YOU PEOPLE?
ISN'T IT OBVIOUS?

!

...

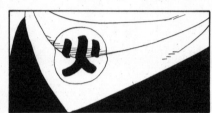

SLUMP

?

...LOOKS LIKE I'M GOING BACK TO THAT STINKY COLLECTION OFFICE...

OH. TERRIFIC...

CHIRIKU...

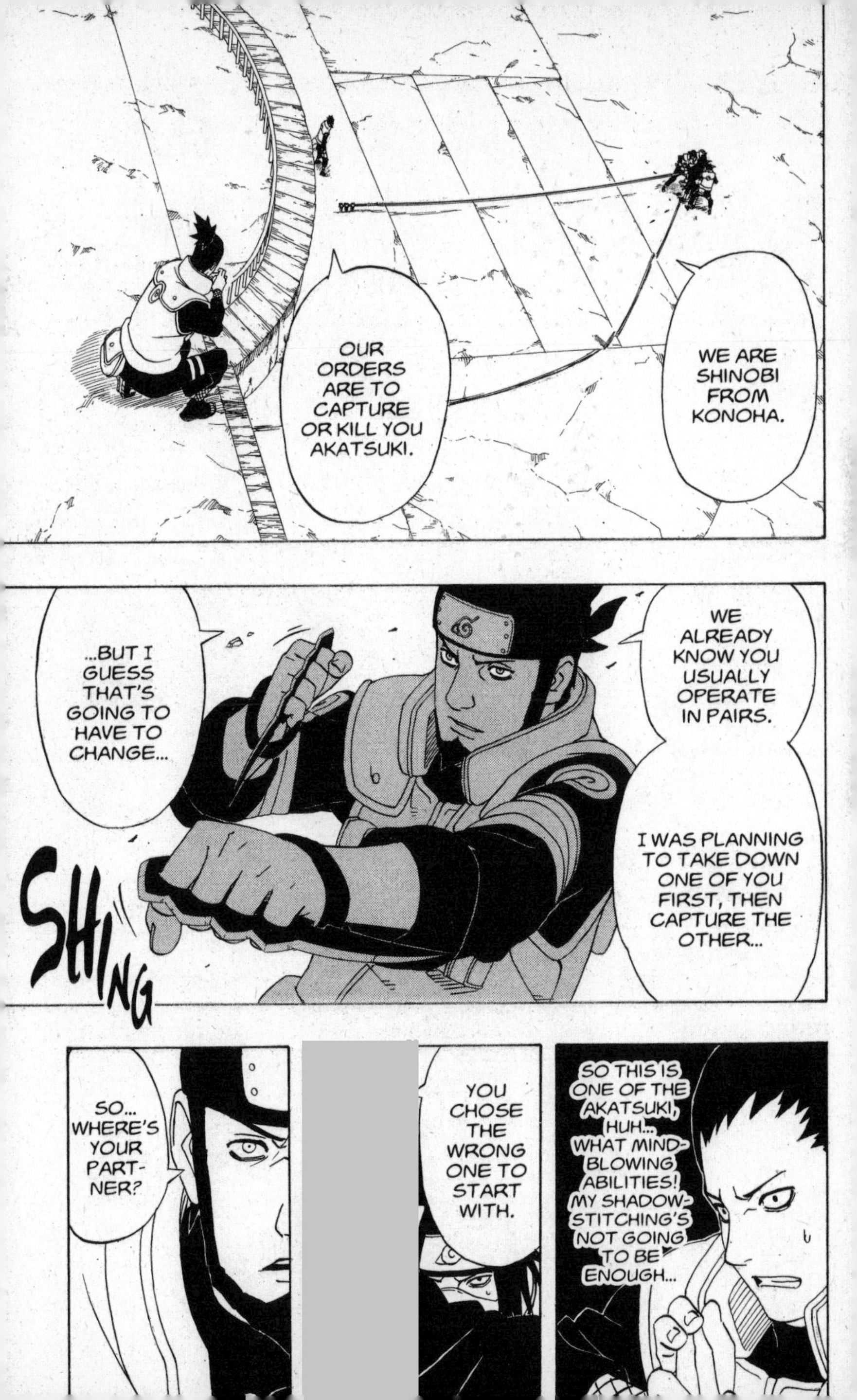
WE ARE SHINOBI FROM KONOHA.
OUR ORDERS ARE TO CAPTURE OR KILL YOU AKATSUKI.
WE ALREADY KNOW YOU USUALLY OPERATE IN PAIRS.
I WAS PLANNING TO TAKE DOWN ONE OF YOU FIRST, THEN CAPTURE THE OTHER...
...BUT I GUESS THAT'S GOING TO HAVE TO CHANGE...
SHING
SO THIS IS ONE OF THE AKATSUKI, HUH... WHAT MIND-BLOWING ABILITIES! MY SHADOW-STITCHING'S NOT GOING TO BE ENOUGH...
YOU CHOSE THE WRONG ONE TO START WITH.
SO... WHERE'S YOUR PARTNER?

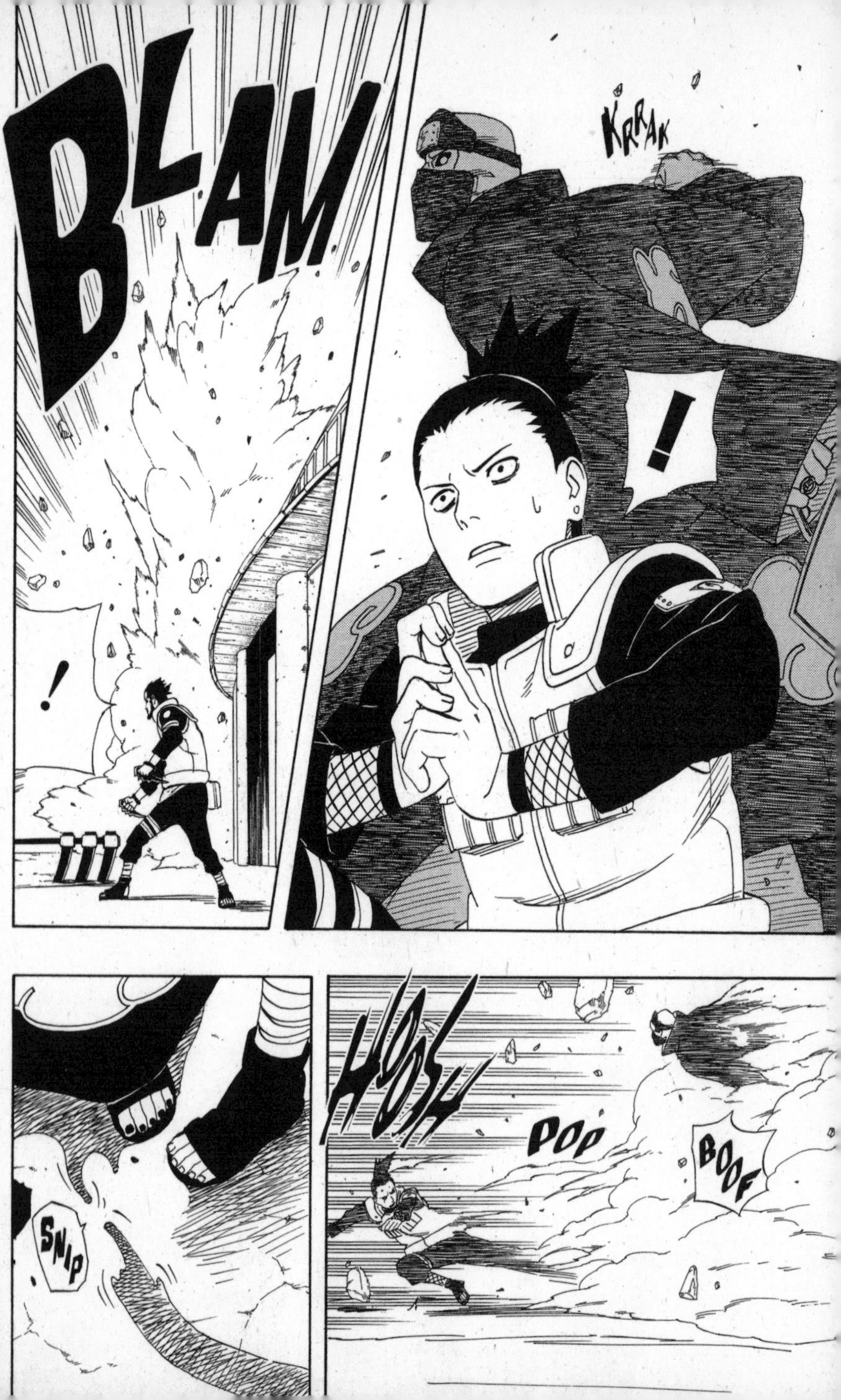
KRRAK
!
BLAM
!
HOSH
POP
BOOF
SNIP

READ THIS WAY

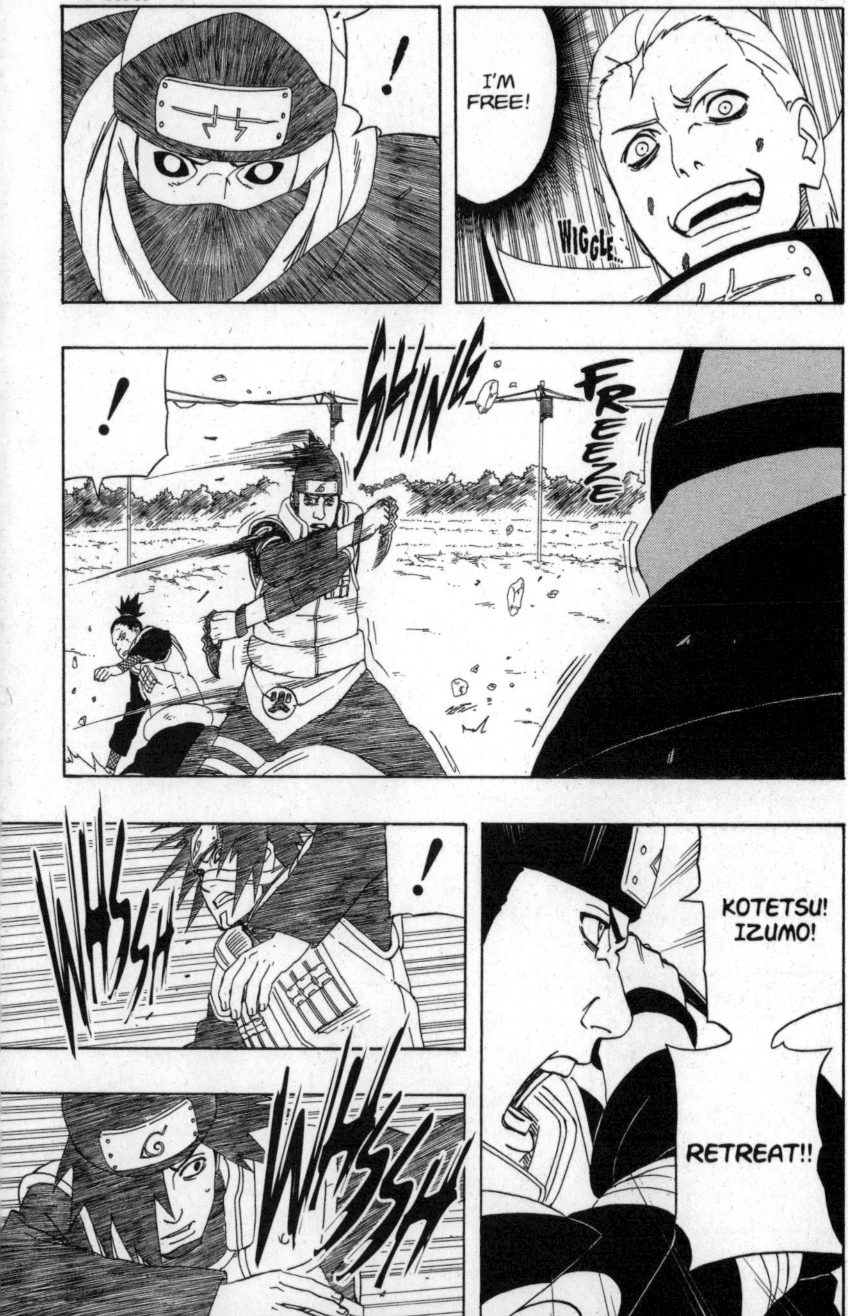
I'M FREE!
WIGGLE...
!
FREEZE
SHING
!
KOTETSU! IZUMO!
RETREAT!!
WHSSH
!
WHSSH

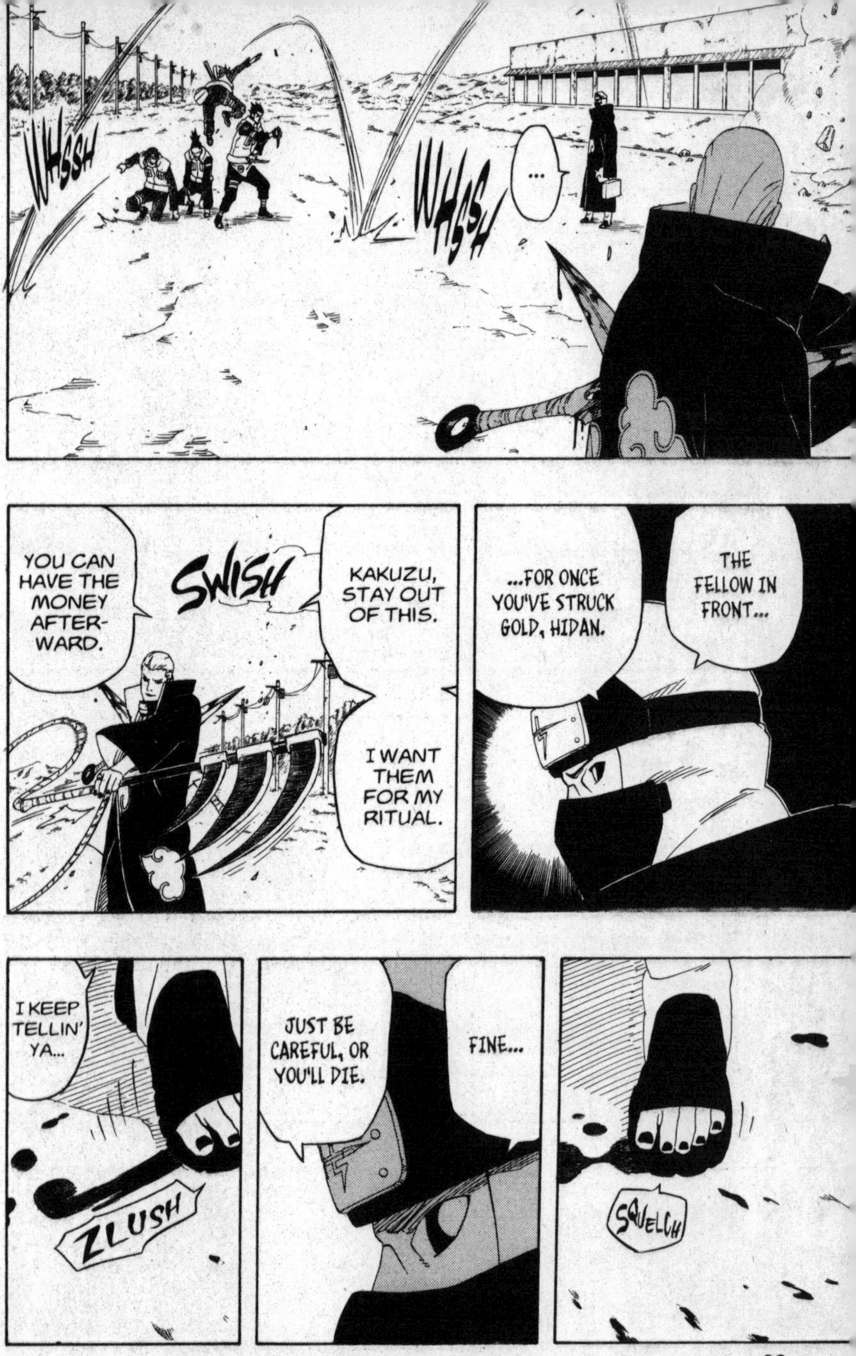
...
WHSSH
WHSSH
THE FELLOW IN FRONT...
...FOR ONCE YOU'VE STRUCK GOLD, HIDAN.
KAKUZU, STAY OUT OF THIS.
I WANT THEM FOR MY RITUAL.
SWISH
YOU CAN HAVE THE MONEY AFTER-WARD.
SQUELCH
FINE...
JUST BE CAREFUL, OR YOU'LL DIE.
I KEEP TELLIN' YA...
ZLUSH

READ THIS WAY

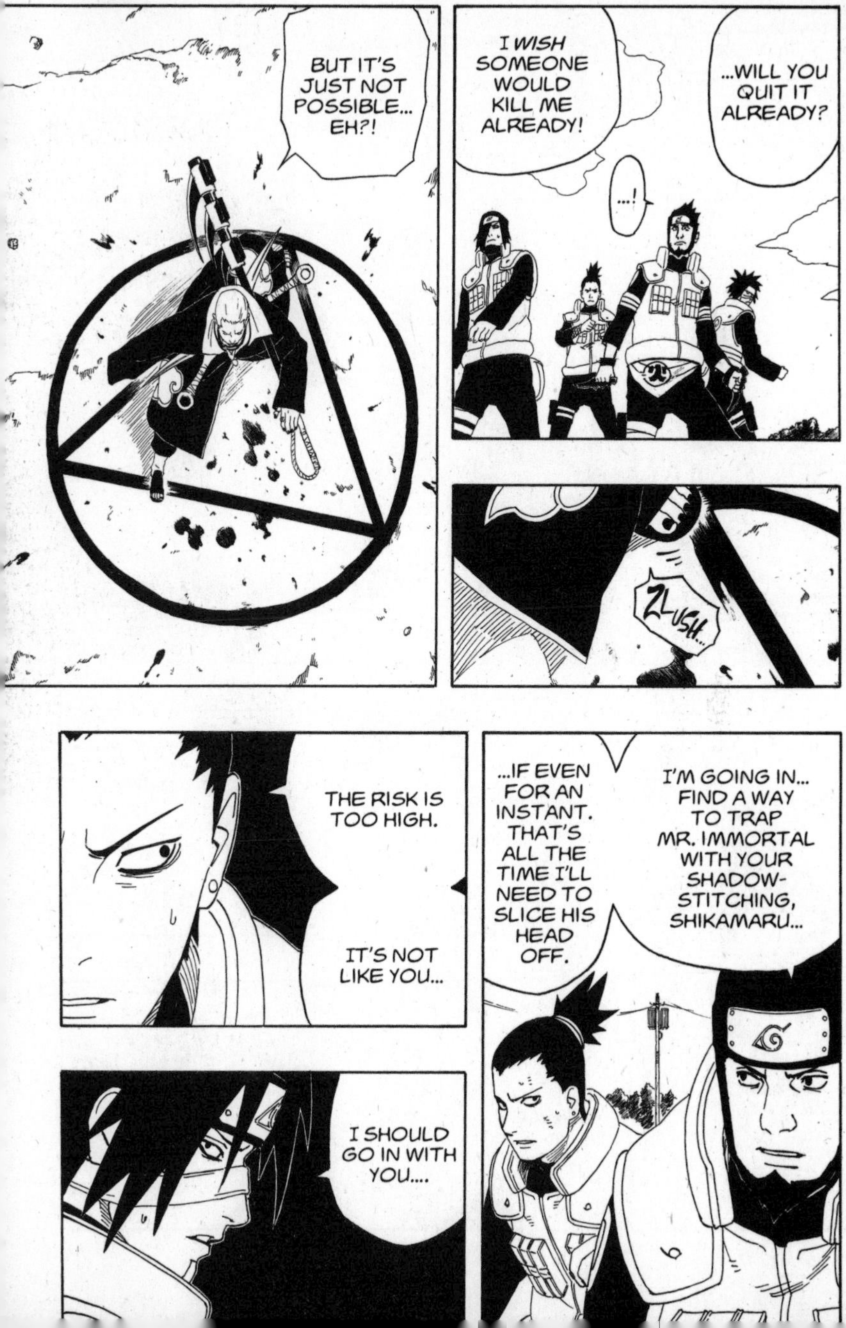
...WILL YOU QUIT IT ALREADY?
I WISH SOMEONE WOULD KILL ME ALREADY!
...!
ZLUSH...
BUT IT'S JUST NOT POSSIBLE... EH?!
I'M GOING IN... FIND A WAY TO TRAP MR. IMMORTAL WITH YOUR SHADOW-STITCHING, SHIKAMARU...
...IF EVEN FOR AN INSTANT. THAT'S ALL THE TIME I'LL NEED TO SLICE HIS HEAD OFF.
THE RISK IS TOO HIGH.
IT'S NOT LIKE YOU...
I SHOULD GO IN WITH YOU....

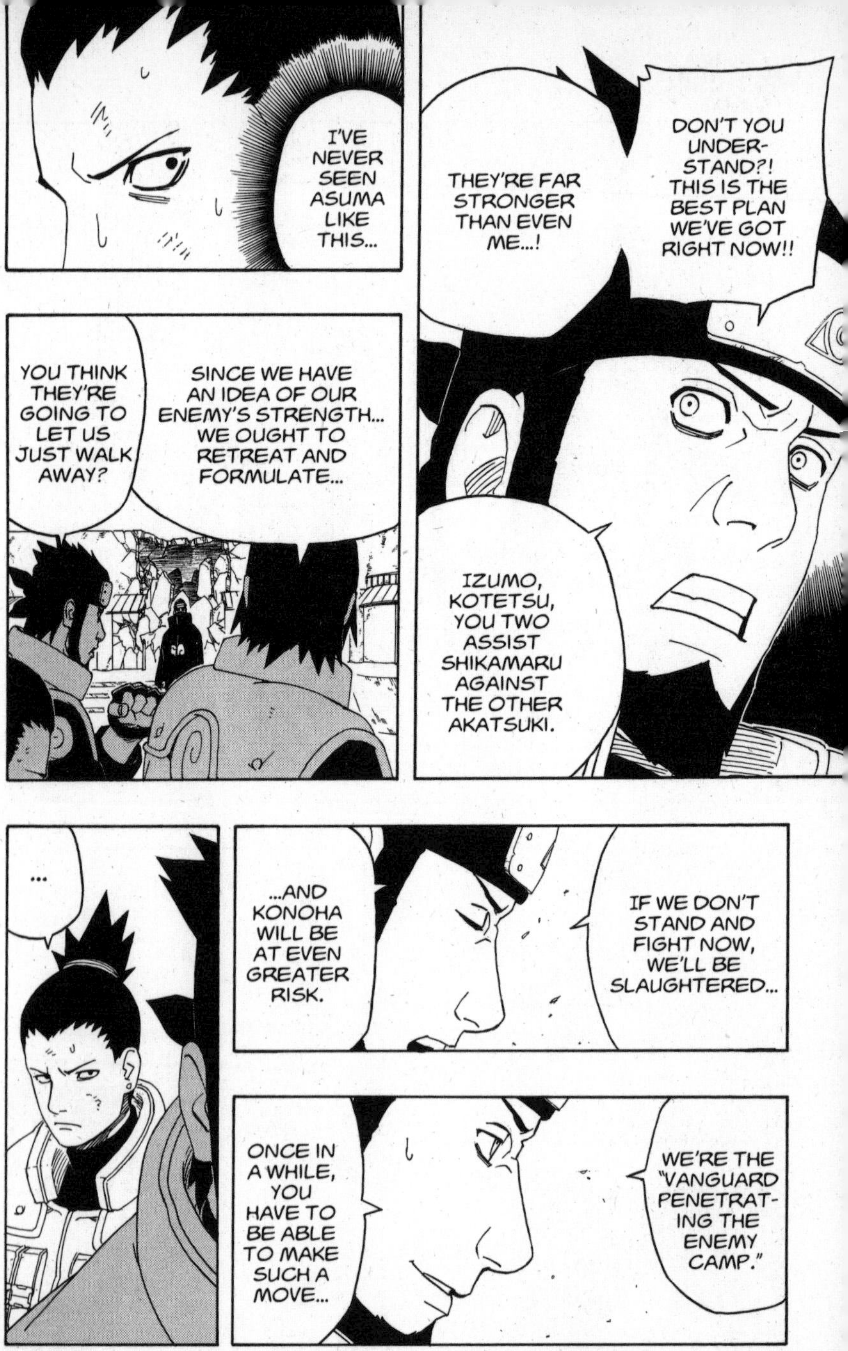
DON'T YOU UNDER-STAND?! THIS IS THE BEST PLAN WE'VE GOT RIGHT NOW!!
THEY'RE FAR STRONGER THAN EVEN ME...!
IZUMO, KOTETSU, YOU TWO ASSIST SHIKAMARU AGAINST THE OTHER AKATSUKI.
I'VE NEVER SEEN ASUMA LIKE THIS...
SINCE WE HAVE AN IDEA OF OUR ENEMY'S STRENGTH... WE OUGHT TO RETREAT AND FORMULATE...
YOU THINK THEY'RE GOING TO LET US JUST WALK AWAY?
IF WE DON'T STAND AND FIGHT NOW, WE'LL BE SLAUGHTERED...
...AND KONOHA WILL BE AT EVEN GREATER RISK.
WE'RE THE "VANGUARD PENETRAT-ING THE ENEMY CAMP."
ONCE IN A WHILE, YOU HAVE TO BE ABLE TO MAKE SUCH A MOVE...
...

READ THIS WAY

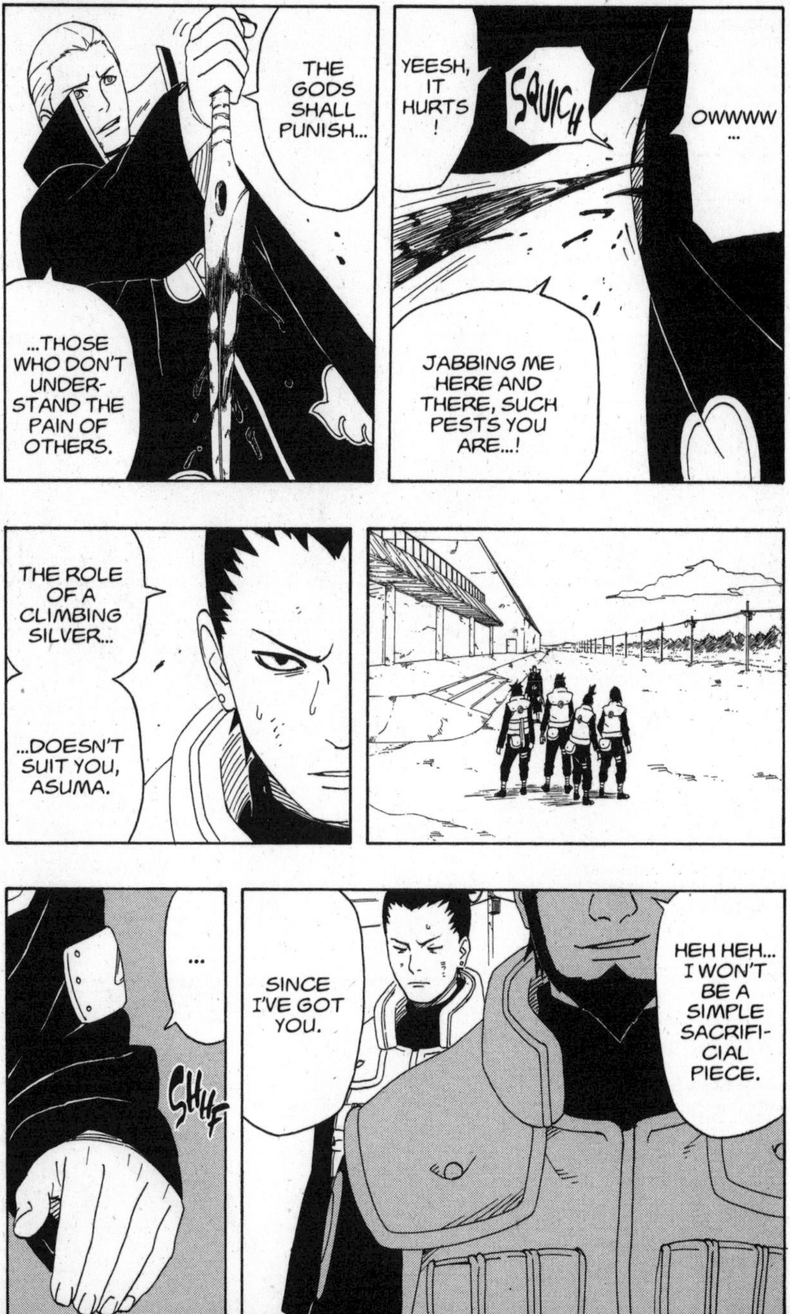
OWWWW...
SQUICH
YEESH, IT HURTS!
JABBING ME HERE AND THERE, SUCH PESTS YOU ARE...!
THE GODS SHALL PUNISH...
...THOSE WHO DON'T UNDER-STAND THE PAIN OF OTHERS.
THE ROLE OF A CLIMBING SILVER...
...DOESN'T SUIT YOU, ASUMA.
HEH HEH... I WON'T BE A SIMPLE SACRIFI-CIAL PIECE.
SINCE I'VE GOT YOU.
...
SHHF

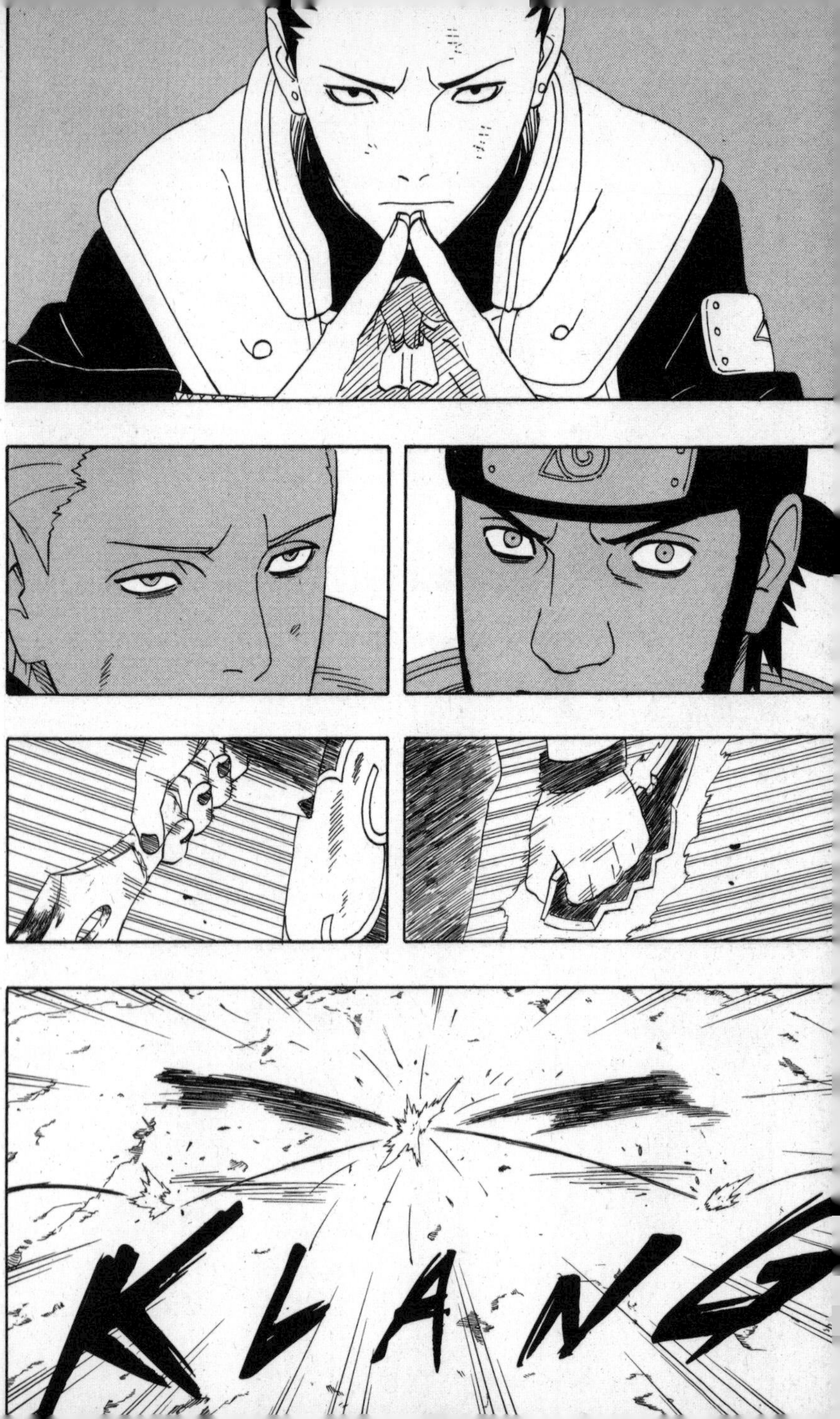
KLANG

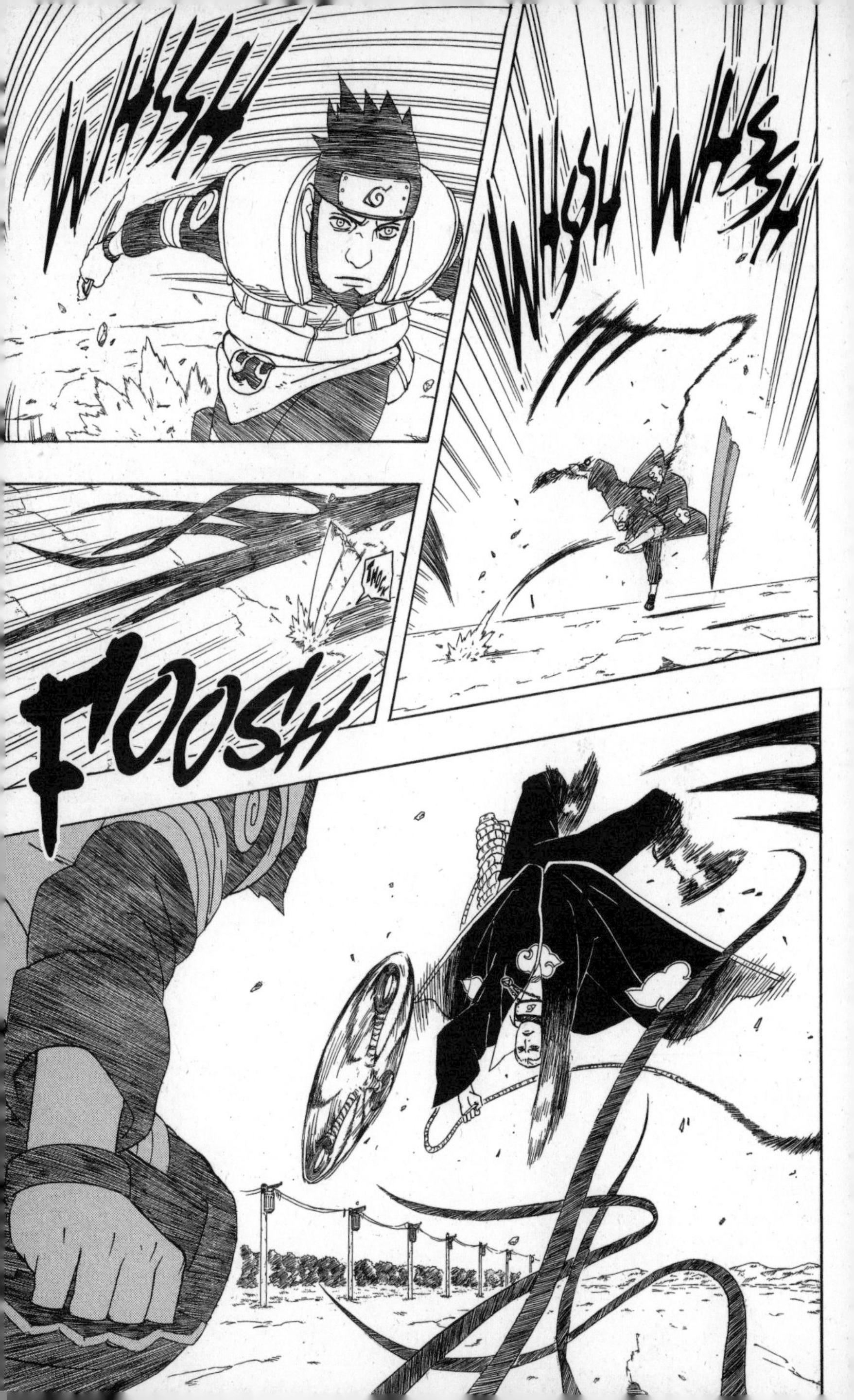
WHSH WHSH
WHSSH
THOCK
FOOSH

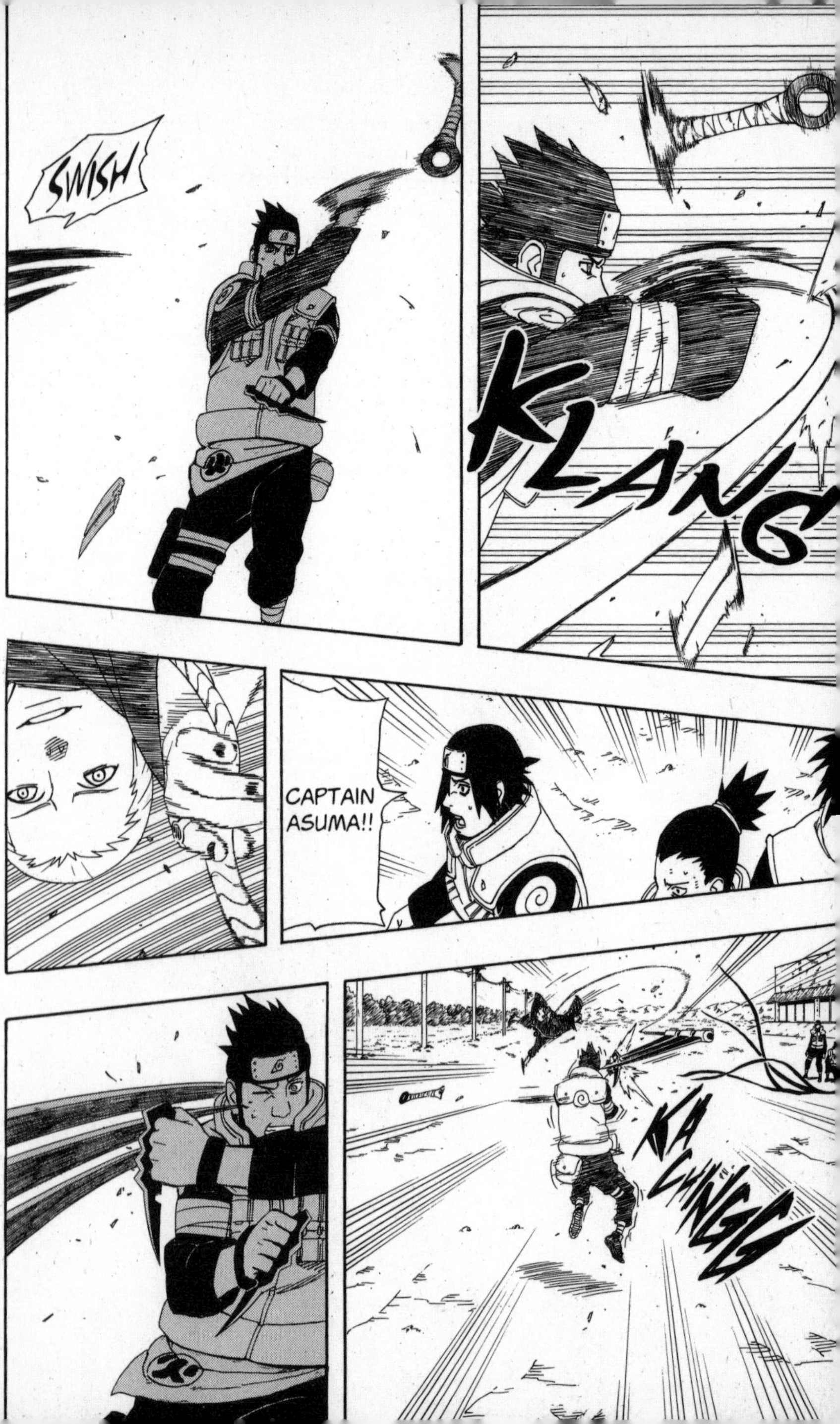
KLANG
SWISH
CAPTAIN ASUMA!!
KA CHING

READ THIS WAY

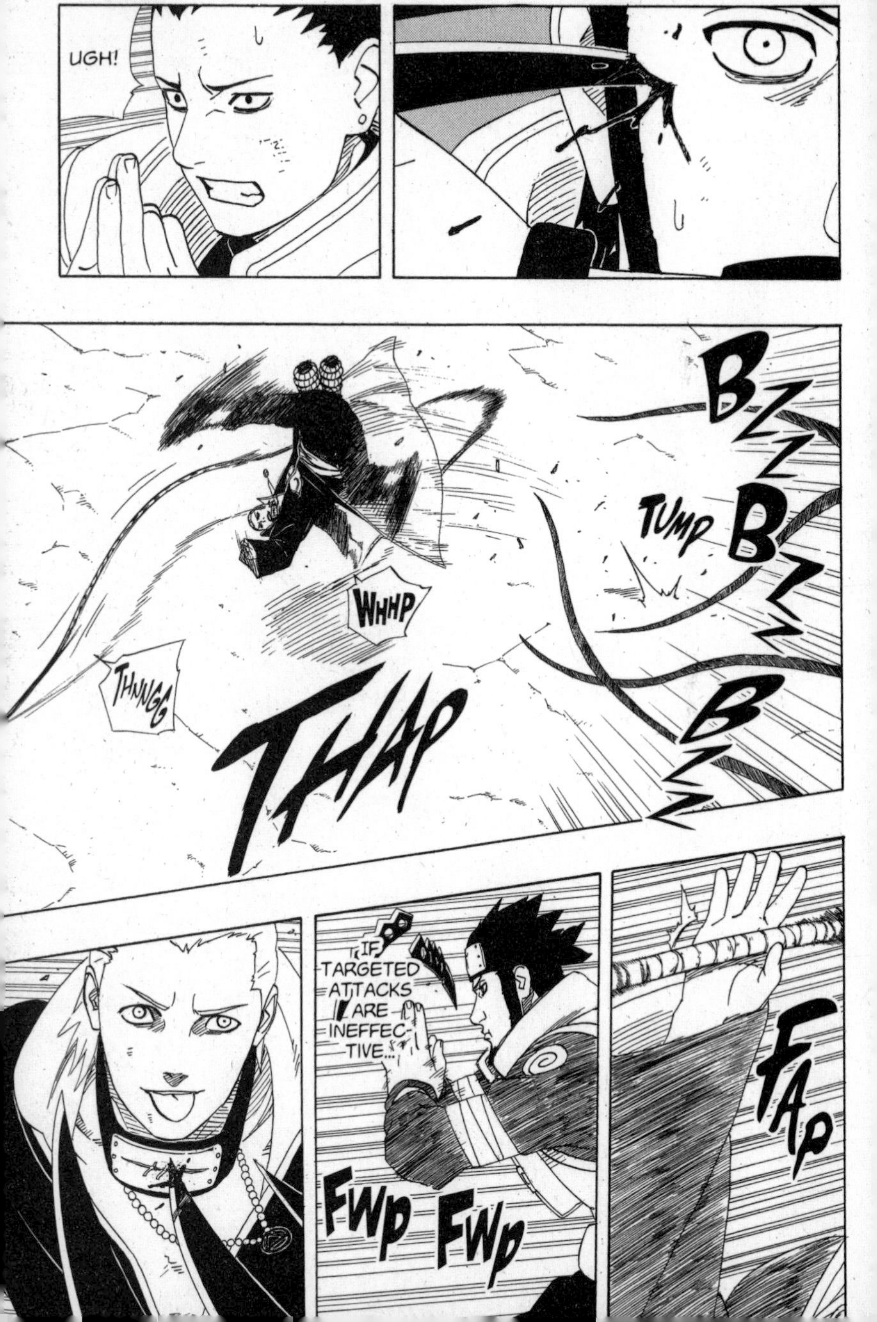

UGH!
BZZZBZZZBZZZ
TUMP
WHHP
THNNGG
THAP
FAP
IF TARGETED ATTACKS ARE INEFFECTIVE...
FWP FWP

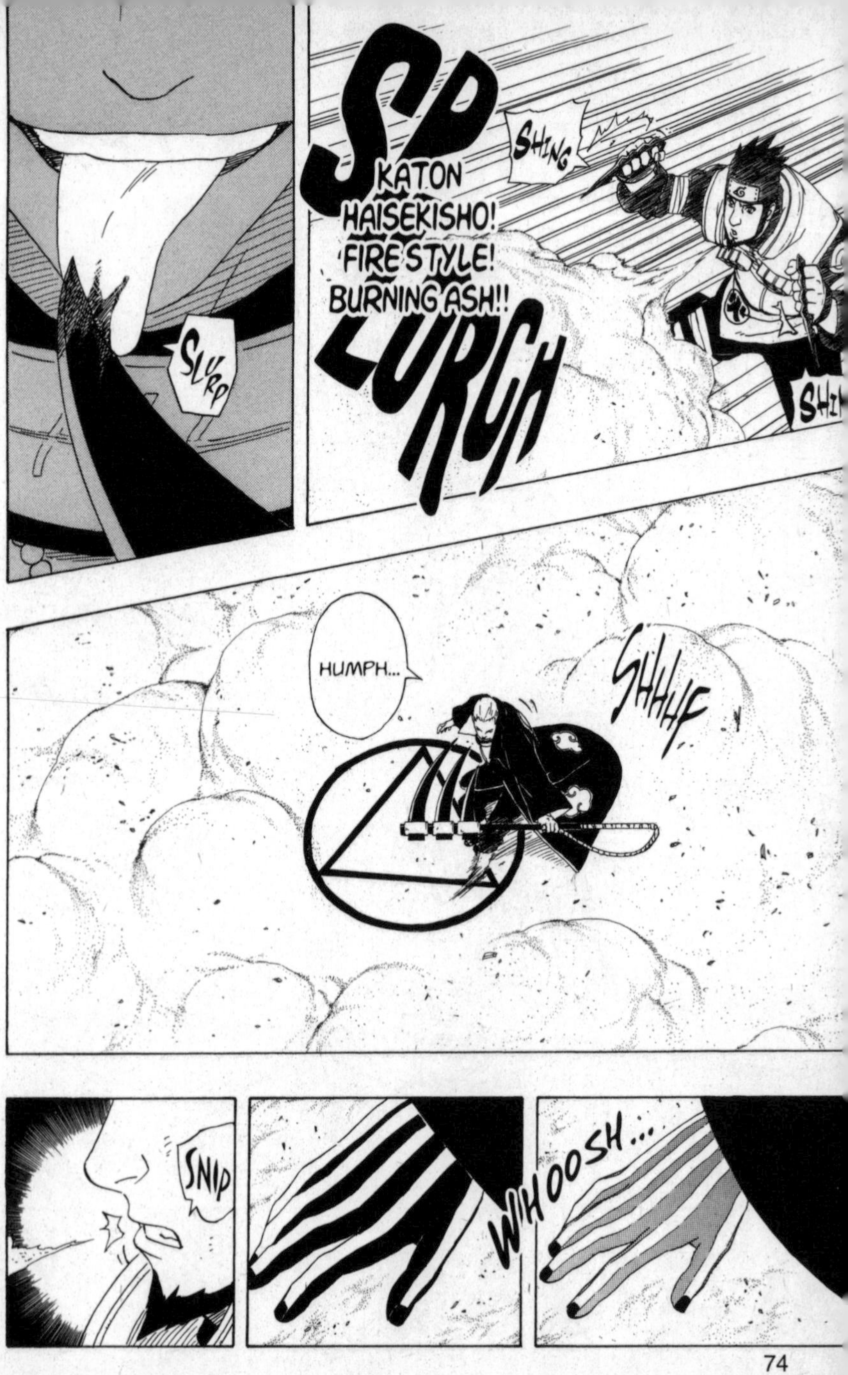
SHING
SP
KATON HAISEKISHO! FIRE STYLE! BURNING ASH!!
SHI
LURCH
SLURP
SHHHF
HUMPH...
WHOOSH...
SNIP

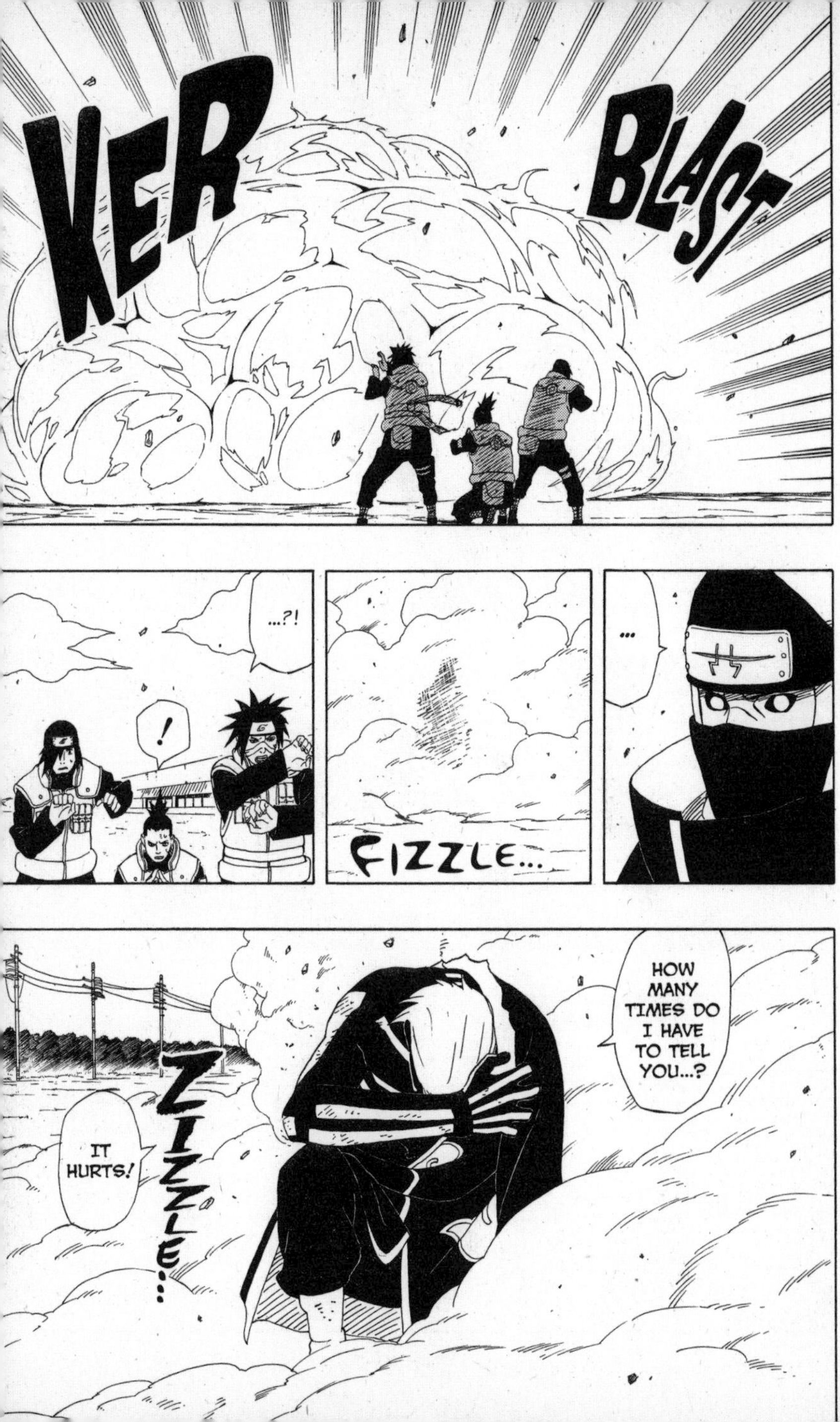
KER BLAST
...
FIZZLE...
...?!
!
HOW MANY TIMES DO I HAVE TO TELL YOU...?
ZIZZLE...
IT HURTS!

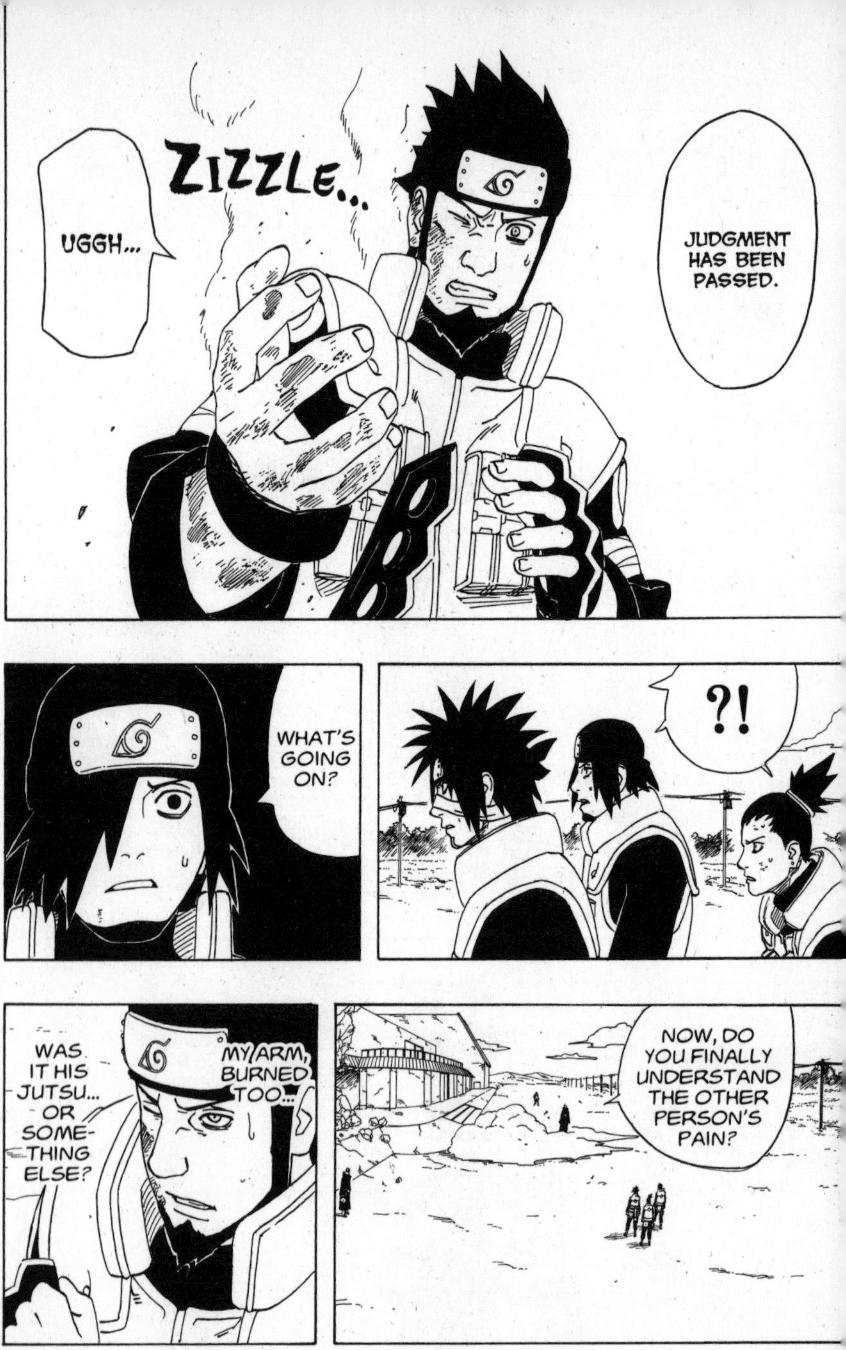
JUDGMENT HAS BEEN PASSED.
ZIZZLE...
UGGH...
?!
WHAT'S GOING ON?
NOW, DO YOU FINALLY UNDERSTAND THE OTHER PERSON'S PAIN?
MY ARM, BURNED TOO...
WAS IT HIS JUTSU... OR SOME-THING ELSE?

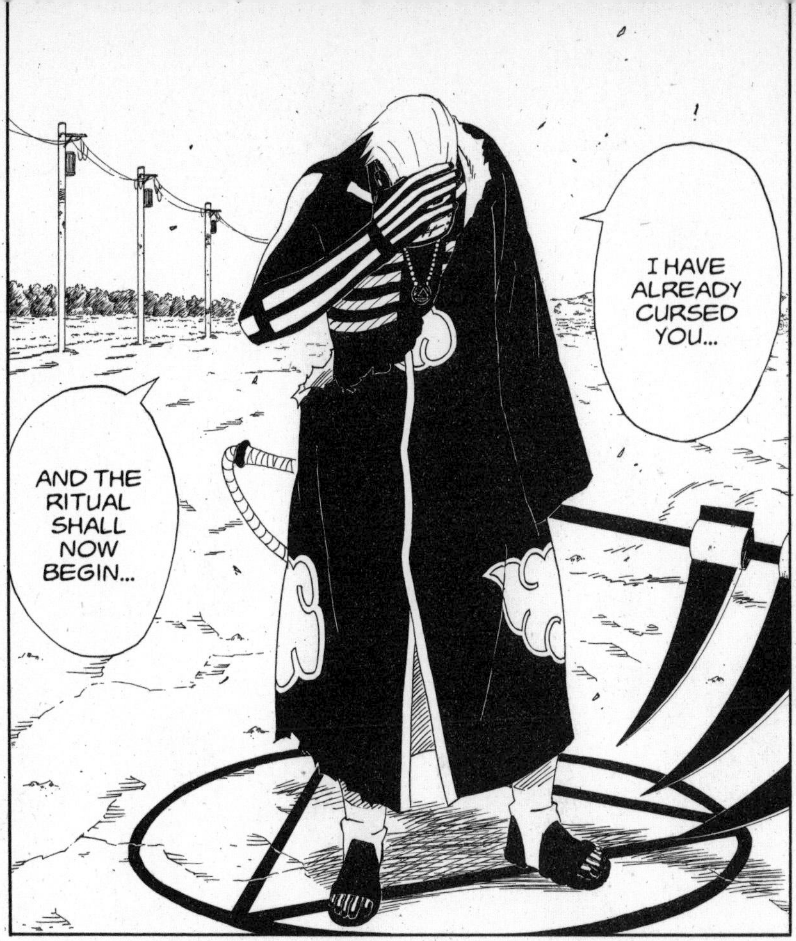
I HAVE ALREADY CURSED YOU...
AND THE RITUAL SHALL NOW BEGIN...

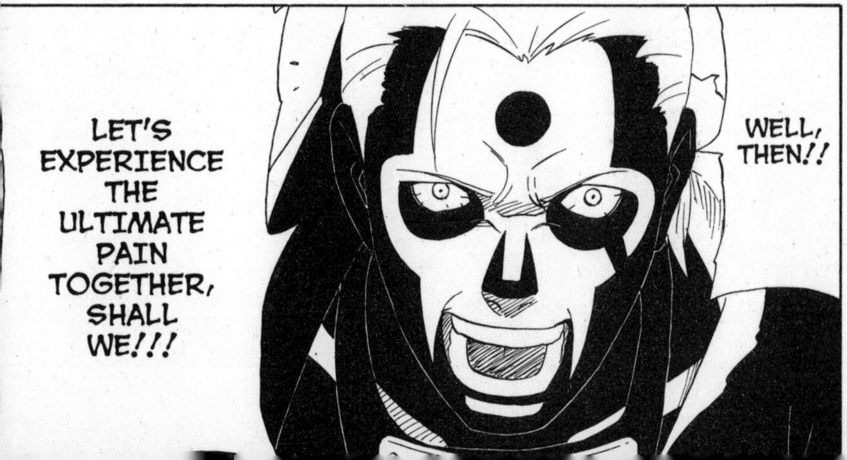
WELL, THEN!!
LET'S EXPERIENCE THE ULTIMATE PAIN TOGETHER, SHALL WE!!!

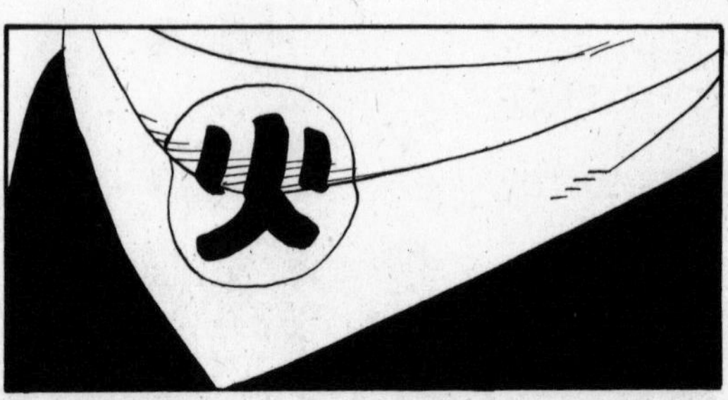
火

Number 324: Shikamaru's Analysis!!

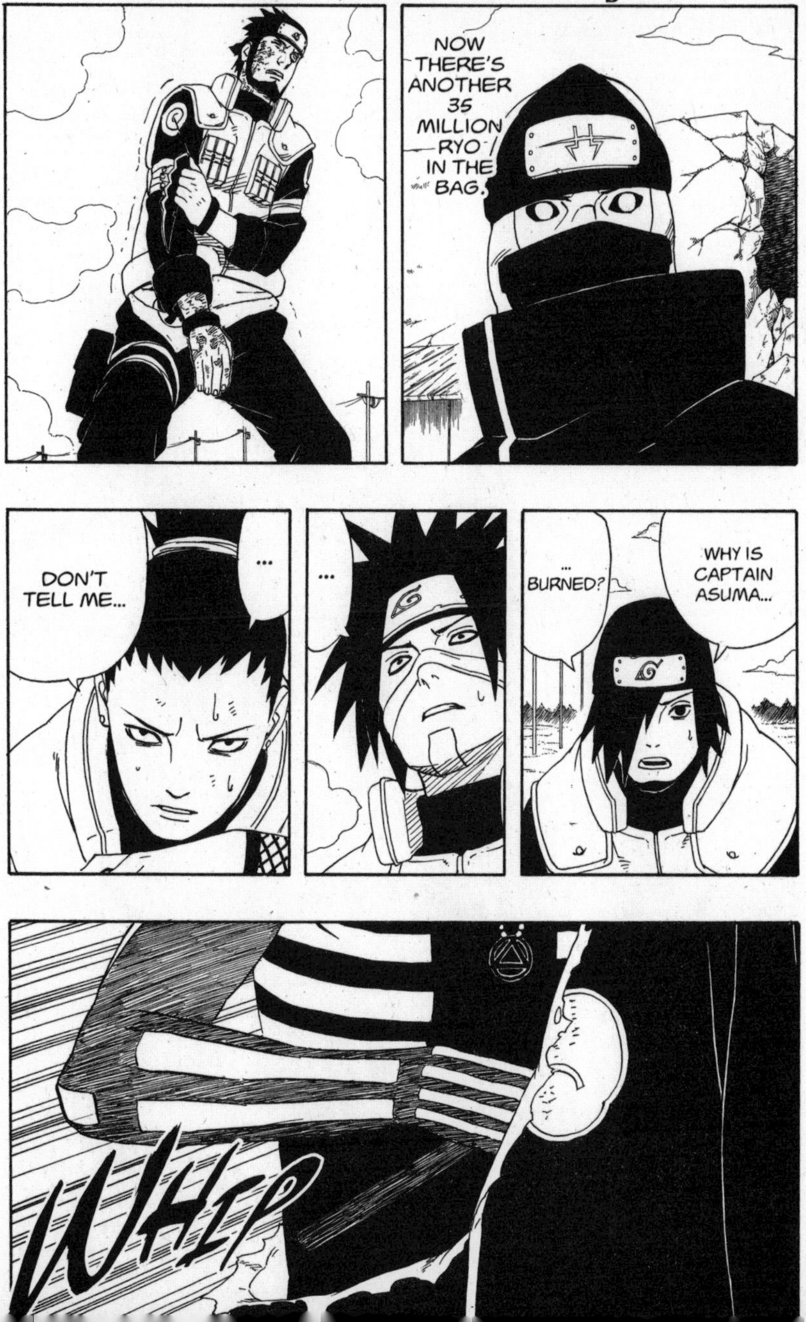
NOW THERE'S ANOTHER 35 MILLION RYO IN THE BAG.
WHY IS CAPTAIN ASUMA...
... BURNED?
...
...
DON'T TELL ME...
WHIP

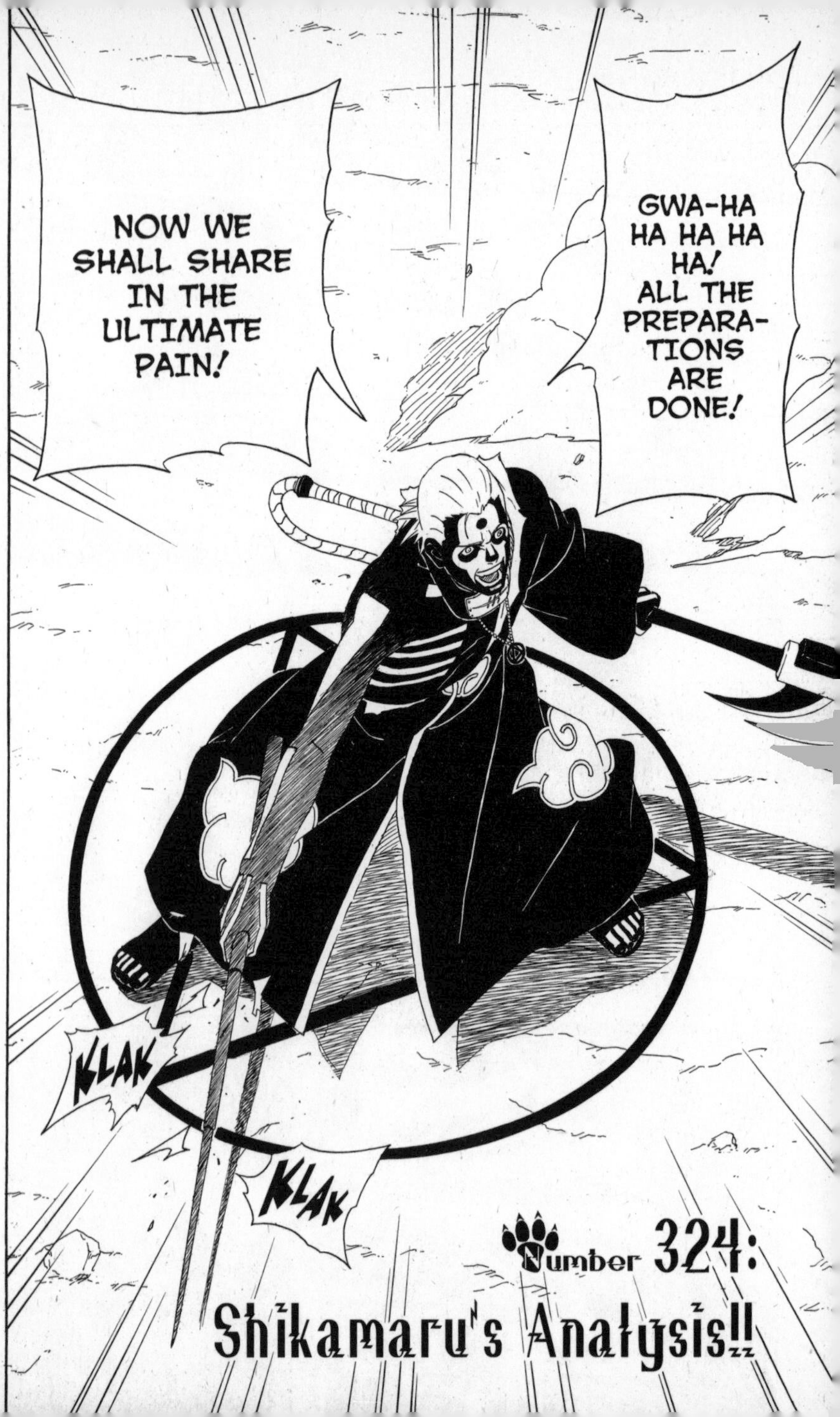
GWA-HA HA HA HA HA! ALL THE PREPARATIONS ARE DONE!
NOW WE SHALL SHARE IN THE ULTIMATE PAIN!
KLAK
KLAK

Number 324: Shikamaru's Analysis!!

READ THIS WAY

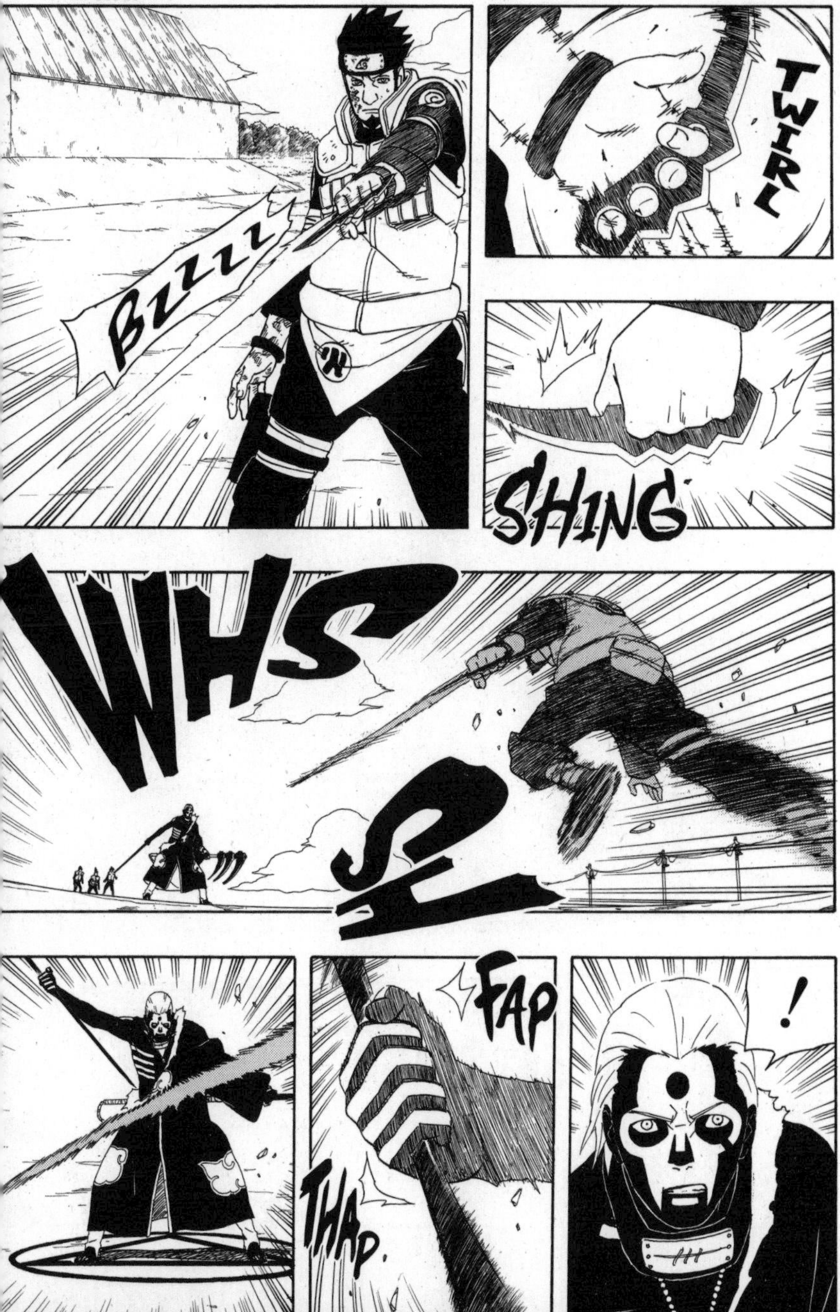
TWIRL
SHING
BZZZZ
WHSSH
!
FAP
THAP

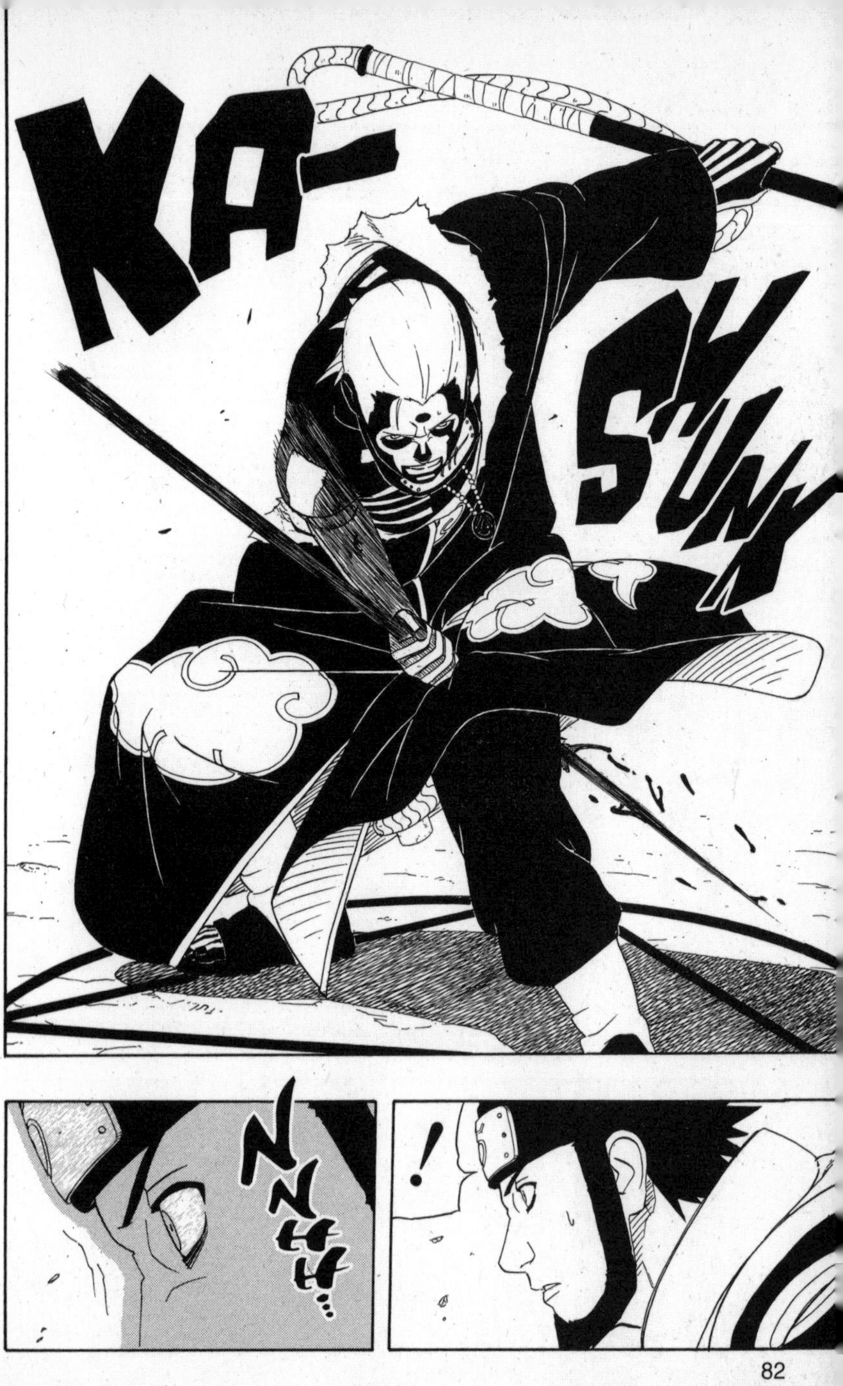
KA-SHUNK
!
NNHH...

READ THIS WAY

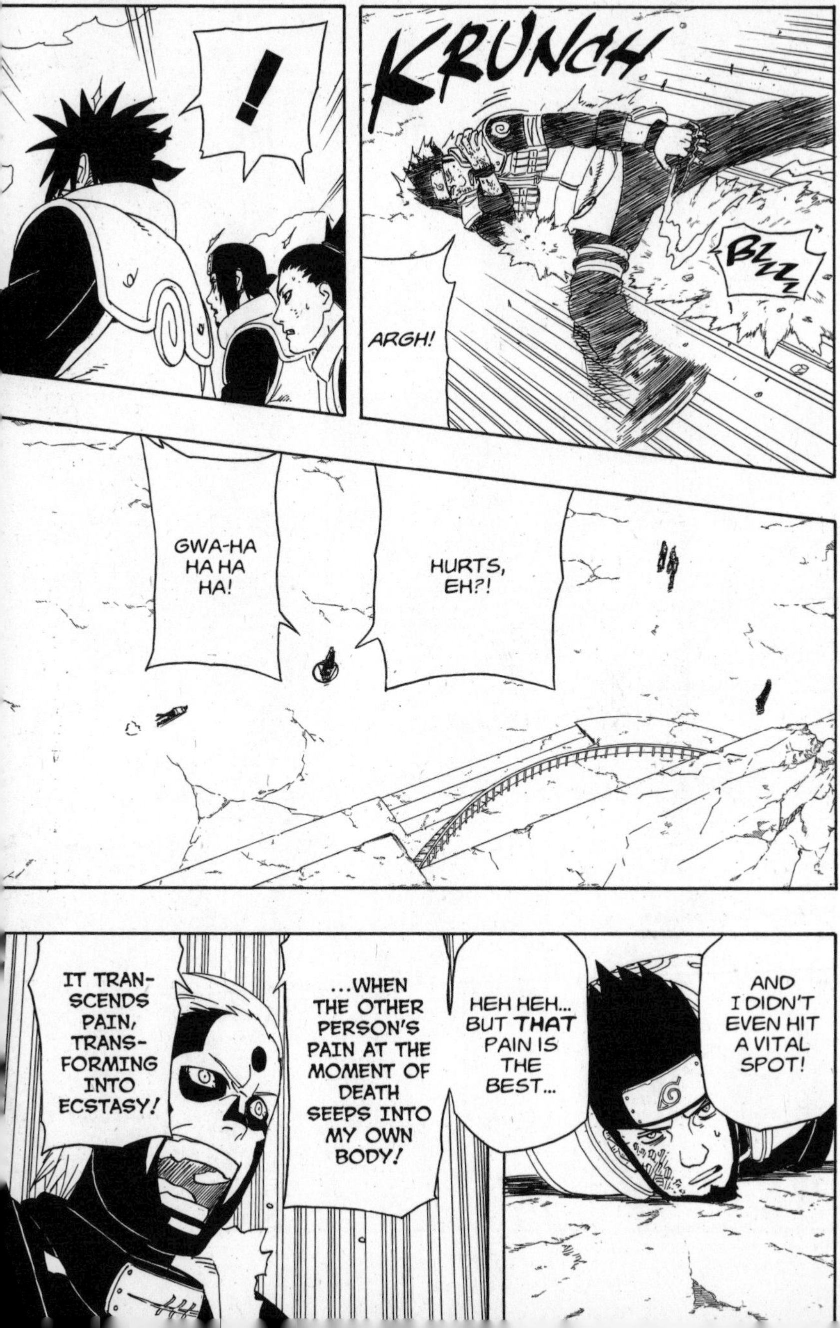
KRUNCH
BZZZ
ARGH!
!
HURTS, EH?!
GWA-HA HA HA HA!
AND I DIDN'T EVEN HIT A VITAL SPOT!
HEH HEH... BUT **THAT** PAIN IS THE BEST...
...WHEN THE OTHER PERSON'S PAIN AT THE MOMENT OF DEATH SEEPS INTO MY OWN BODY!
IT TRANSCENDS PAIN, TRANSFORMING INTO ECSTASY!

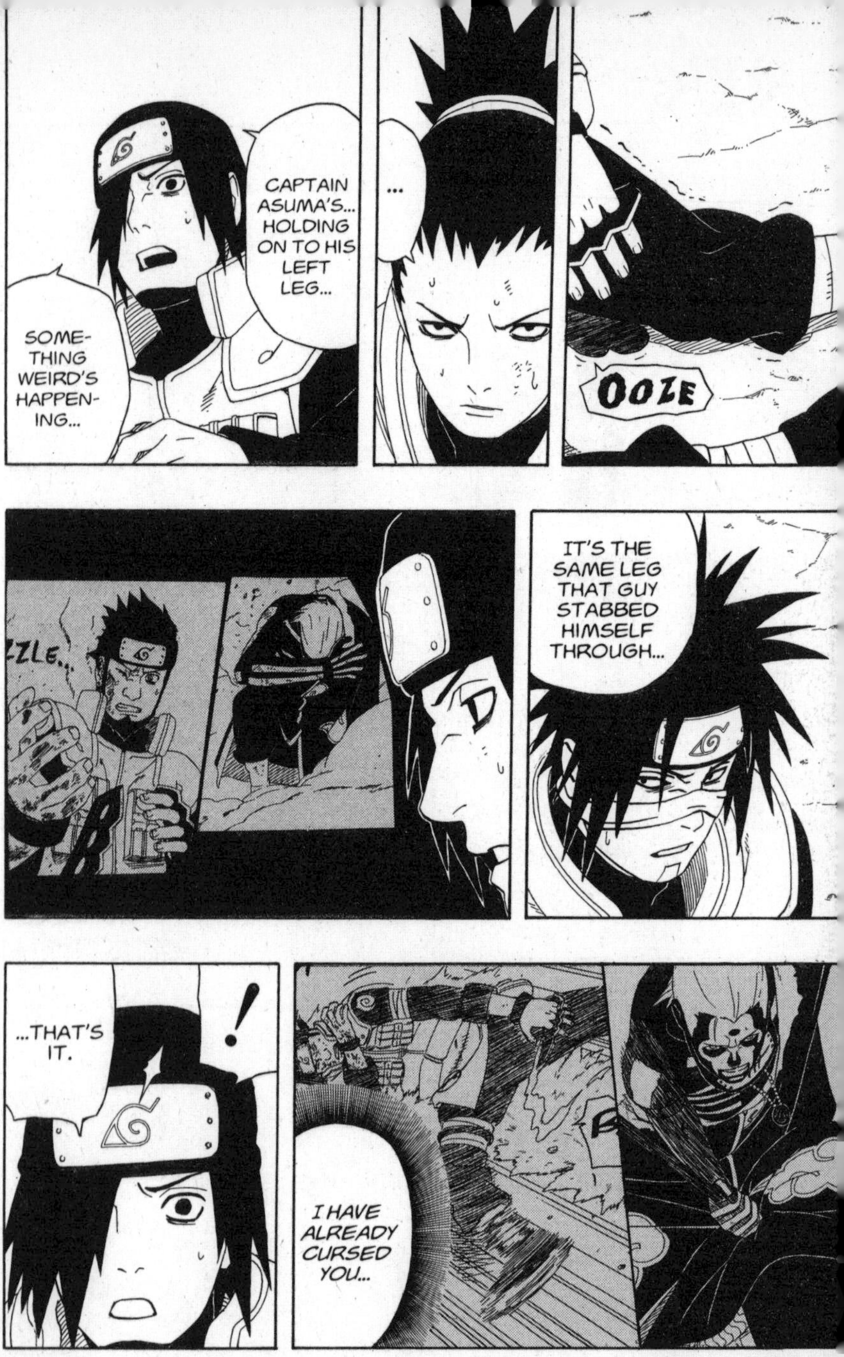
OOZE
...
CAPTAIN ASUMA'S... HOLDING ON TO HIS LEFT LEG...
SOME-THING WEIRD'S HAPPEN-ING...
IT'S THE SAME LEG THAT GUY STABBED HIMSELF THROUGH...
ZZLE...
I HAVE ALREADY CURSED YOU...
!
...THAT'S IT.

READ THIS WAY

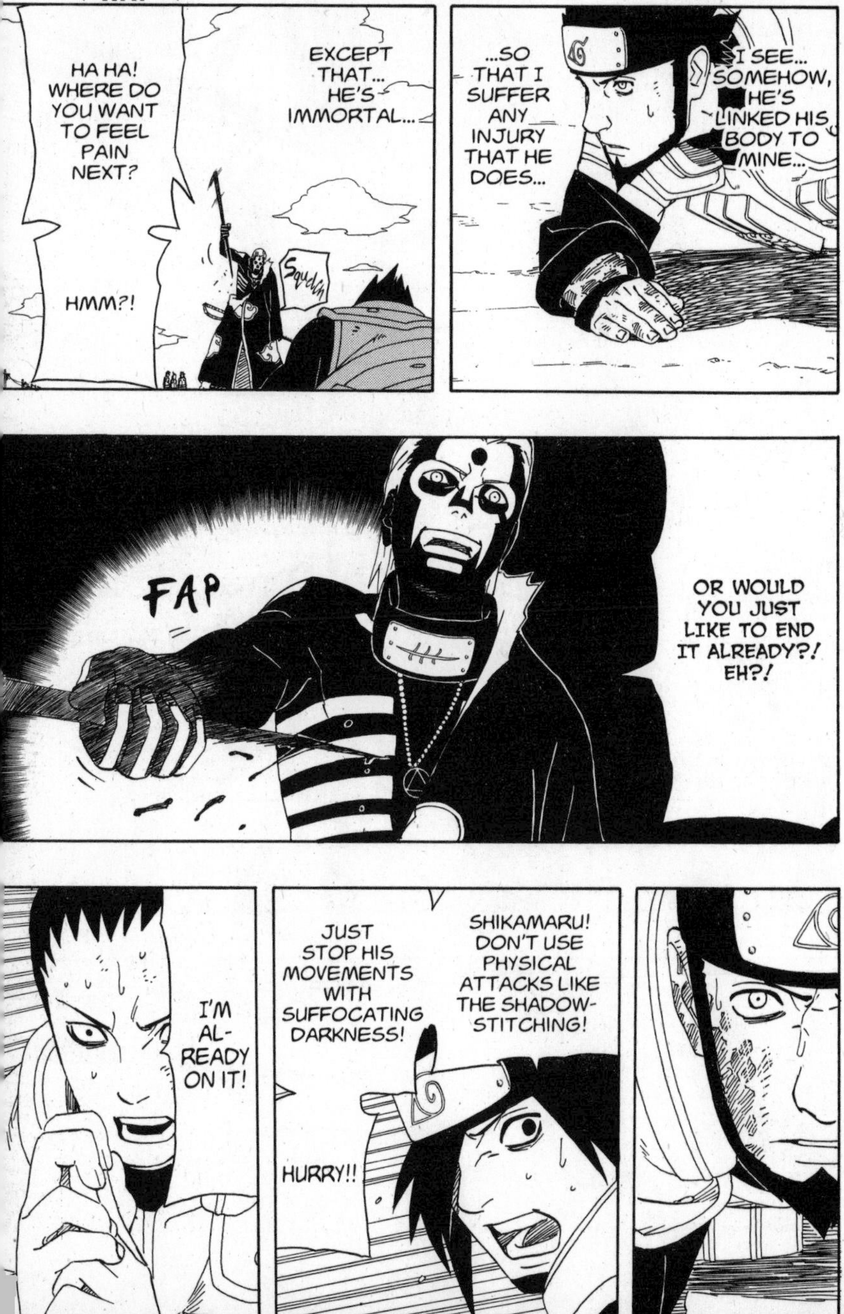

...I SEE... SOMEHOW, HE'S LINKED HIS BODY TO MINE...
...SO THAT I SUFFER ANY INJURY THAT HE DOES...
EXCEPT THAT... HE'S IMMORTAL...
HA HA! WHERE DO YOU WANT TO FEEL PAIN NEXT?
Squelch
HMM?!
OR WOULD YOU JUST LIKE TO END IT ALREADY?! EH?!
FAP
SHIKAMARU! DON'T USE PHYSICAL ATTACKS LIKE THE SHADOW-STITCHING!
JUST STOP HIS MOVEMENTS WITH SUFFOCATING DARKNESS!
HURRY!!
I'M AL-READY ON IT!

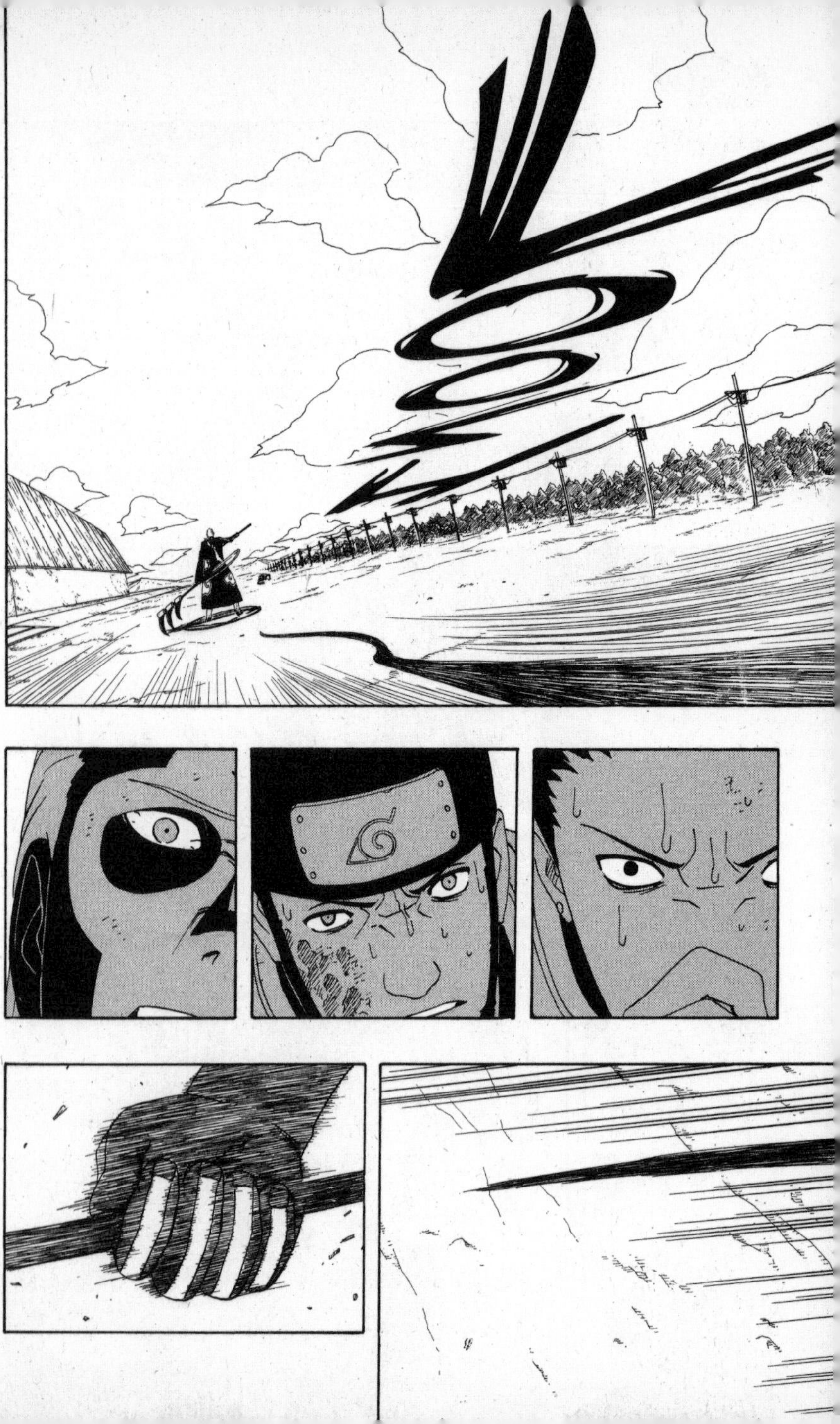

READ THIS WAY

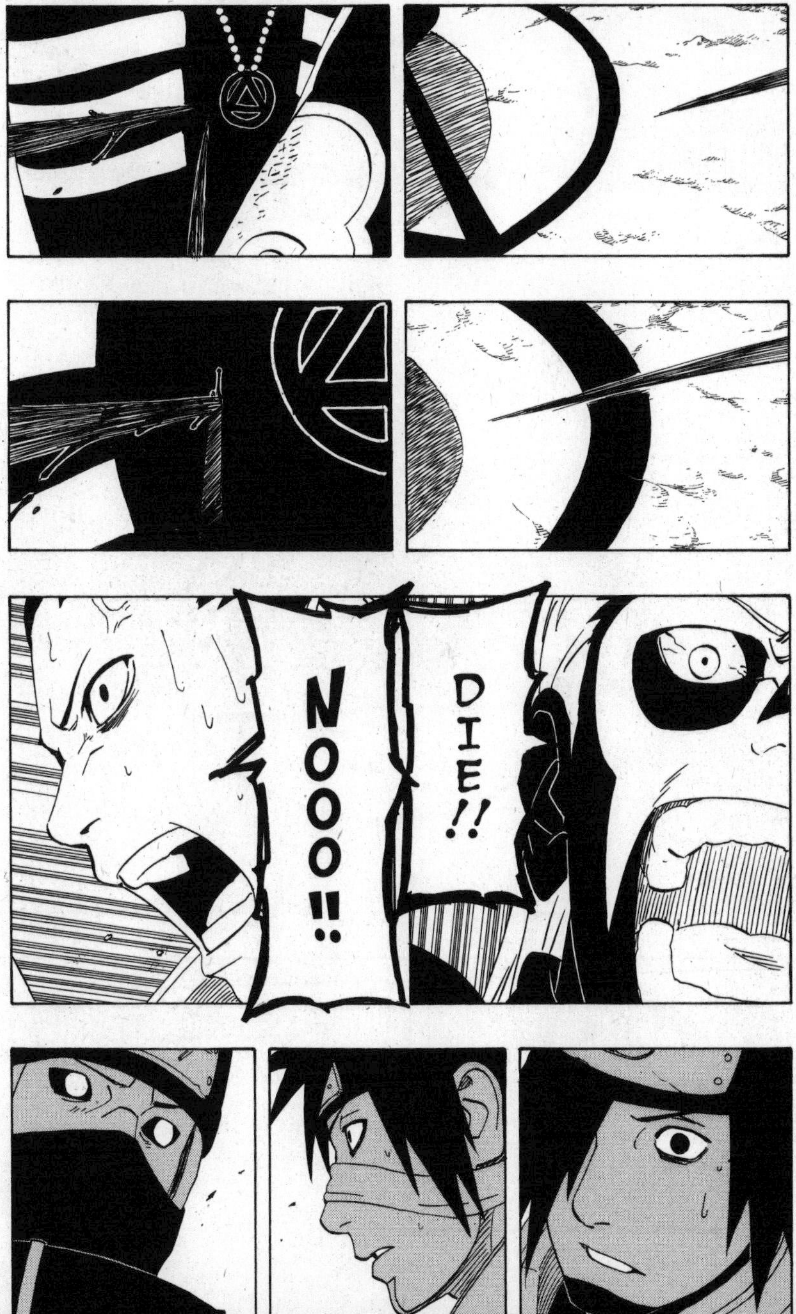
DIE!!
NOOO!!

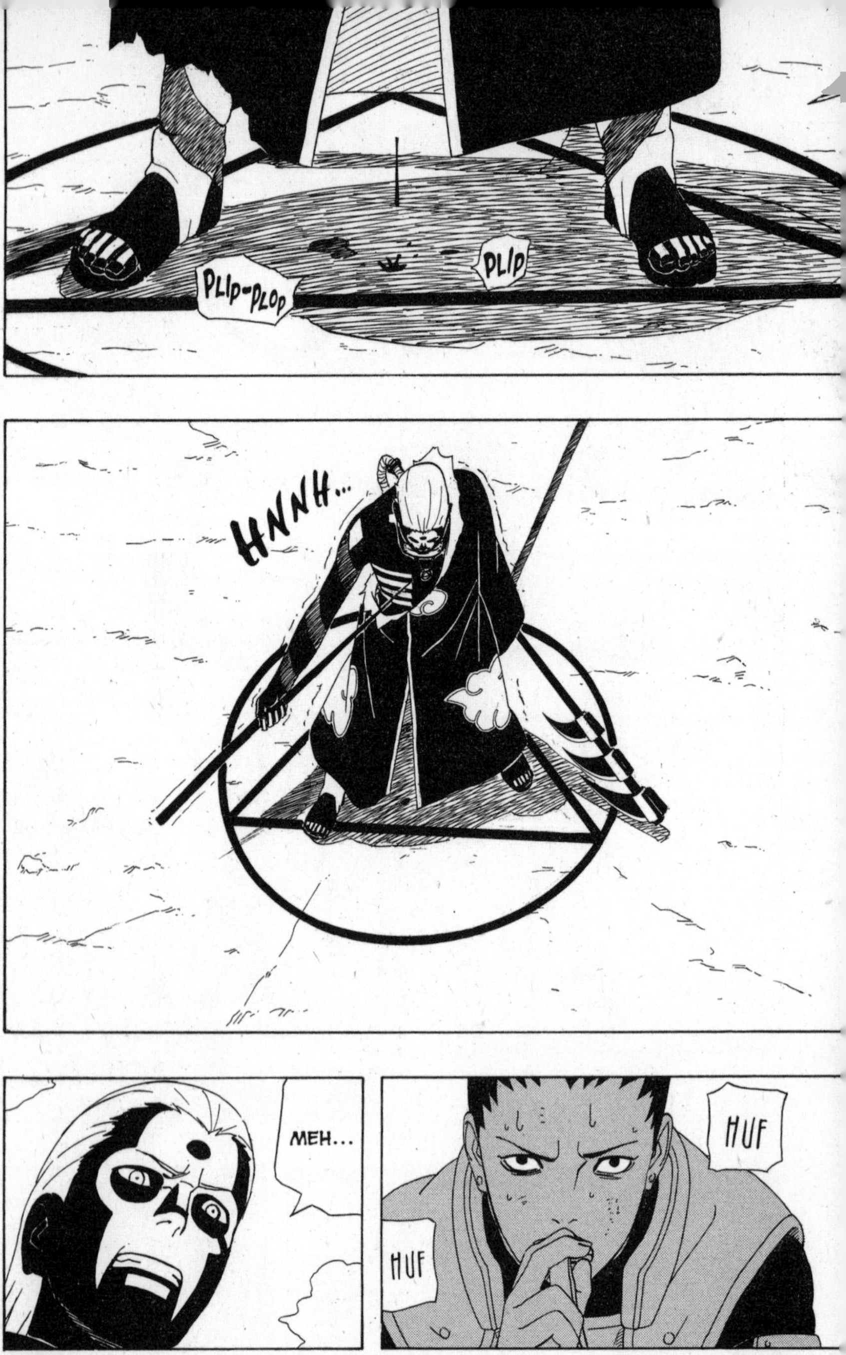
PLIP
PLIP-PLOP
HNNH...
HUF
HUF
MEH...

READ THIS WAY

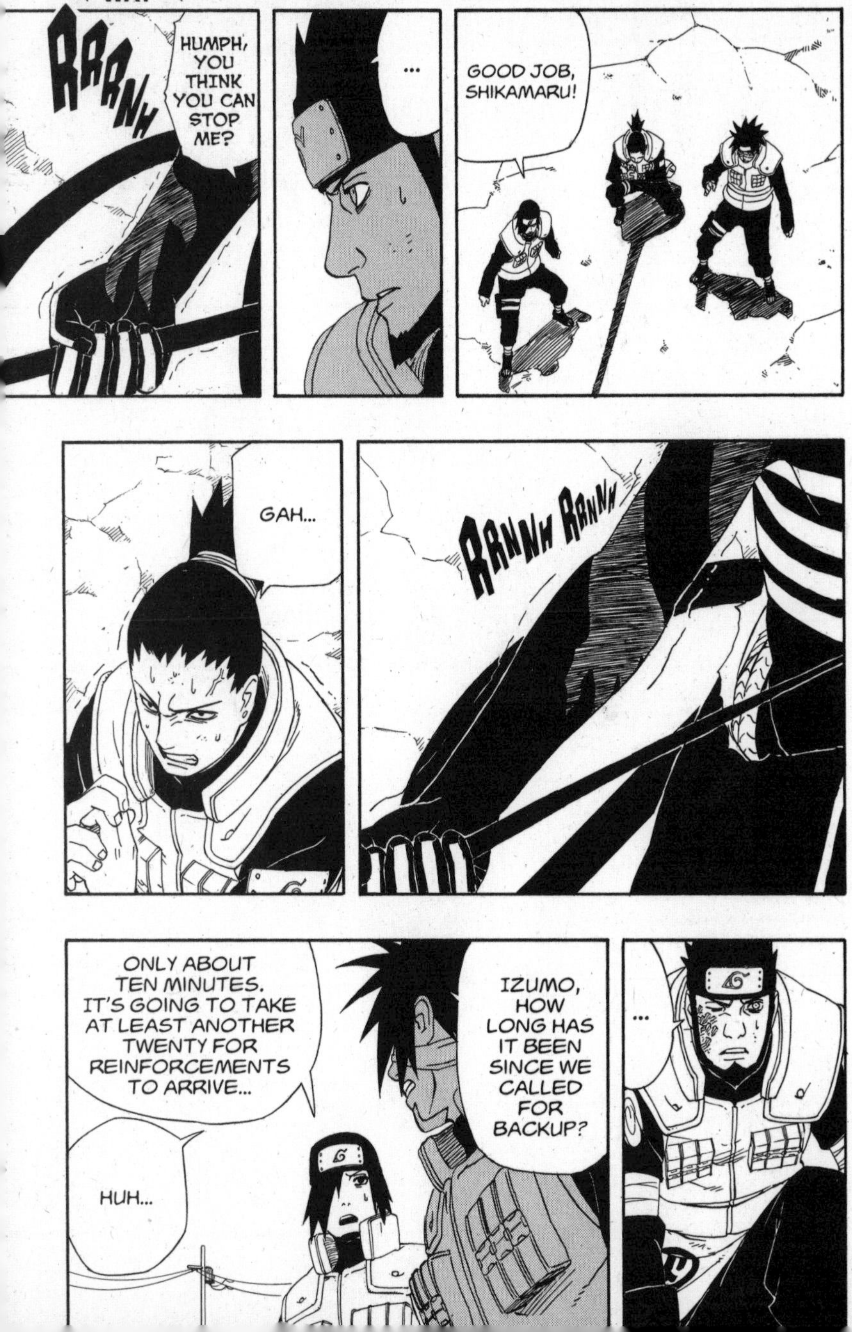
GOOD JOB, SHIKAMARU!
...
RRRNH
HUMPH, YOU THINK YOU CAN STOP ME?
RRNNH RRNNH
GAH...
...
IZUMO, HOW LONG HAS IT BEEN SINCE WE CALLED FOR BACKUP?
ONLY ABOUT TEN MINUTES. IT'S GOING TO TAKE AT LEAST ANOTHER TWENTY FOR REINFORCEMENTS TO ARRIVE...
HUH...

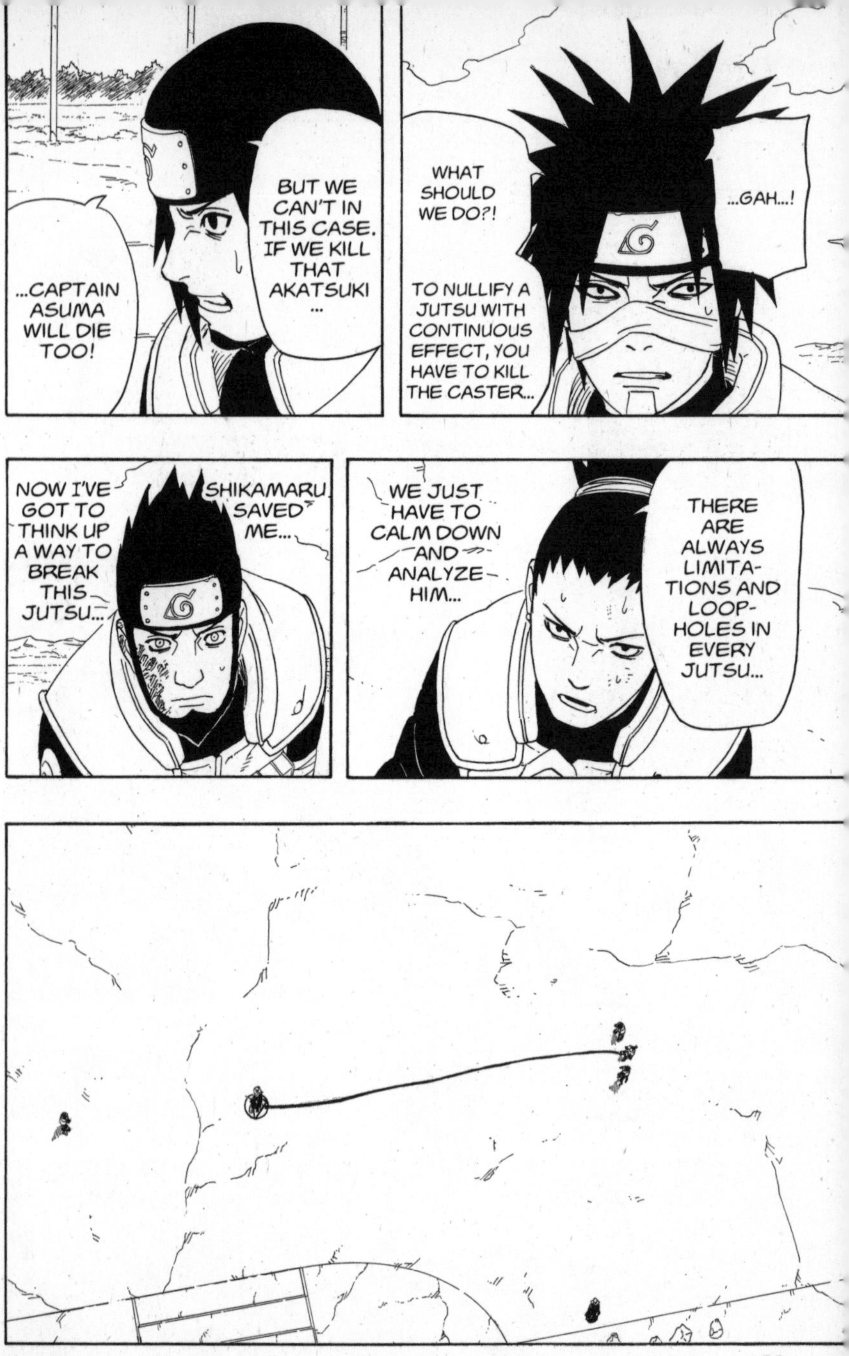
...GAH...!
WHAT SHOULD WE DO?!
TO NULLIFY A JUTSU WITH CONTINUOUS EFFECT, YOU HAVE TO KILL THE CASTER...
BUT WE CAN'T IN THIS CASE. IF WE KILL THAT AKATSUKI ...
...CAPTAIN ASUMA WILL DIE TOO!
THERE ARE ALWAYS LIMITATIONS AND LOOPHOLES IN EVERY JUTSU...
WE JUST HAVE TO CALM DOWN AND ANALYZE HIM...
SHIKAMARU SAVED ME...
NOW I'VE GOT TO THINK UP A WAY TO BREAK THIS JUTSU...

READ THIS WAY

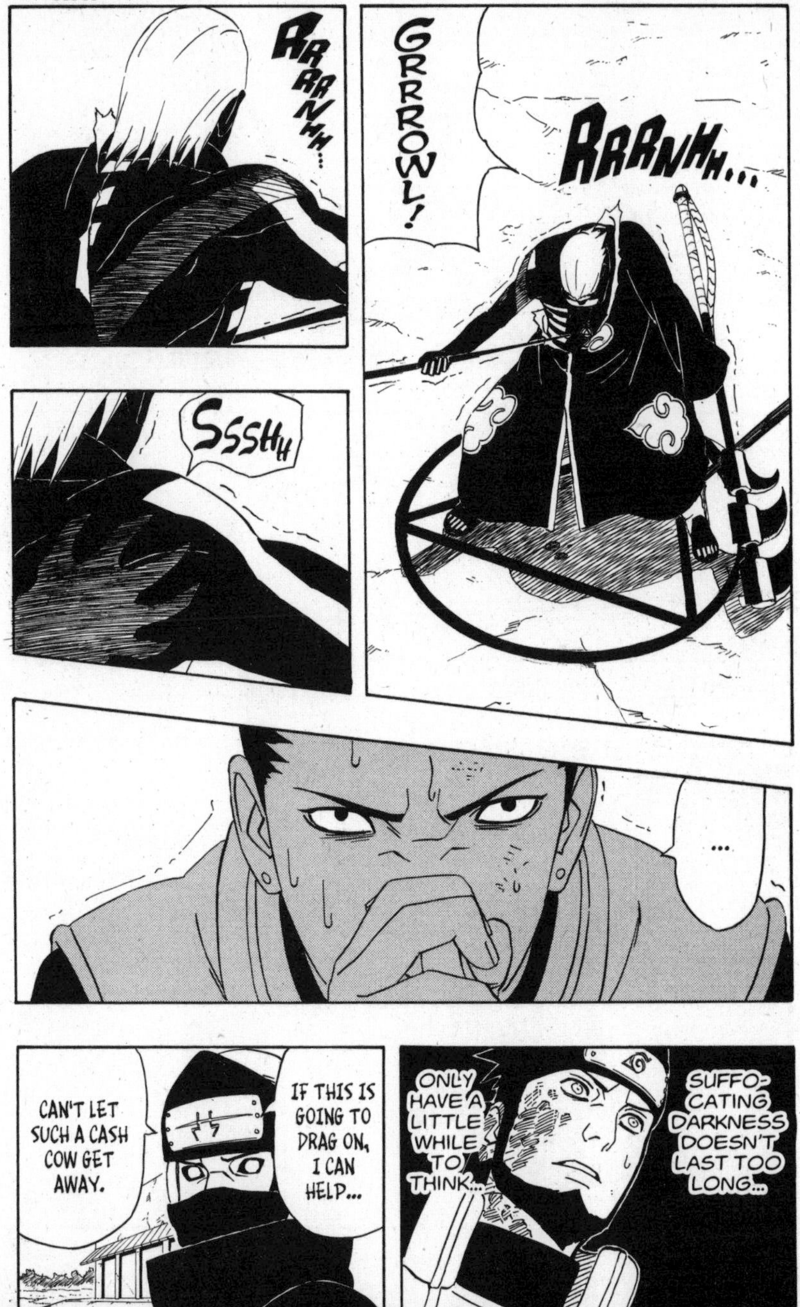
GRRROWL!
RRRNHH...
RRRNHH...
SSSHH
...
SUFFOCATING DARKNESS DOESN'T LAST TOO LONG...
ONLY HAVE A LITTLE WHILE TO THINK...
IF THIS IS GOING TO DRAG ON, I CAN HELP...
CAN'T LET SUCH A CASH COW GET AWAY.

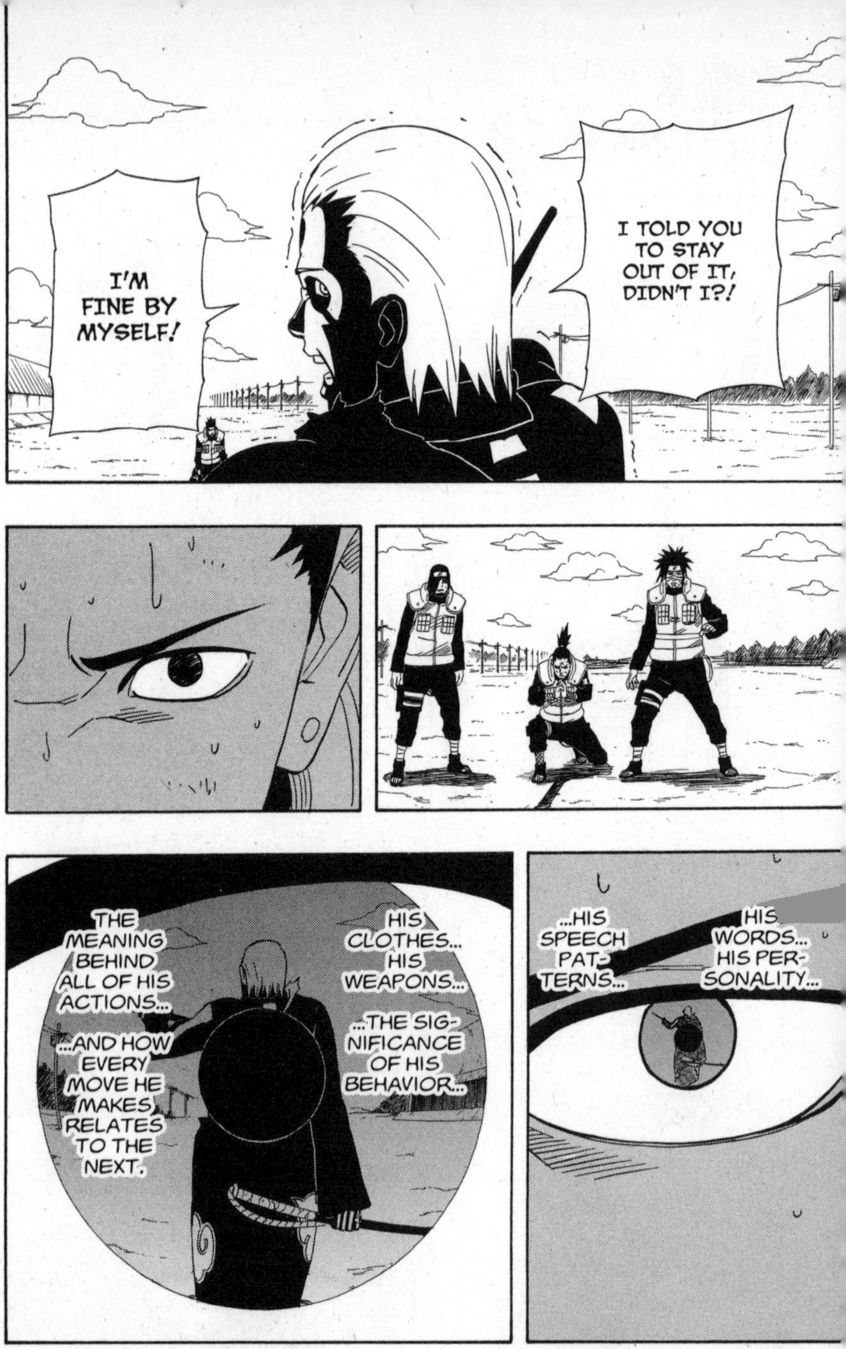
I TOLD YOU TO STAY OUT OF IT, DIDN'T I?!
I'M FINE BY MYSELF!
HIS WORDS... HIS PERSONALITY...
...HIS SPEECH PATTERNS...
HIS CLOTHES... HIS WEAPONS...
...THE SIGNIFICANCE OF HIS BEHAVIOR...
THE MEANING BEHIND ALL OF HIS ACTIONS...
...AND HOW EVERY MOVE HE MAKES RELATES TO THE NEXT.

READ THIS WAY

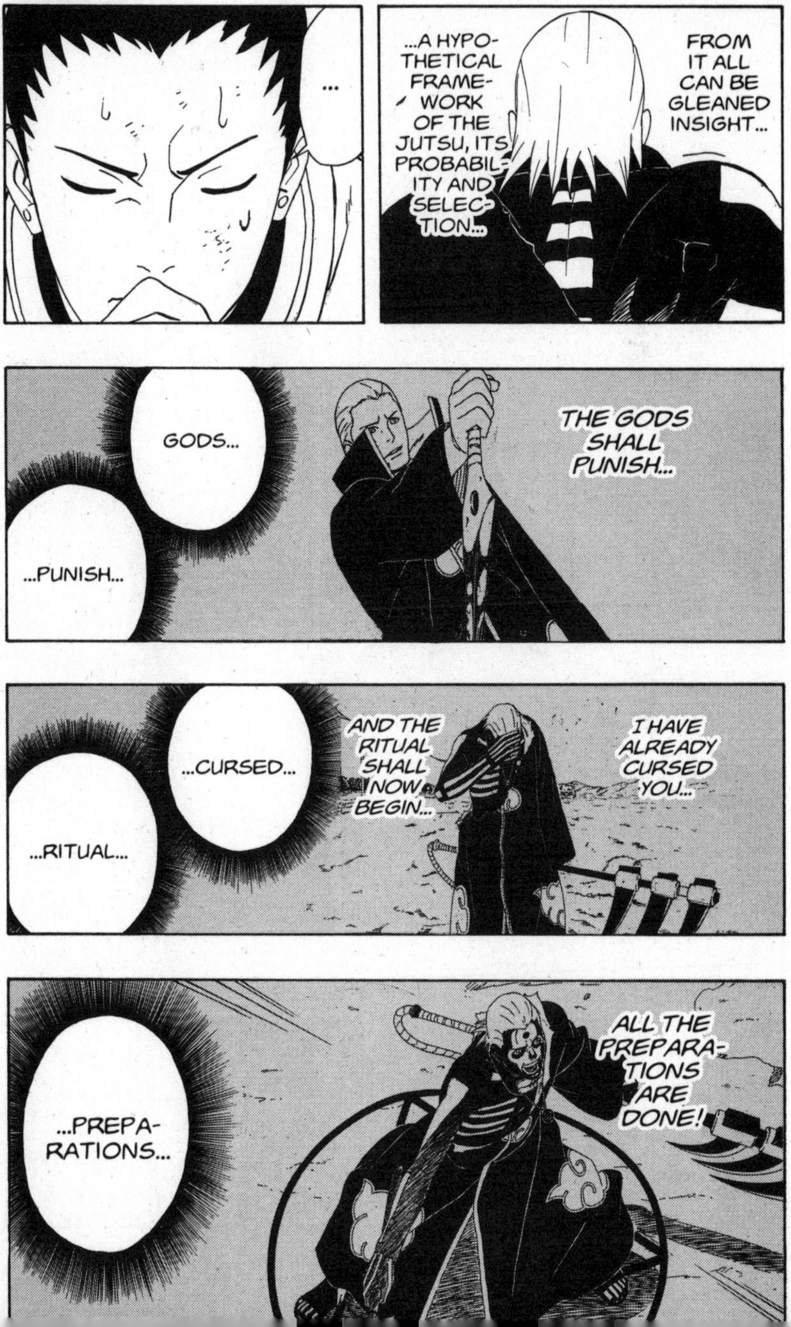
FROM IT ALL CAN BE GLEANED INSIGHT...
...A HYPOTHETICAL FRAMEWORK OF THE JUTSU, ITS PROBABILITY AND SELECTION...
...
THE GODS SHALL PUNISH...
GODS...
...PUNISH...
I HAVE ALREADY CURSED YOU...
AND THE RITUAL SHALL NOW BEGIN...
...CURSED...
...RITUAL...
ALL THE PREPARATIONS ARE DONE!
...PREPARATIONS...

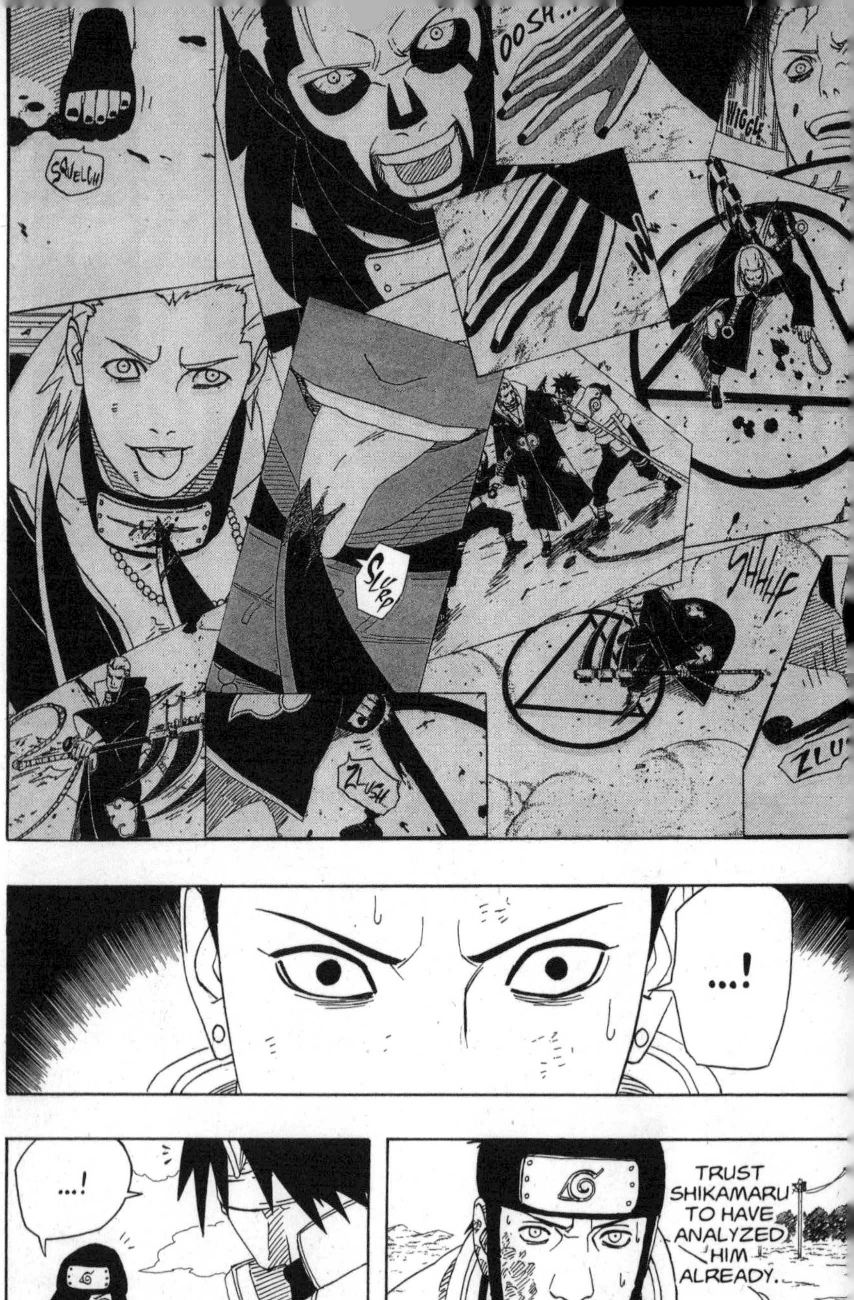
WIGGLE
OOSH...
SQUELCH
SHHHF
SLURP
ZLU
ZLUSH
...!
TRUST SHIKAMARU TO HAVE ANALYZED HIM ALREADY.
...!

READ THIS WAY

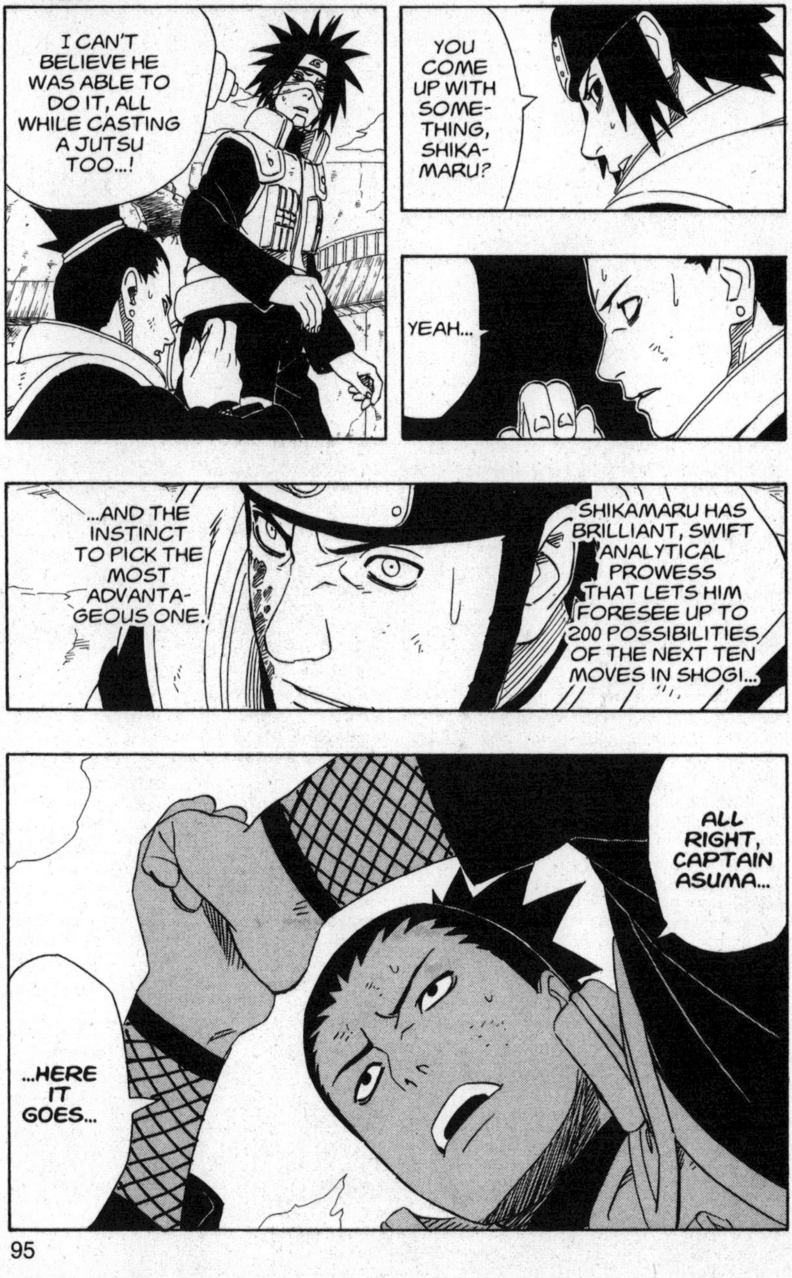
YOU COME UP WITH SOME-THING, SHIKA-MARU?
YEAH...
I CAN'T BELIEVE HE WAS ABLE TO DO IT, ALL WHILE CASTING A JUTSU TOO...!
SHIKAMARU HAS BRILLIANT, SWIFT ANALYTICAL PROWESS THAT LETS HIM FORESEE UP TO 200 POSSIBILITIES OF THE NEXT TEN MOVES IN SHOGI...
...AND THE INSTINCT TO PICK THE MOST ADVANTA-GEOUS ONE.
ALL RIGHT, CAPTAIN ASUMA...
...HERE IT GOES...

NARUTO

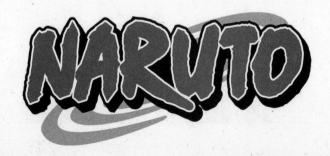

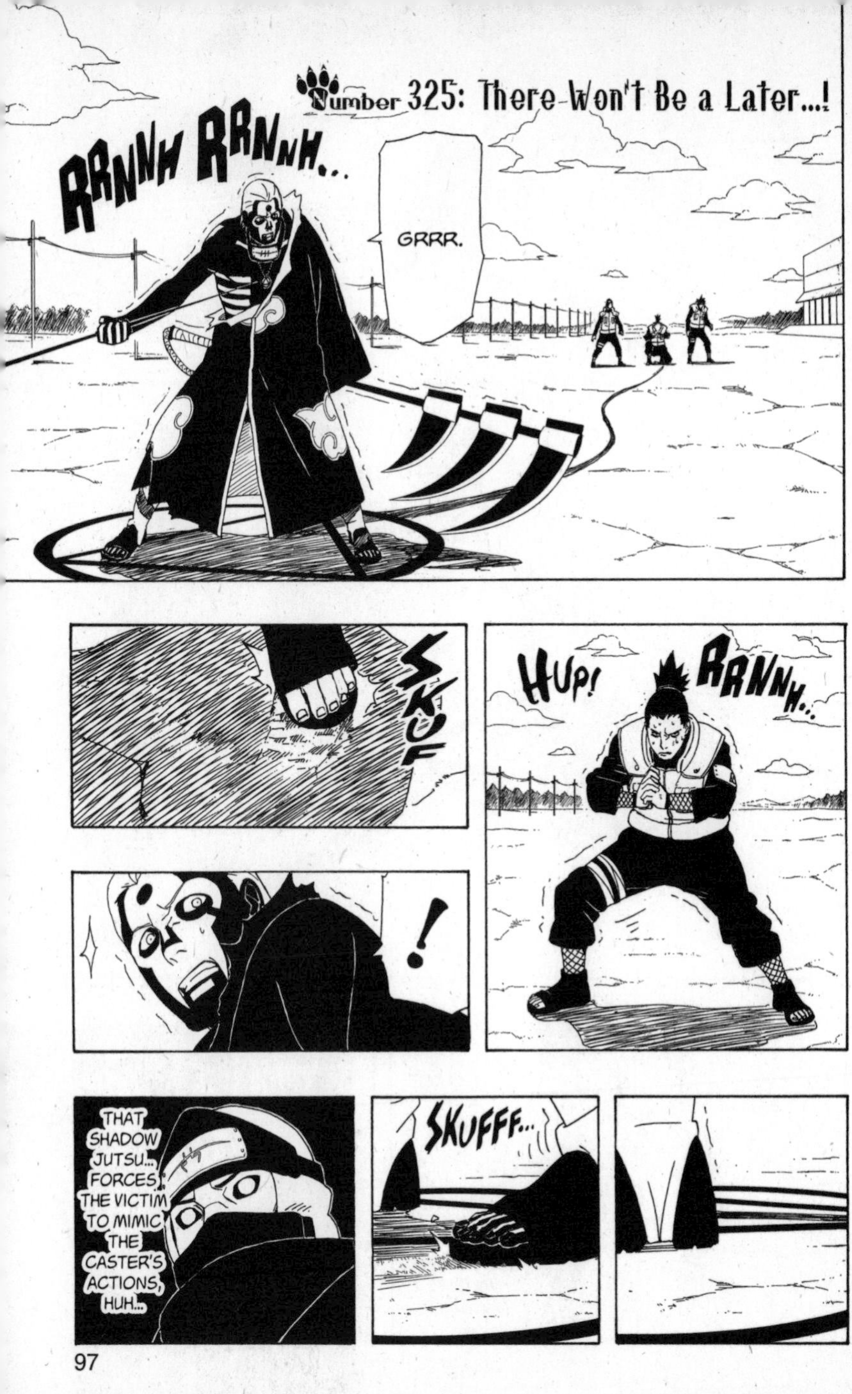
Number 325: There Won't Be a Later...!
GRRR.
RRNNH RRNNH...
RRNNH...
HUP!
SKUF
!
SKUFFF...
THAT SHADOW JUTSU... FORCES THE VICTIM TO MIMIC THE CASTER'S ACTIONS, HUH...

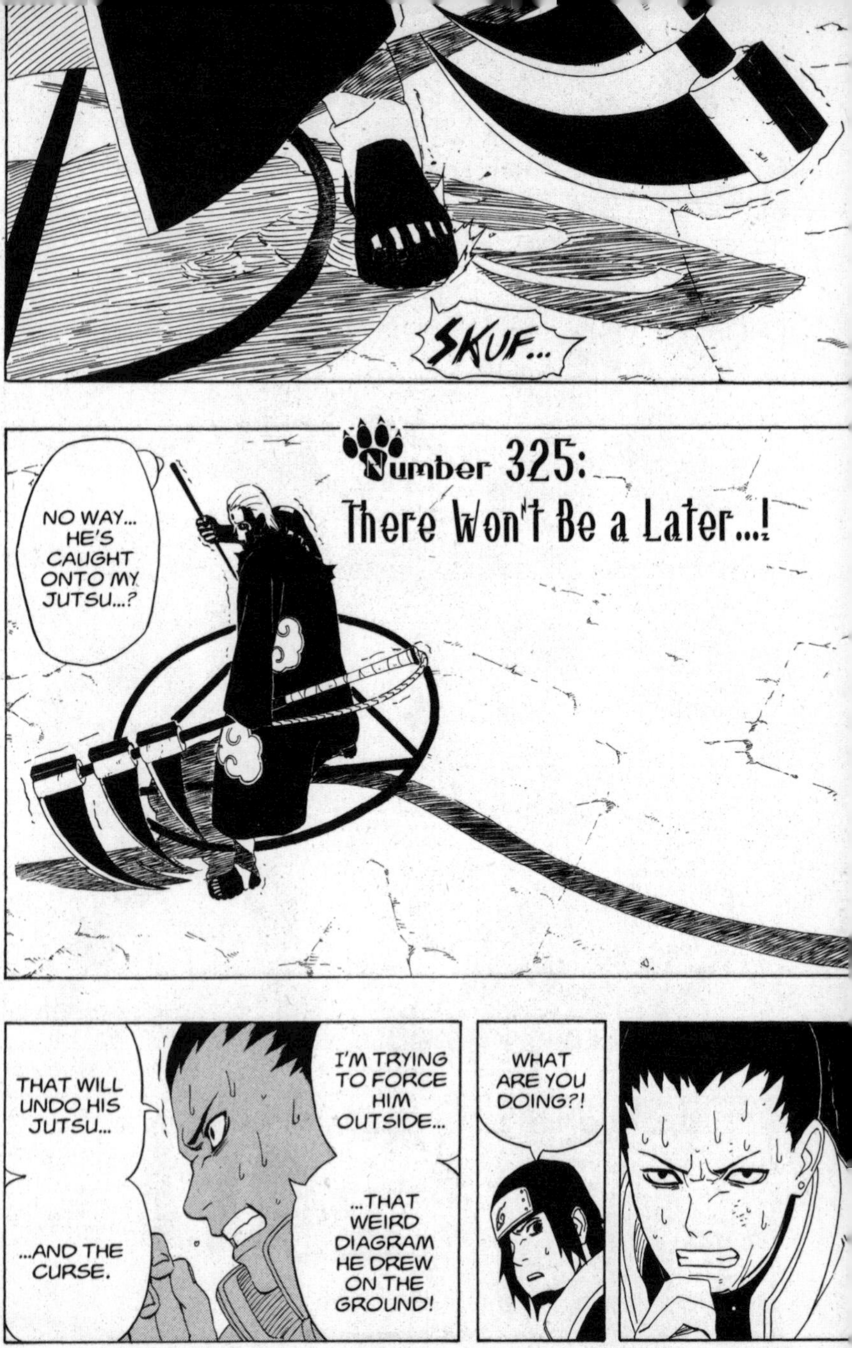
SKUF...
Number 325:
There Won't Be a Later...!
NO WAY... HE'S CAUGHT ONTO MY JUTSU...?
WHAT ARE YOU DOING?!
I'M TRYING TO FORCE HIM OUTSIDE...
...THAT WEIRD DIAGRAM HE DREW ON THE GROUND!
THAT WILL UNDO HIS JUTSU...
...AND THE CURSE.

READ THIS WAY

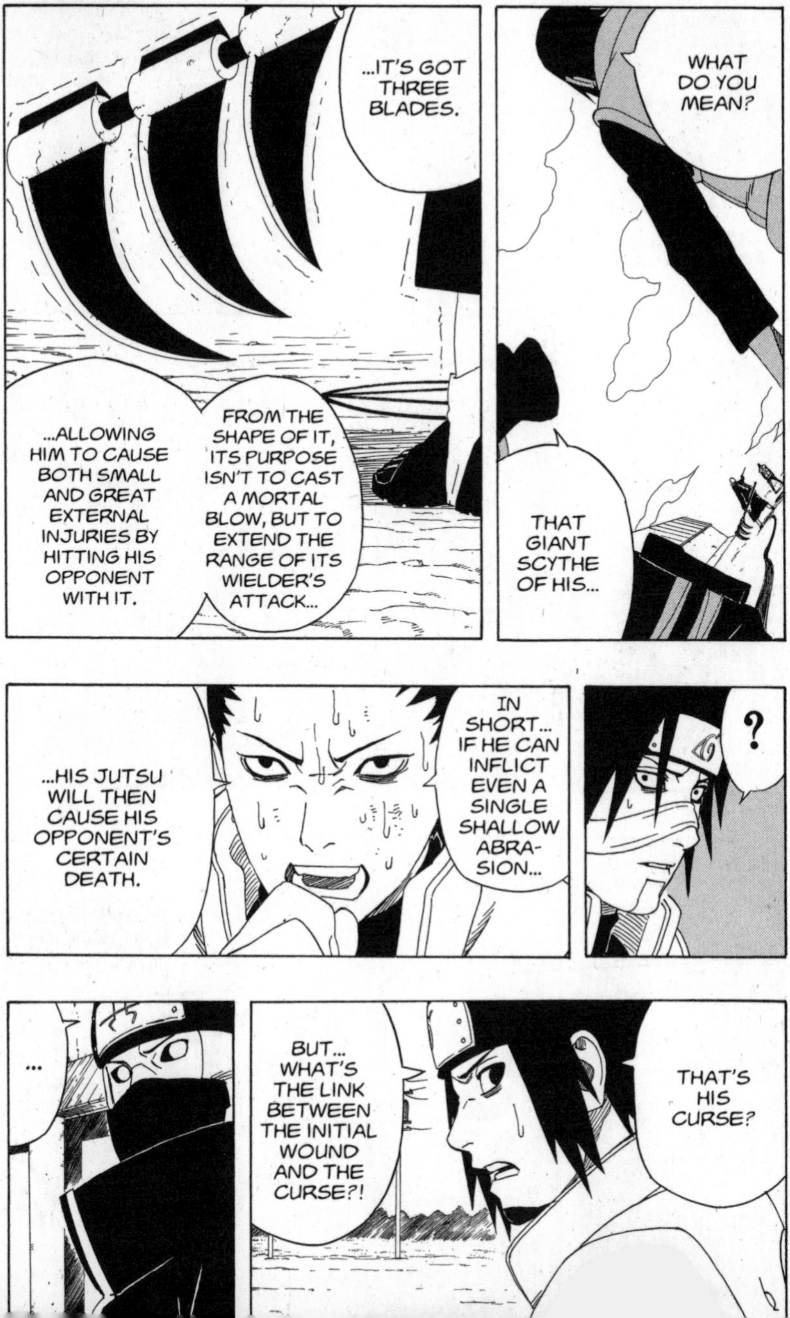
WHAT DO YOU MEAN?
THAT GIANT SCYTHE OF HIS...
...IT'S GOT THREE BLADES.
FROM THE SHAPE OF IT, ITS PURPOSE ISN'T TO CAST A MORTAL BLOW, BUT TO EXTEND THE RANGE OF ITS WIELDER'S ATTACK...
...ALLOWING HIM TO CAUSE BOTH SMALL AND GREAT EXTERNAL INJURIES BY HITTING HIS OPPONENT WITH IT.
?
IN SHORT... IF HE CAN INFLICT EVEN A SINGLE SHALLOW ABRA-SION...
...HIS JUTSU WILL THEN CAUSE HIS OPPONENT'S CERTAIN DEATH.
THAT'S HIS CURSE?
BUT... WHAT'S THE LINK BETWEEN THE INITIAL WOUND AND THE CURSE?!
...

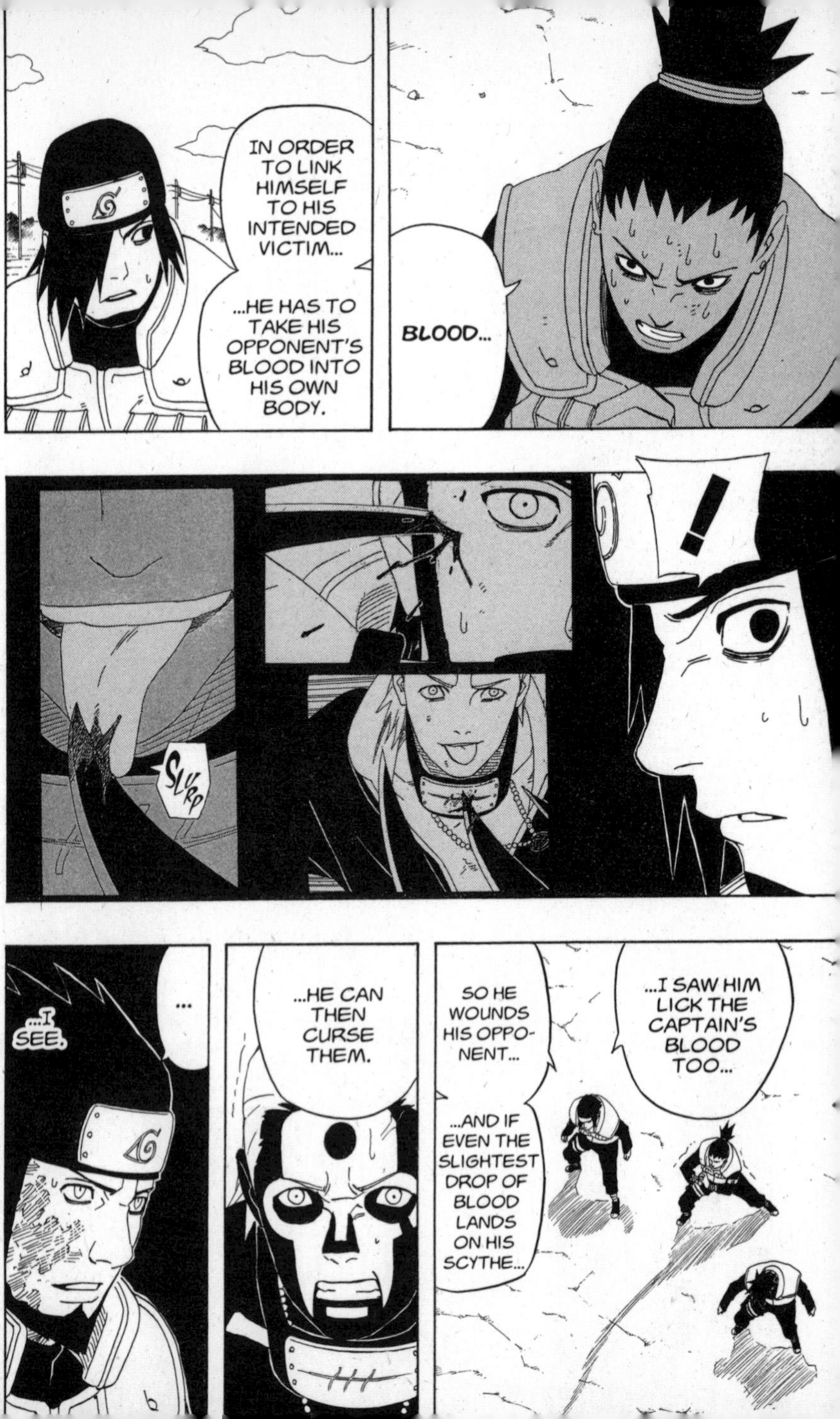
BLOOD...
IN ORDER TO LINK HIMSELF TO HIS INTENDED VICTIM...
...HE HAS TO TAKE HIS OPPONENT'S BLOOD INTO HIS OWN BODY.
!
SLURP
...I SAW HIM LICK THE CAPTAIN'S BLOOD TOO...
SO HE WOUNDS HIS OPPO-NENT...
...AND IF EVEN THE SLIGHTEST DROP OF BLOOD LANDS ON HIS SCYTHE...
...HE CAN THEN CURSE THEM.
...
...I SEE.

READ THIS WAY

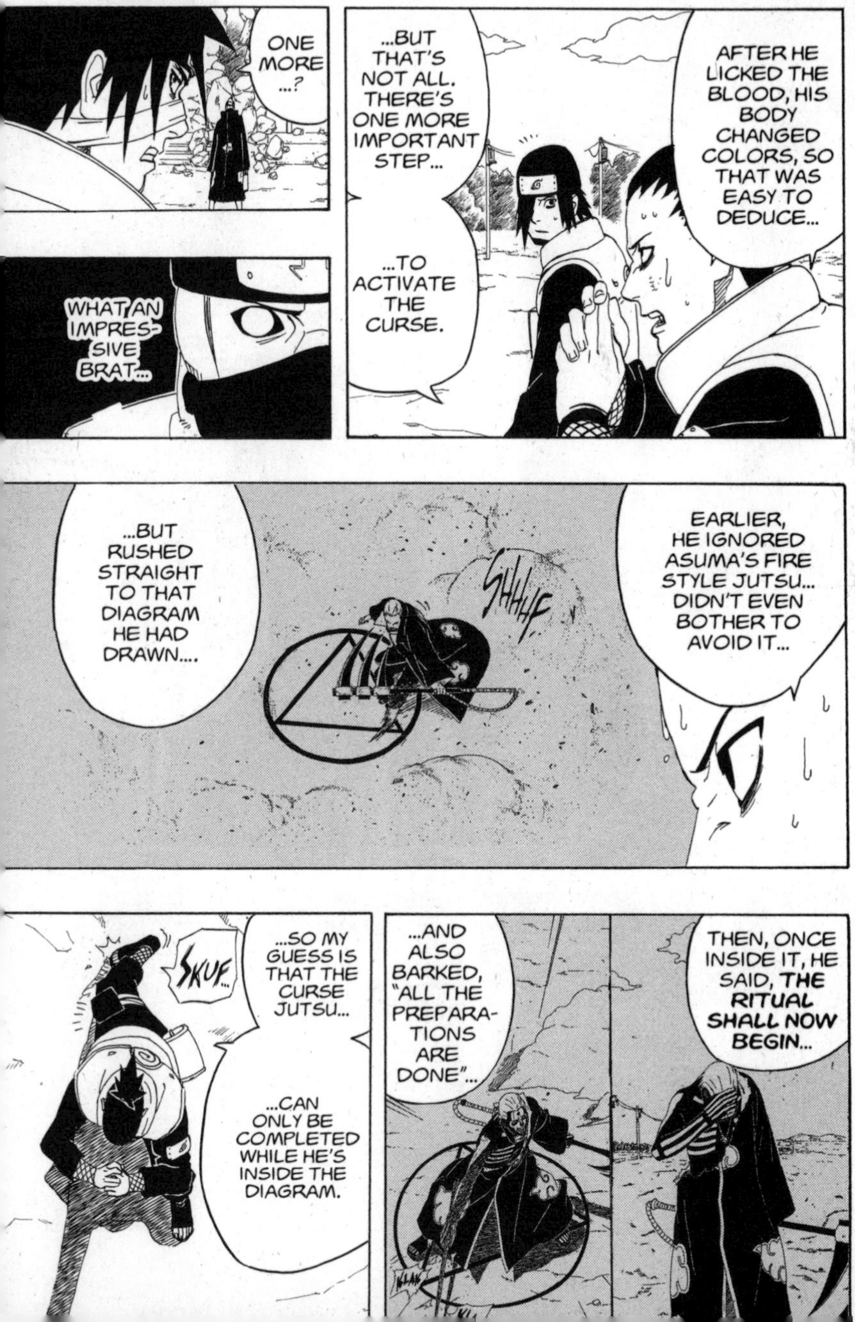
AFTER HE LICKED THE BLOOD, HIS BODY CHANGED COLORS, SO THAT WAS EASY TO DEDUCE...
...BUT THAT'S NOT ALL. THERE'S ONE MORE IMPORTANT STEP...
...TO ACTIVATE THE CURSE.
ONE MORE ...?
WHAT AN IMPRESSIVE BRAT...
EARLIER, HE IGNORED ASUMA'S FIRE STYLE JUTSU... DIDN'T EVEN BOTHER TO AVOID IT...
SHHUF
...BUT RUSHED STRAIGHT TO THAT DIAGRAM HE HAD DRAWN....
THEN, ONCE INSIDE IT, HE SAID, **THE RITUAL SHALL NOW BEGIN...**
...AND ALSO BARKED, "ALL THE PREPARATIONS ARE DONE"...
...SO MY GUESS IS THAT THE CURSE JUTSU...
SKUF...
...CAN ONLY BE COMPLETED WHILE HE'S INSIDE THE DIAGRAM.

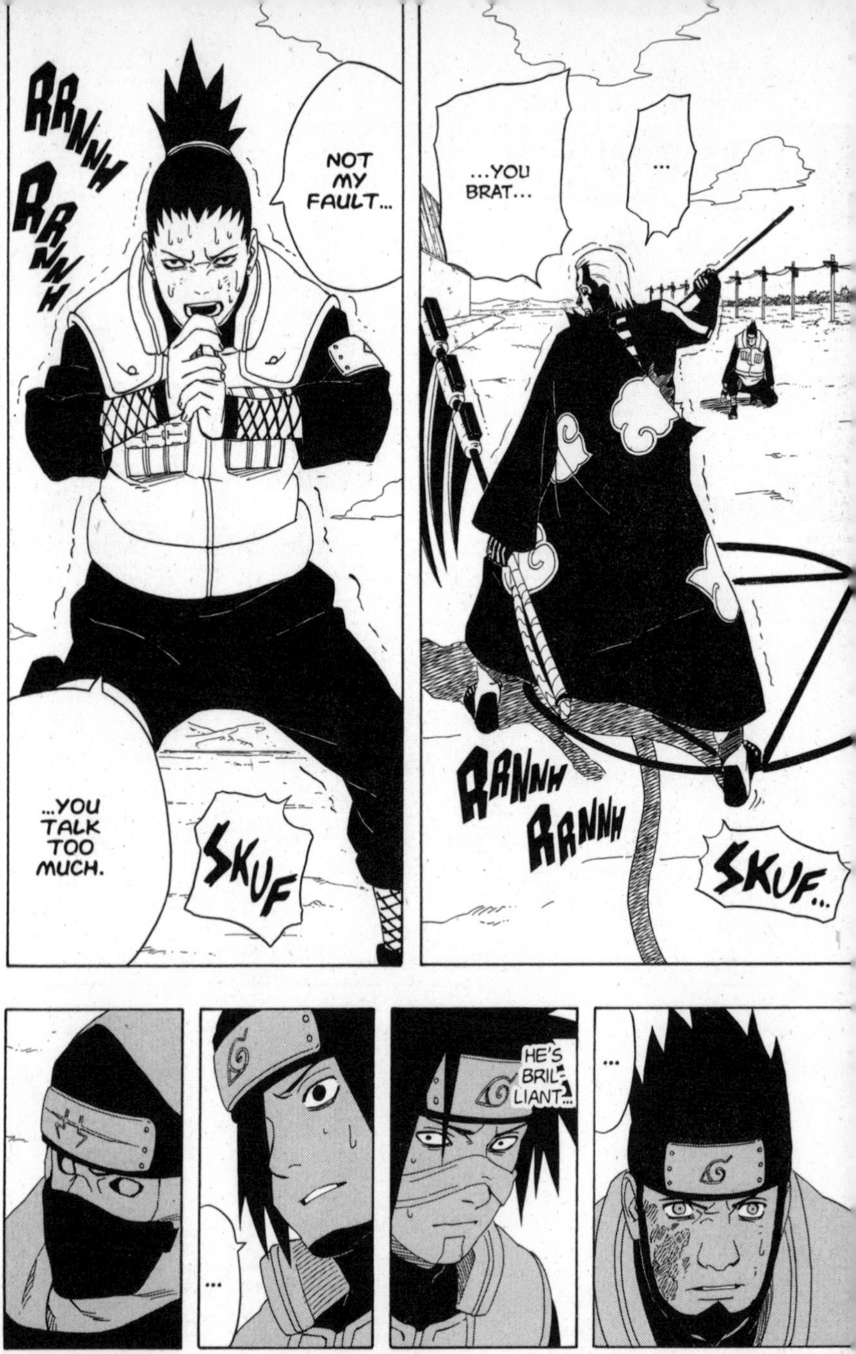
...YOU BRAT...
...
RRNNH RRNNH
SKUF...
NOT MY FAULT...
RRNNH RRNNH
...YOU TALK TOO MUCH.
SKUF
...
HE'S BRILLIANT...
...

READ THIS WAY

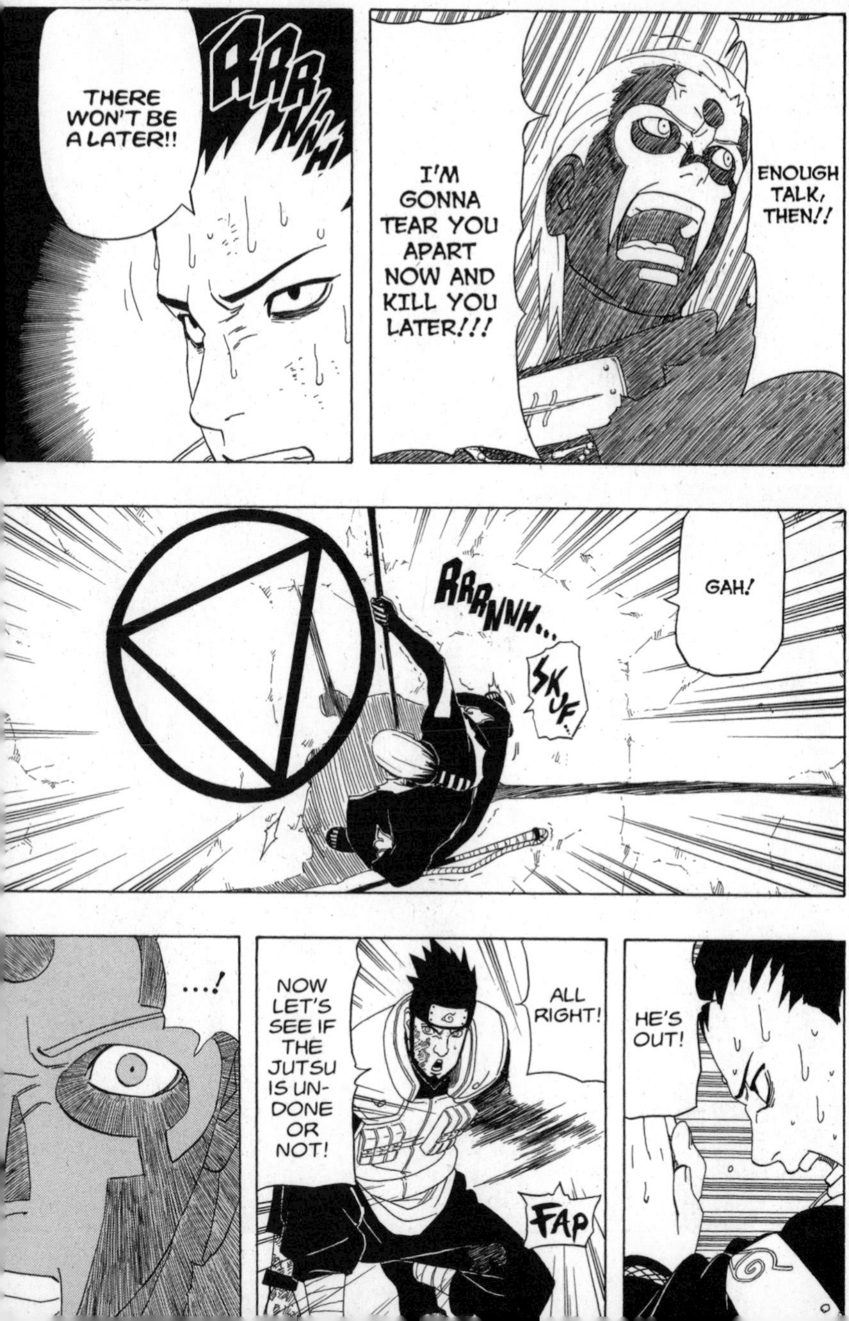
ENOUGH TALK, THEN!!
I'M GONNA TEAR YOU APART NOW AND KILL YOU LATER!!!
RRRNNH
THERE WON'T BE A LATER!!
GAH!
RRRNNH...
SKUF...
HE'S OUT!
ALL RIGHT!
NOW LET'S SEE IF THE JUTSU IS UN-DONE OR NOT!
FAP
...!

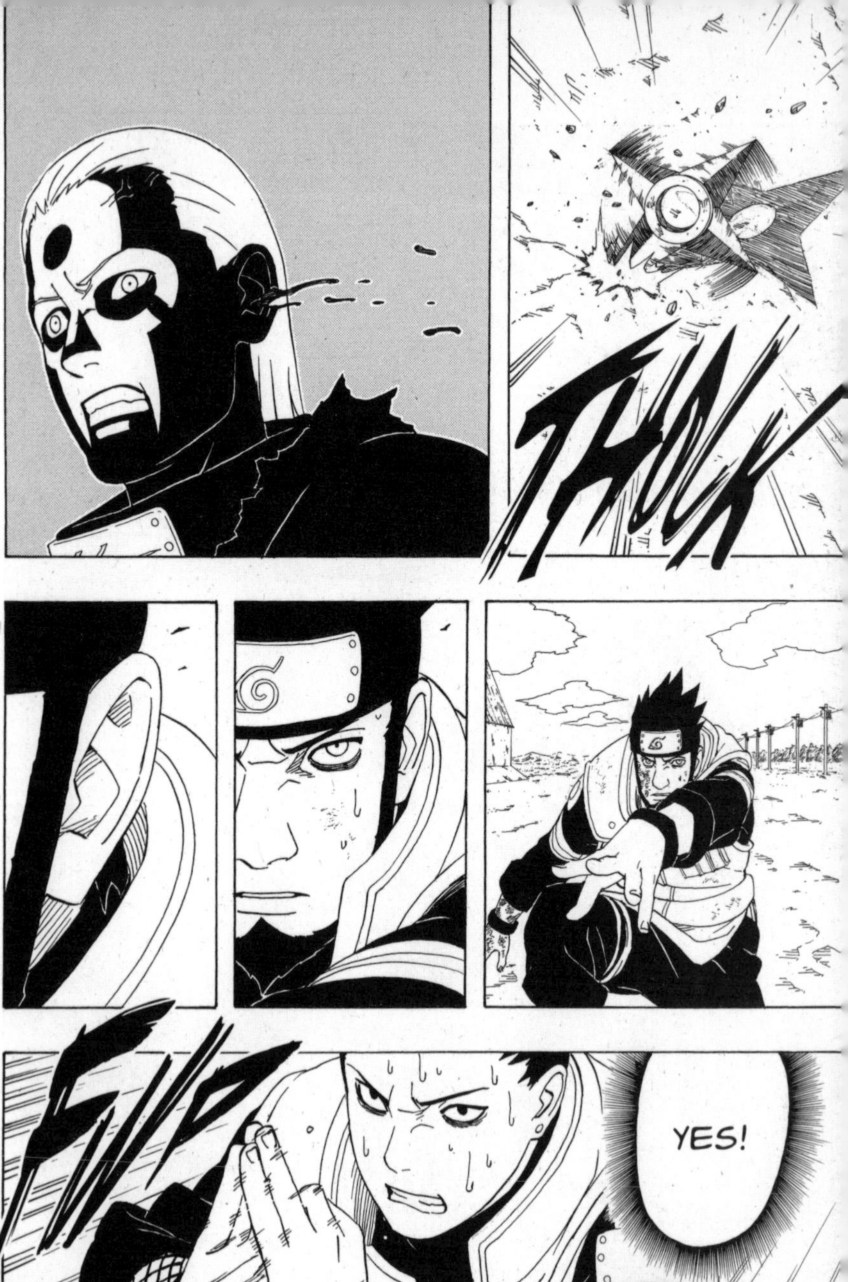
THUNK
SHIP
YES!

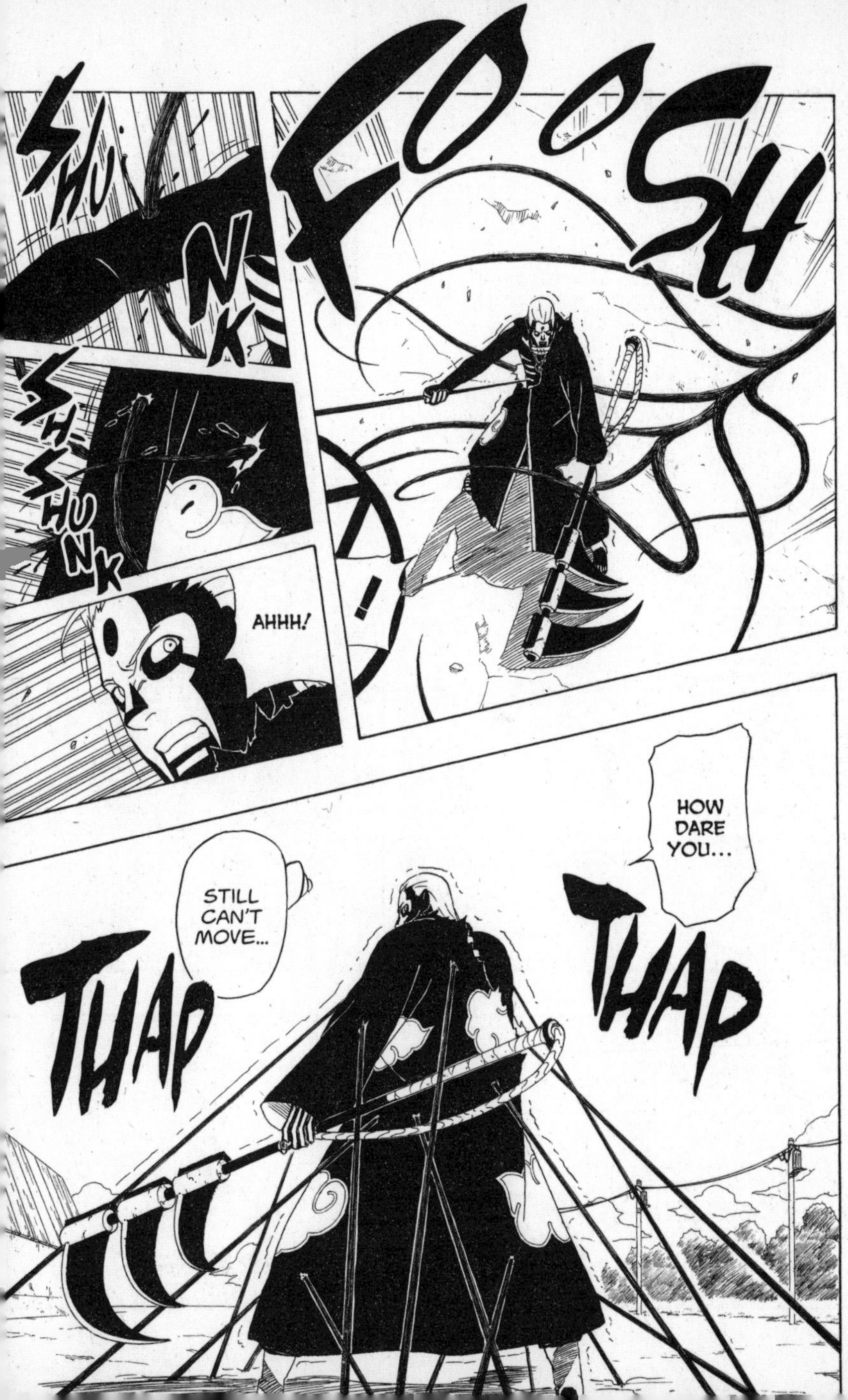
FOOSH
SHUNK
SHHSHUNK
AHHH!
HOW DARE YOU...
THAP
STILL CAN'T MOVE...
THAP

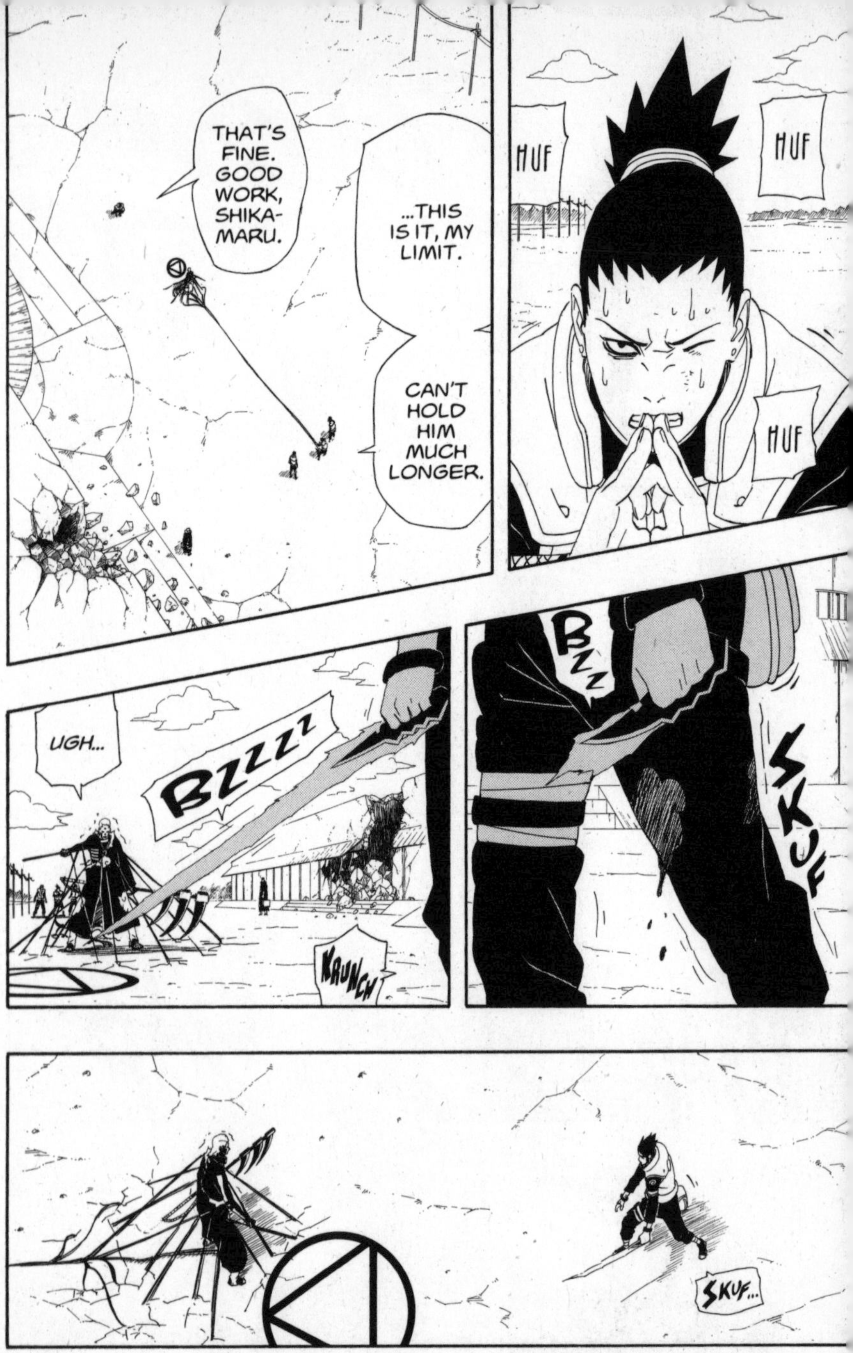
HUF
HUF
HUF
...THIS IS IT, MY LIMIT.
CAN'T HOLD HIM MUCH LONGER.
THAT'S FINE. GOOD WORK, SHIKAMARU.
BZZ
SKUF
BZZZZZ
UGH...
KRUNCH
SKUF...

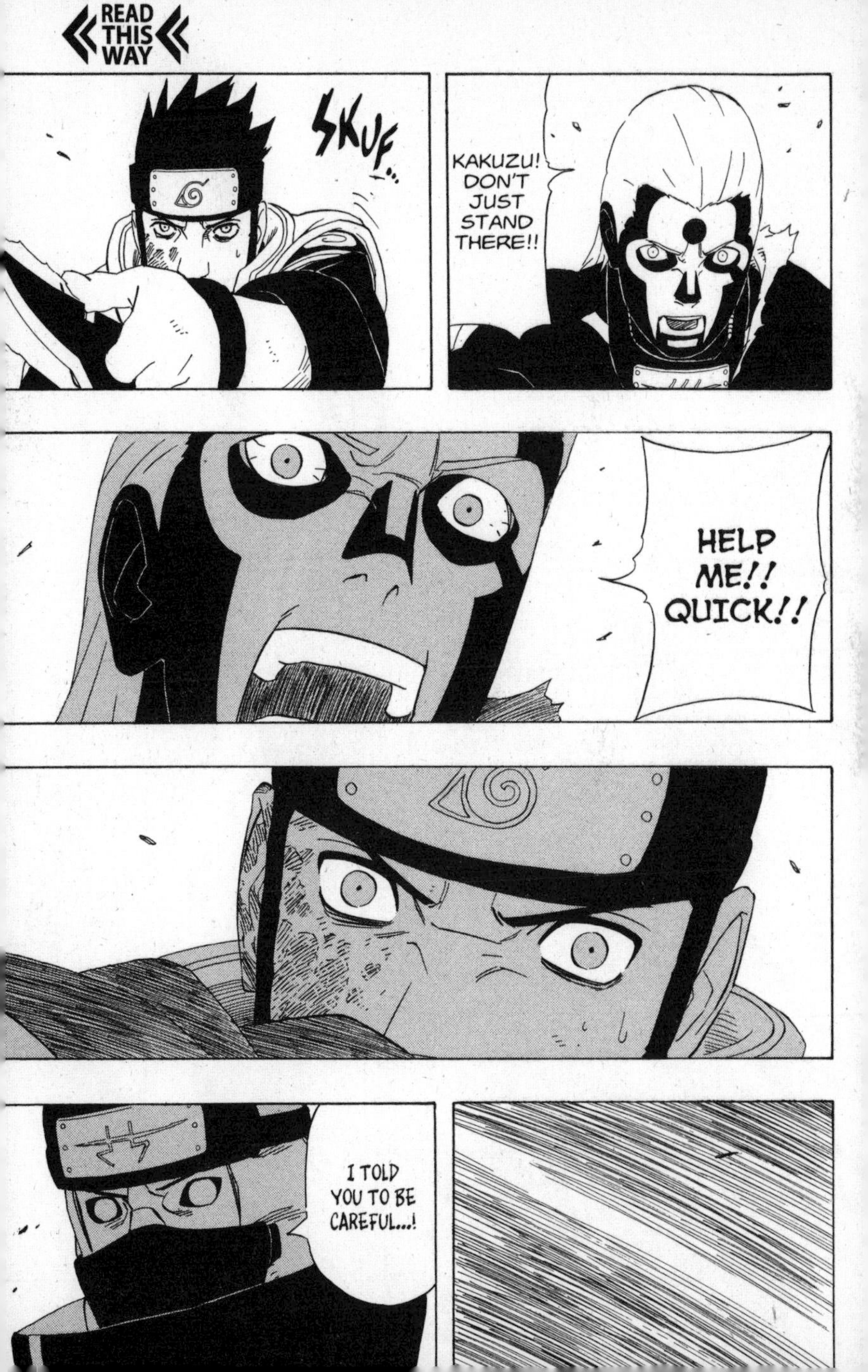
READ THIS WAY
KAKUZU! DON'T JUST STAND THERE!!
SKUF
HELP ME!! QUICK!!
I TOLD YOU TO BE CAREFUL...!

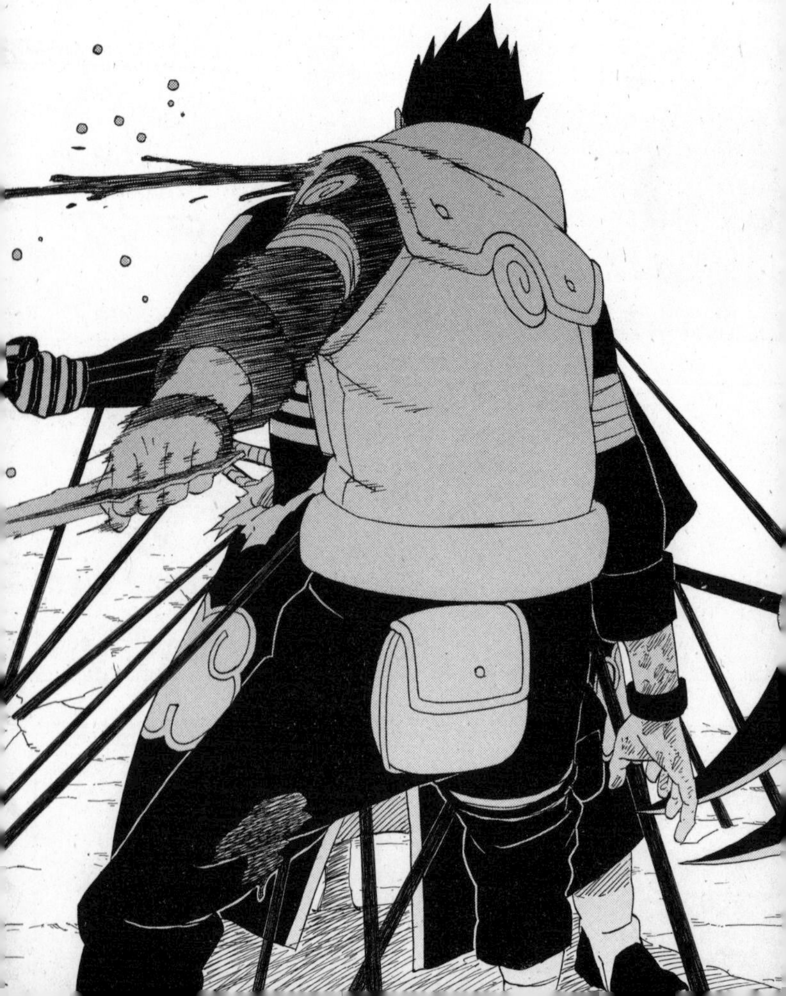

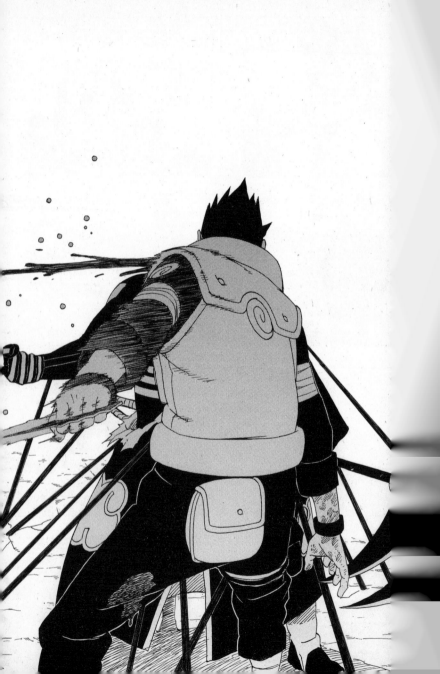

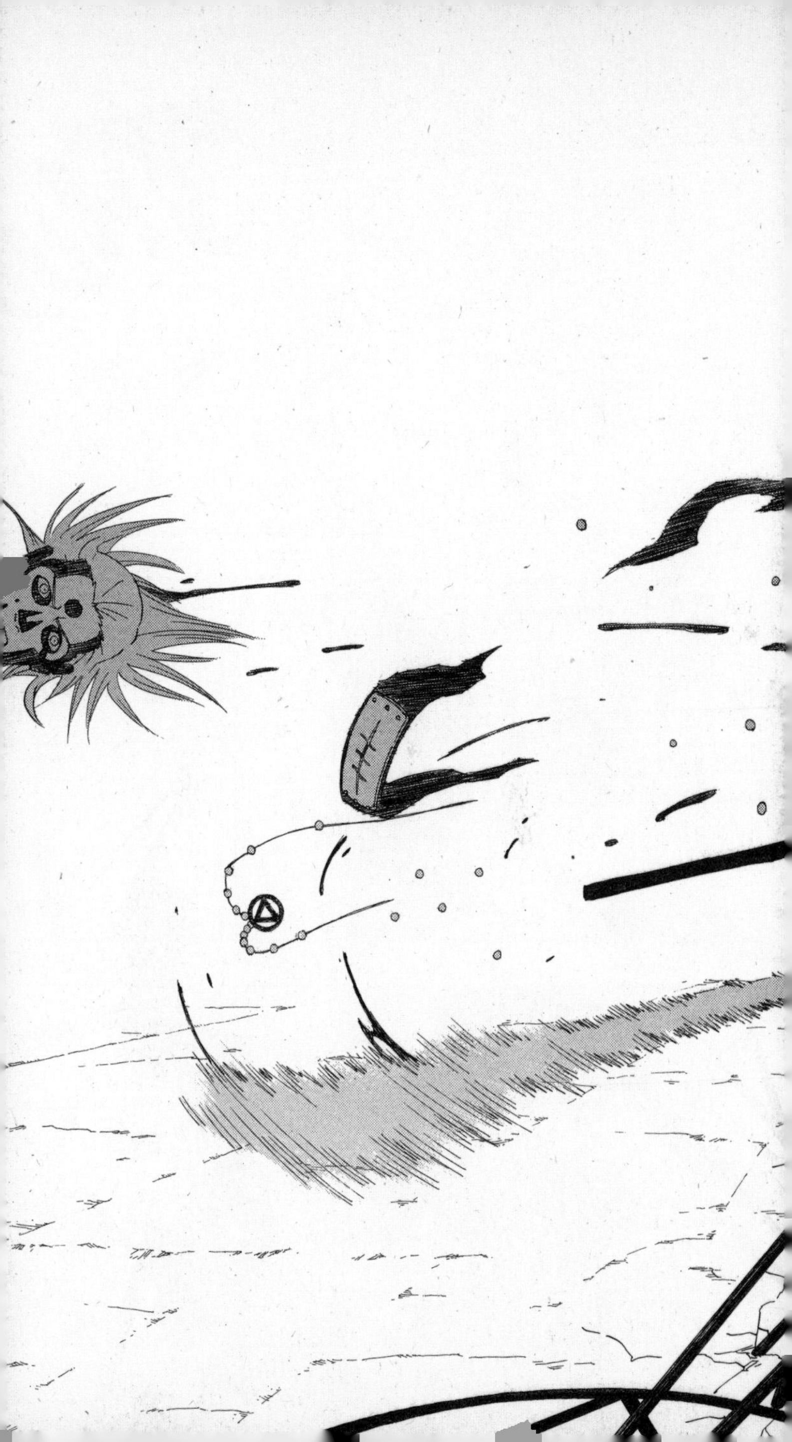

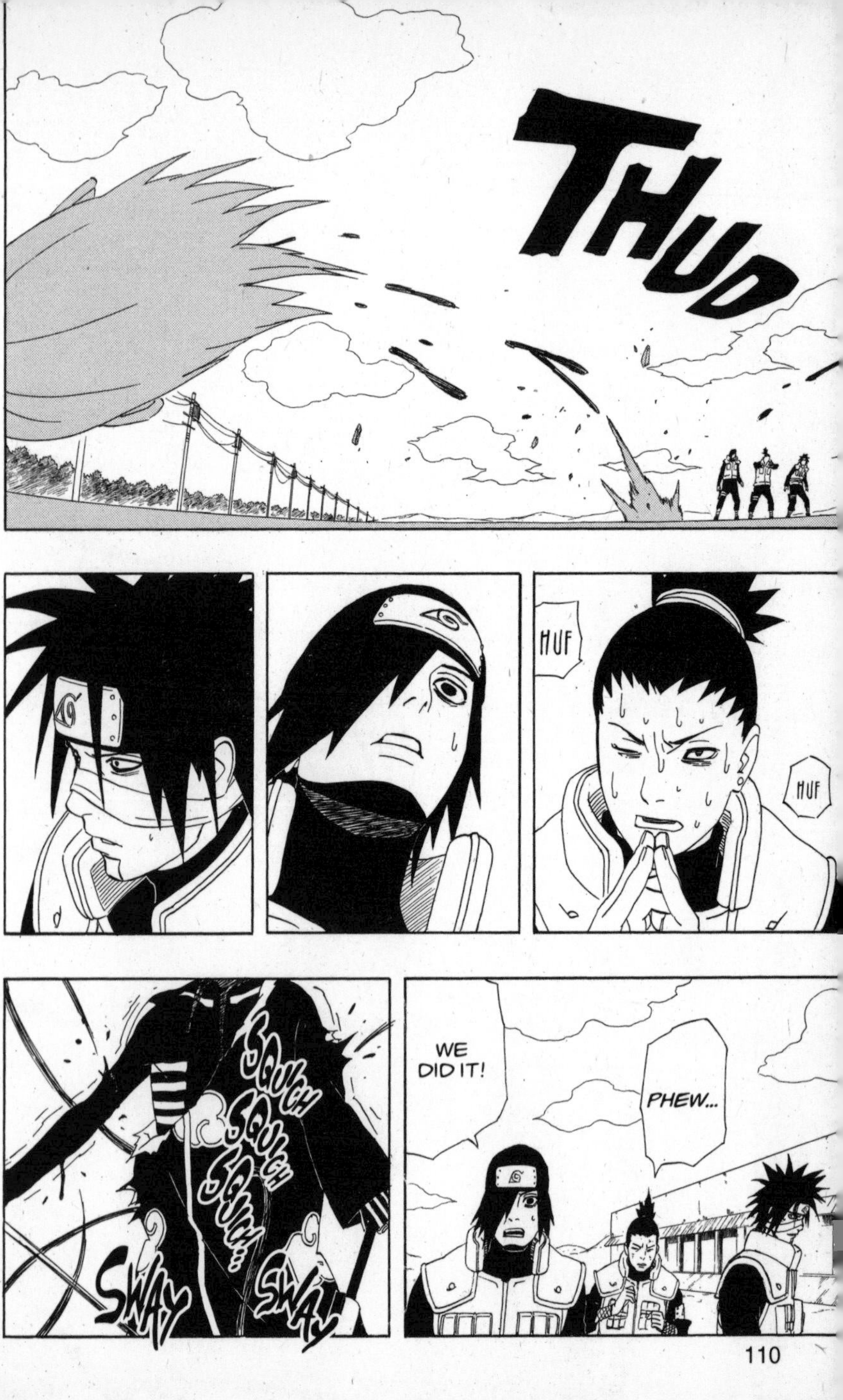
THUD
HUF
HUF
PHEW...
WE DID IT!
SQUISH SQUISH SQUISH...
SWAY
SWAY

READ THIS WAY

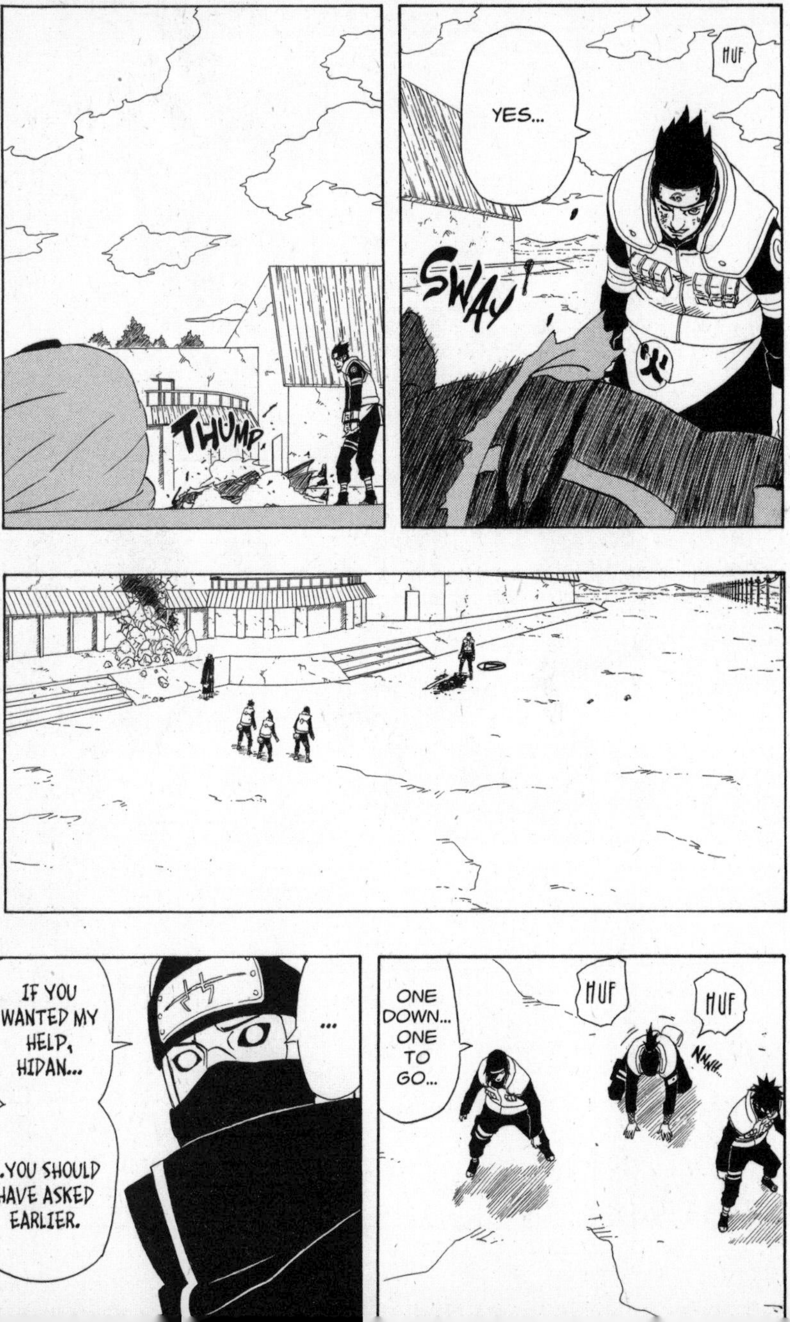
HUF
YES...
SWAY
THUMP
HUF
HUF
NNNH...
ONE DOWN... ONE TO GO...
...
IF YOU WANTED MY HELP, HIDAN...
...YOU SHOULD HAVE ASKED EARLIER.

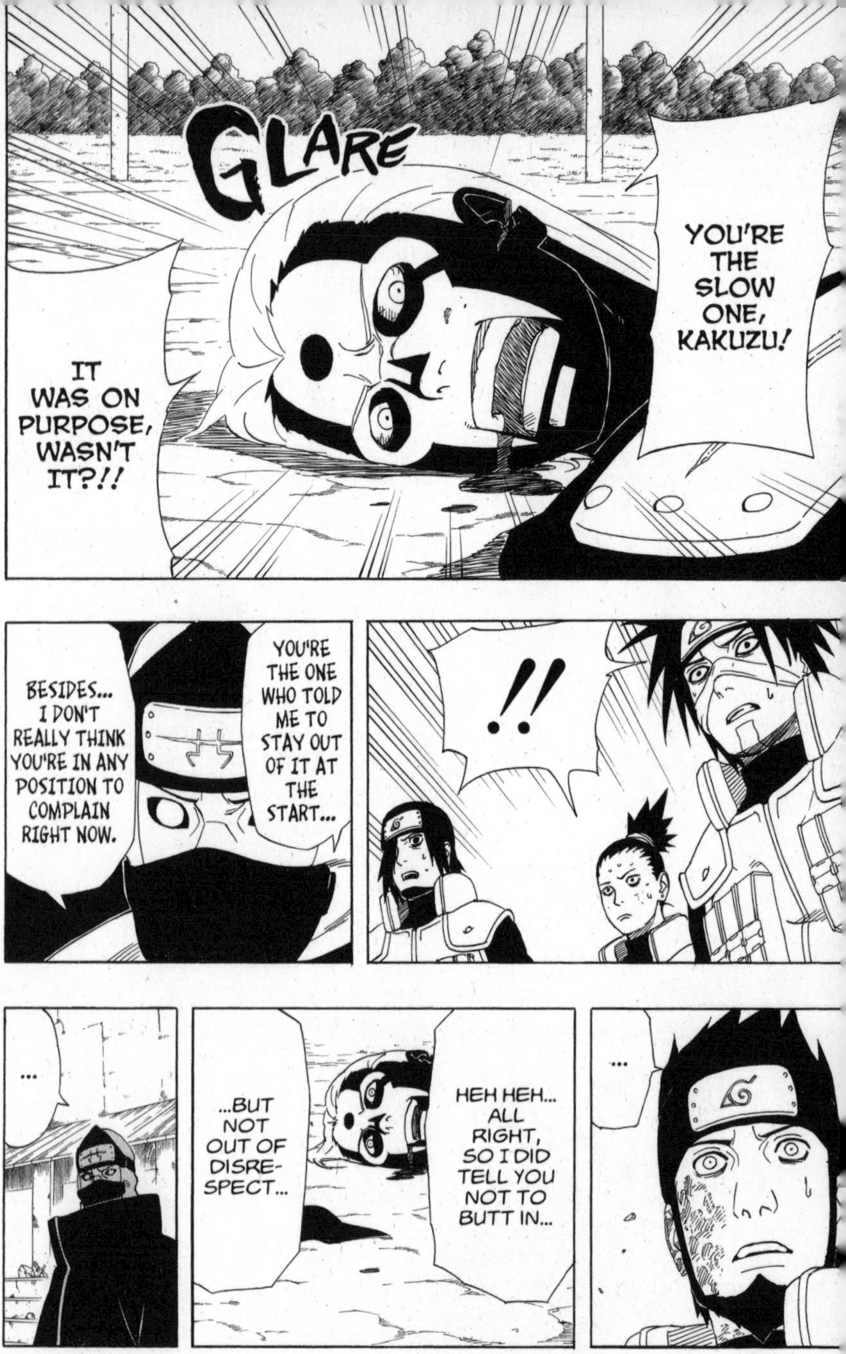
YOU'RE THE SLOW ONE, KAKUZU!
GLARE
IT WAS ON PURPOSE, WASN'T IT?!!
!!
YOU'RE THE ONE WHO TOLD ME TO STAY OUT OF IT AT THE START...
BESIDES... I DON'T REALLY THINK YOU'RE IN ANY POSITION TO COMPLAIN RIGHT NOW.
...
HEH HEH... ALL RIGHT, SO I DID TELL YOU NOT TO BUTT IN...
...BUT NOT OUT OF DISRESPECT...
...

READ THIS WAY

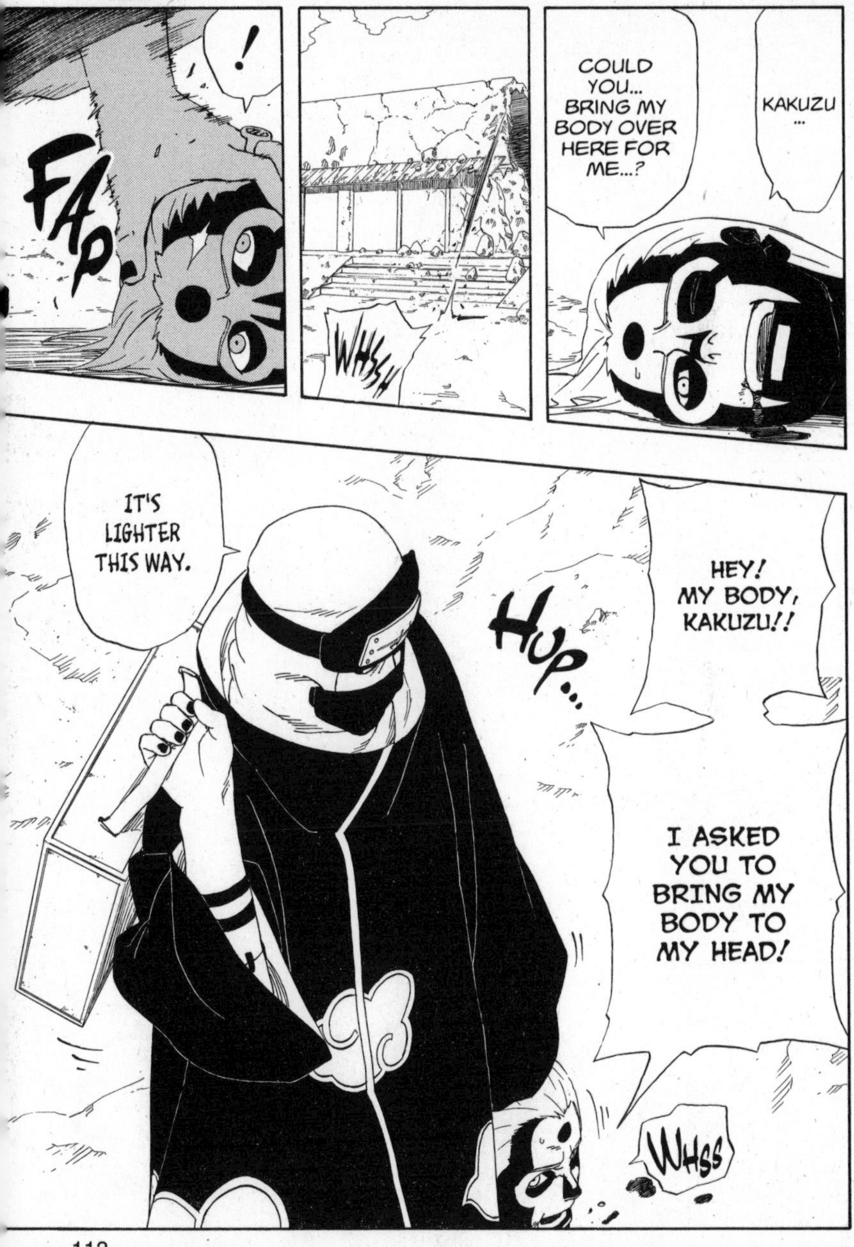
KAKUZU ...
COULD YOU... BRING MY BODY OVER HERE FOR ME...?
WHSSH
!
FAP
HEY! MY BODY, KAKUZU!!
I ASKED YOU TO BRING MY BODY TO MY HEAD!
HUP...
IT'S LIGHTER THIS WAY.
WHSS

NARUTO

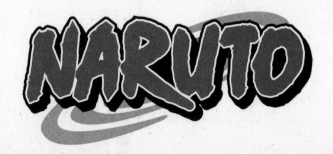

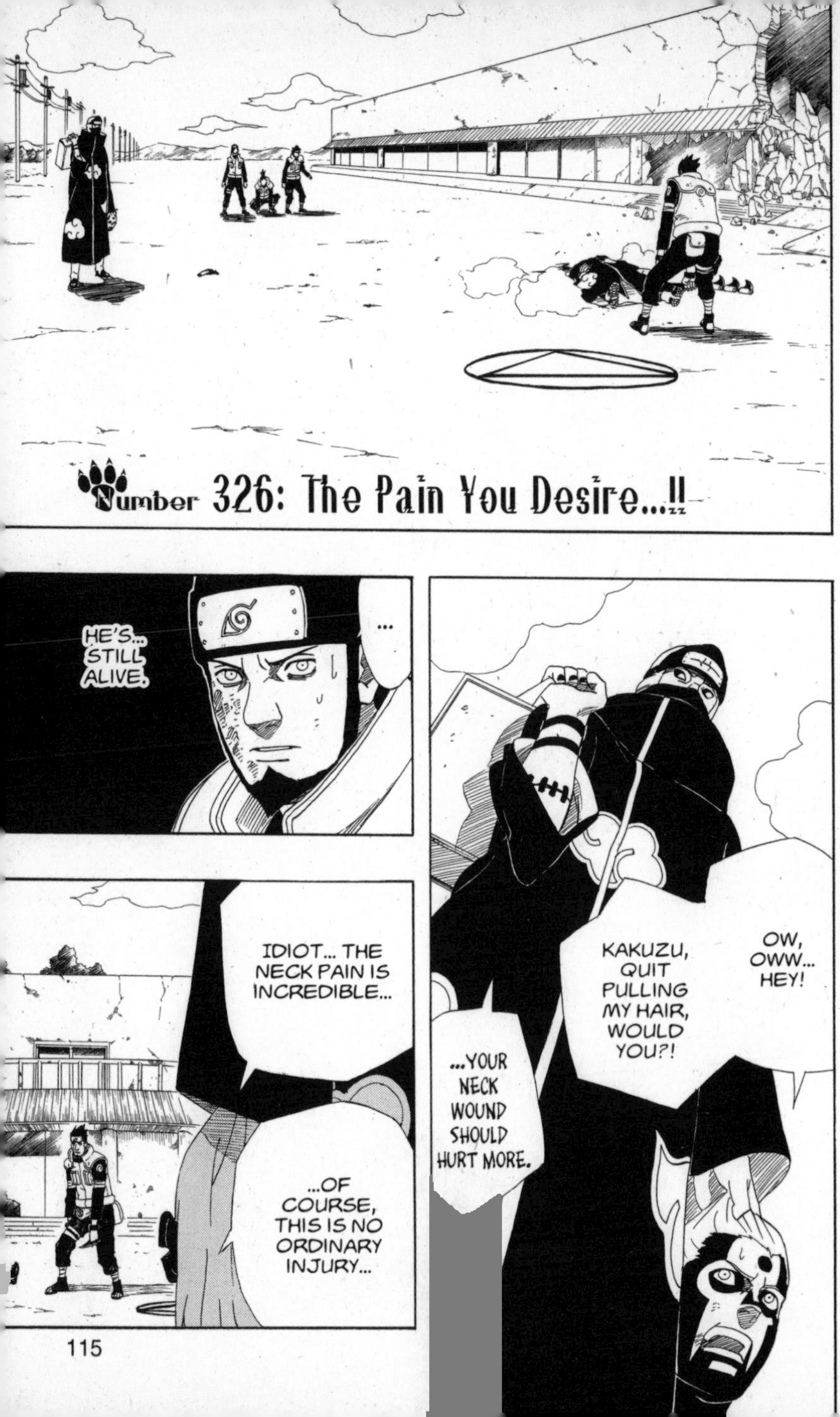
Number 326: The Pain You Desire...!!
OW, OWW... HEY!
KAKUZU, QUIT PULLING MY HAIR, WOULD YOU?!
...YOUR NECK WOUND SHOULD HURT MORE.
...
HE'S... STILL ALIVE.
IDIOT... THE NECK PAIN IS INCREDIBLE...
...OF COURSE, THIS IS NO ORDINARY INJURY...

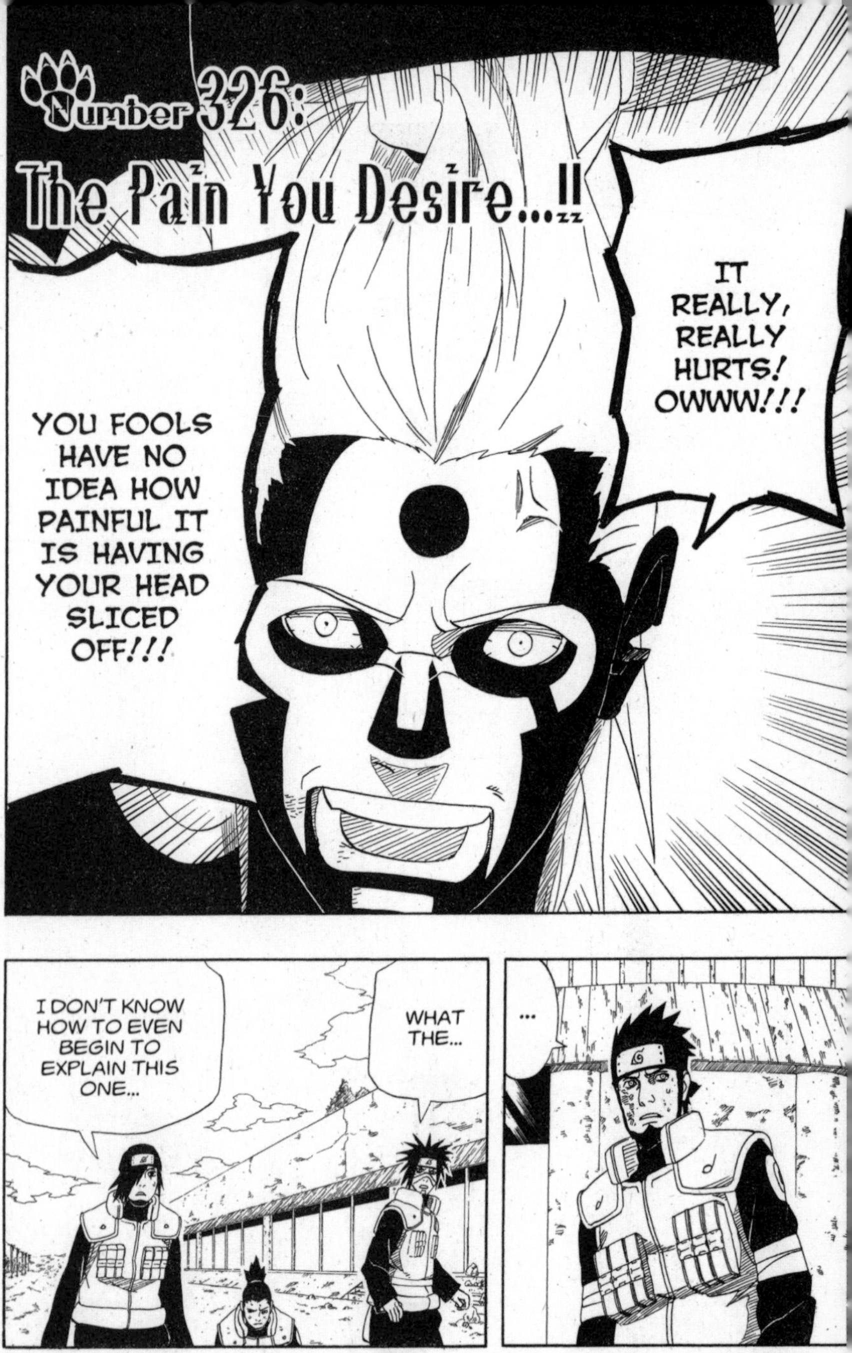
Number 326: The Pain You Desire...!!
IT REALLY, REALLY HURTS! OWWW!!!
YOU FOOLS HAVE NO IDEA HOW PAINFUL IT IS HAVING YOUR HEAD SLICED OFF!!!
...
WHAT THE...
I DON'T KNOW HOW TO EVEN BEGIN TO EXPLAIN THIS ONE...

READ THIS WAY

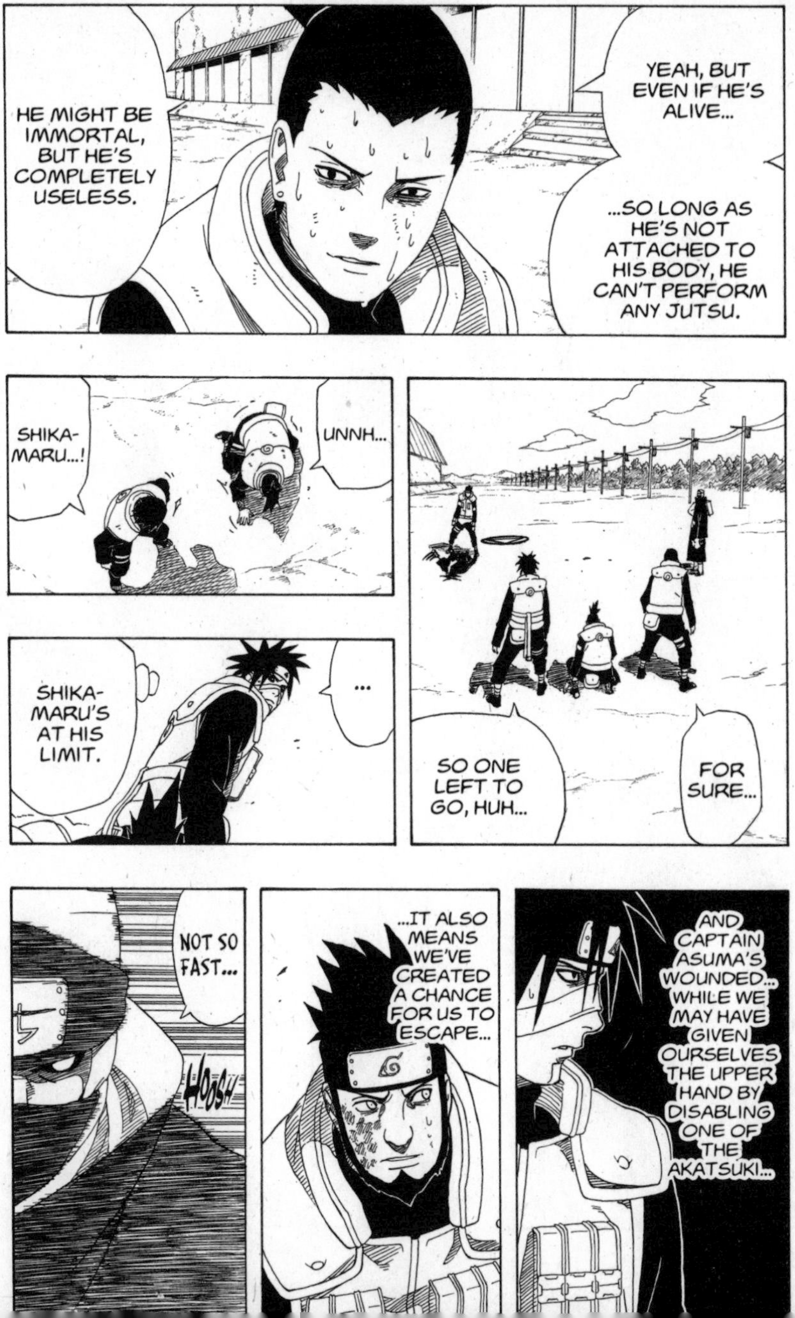
YEAH, BUT EVEN IF HE'S ALIVE...
...SO LONG AS HE'S NOT ATTACHED TO HIS BODY, HE CAN'T PERFORM ANY JUTSU.
HE MIGHT BE IMMORTAL, BUT HE'S COMPLETELY USELESS.
FOR SURE...
SO ONE LEFT TO GO, HUH...
UNNH...
SHIKAMARU...!
...
SHIKAMARU'S AT HIS LIMIT.
AND CAPTAIN ASUMA'S WOUNDED... WHILE WE MAY HAVE GIVEN OURSELVES THE UPPER HAND BY DISABLING ONE OF THE AKATSUKI...
...IT ALSO MEANS WE'VE CREATED A CHANCE FOR US TO ESCAPE...
NOT SO FAST...
HOOSH

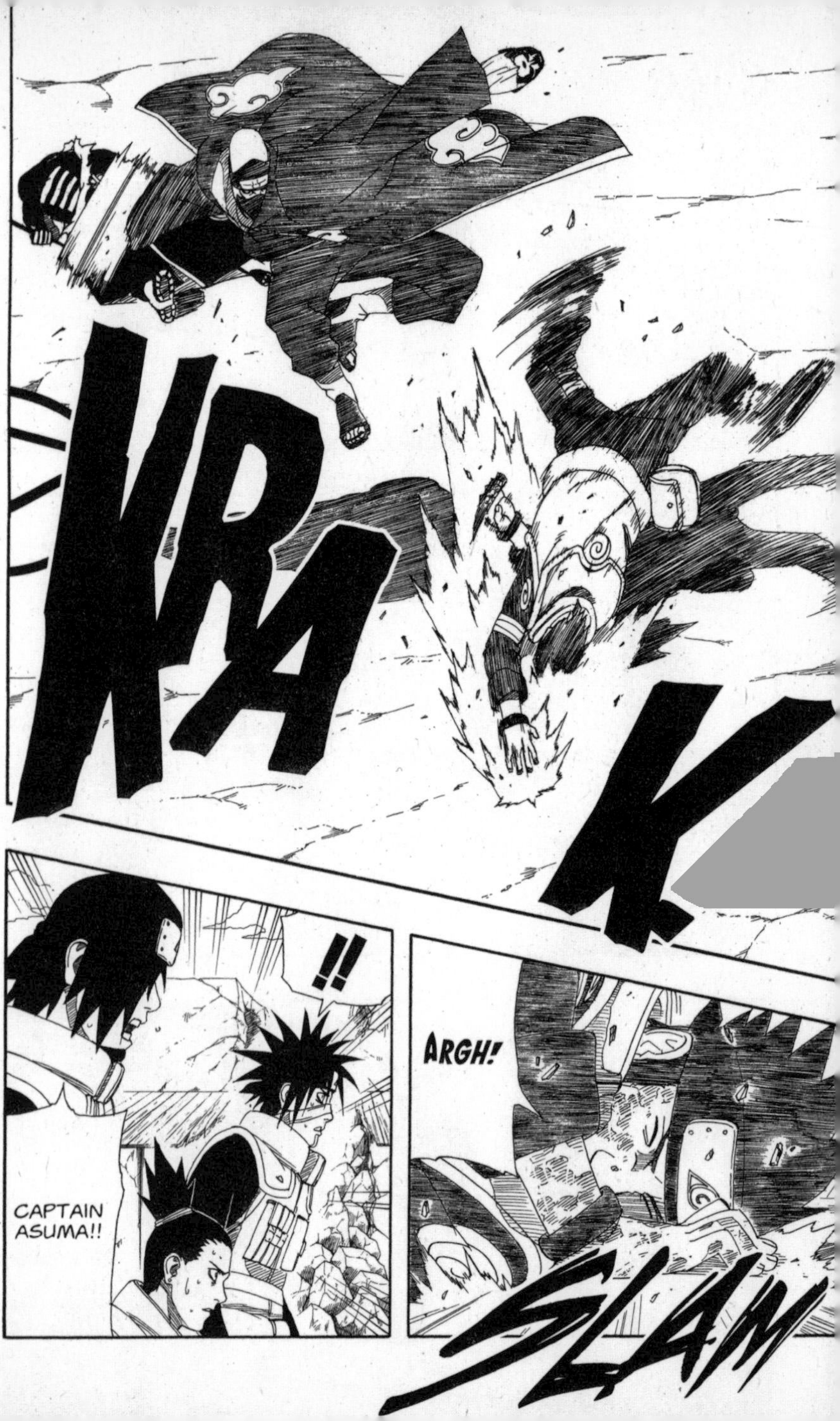
KRAK
ARGH!
SLAM
!!
CAPTAIN ASUMA!!

READ THIS WAY

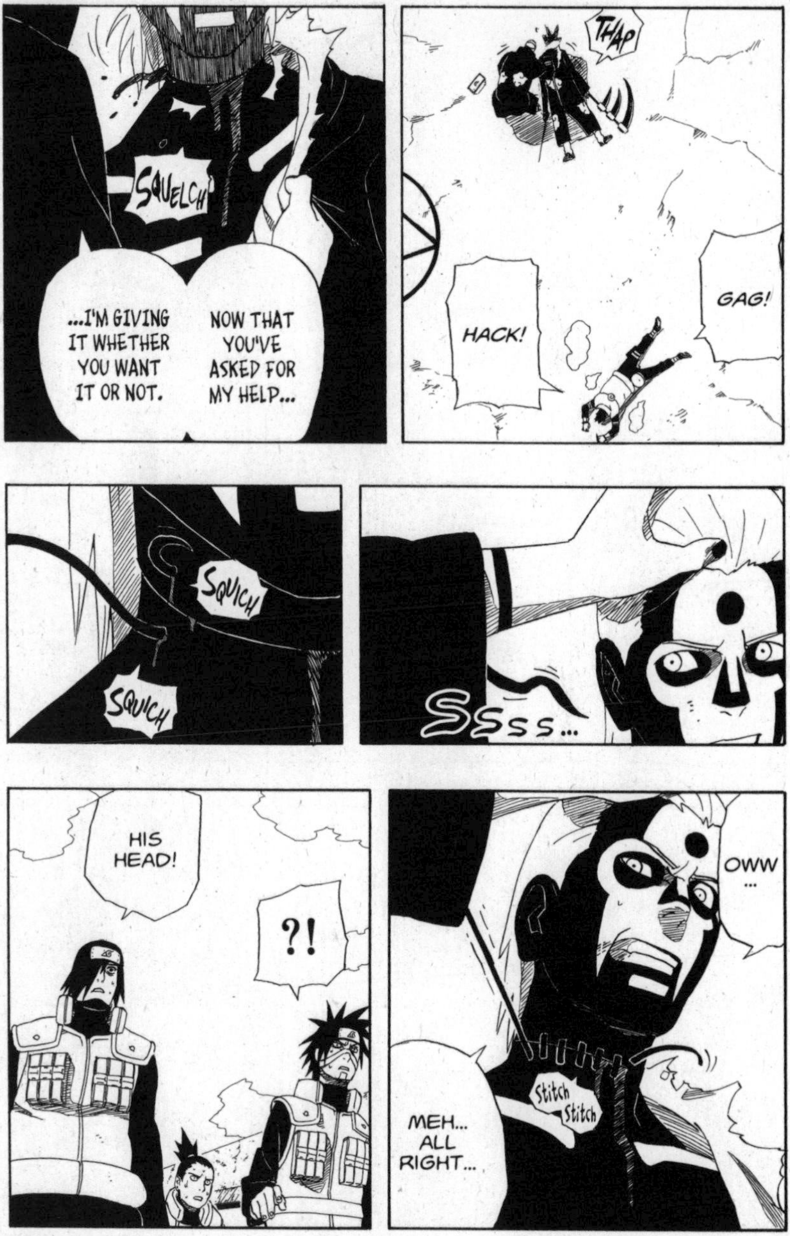
THAP
GAG!
HACK!
SQUELCH
NOW THAT YOU'VE ASKED FOR MY HELP...
...I'M GIVING IT WHETHER YOU WANT IT OR NOT.
SSSS...
SQUICH
SQUICH
OWW ...
Stitch Stitch
MEH... ALL RIGHT...
?!
HIS HEAD!

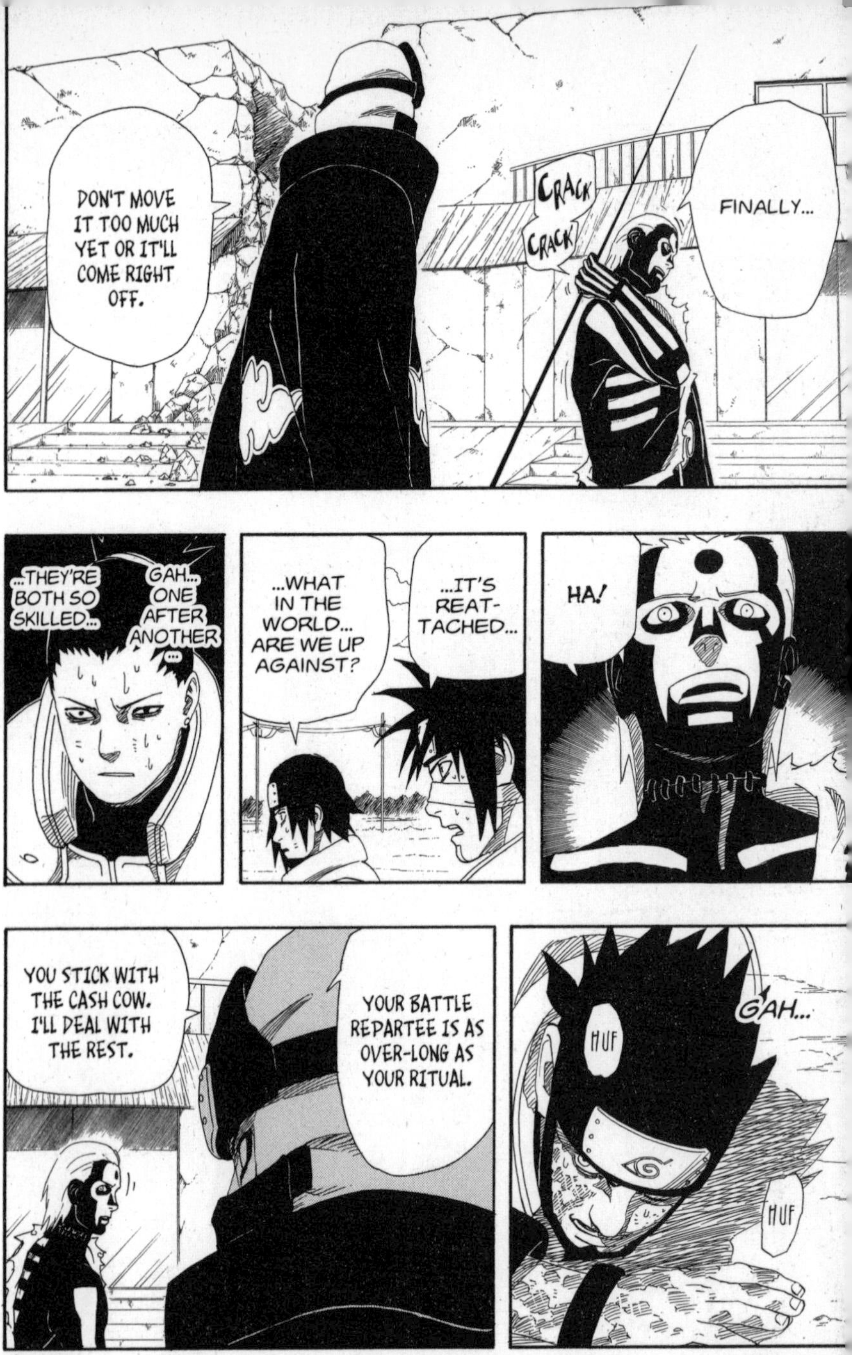
FINALLY...
CRACK
CRACK
DON'T MOVE IT TOO MUCH YET OR IT'LL COME RIGHT OFF.
HA!
...IT'S REAT-TACHED...
...WHAT IN THE WORLD... ARE WE UP AGAINST?
GAH... ONE AFTER ANOTHER...
...THEY'RE BOTH SO SKILLED...
GAH...
HUF
HUF
YOUR BATTLE REPARTEE IS AS OVER-LONG AS YOUR RITUAL.
YOU STICK WITH THE CASH COW. I'LL DEAL WITH THE REST.

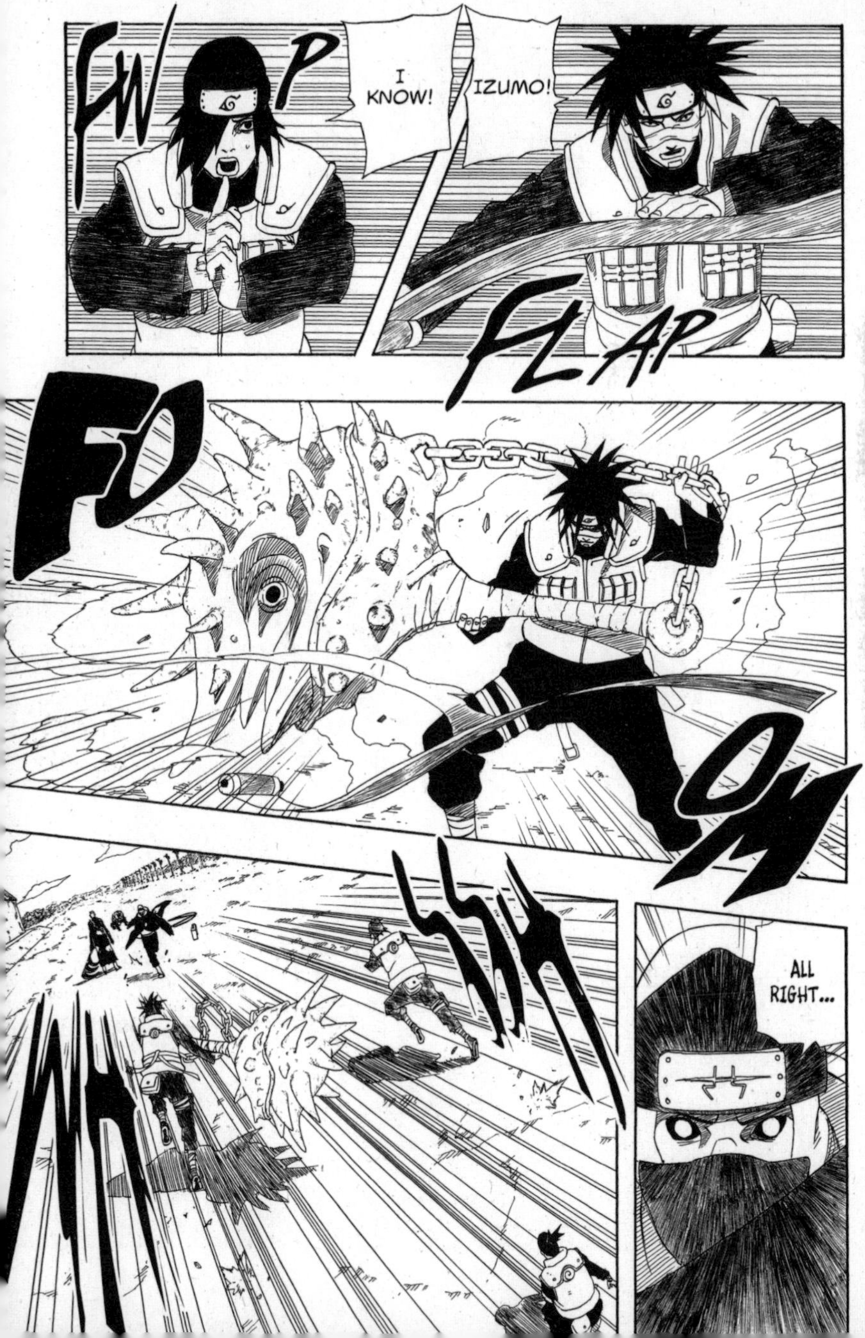
IZUMO!
I KNOW!
FLAP
ALL RIGHT...

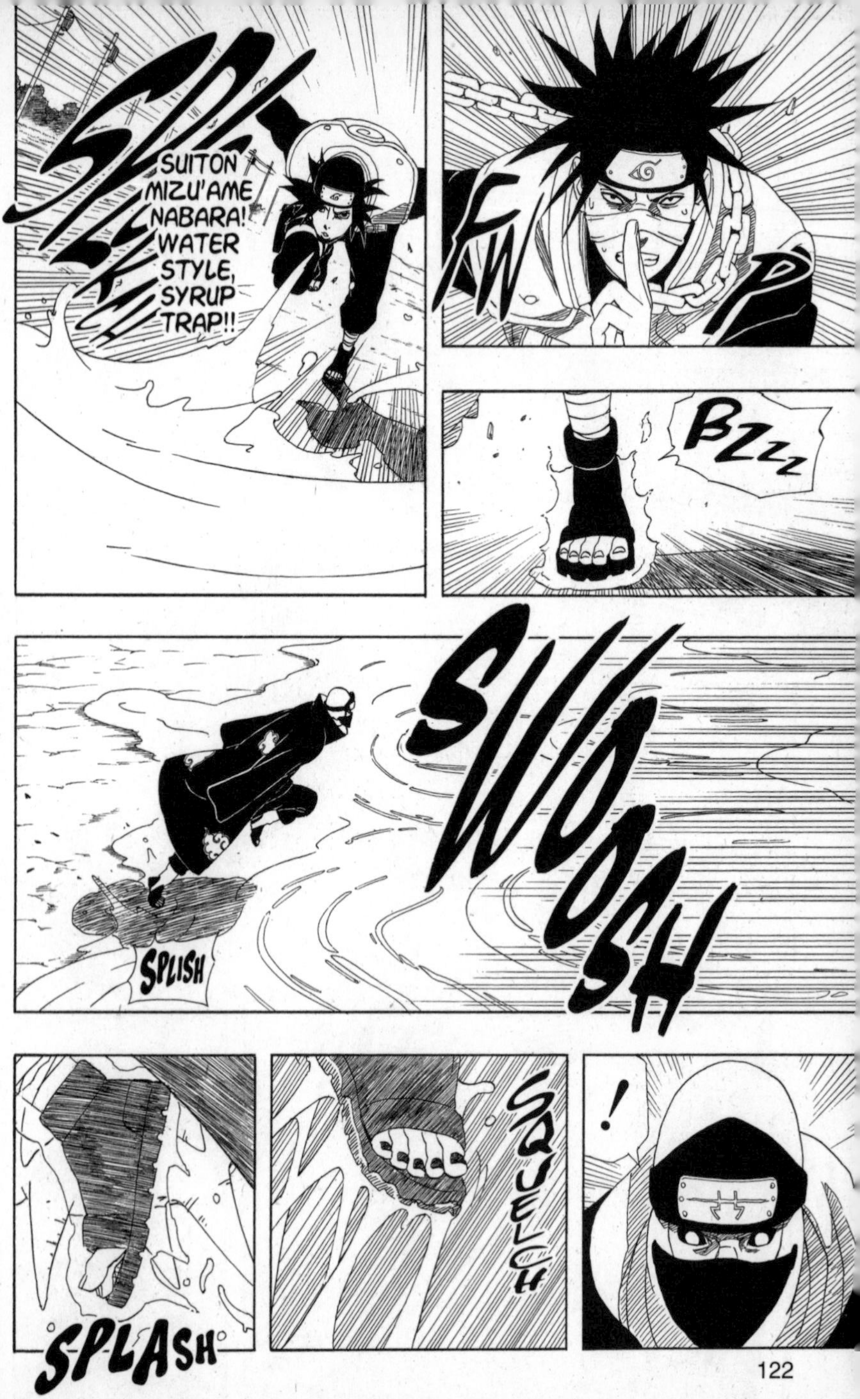
FWIP
BZZZ
SUITON MIZU'AME NABARA! WATER STYLE, SYRUP TRAP!!
SWOOSH
SPLISH
!
SQUELCH
SPLASH

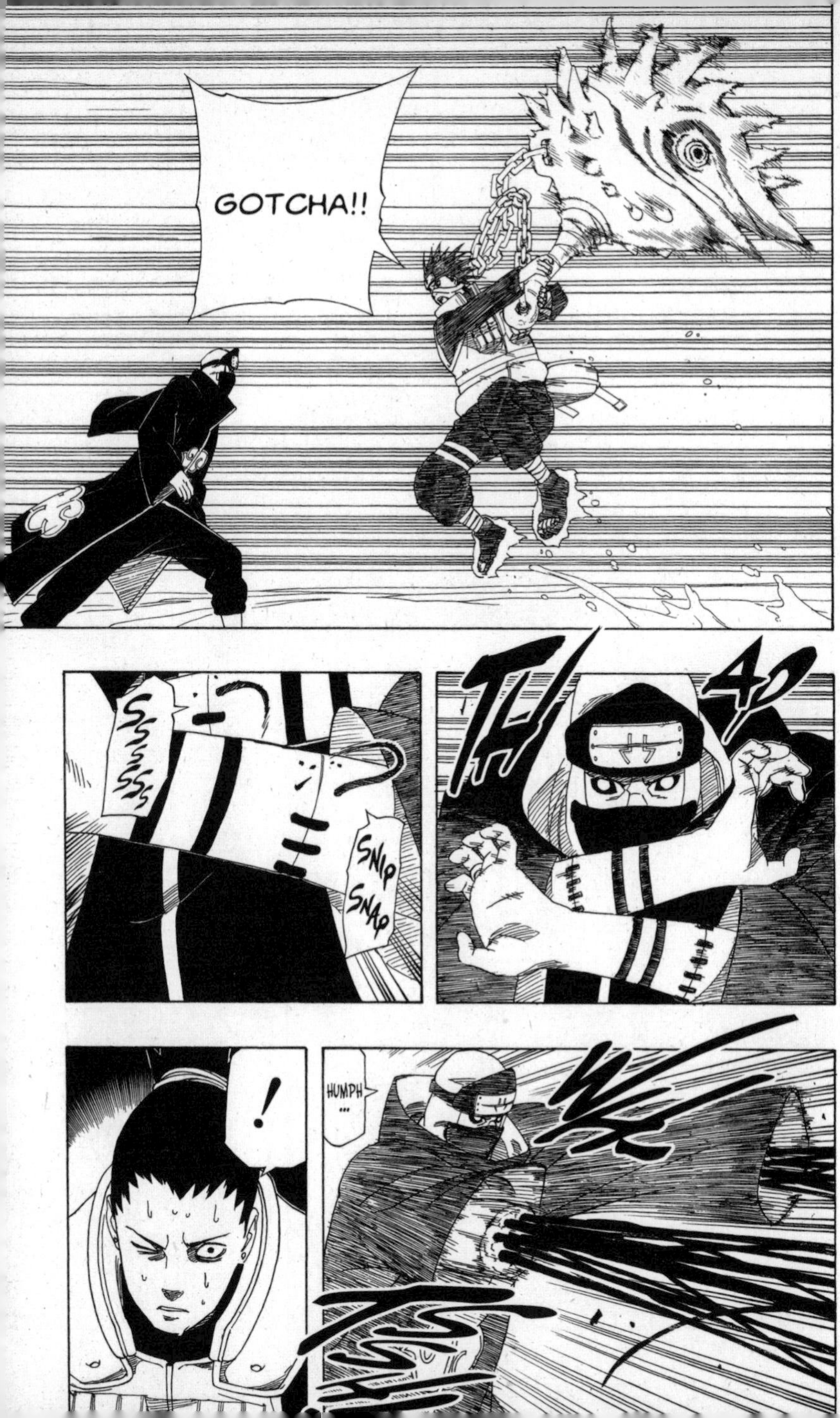
GOTCHA!!
THUD
SSSSSS
SNIP SNAP
HUMPH...
!

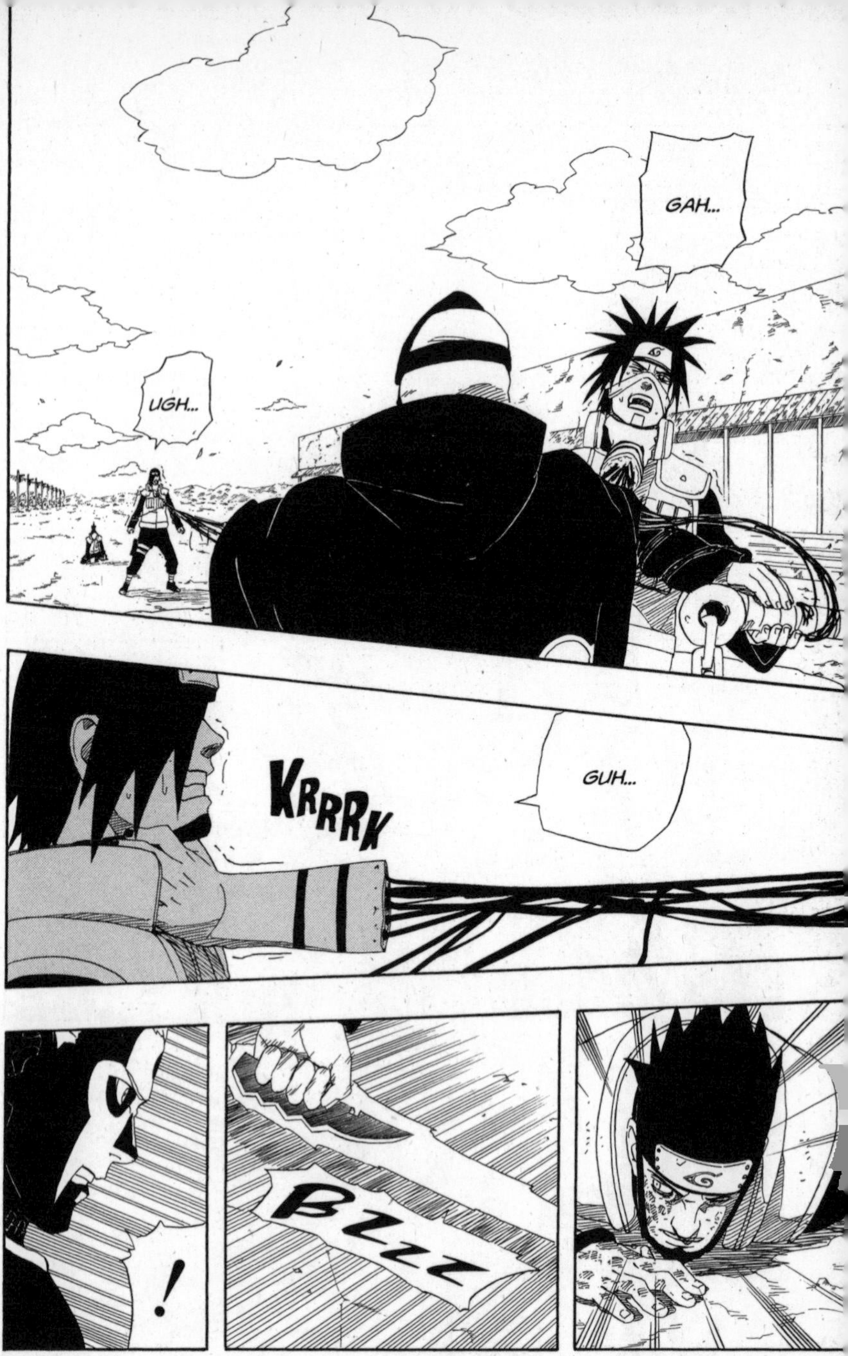
GAH...
UGH...
GUH...
KRRRK
BZZZ
!

READ THIS WAY

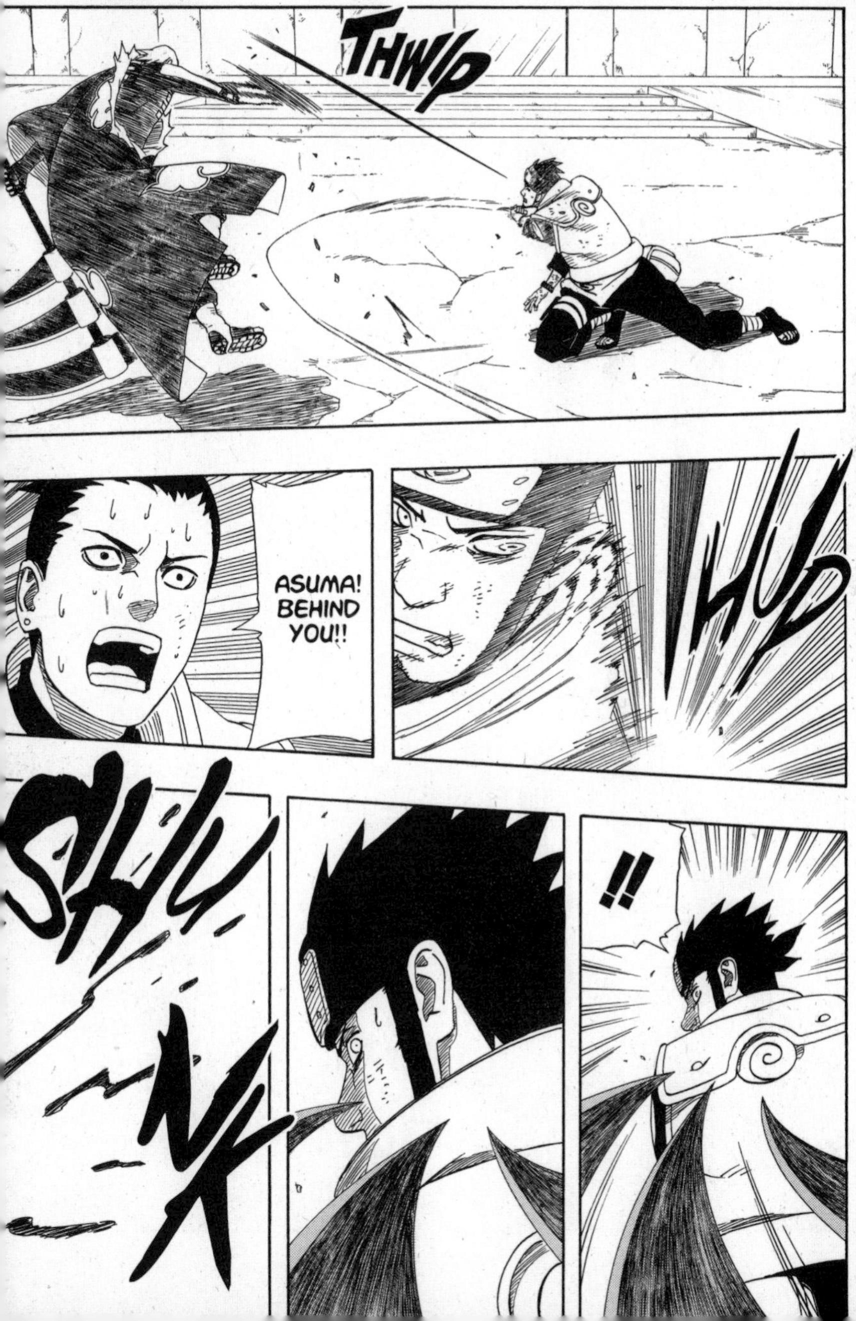
THWIP
WHUD
ASUMA! BEHIND YOU!!
!!
SHUNK

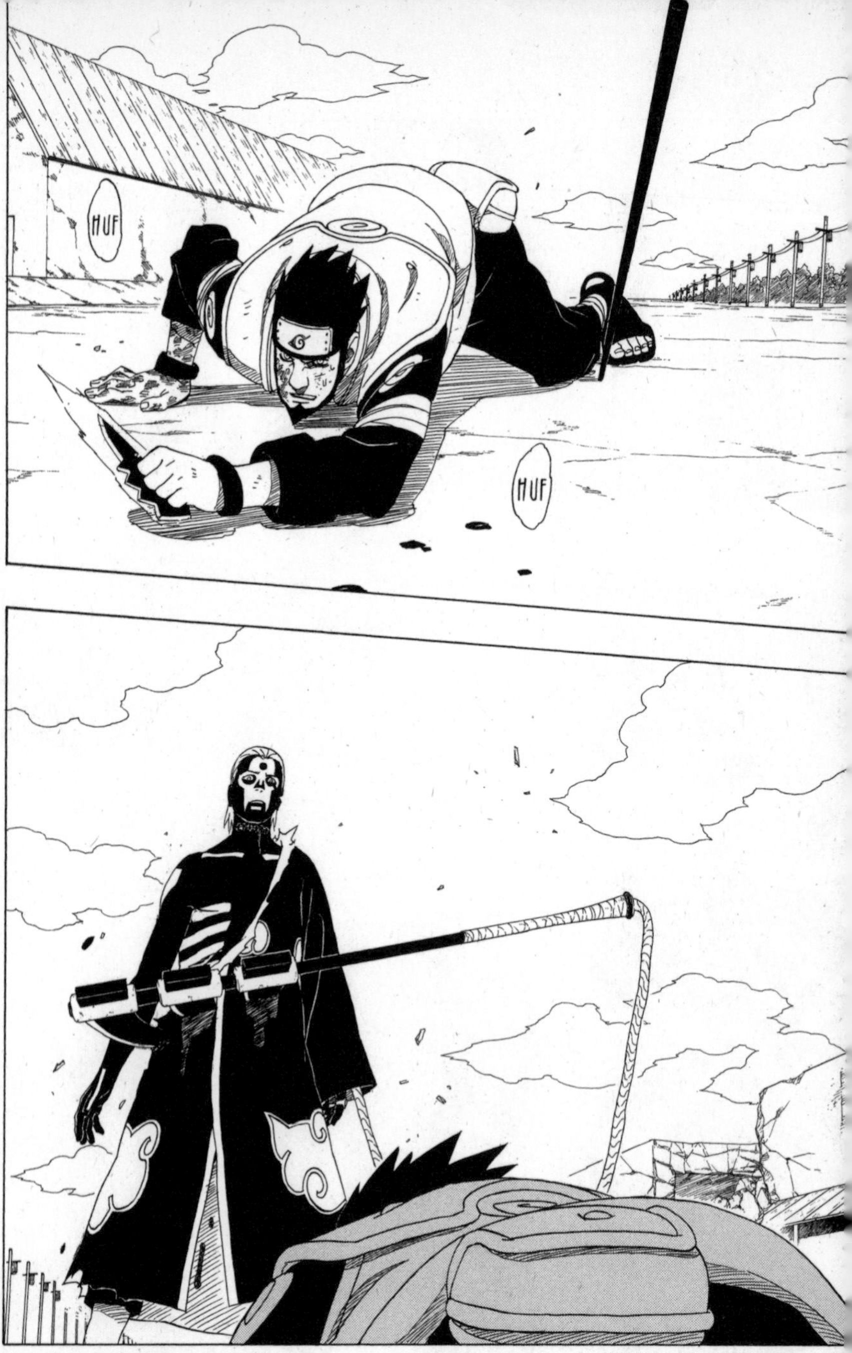
HUF
HUF

!!

HOW MANY TIMES YOU THINK I'M GONNA FALL FOR...

GWA-HA HA HA HA!!

HEH HEH...

...

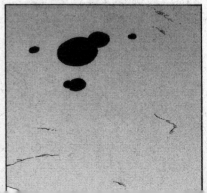

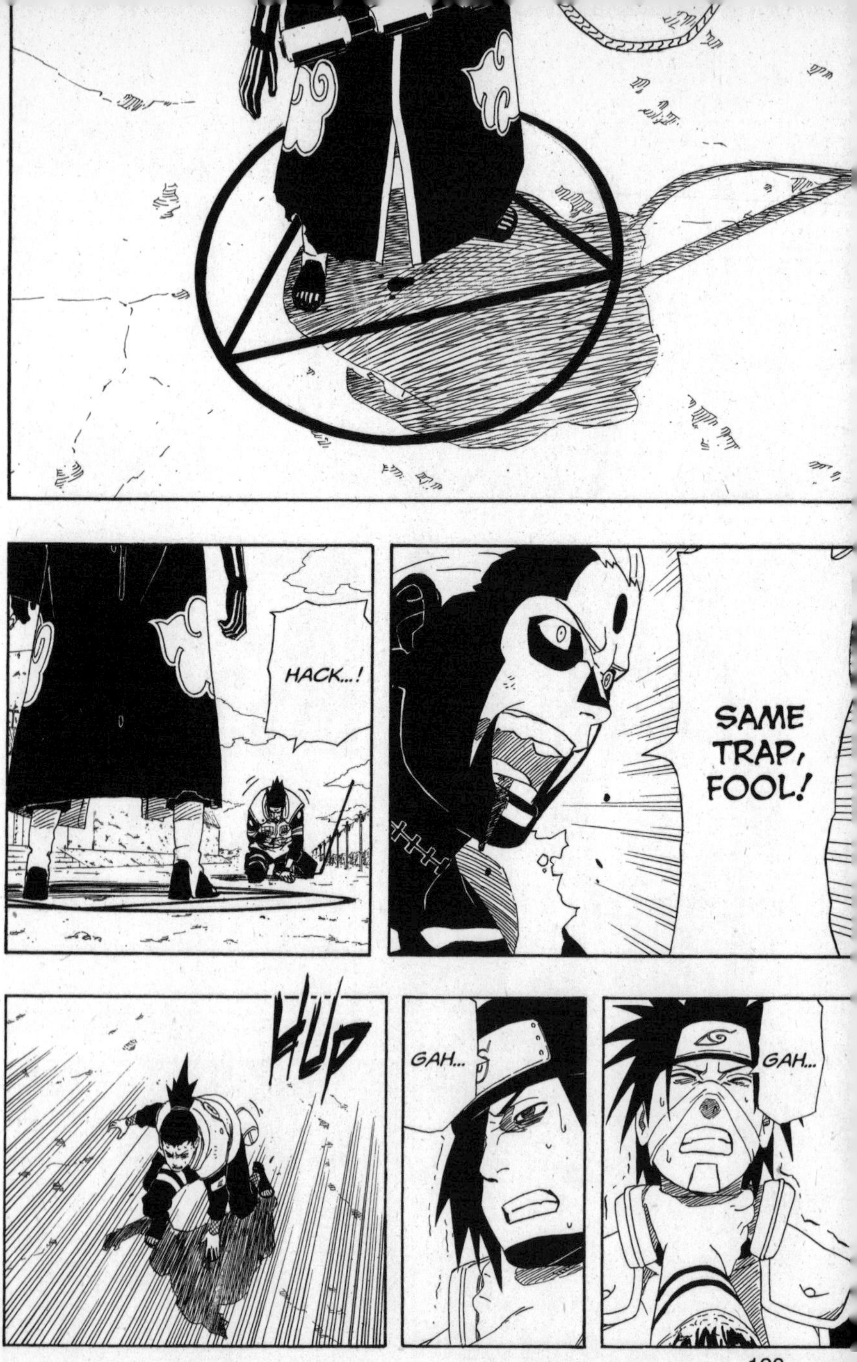
SAME TRAP, FOOL!
HACK...!
GAH...
GAH...
KUP

READ THIS WAY

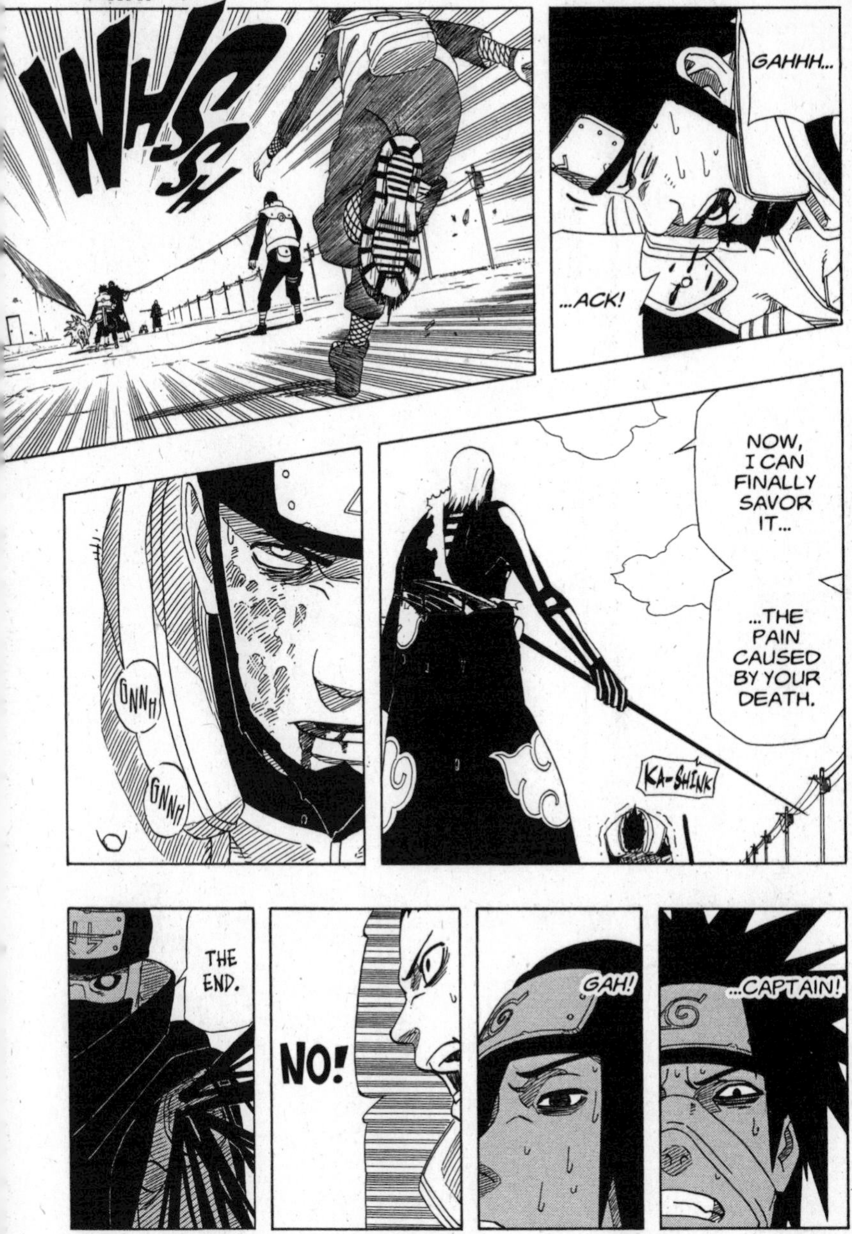

GAHHH...
...ACK!
WHSSH
NOW, I CAN FINALLY SAVOR IT...
...THE PAIN CAUSED BY YOUR DEATH.
KA-SHINK
GNNH
GNNH
...CAPTAIN!
GAH!
NO!
THE END.

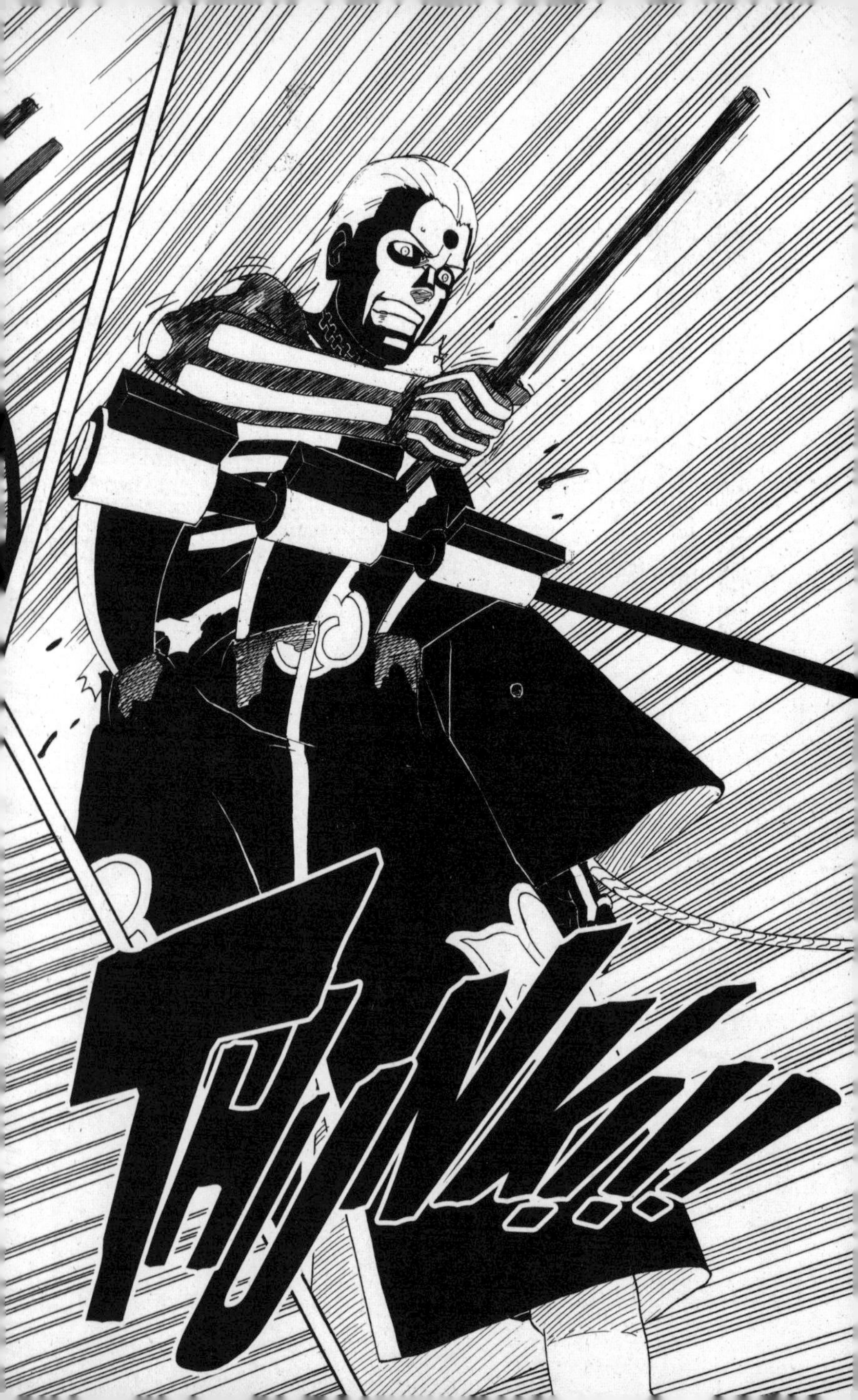
THWAK!!

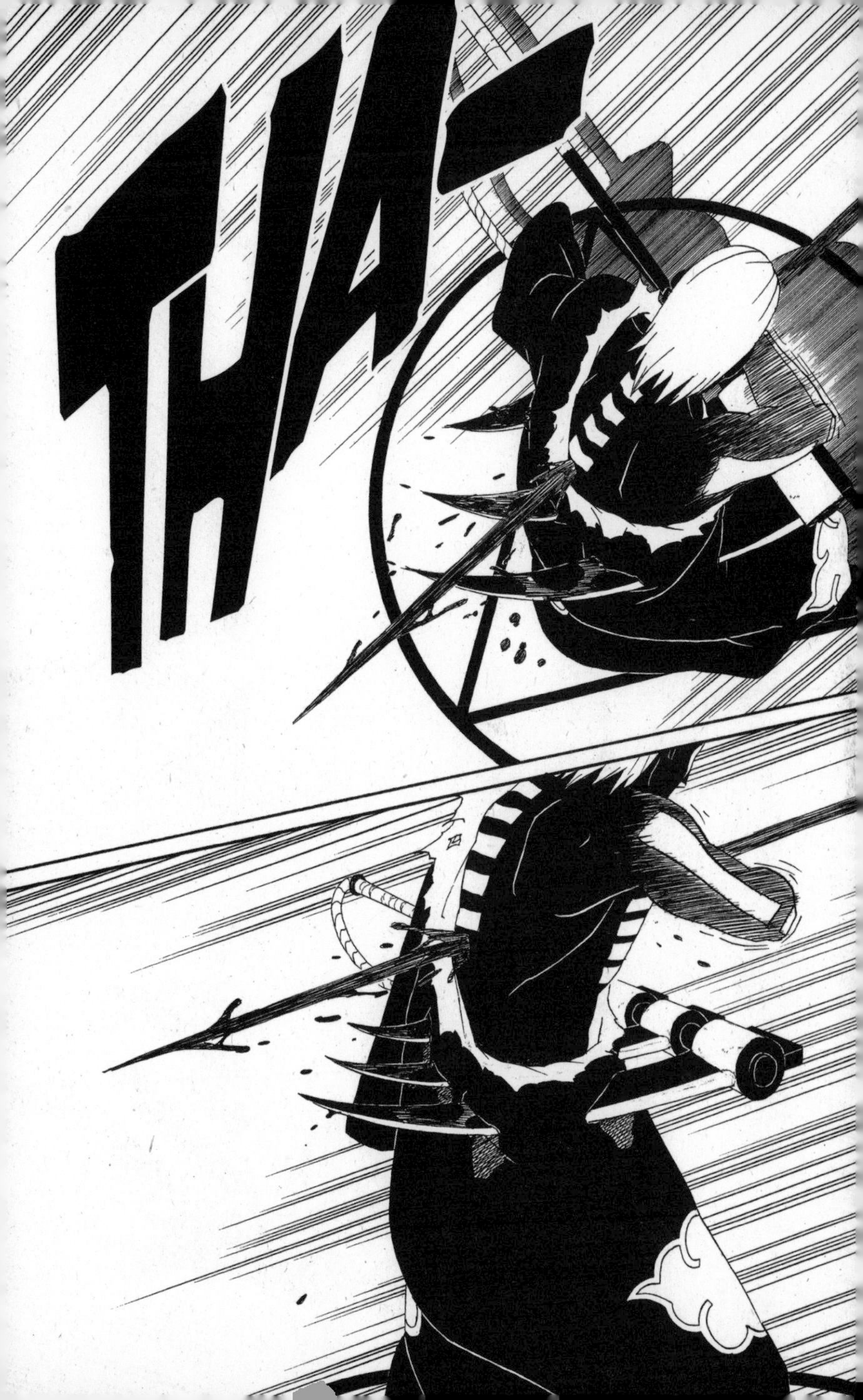
THA-

NARUTO

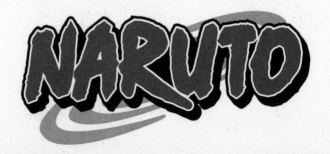

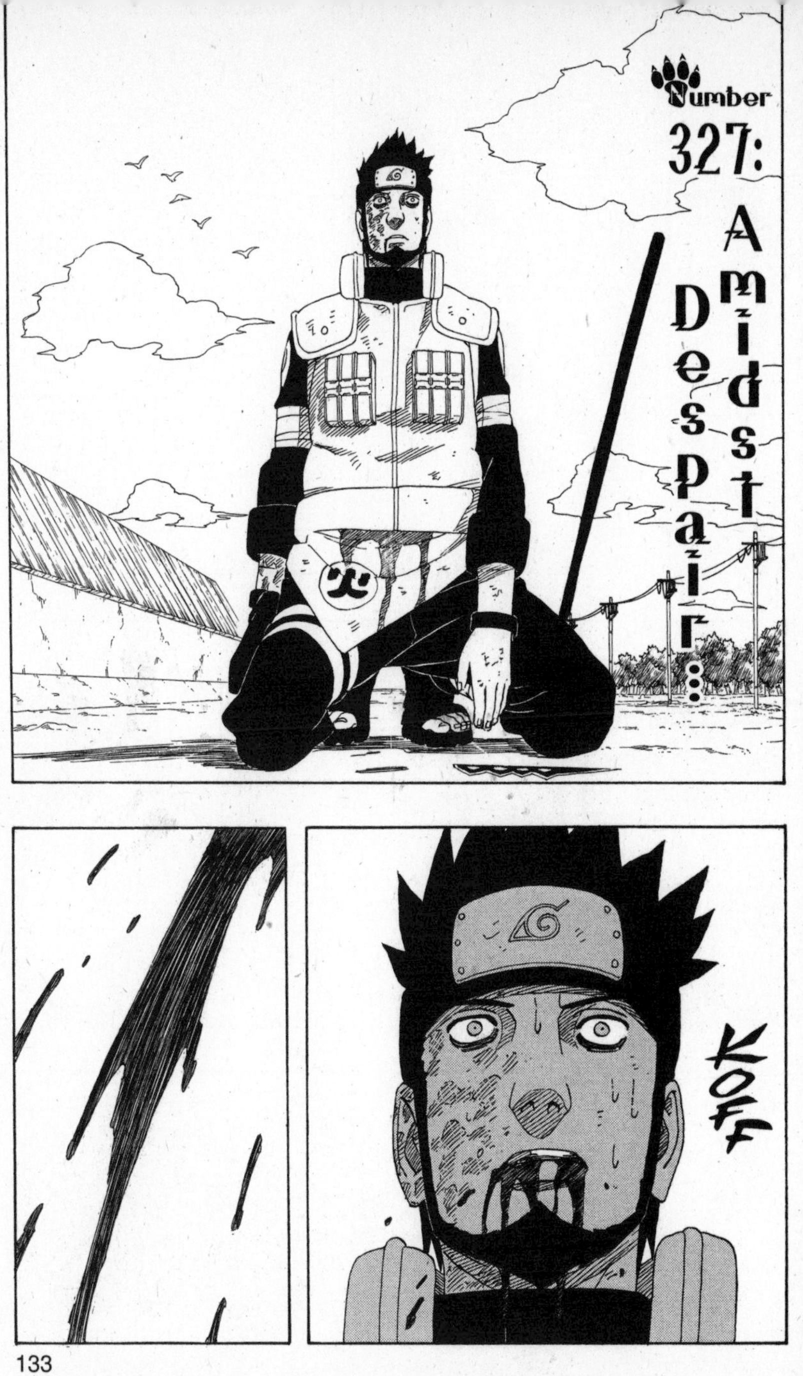
Number 327: Amidst Despair...
KOFF

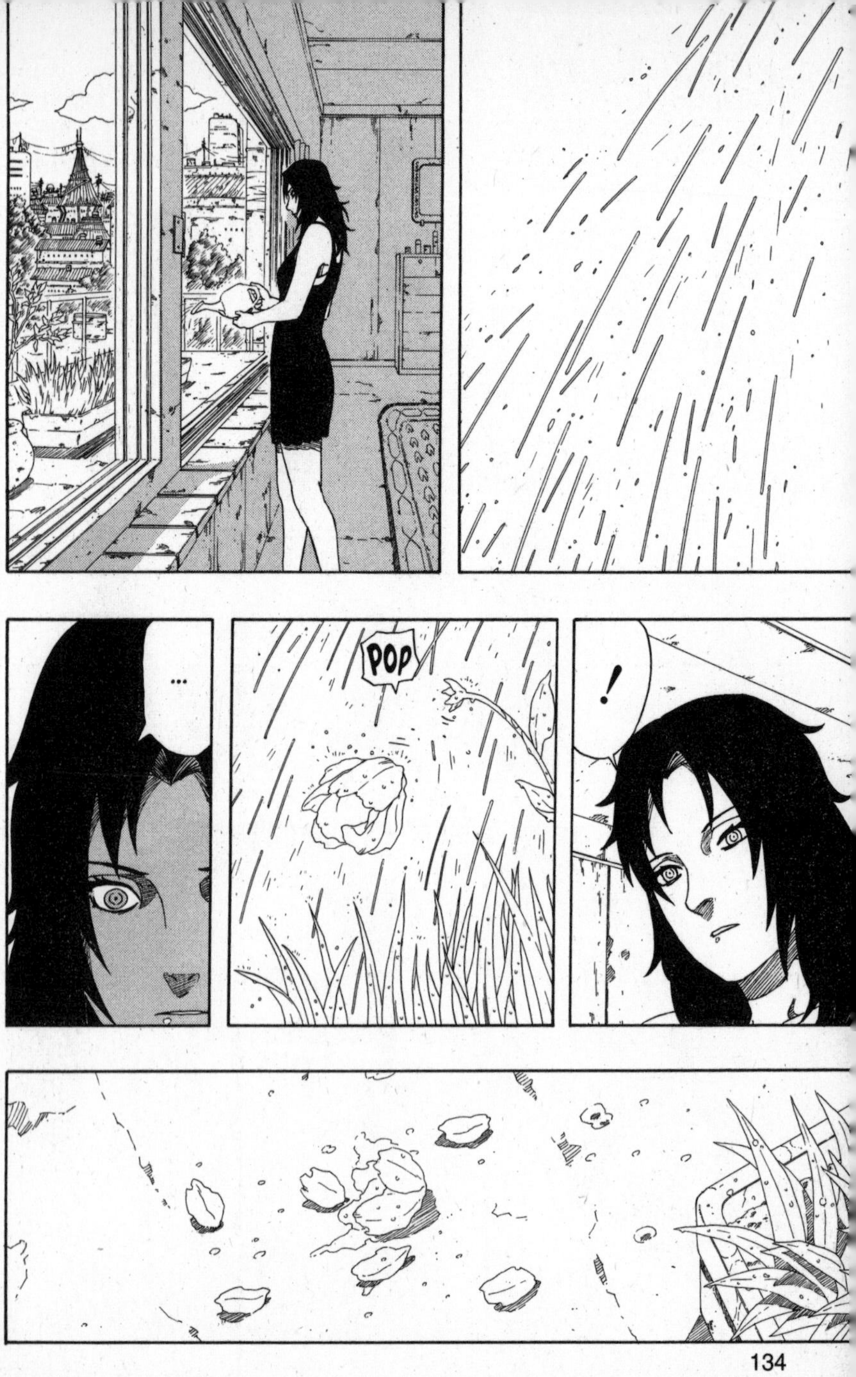
!
POP
...

READ THIS WAY

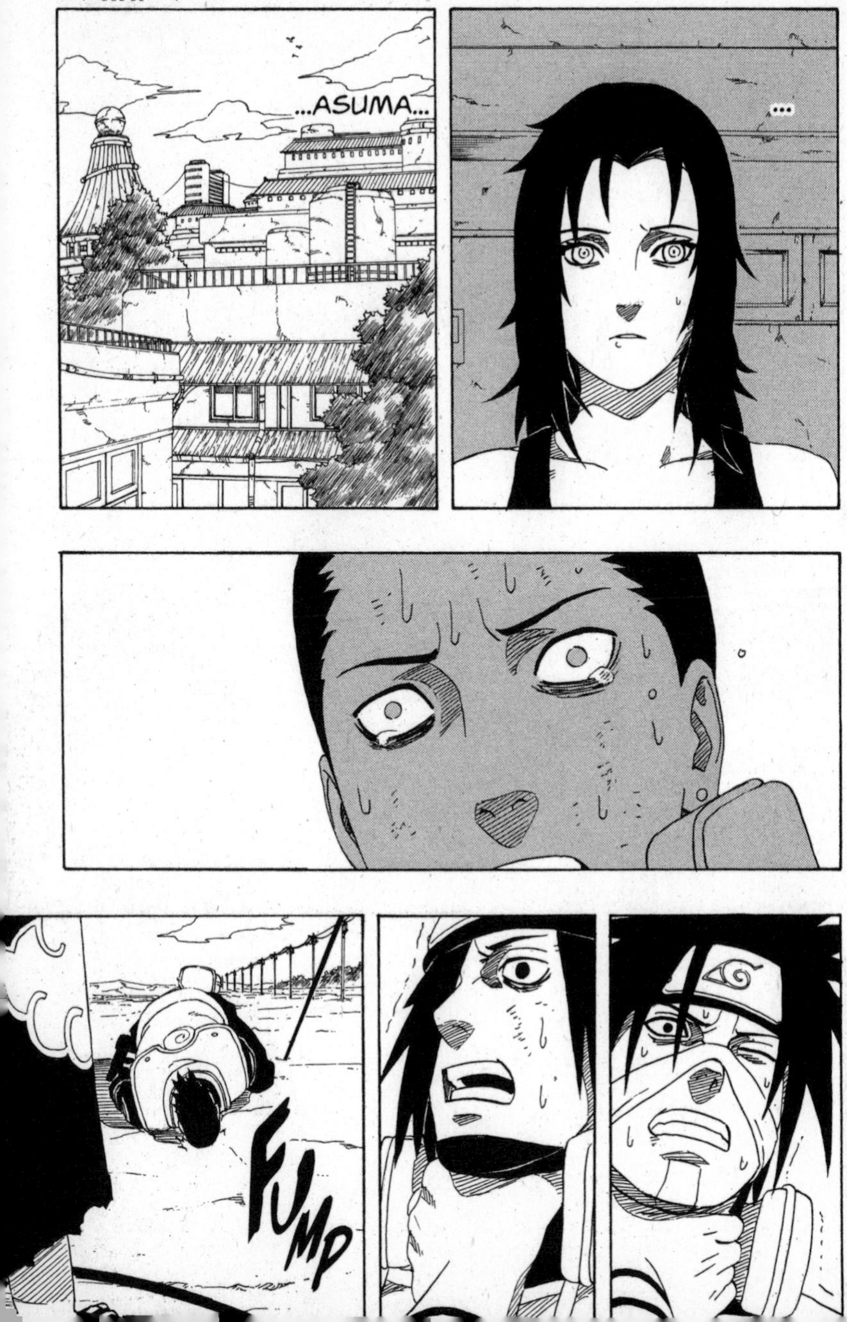
...
...ASUMA...
FUMP

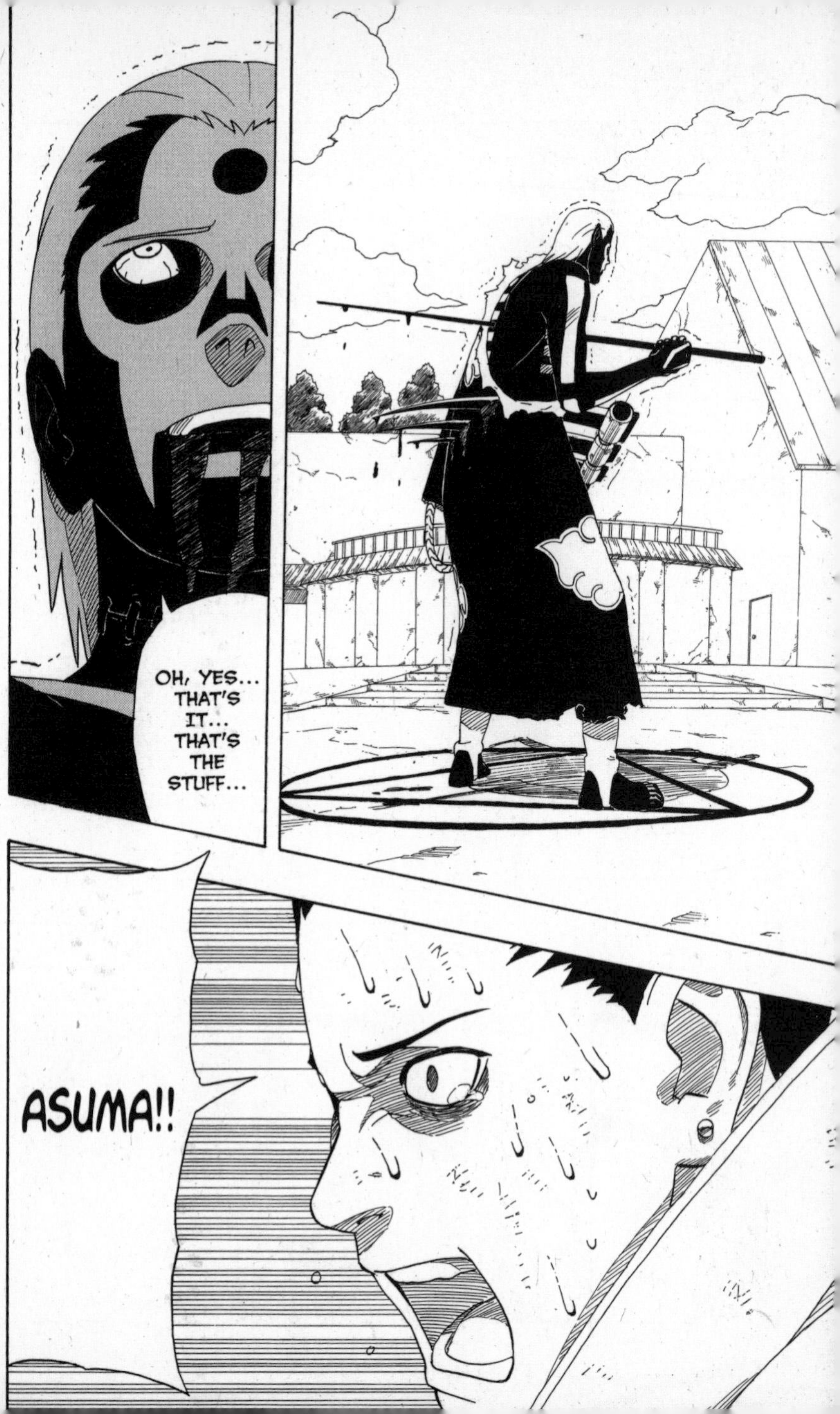
OH, YES... THAT'S IT... THAT'S THE STUFF...
ASUMA!!

READ THIS WAY

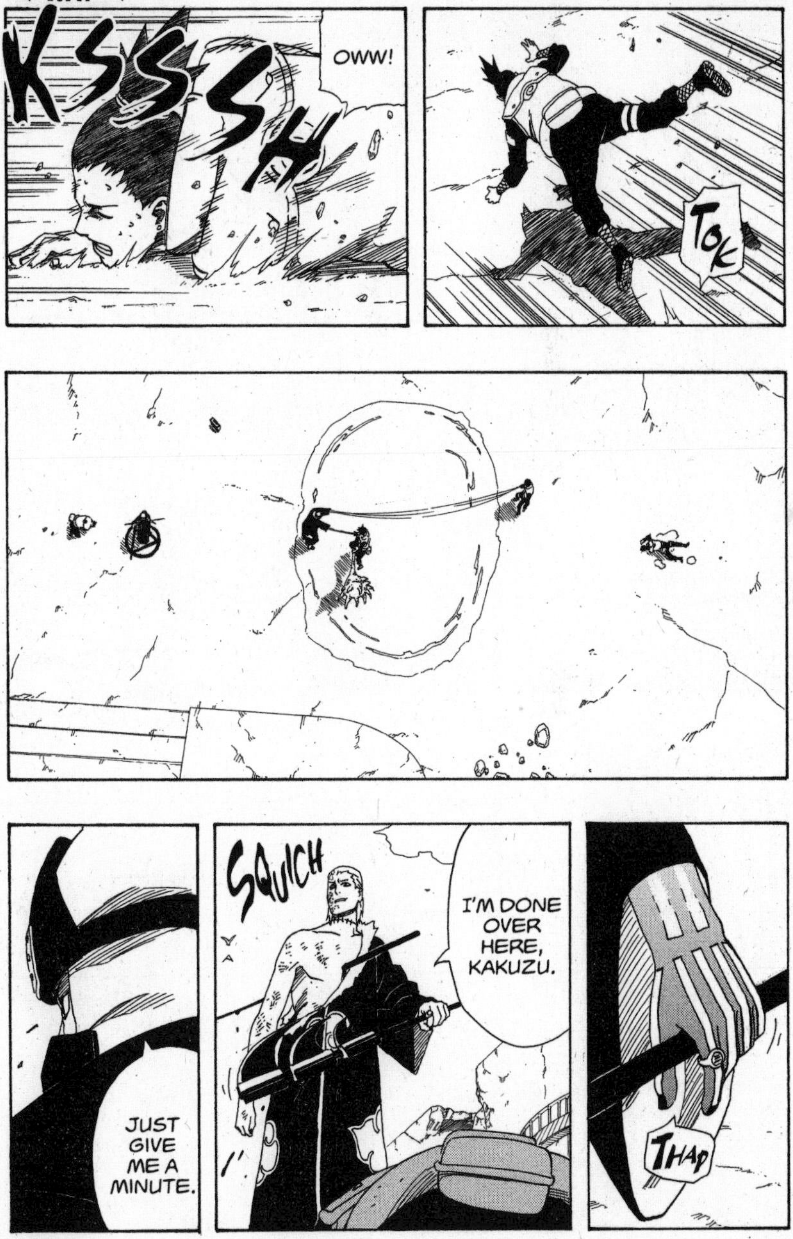
TOK
KSSSH
OWW!
THAP
SQUICH
I'M DONE OVER HERE, KAKUZU.
JUST GIVE ME A MINUTE.

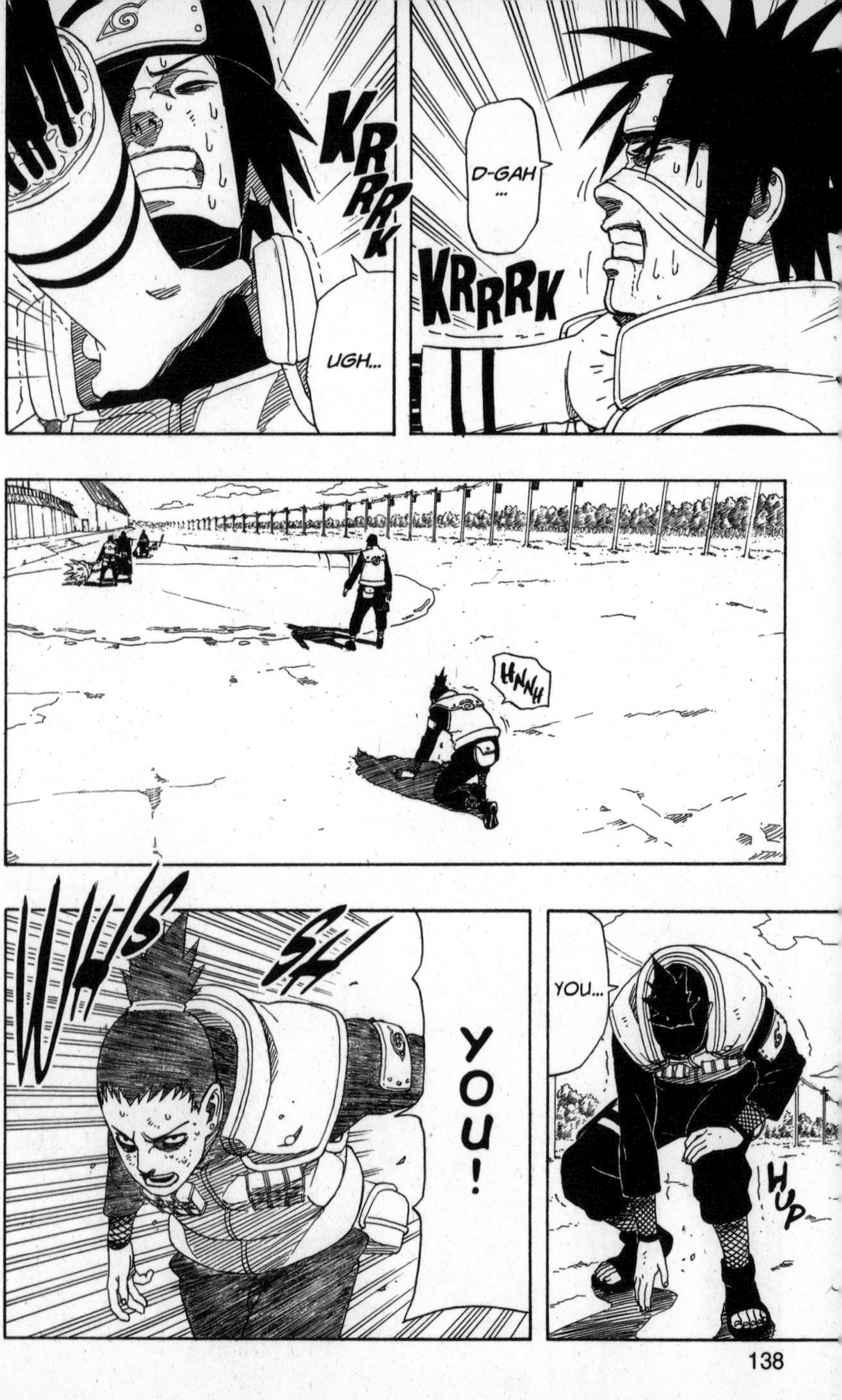
D-GAH ...
KRRRK
KRRRK
UGH...
HNNH
YOU...
HUP
WHUSSH
YOU!

READ THIS WAY

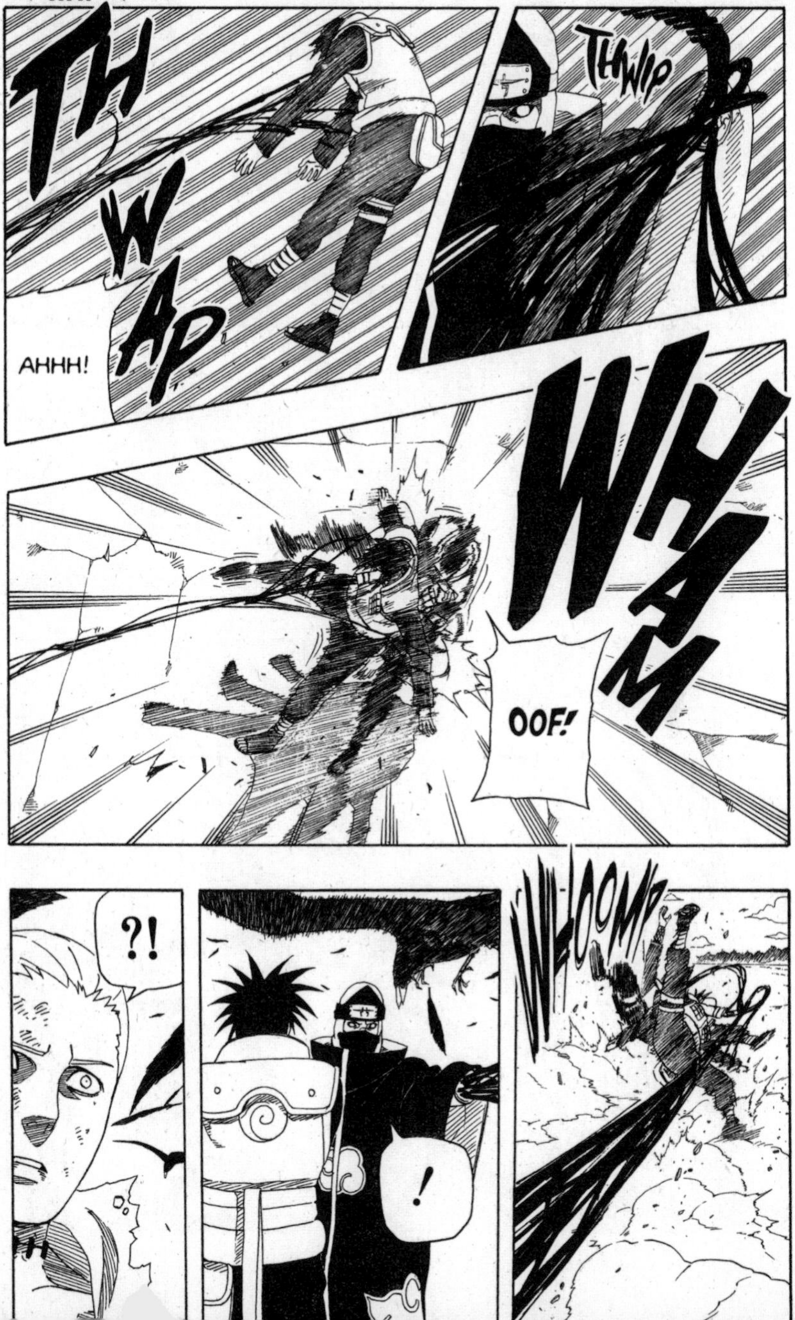
THWIP
THWAP
AHHH!
WHAM
OOF!
WHOOMP
!
?!

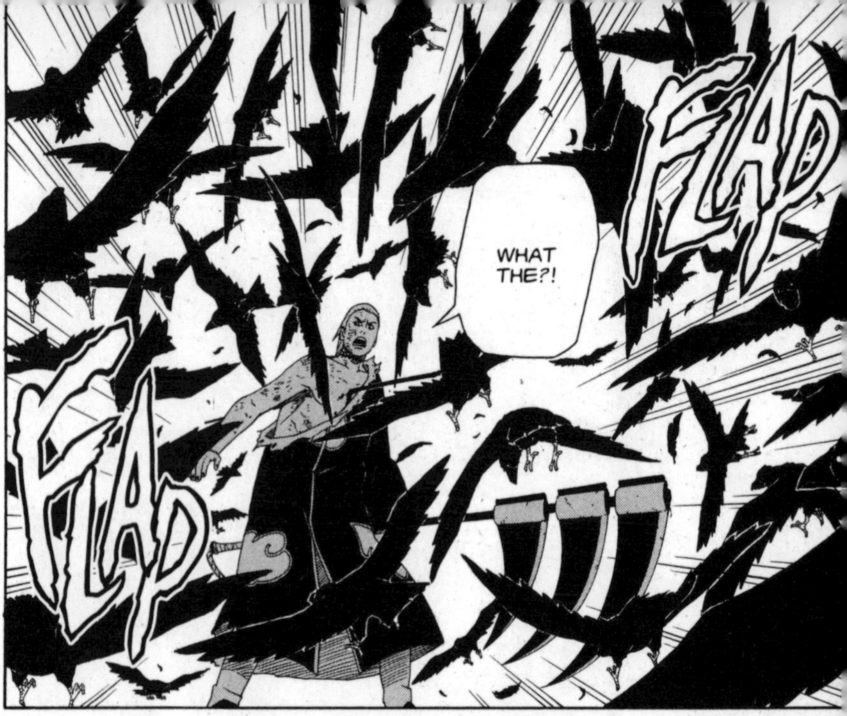
FLAP
WHAT THE?!
FLAP

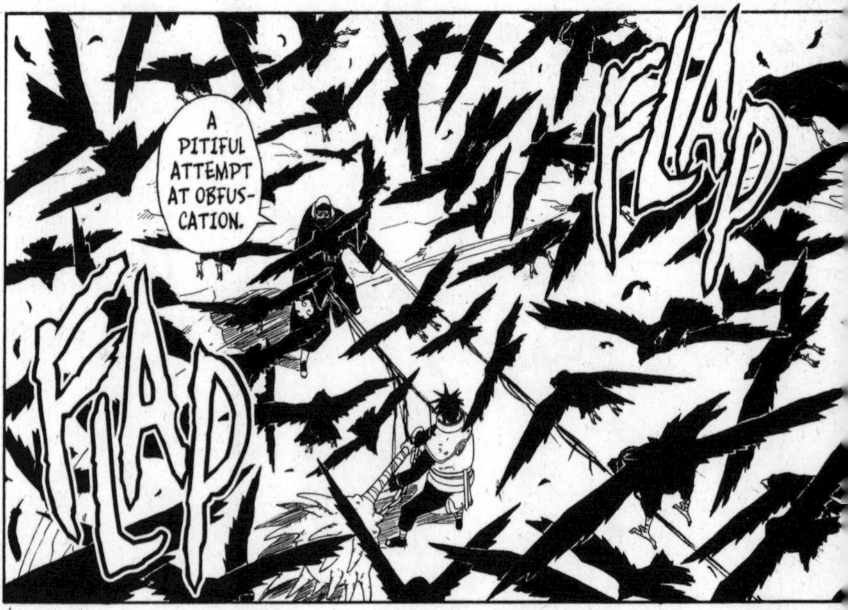
FLAP
A PITIFUL ATTEMPT AT OBFUS-CATION.
FLAP

READ THIS WAY

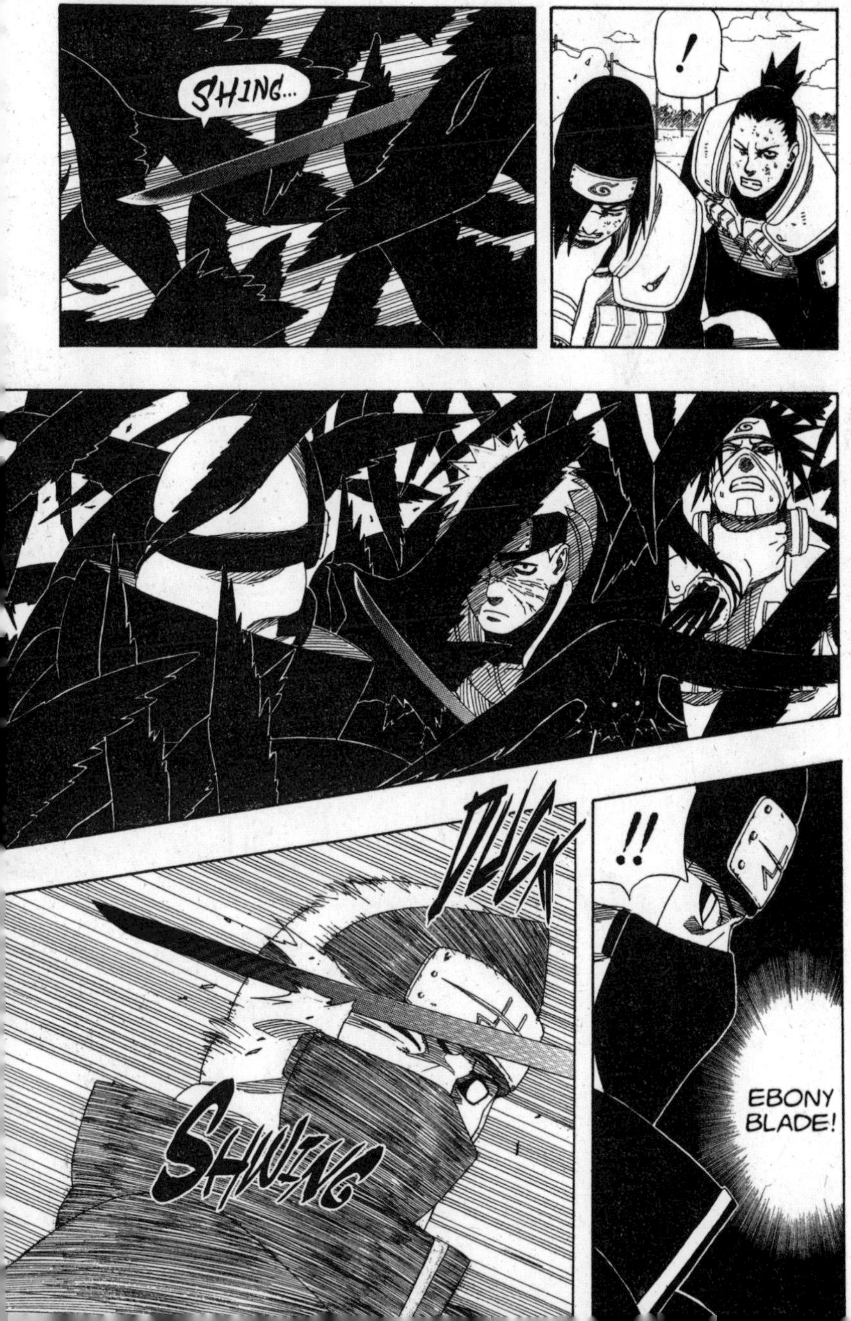
!
SHING...
!!
EBONY BLADE!
DUCK
SHWING

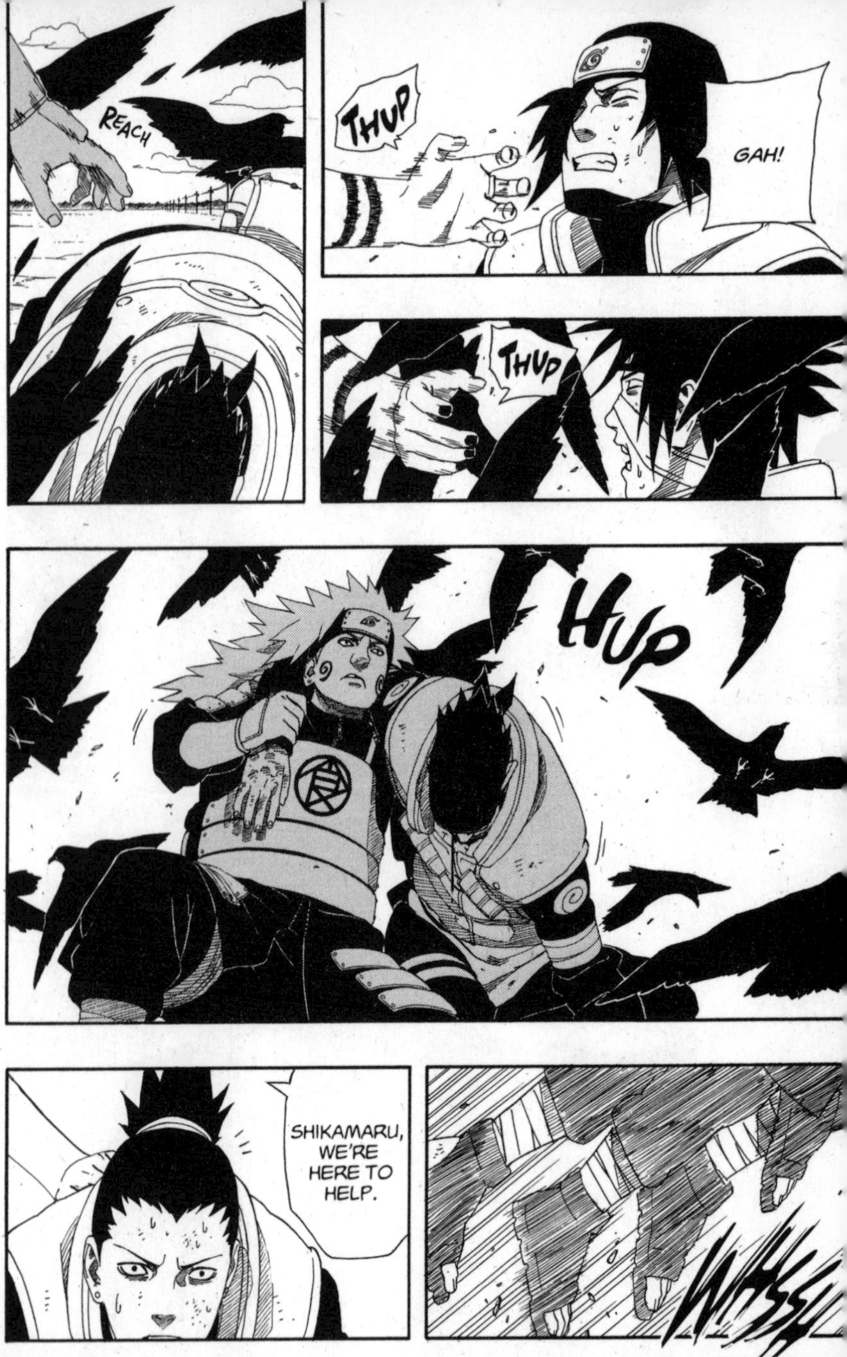
GAH!
THUP
THUP
REACH
HUP
WHSSH
SHIKAMARU, WE'RE HERE TO HELP.

READ THIS WAY

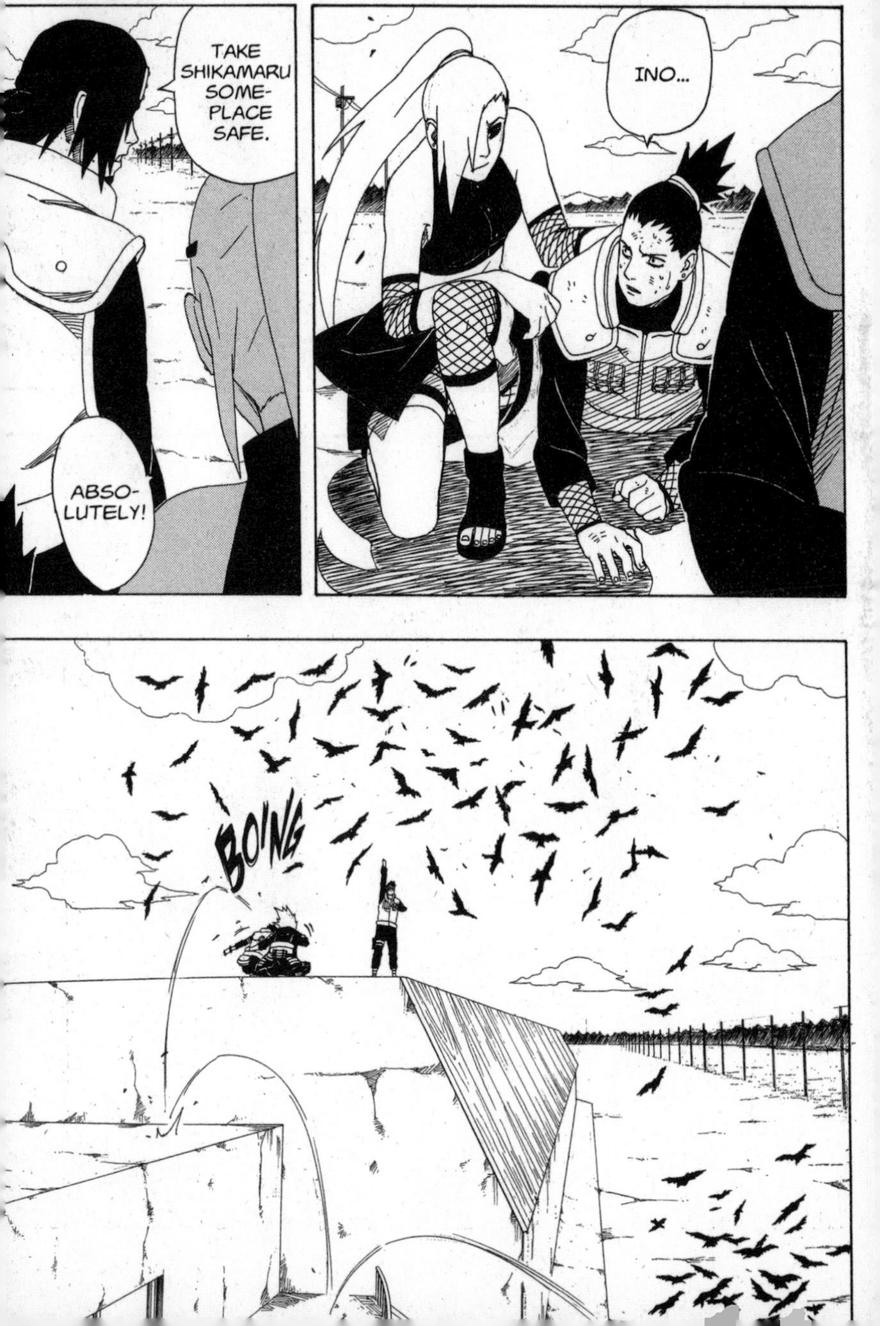
INO...
TAKE SHIKAMARU SOME-PLACE SAFE.
ABSO-LUTELY!
BOING

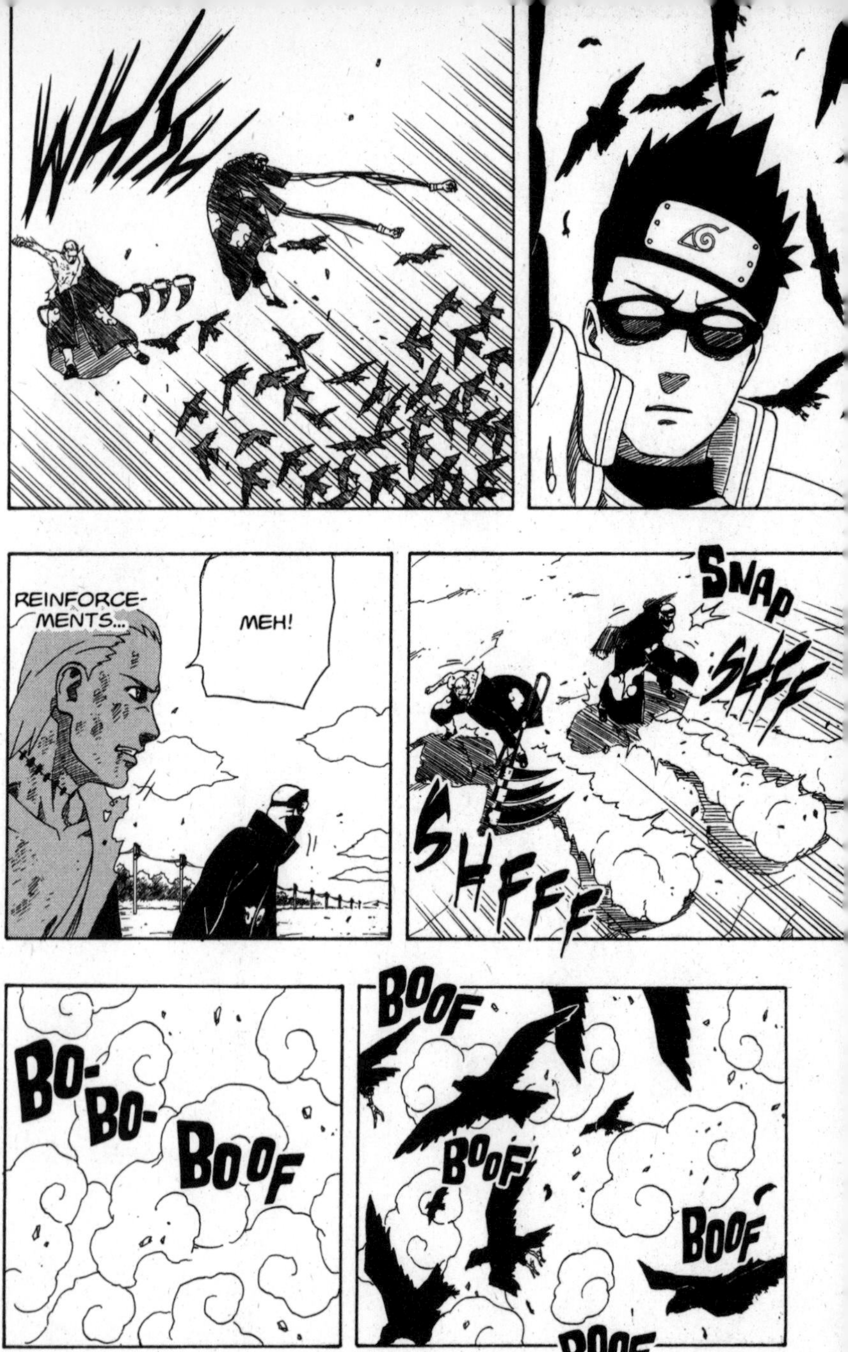
WHSSH
SNAP
SHFF
SHFFF
REINFORCE-MENTS...
MEH!
BOOF
BOOF
BOOF
BOOF
BO-BO-BOOF

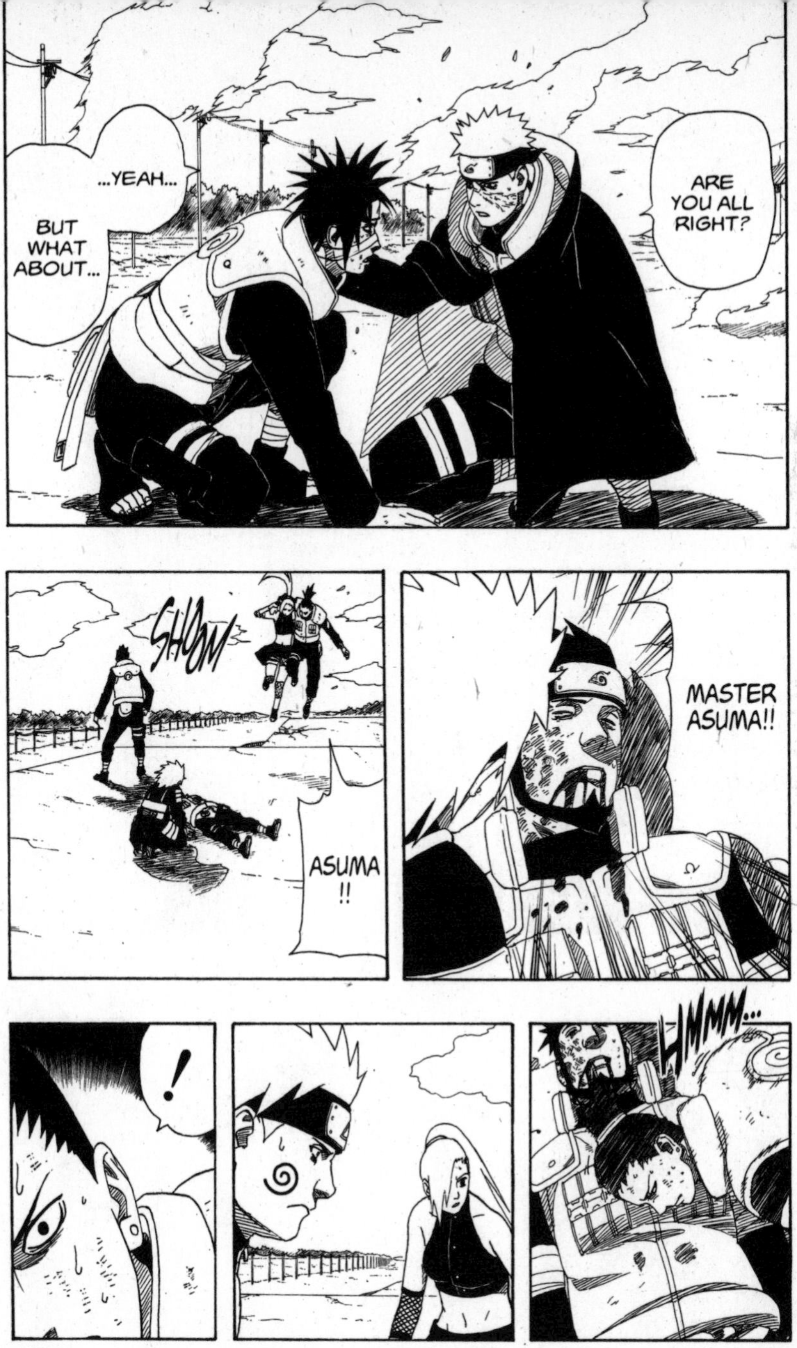
ARE YOU ALL RIGHT?
...YEAH...
BUT WHAT ABOUT...
MASTER ASUMA!!
SHOOM
ASUMA !!
HMMM...
!

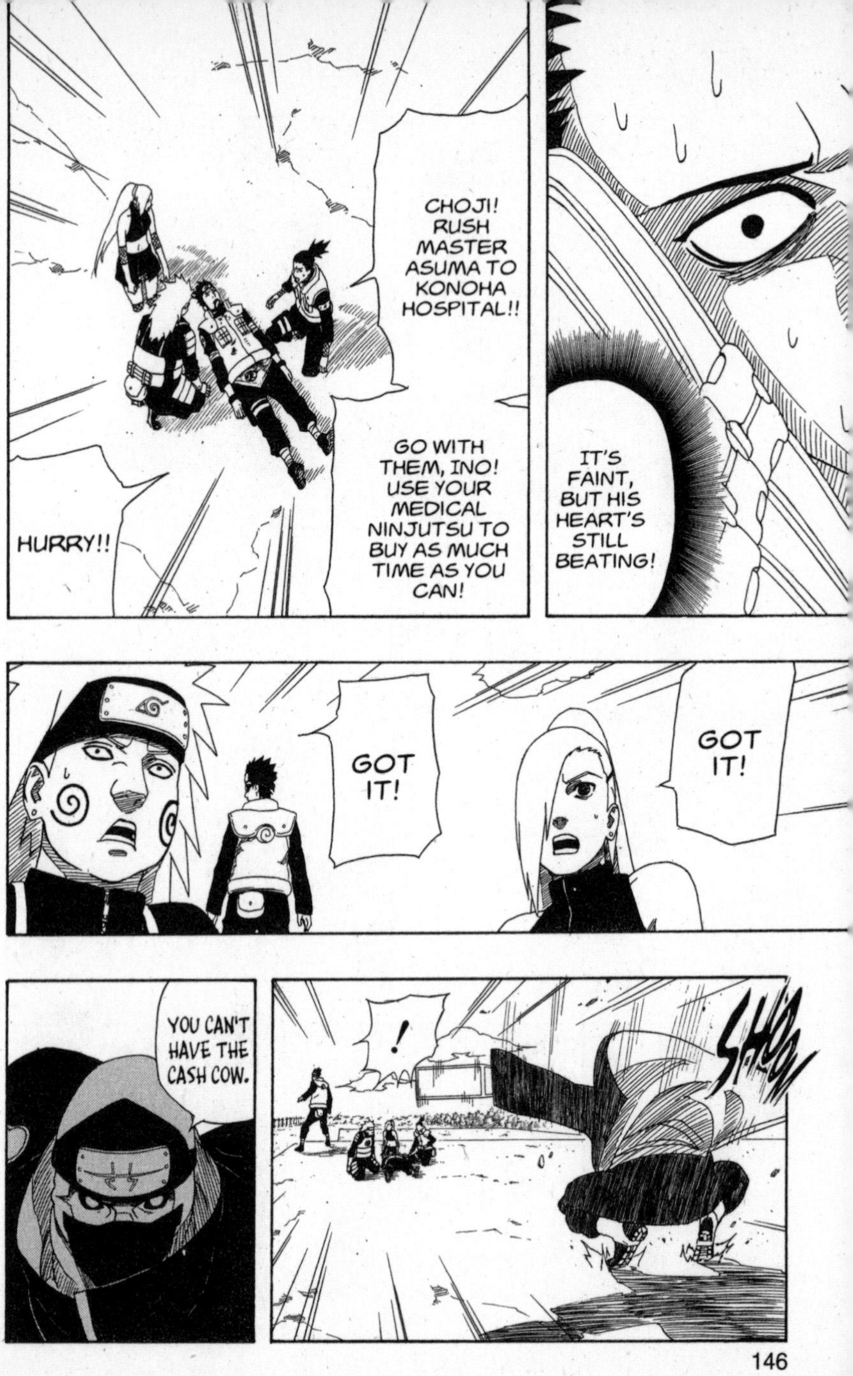
IT'S FAINT, BUT HIS HEART'S STILL BEATING!
CHOJI! RUSH MASTER ASUMA TO KONOHA HOSPITAL!!
GO WITH THEM, INO! USE YOUR MEDICAL NINJUTSU TO BUY AS MUCH TIME AS YOU CAN!
HURRY!!
GOT IT!
GOT IT!
!
SHOOM
YOU CAN'T HAVE THE CASH COW.

READ THIS WAY

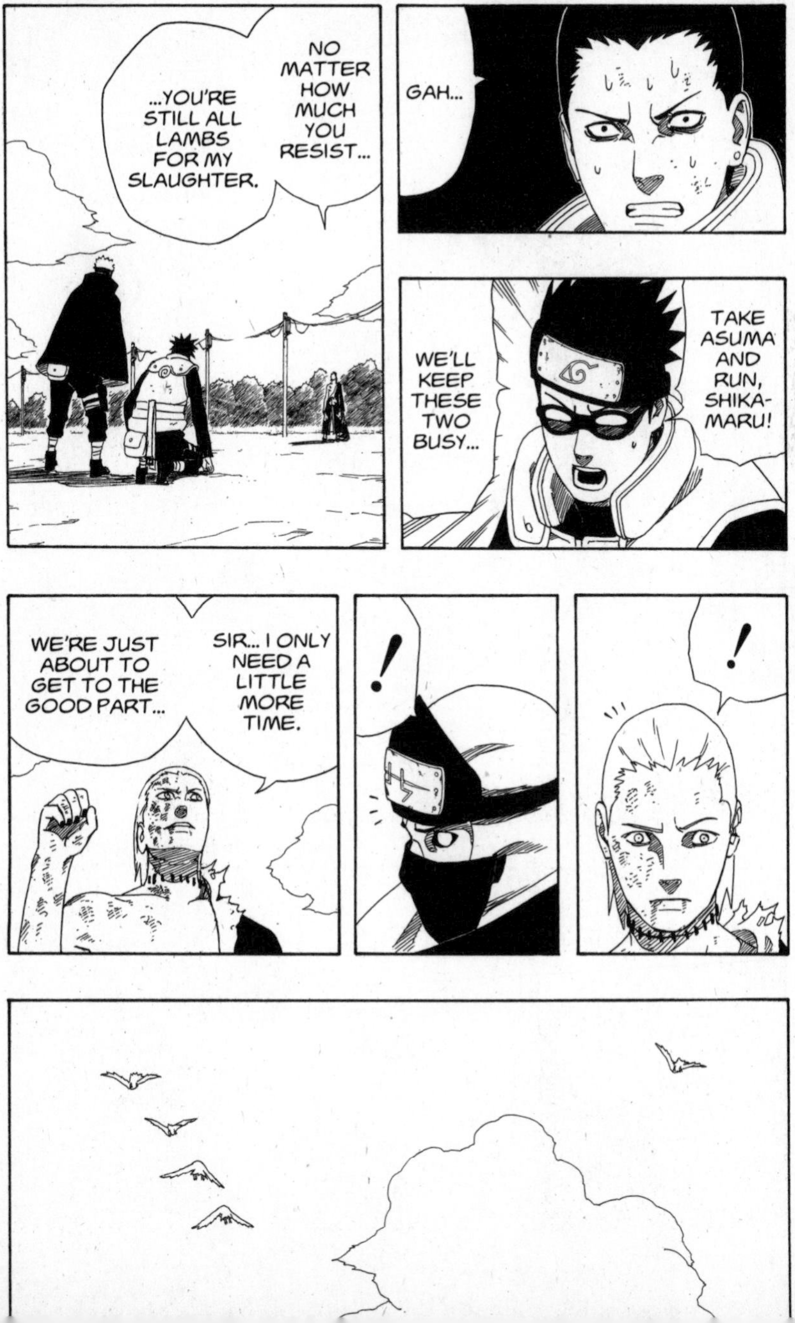
GAH...
TAKE ASUMA AND RUN, SHIKAMARU!
WE'LL KEEP THESE TWO BUSY...
NO MATTER HOW MUCH YOU RESIST...
...YOU'RE STILL ALL LAMBS FOR MY SLAUGHTER.
!
!
SIR... I ONLY NEED A LITTLE MORE TIME.
WE'RE JUST ABOUT TO GET TO THE GOOD PART...

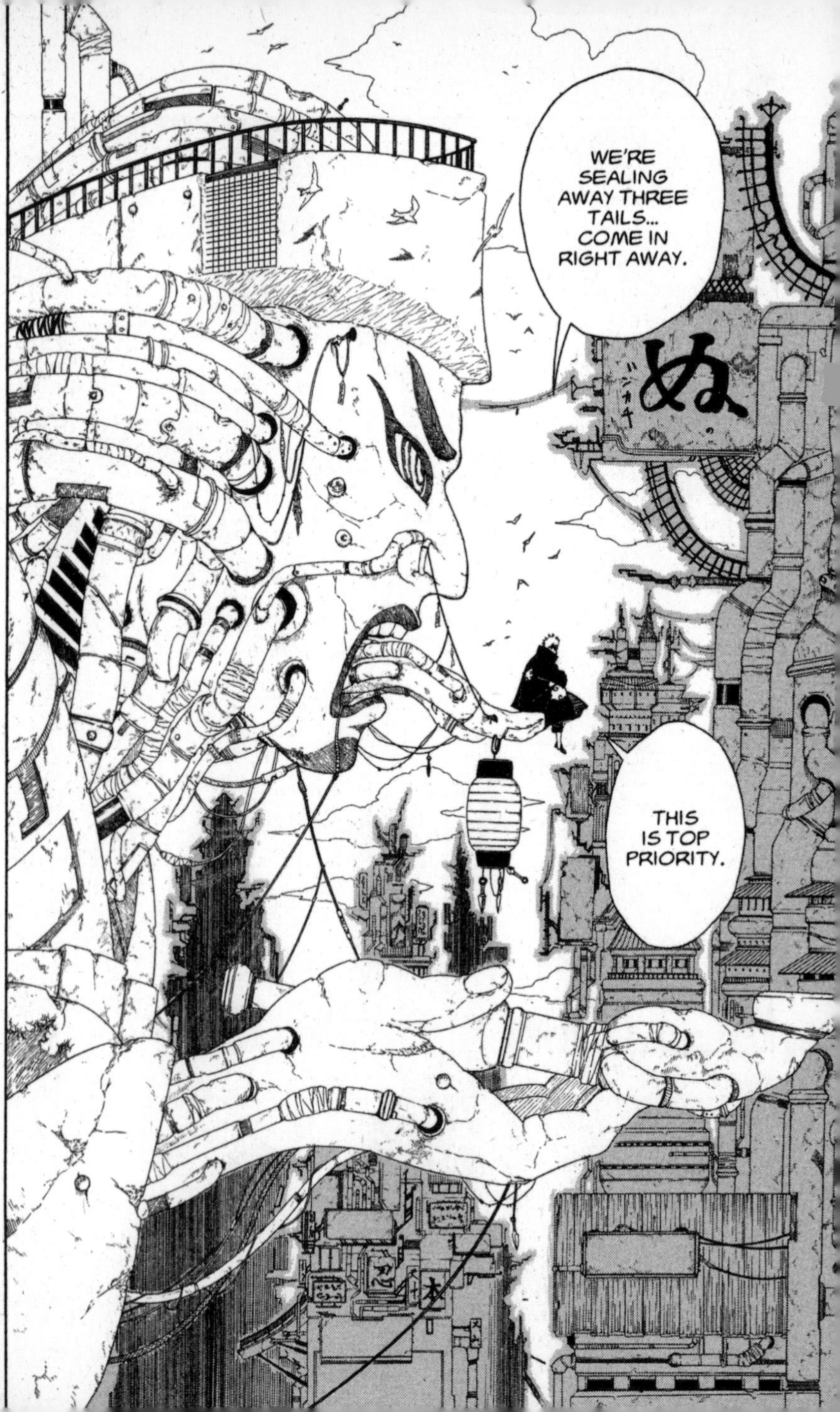
WE'RE SEALING AWAY THREE TAILS... COME IN RIGHT AWAY.
THIS IS TOP PRIORITY.

READ THIS WAY

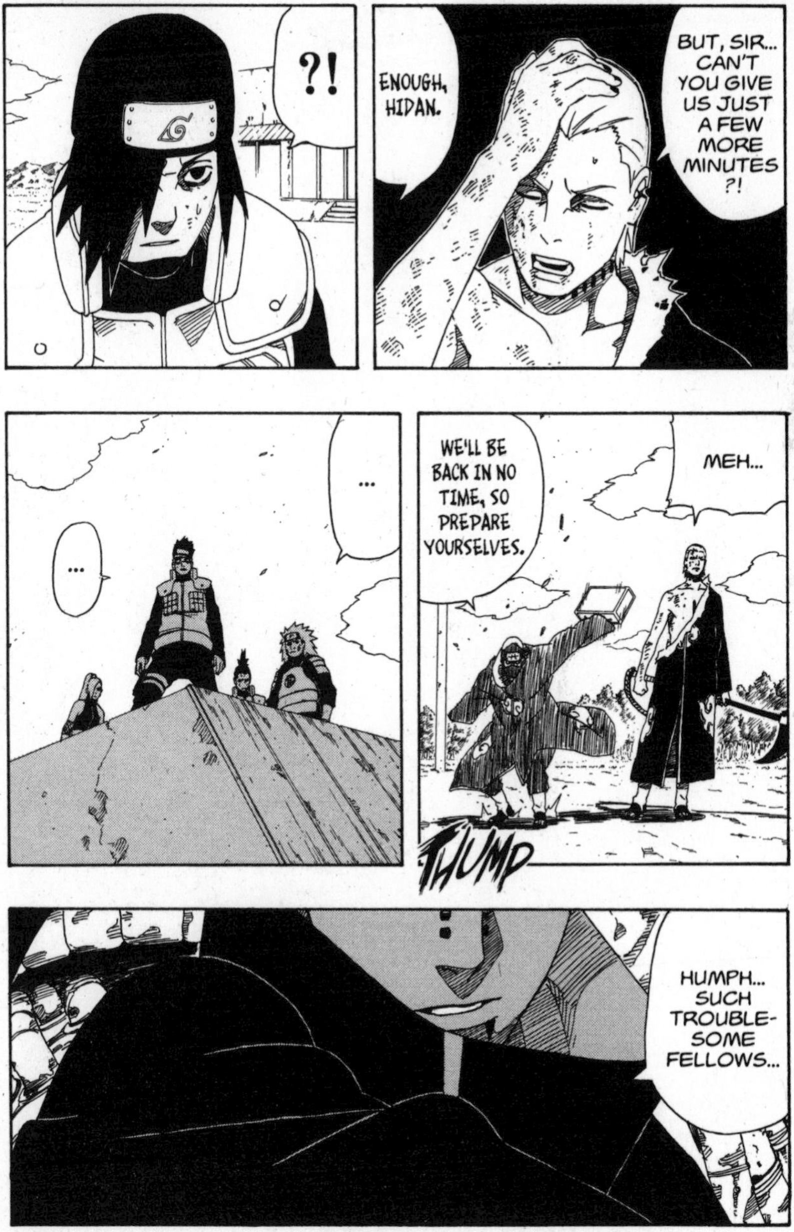

BUT, SIR... CAN'T YOU GIVE US JUST A FEW MORE MINUTES?!
ENOUGH, HIDAN.
?!
MEH...
WE'LL BE BACK IN NO TIME, SO PREPARE YOURSELVES.
THUMP
...
...
HUMPH... SUCH TROUBLE-SOME FELLOWS...

NARUTO

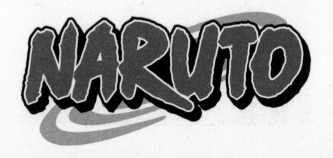

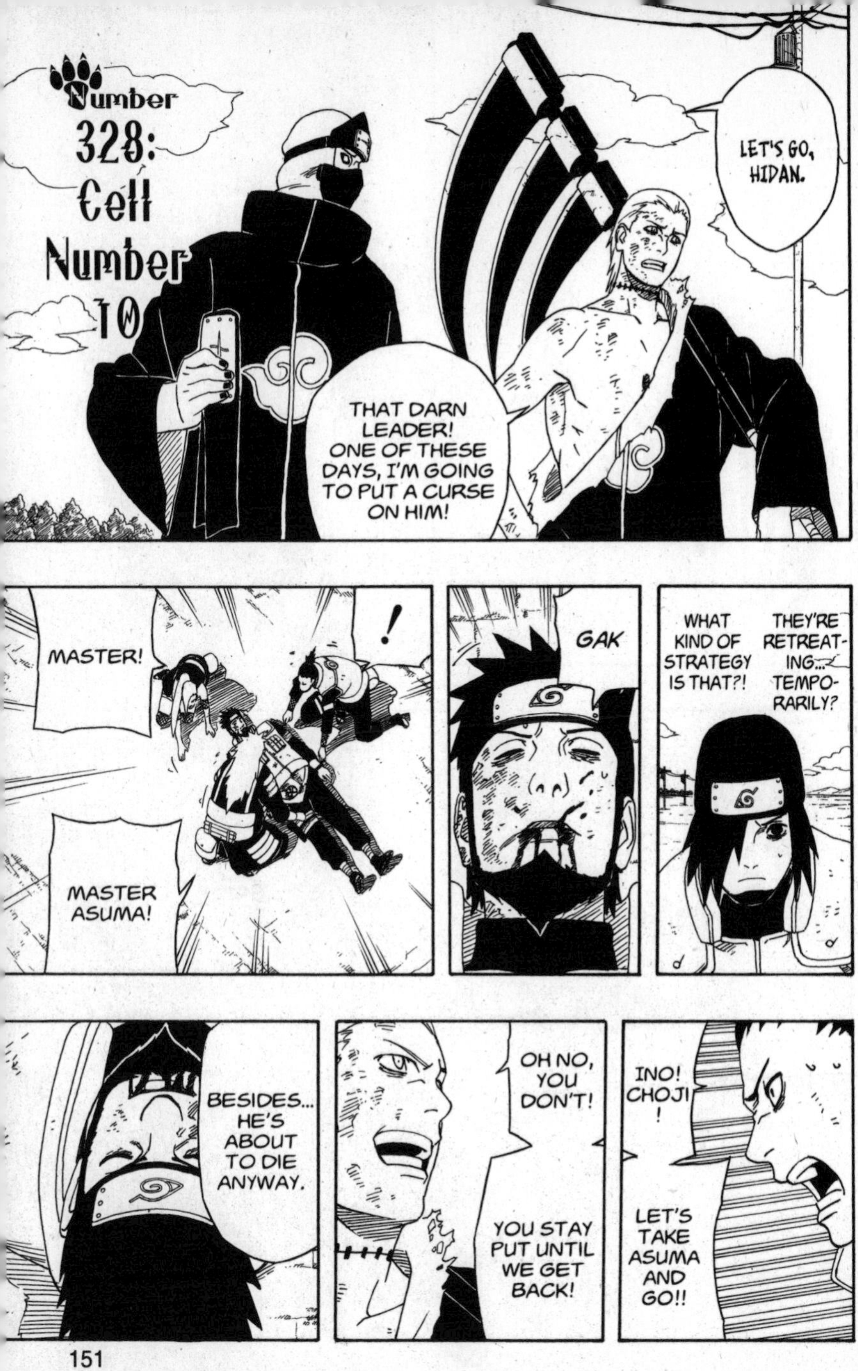
Number 328: Cell Number 10
LET'S GO, HIDAN.
THAT DARN LEADER! ONE OF THESE DAYS, I'M GOING TO PUT A CURSE ON HIM!
THEY'RE RETREATING... TEMPORARILY?
WHAT KIND OF STRATEGY IS THAT?!
GAK
!
MASTER!
MASTER ASUMA!
INO! CHOJI!
LET'S TAKE ASUMA AND GO!!
OH NO, YOU DON'T!
YOU STAY PUT UNTIL WE GET BACK!
BESIDES... HE'S ABOUT TO DIE ANYWAY.

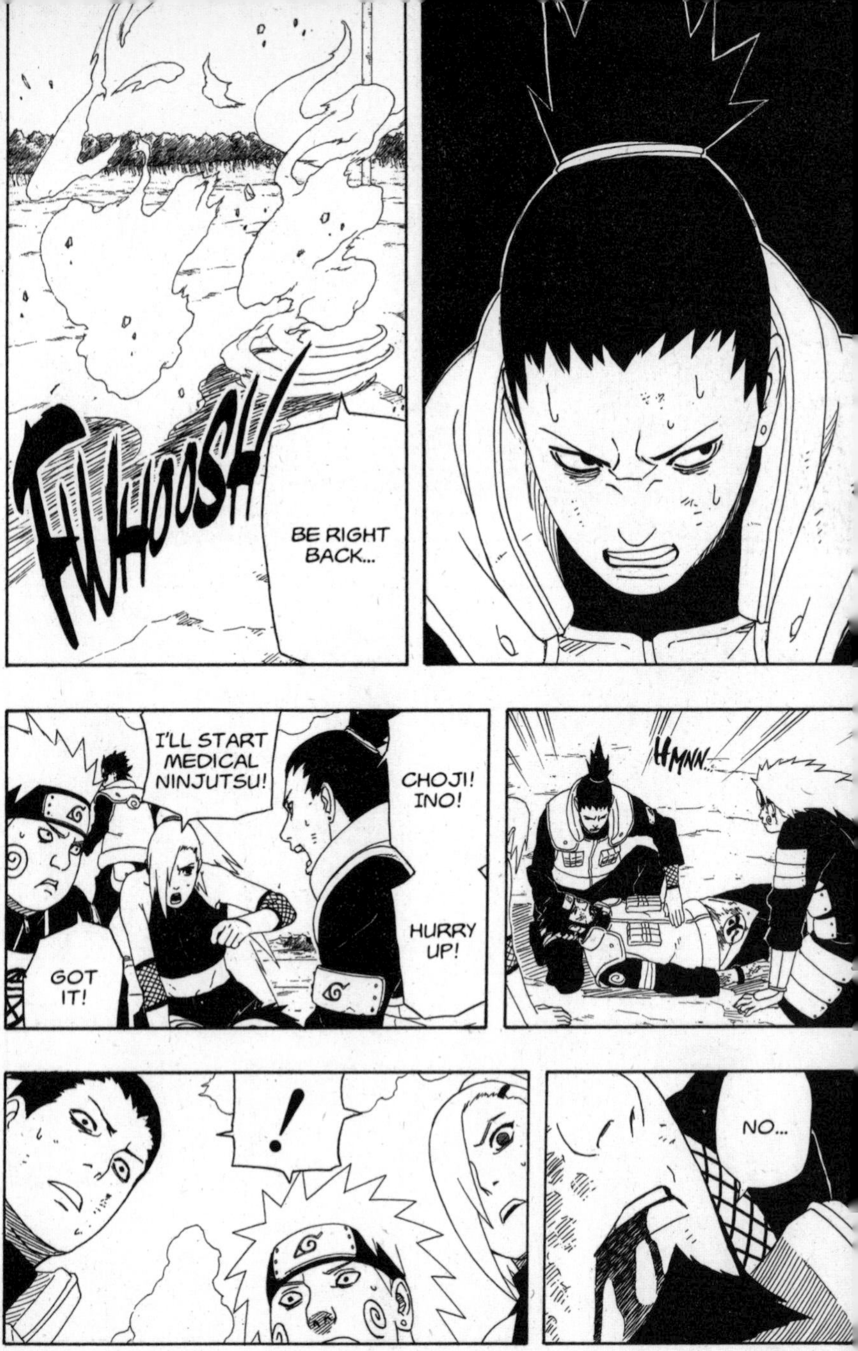
BE RIGHT BACK...
FWHOOSH
HMNN...
CHOJI! INO!
HURRY UP!
I'LL START MEDICAL NINJUTSU!
GOT IT!
NO...
!

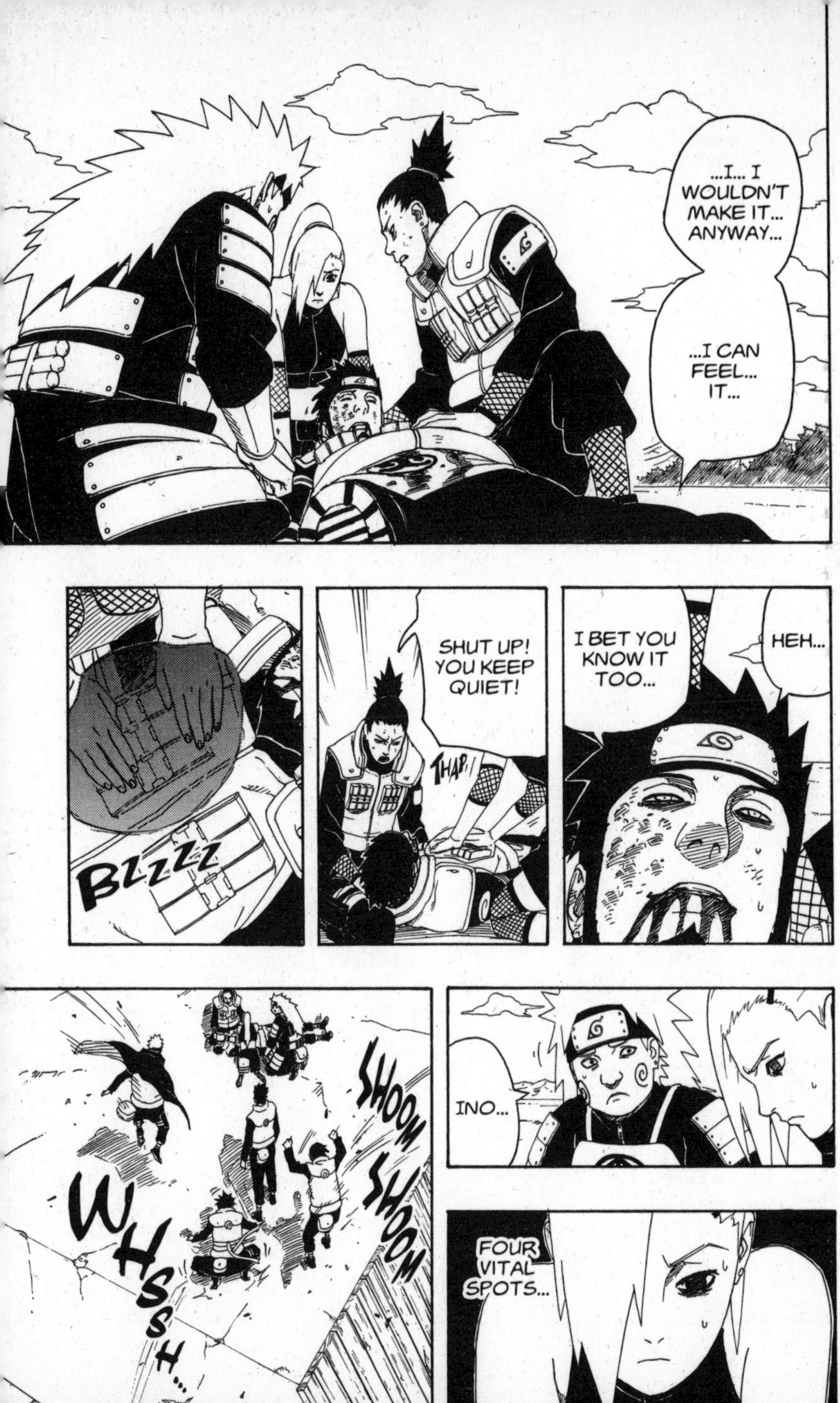
...I... I WOULDN'T MAKE IT... ANYWAY...
...I CAN FEEL... IT...
HEH...
I BET YOU KNOW IT TOO...
SHUT UP! YOU KEEP QUIET!
THAP
BLZZZ
INO...
FOUR VITAL SPOTS...
SHOOM
SHOOM
WHSSH...

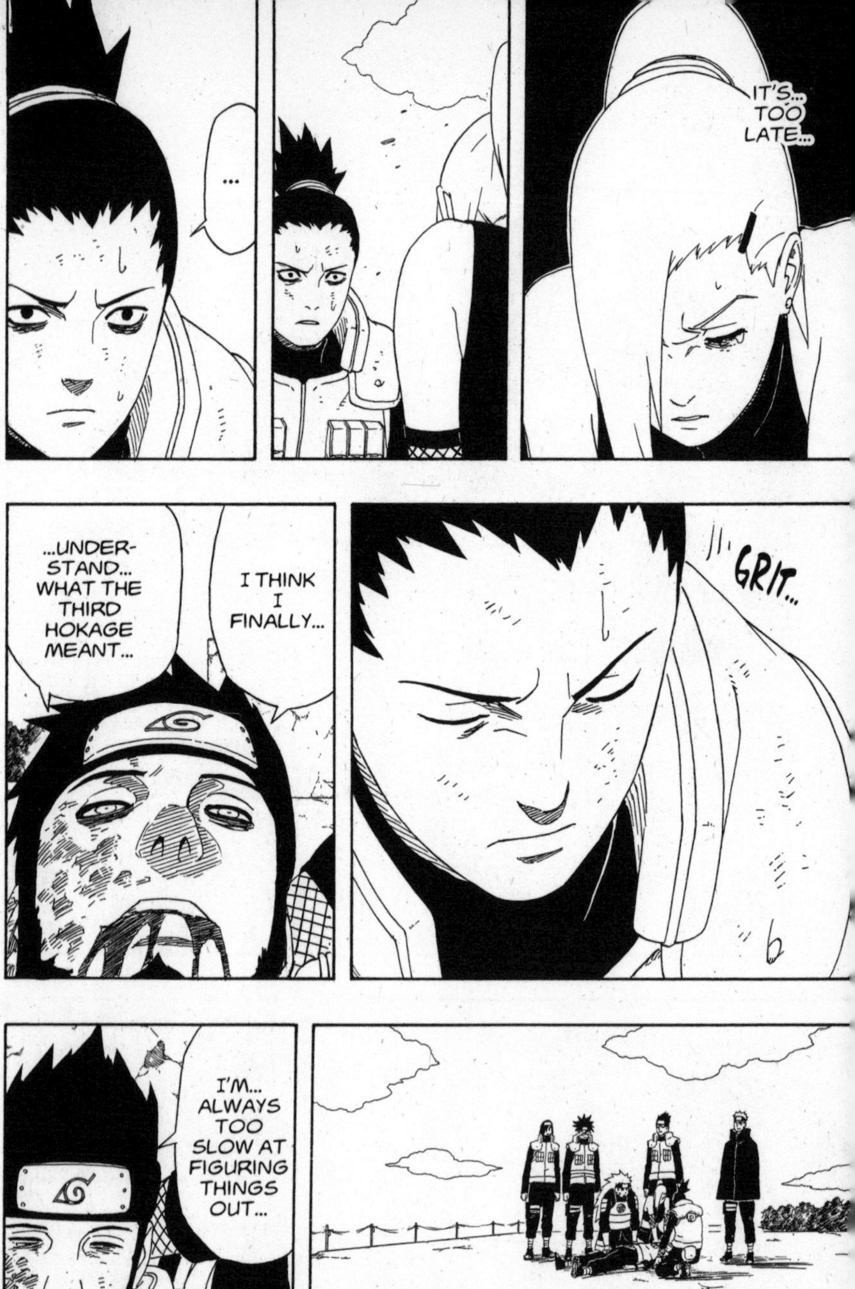
IT'S... TOO LATE...
...
GRIT...
I THINK I FINALLY...
...UNDER-STAND... WHAT THE THIRD HOKAGE MEANT...
I'M... ALWAYS TOO SLOW AT FIGURING THINGS OUT...

READ THIS WAY

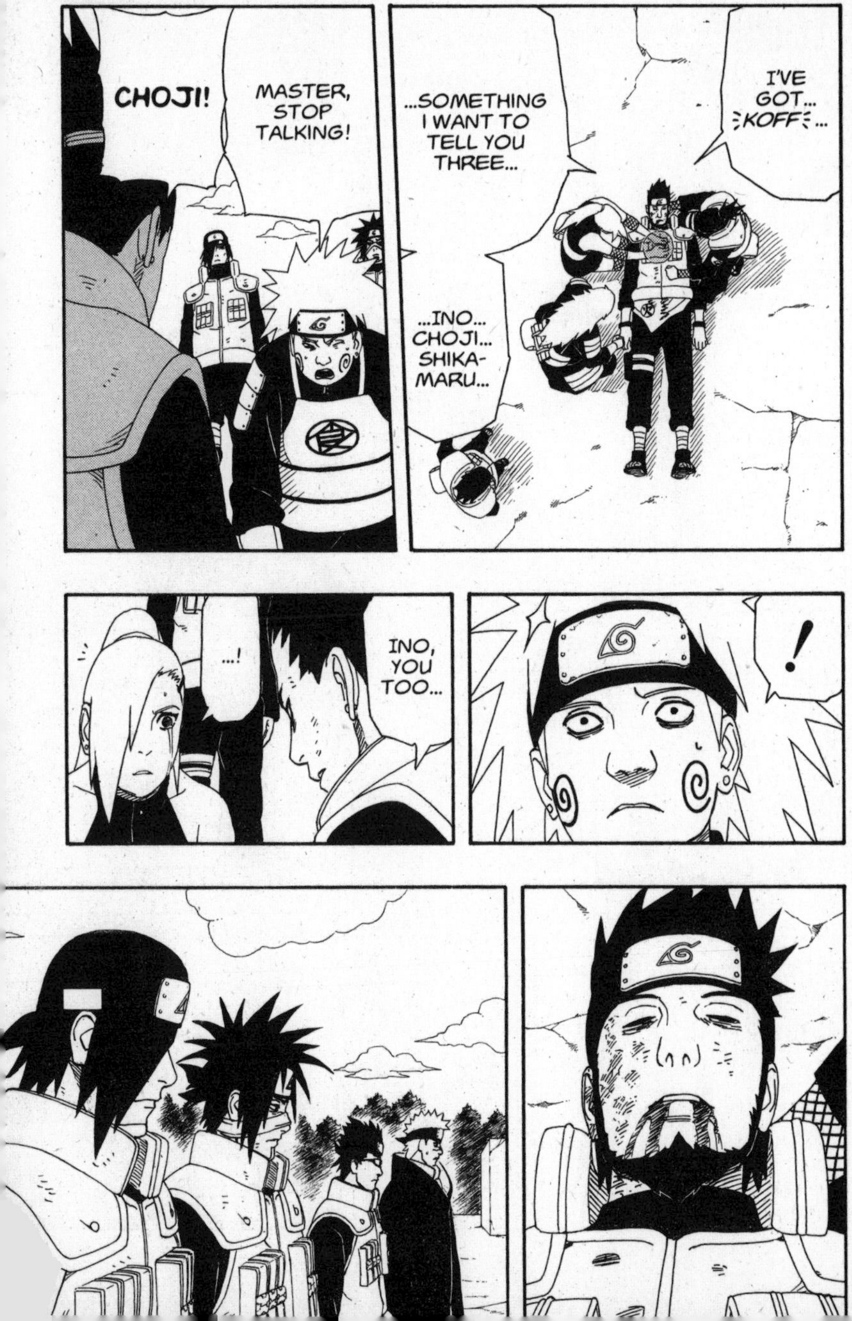
I'VE GOT... KOFF ...
...SOMETHING I WANT TO TELL YOU THREE...
...INO... CHOJI... SHIKA-MARU...
MASTER, STOP TALKING!
CHOJI!
!
INO, YOU TOO...
...!

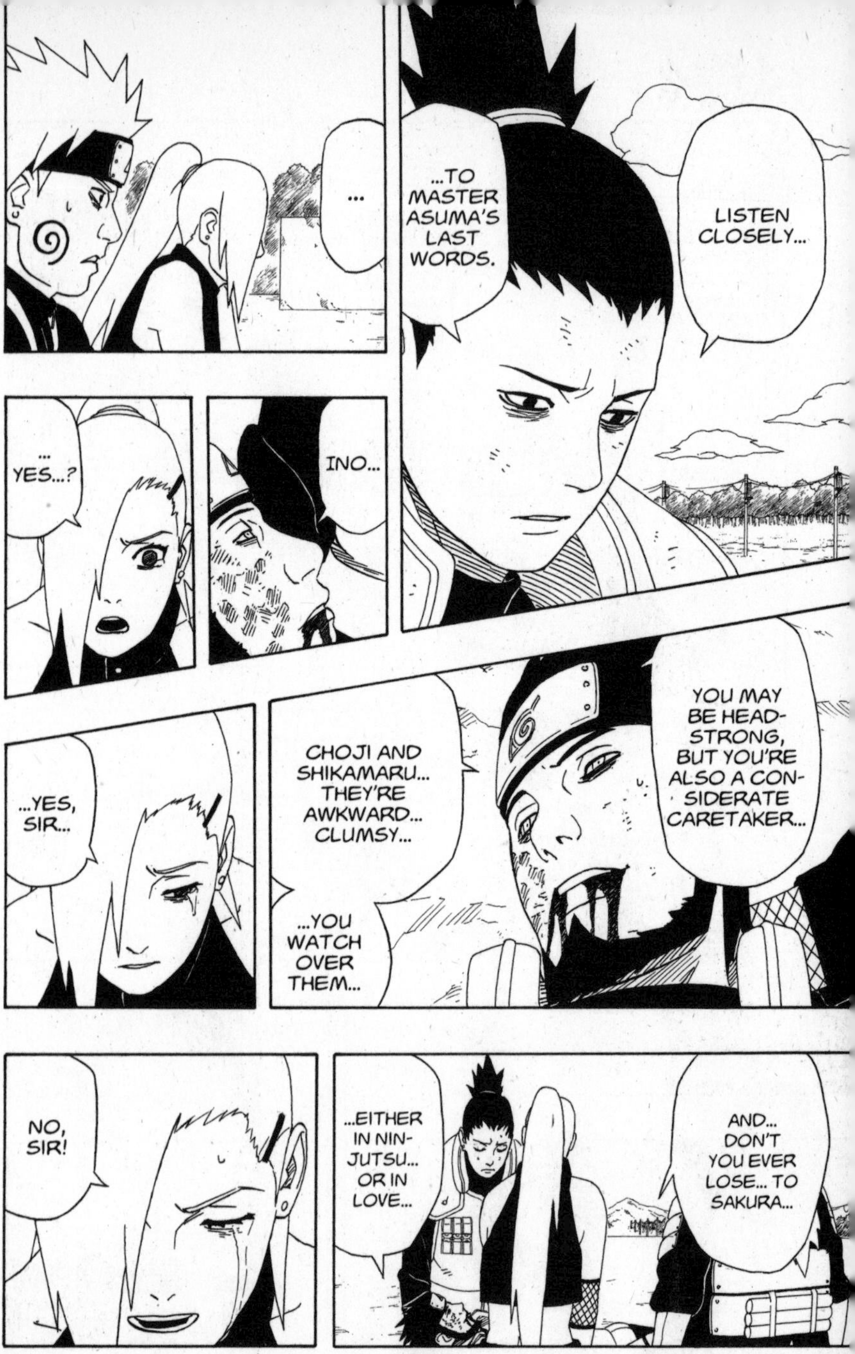
LISTEN CLOSELY...
...TO MASTER ASUMA'S LAST WORDS.
...
INO...
...
YES...?
YOU MAY BE HEAD-STRONG, BUT YOU'RE ALSO A CON-SIDERATE CARETAKER...
CHOJI AND SHIKAMARU... THEY'RE AWKWARD... CLUMSY...
...YOU WATCH OVER THEM...
...YES, SIR...
AND... DON'T YOU EVER LOSE... TO SAKURA...
...EITHER IN NIN-JUTSU... OR IN LOVE...
NO, SIR!

READ THIS WAY

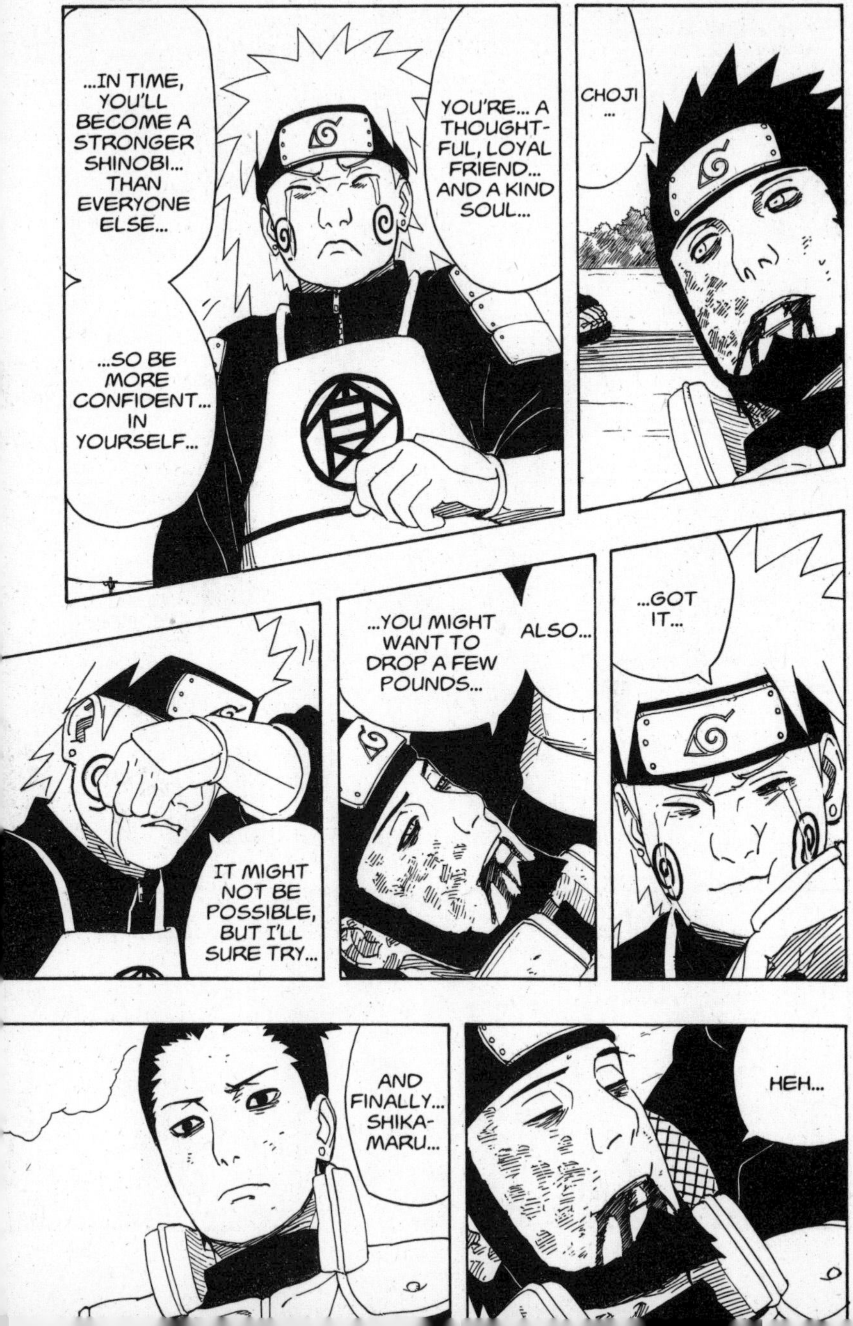
CHOJI ...
YOU'RE... A THOUGHTFUL, LOYAL FRIEND... AND A KIND SOUL...
...IN TIME, YOU'LL BECOME A STRONGER SHINOBI... THAN EVERYONE ELSE...
...SO BE MORE CONFIDENT... IN YOURSELF...
...GOT IT...
ALSO...
...YOU MIGHT WANT TO DROP A FEW POUNDS...
IT MIGHT NOT BE POSSIBLE, BUT I'LL SURE TRY...
HEH...
AND FINALLY... SHIKAMARU...

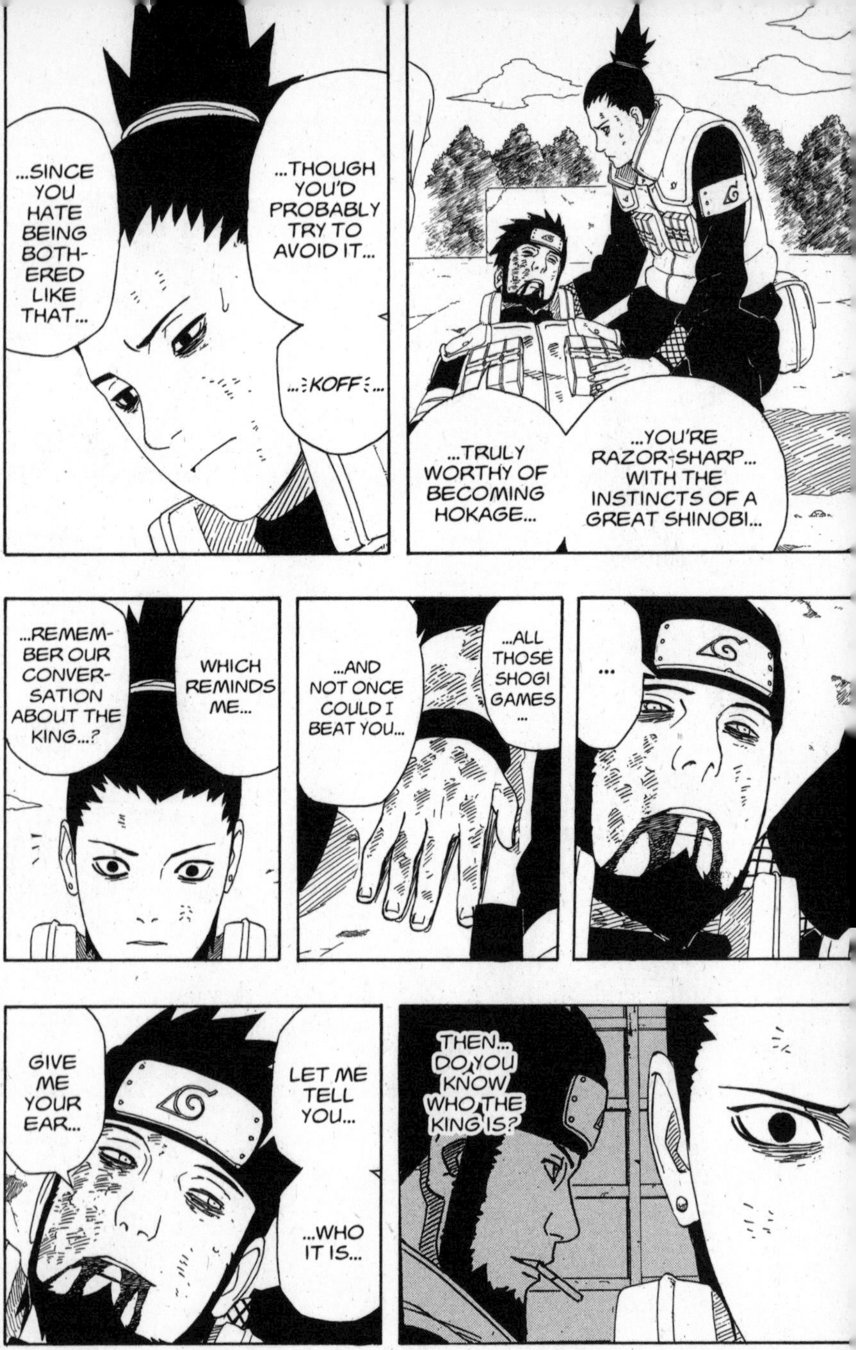
...YOU'RE RAZOR-SHARP... WITH THE INSTINCTS OF A GREAT SHINOBI...
...TRULY WORTHY OF BECOMING HOKAGE...
...THOUGH YOU'D PROBABLY TRY TO AVOID IT...
...KOFF...
...SINCE YOU HATE BEING BOTHERED LIKE THAT...
...
...ALL THOSE SHOGI GAMES...
...AND NOT ONCE COULD I BEAT YOU...
WHICH REMINDS ME...
...REMEMBER OUR CONVERSATION ABOUT THE KING...?
THEN... DO YOU KNOW WHO THE KING IS?
LET ME TELL YOU...
...WHO IT IS...
GIVE ME YOUR EAR...

READ THIS WAY

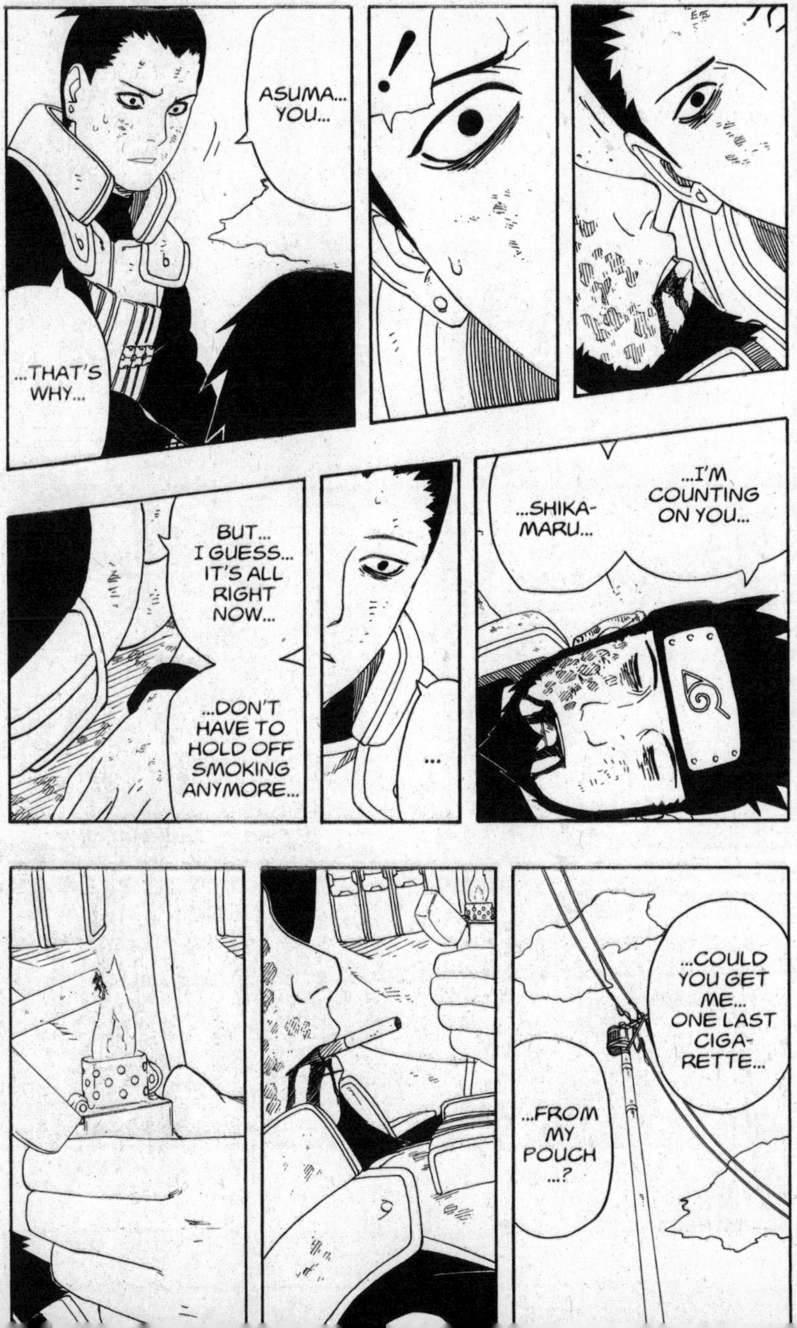
!
ASUMA... YOU...
...THAT'S WHY...
...I'M COUNTING ON YOU...
...SHIKA-MARU...
...
BUT... I GUESS... IT'S ALL RIGHT NOW...
...DON'T HAVE TO HOLD OFF SMOKING ANYMORE...
...COULD YOU GET ME... ONE LAST CIGA-RETTE...
...FROM MY POUCH ...?

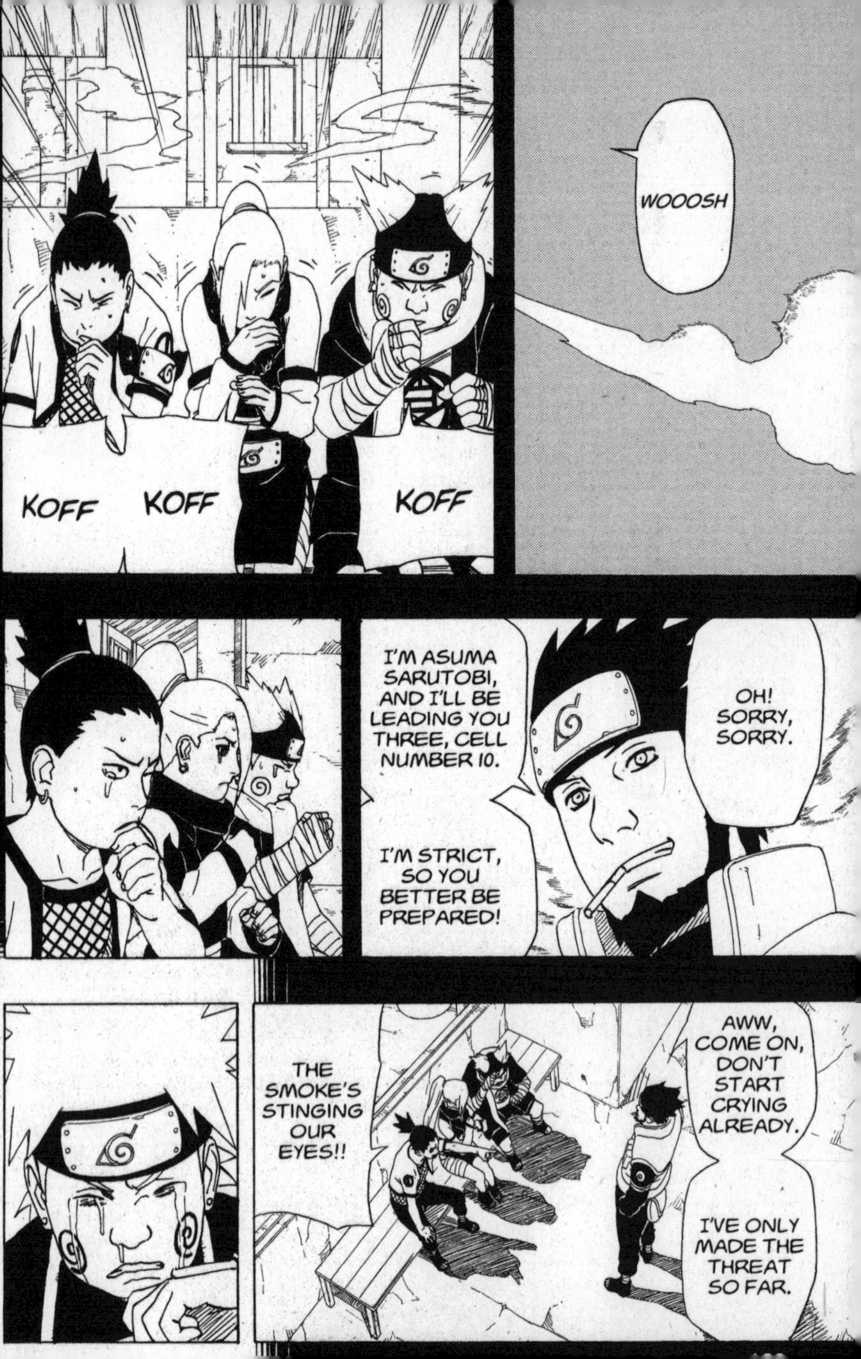
WOOOSH
KOFF
KOFF
KOFF
OH! SORRY, SORRY.
I'M ASUMA SARUTOBI, AND I'LL BE LEADING YOU THREE, CELL NUMBER 10.
I'M STRICT, SO YOU BETTER BE PREPARED!
AWW, COME ON, DON'T START CRYING ALREADY.
I'VE ONLY MADE THE THREAT SO FAR.
THE SMOKE'S STINGING OUR EYES!!

READ THIS WAY

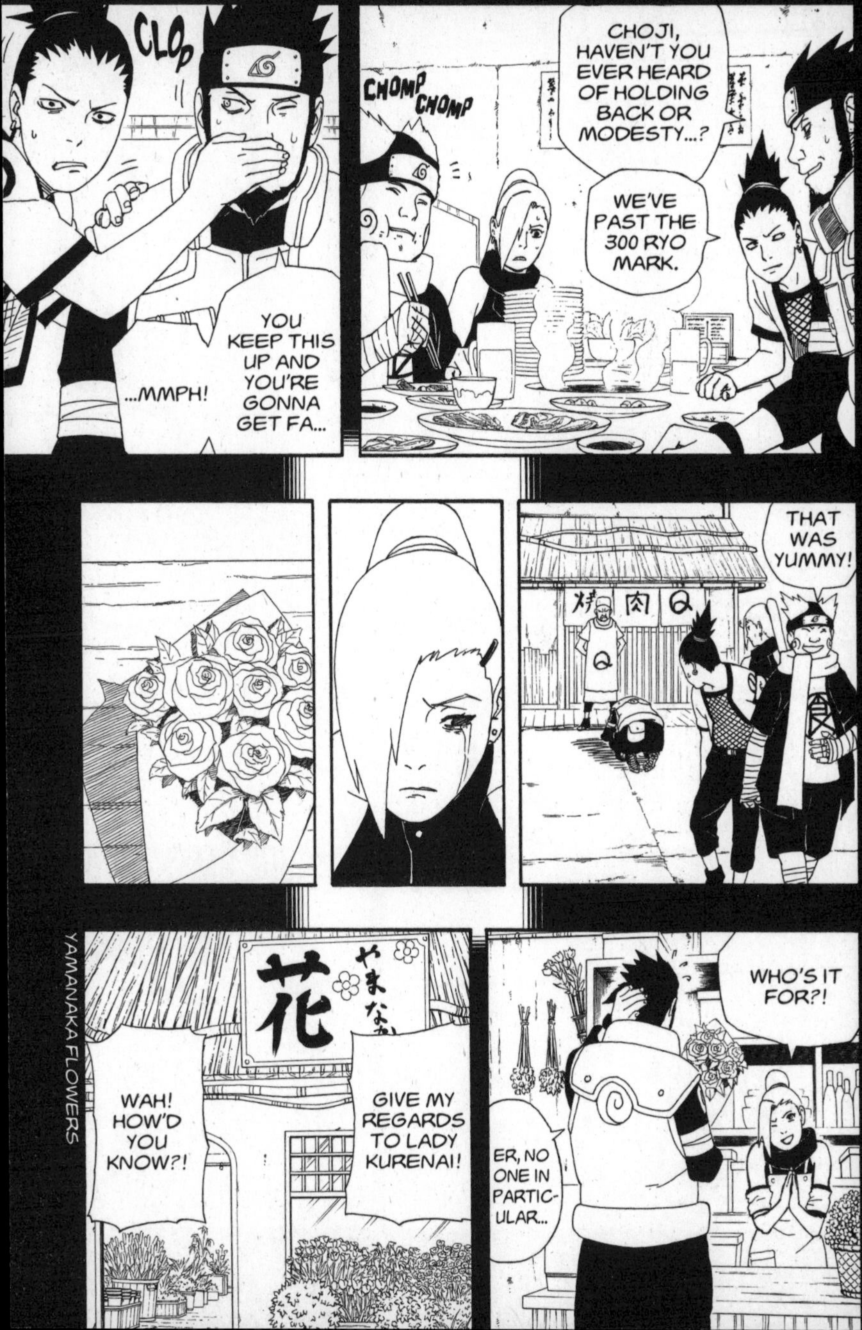
CHOJI, HAVEN'T YOU EVER HEARD OF HOLDING BACK OR MODESTY...?
WE'VE PAST THE 300 RYO MARK.
CHOMP CHOMP
CLOP
YOU KEEP THIS UP AND YOU'RE GONNA GET FA...
...MMPH!
THAT WAS YUMMY!
焼肉 Q
Q
WHO'S IT FOR?!
ER, NO ONE IN PARTICULAR...
花
YAMANAKA FLOWERS
GIVE MY REGARDS TO LADY KURENAI!
WAH! HOW'D YOU KNOW?!

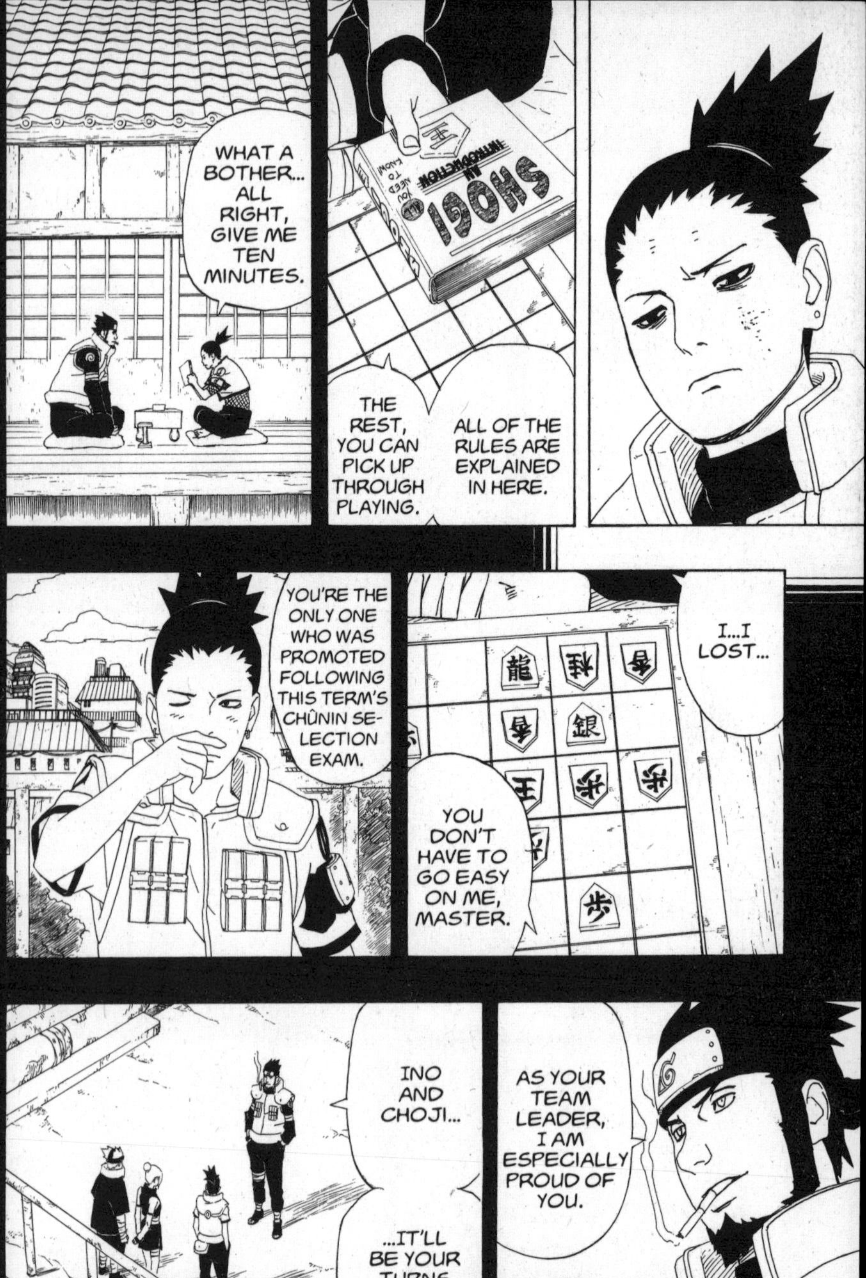
SHOGI
AN INTRODUCTION
ALL YOU NEED TO KNOW!
ALL OF THE RULES ARE EXPLAINED IN HERE.
THE REST, YOU CAN PICK UP THROUGH PLAYING.
WHAT A BOTHER... ALL RIGHT, GIVE ME TEN MINUTES.
I...I LOST...
YOU DON'T HAVE TO GO EASY ON ME, MASTER.
YOU'RE THE ONLY ONE WHO WAS PROMOTED FOLLOWING THIS TERM'S CHÛNIN SE-LECTION EXAM.
AS YOUR TEAM LEADER, I AM ESPECIALLY PROUD OF YOU.
INO AND CHOJI...
...IT'LL BE YOUR TURNS NEXT TIME.

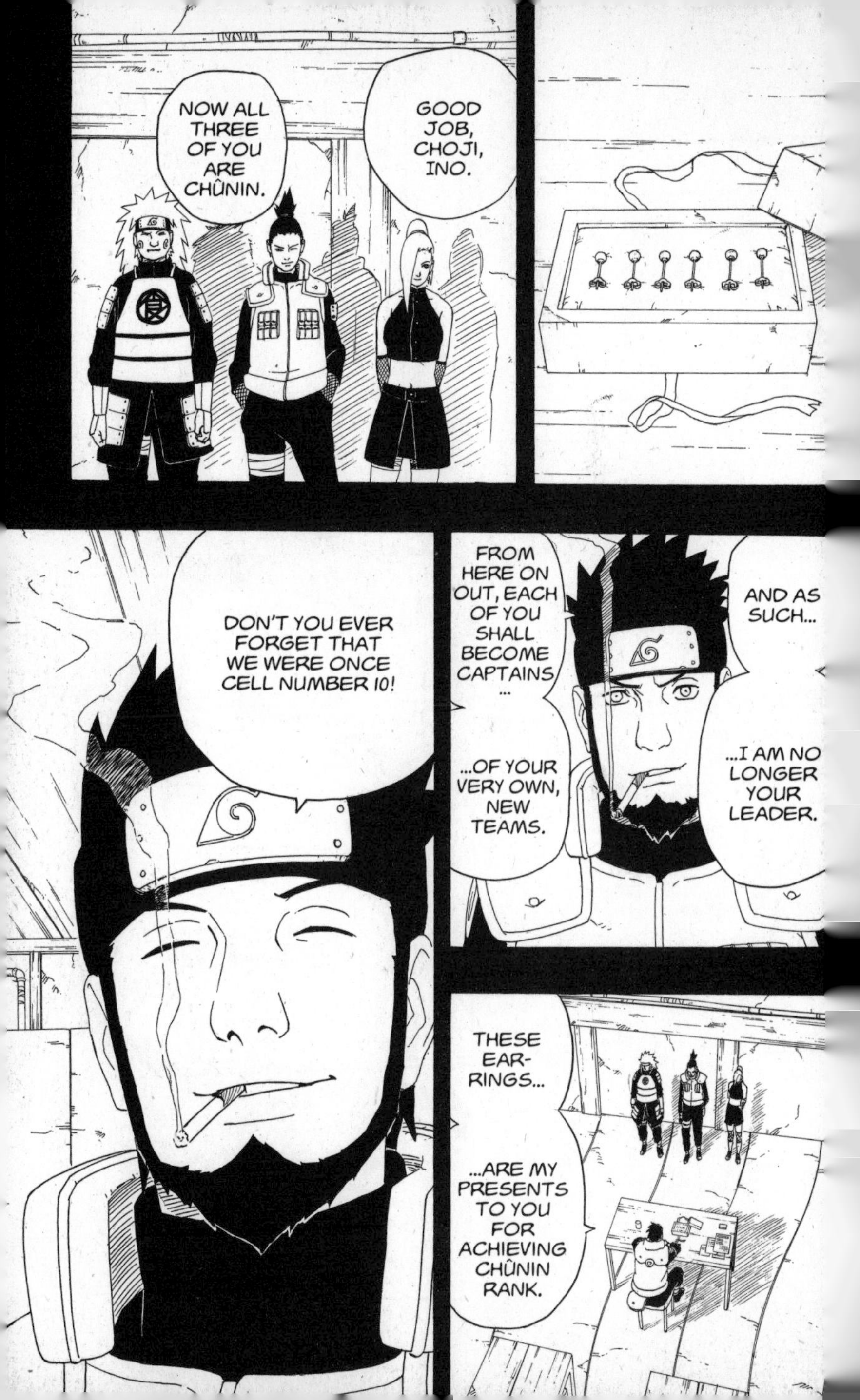
GOOD JOB, CHOJI, INO.
NOW ALL THREE OF YOU ARE CHÛNIN.
FROM HERE ON OUT, EACH OF YOU SHALL BECOME CAPTAINS...
...OF YOUR VERY OWN, NEW TEAMS.
AND AS SUCH...
...I AM NO LONGER YOUR LEADER.
THESE EAR-RINGS...
...ARE MY PRESENTS TO YOU FOR ACHIEVING CHÛNIN RANK.
DON'T YOU EVER FORGET THAT WE WERE ONCE CELL NUMBER 10!

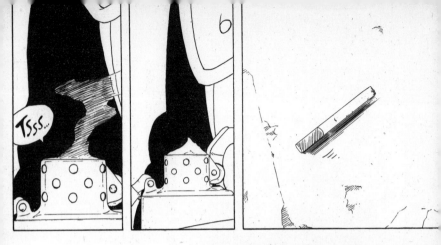

TSSS...

MASTER!!

164

READ THIS WAY

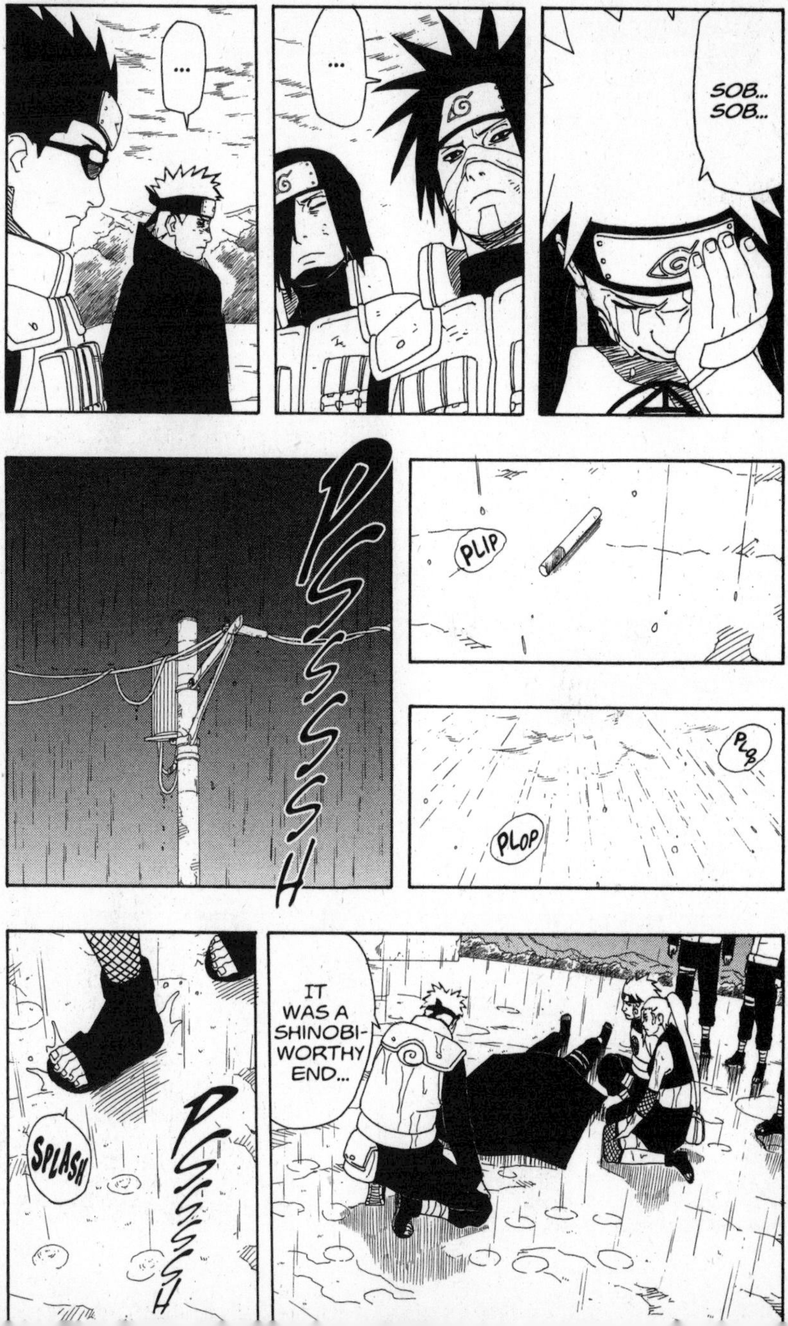
SOB... SOB...
...
...
PLIP
PLOP
PLOP
PSSSSSH
IT WAS A SHINOBI-WORTHY END...
SPLASH
PSSSSSH

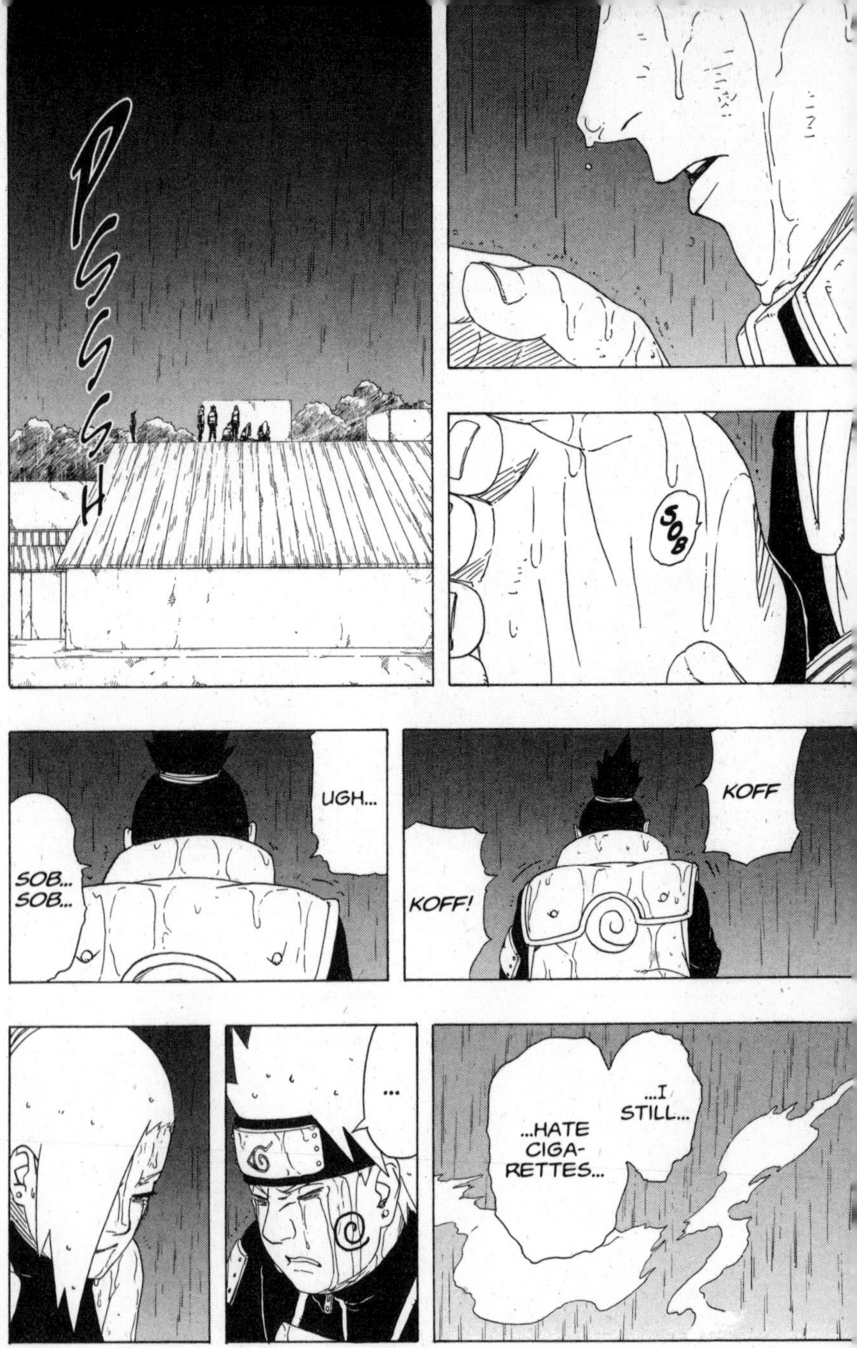
SOB
PSSSH
KOFF
KOFF!
UGH...
SOB... SOB...
...I STILL...
...HATE CIGA-RETTES...
...

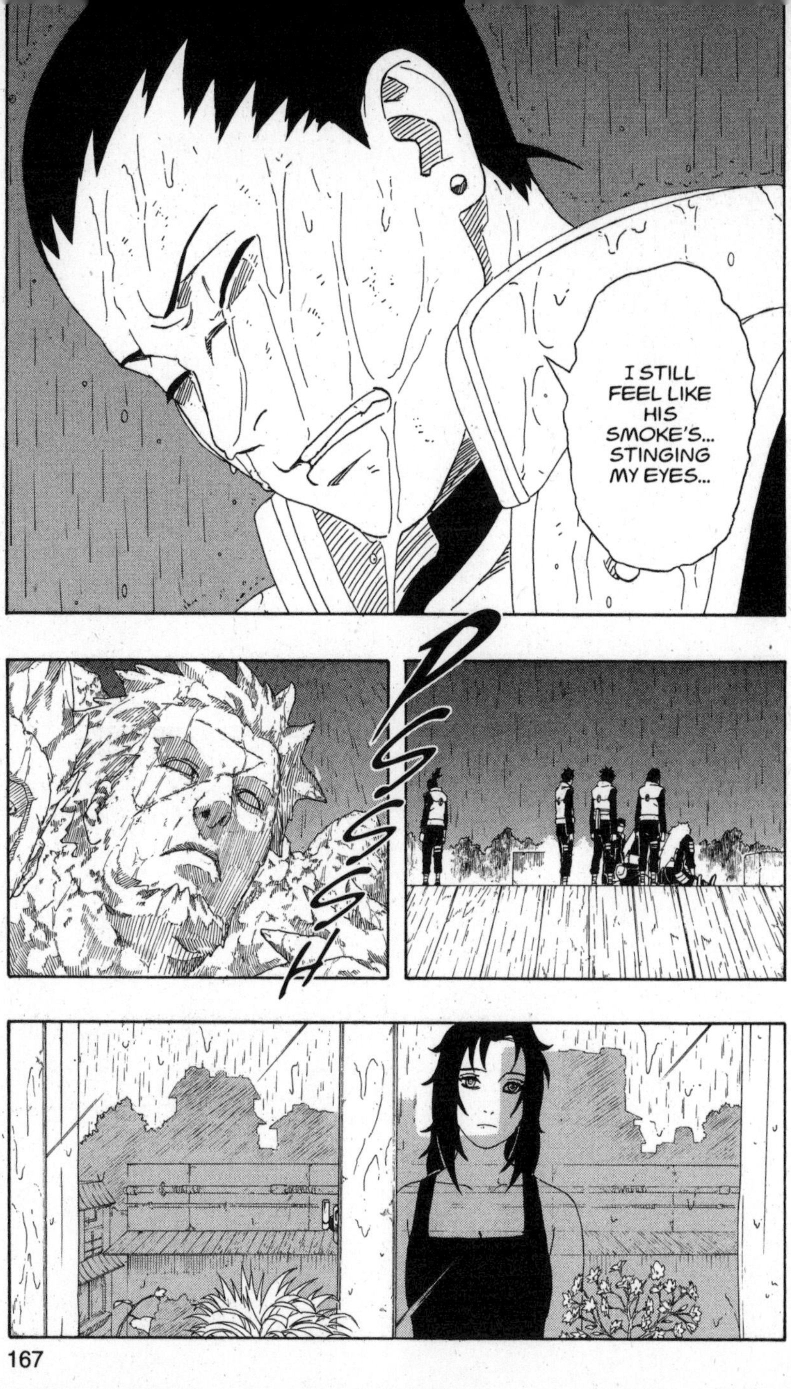
I STILL FEEL LIKE HIS SMOKE'S... STINGING MY EYES...
PSSSSH

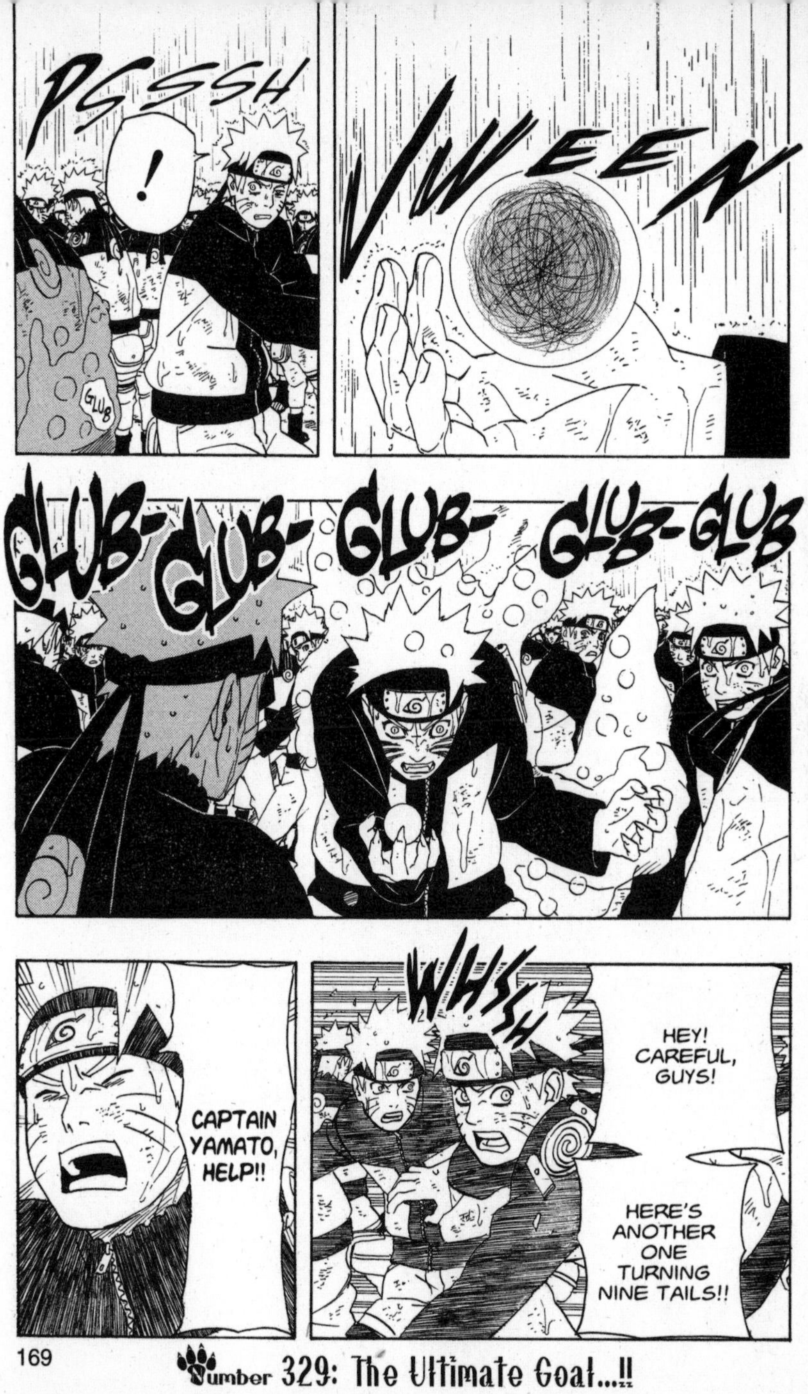
VWEEN
PSSSH
!
GLUB
GLUB-GLUB-GLUB-GLUB-GLUB
WHSSH
HEY! CAREFUL, GUYS!
HERE'S ANOTHER ONE TURNING NINE TAILS!!
CAPTAIN YAMATO, HELP!!

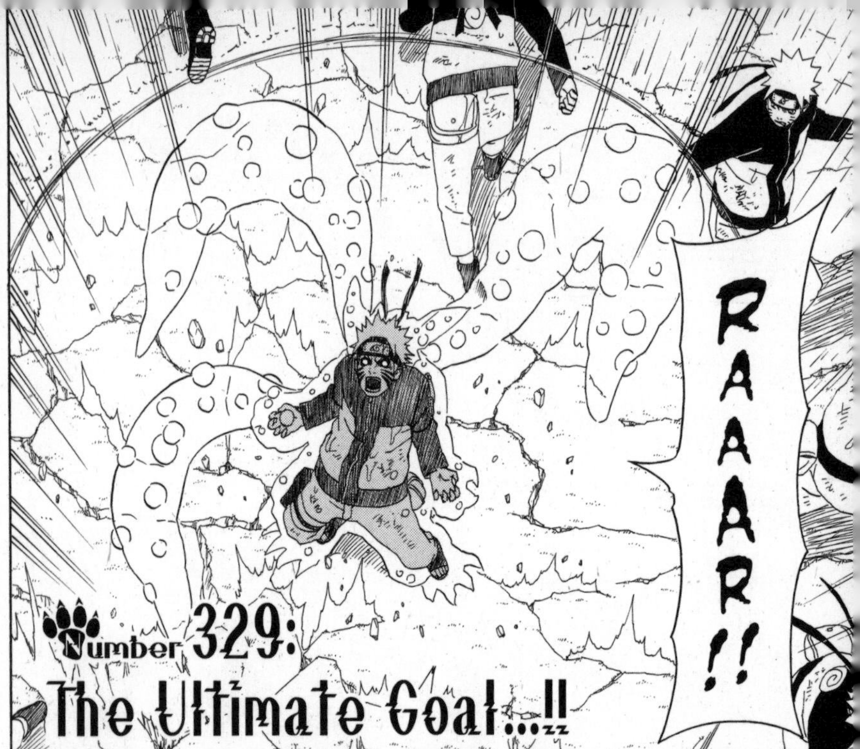
RAAAR!!

Number 329: The Ultimate Goal...!!

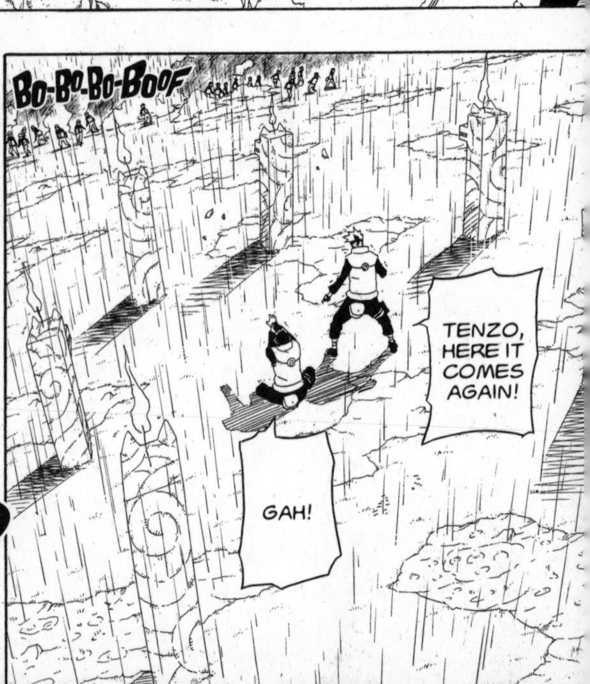
BO-BO-BO-BOOF
TENZO, HERE IT COMES AGAIN!
GAH!

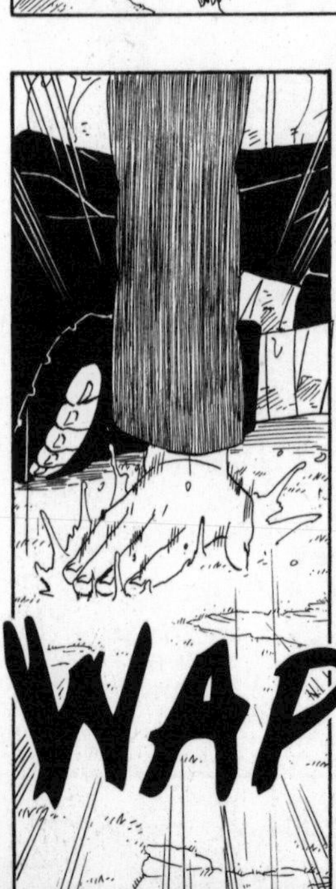
WAP

READ THIS WAY

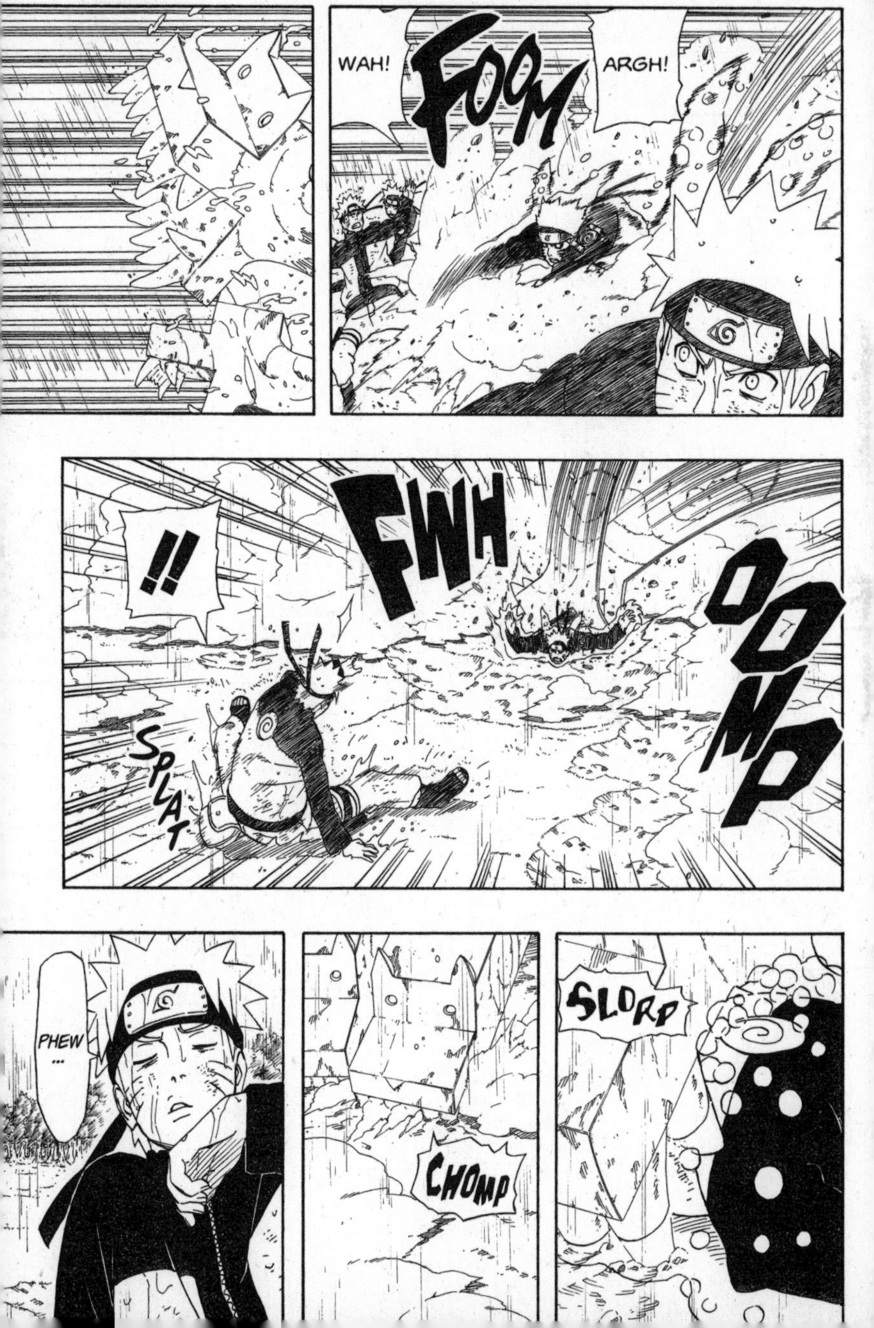
ARGH!
FOOM
WAH!
OOOMP
FWH
!!
SPLAT
SLORP
CHOMP
PHEW...

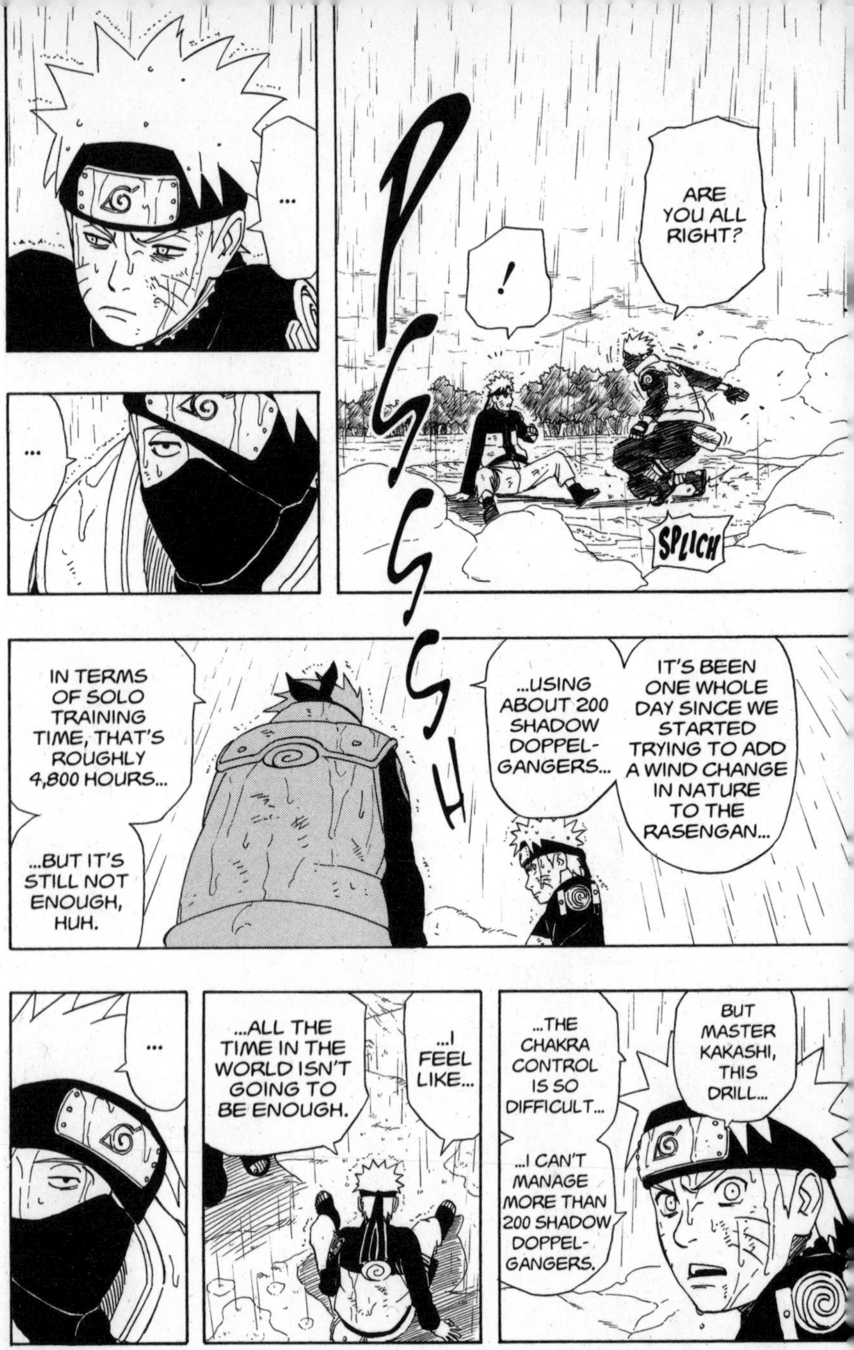
ARE YOU ALL RIGHT?
!
PSSSSH
SPLICH
...
...
IT'S BEEN ONE WHOLE DAY SINCE WE STARTED TRYING TO ADD A WIND CHANGE IN NATURE TO THE RASENGAN...
...USING ABOUT 200 SHADOW DOPPEL-GANGERS...
IN TERMS OF SOLO TRAINING TIME, THAT'S ROUGHLY 4,800 HOURS...
...BUT IT'S STILL NOT ENOUGH, HUH.
BUT MASTER KAKASHI, THIS DRILL...
...THE CHAKRA CONTROL IS SO DIFFICULT...
...I CAN'T MANAGE MORE THAN 200 SHADOW DOPPEL-GANGERS.
...I FEEL LIKE...
...ALL THE TIME IN THE WORLD ISN'T GOING TO BE ENOUGH.
...

READ THIS WAY

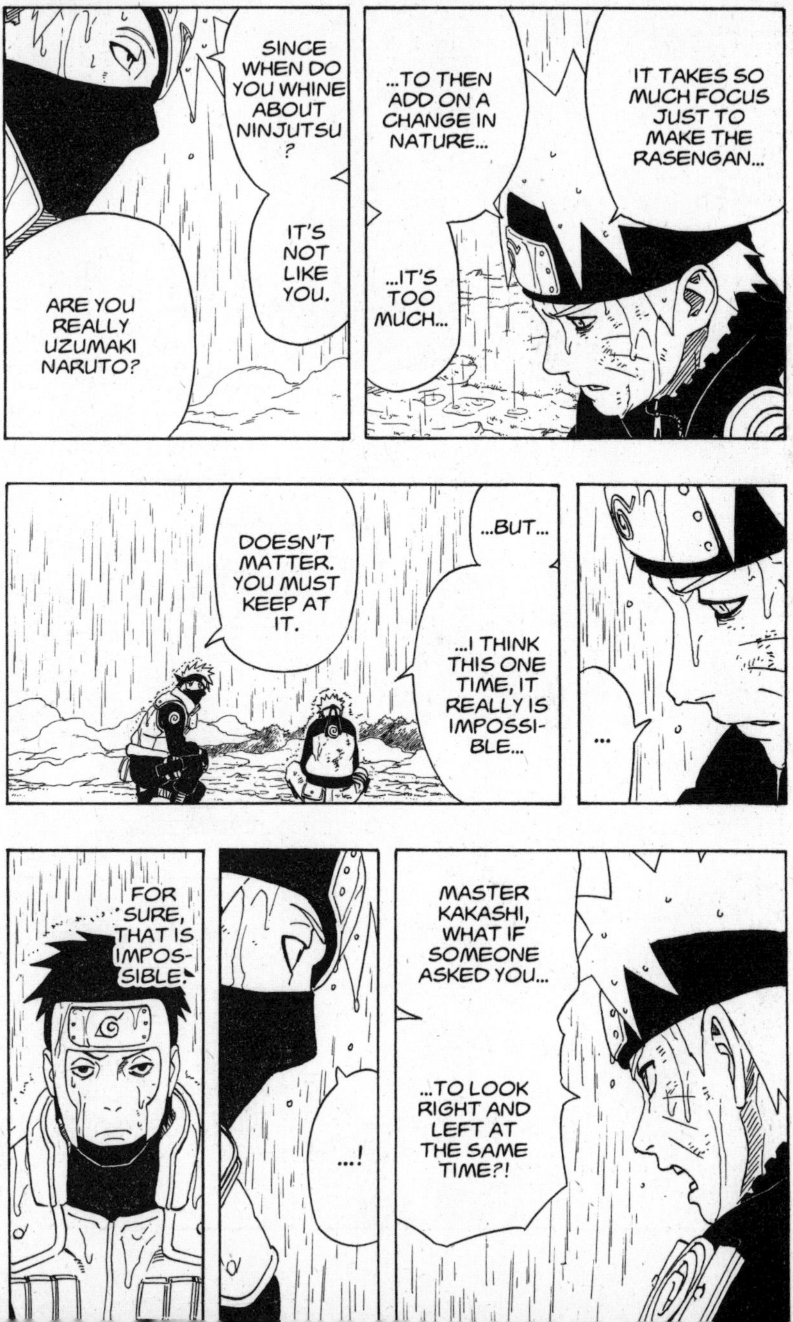
IT TAKES SO MUCH FOCUS JUST TO MAKE THE RASENGAN...
...TO THEN ADD ON A CHANGE IN NATURE...
...IT'S TOO MUCH...
SINCE WHEN DO YOU WHINE ABOUT NINJUTSU?
IT'S NOT LIKE YOU.
ARE YOU REALLY UZUMAKI NARUTO?
...
...BUT...
...I THINK THIS ONE TIME, IT REALLY IS IMPOSSIBLE...
DOESN'T MATTER. YOU MUST KEEP AT IT.
MASTER KAKASHI, WHAT IF SOMEONE ASKED YOU...
...TO LOOK RIGHT AND LEFT AT THE SAME TIME?!
...!
FOR SURE, THAT IS IMPOSSIBLE.

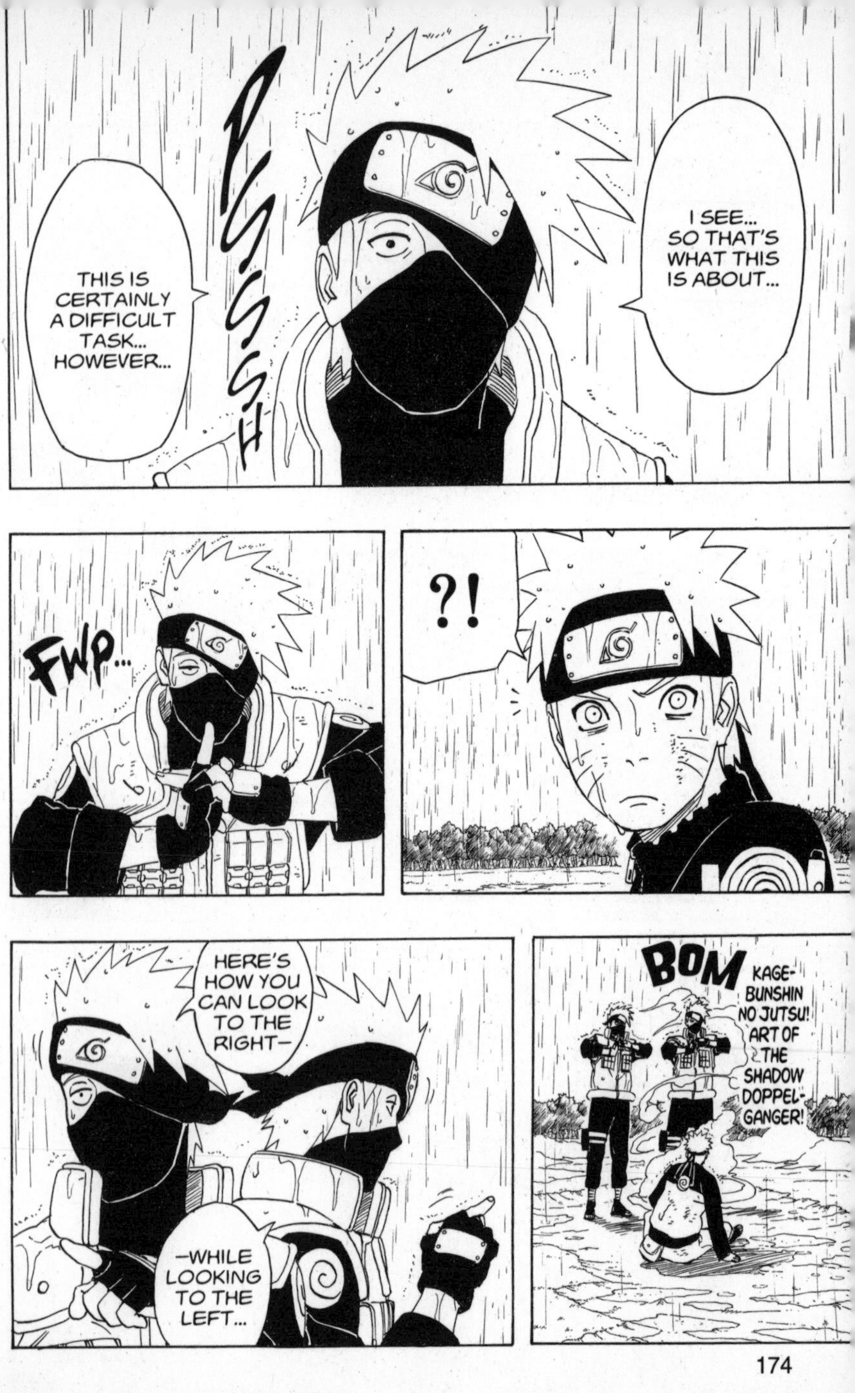
I SEE... SO THAT'S WHAT THIS IS ABOUT...
PSSSH
THIS IS CERTAINLY A DIFFICULT TASK... HOWEVER...
?!
FWP...
BOM
KAGE-BUNSHIN NO JUTSU! ART OF THE SHADOW DOPPELGANGER!
HERE'S HOW YOU CAN LOOK TO THE RIGHT—
—WHILE LOOKING TO THE LEFT...

READ THIS WAY

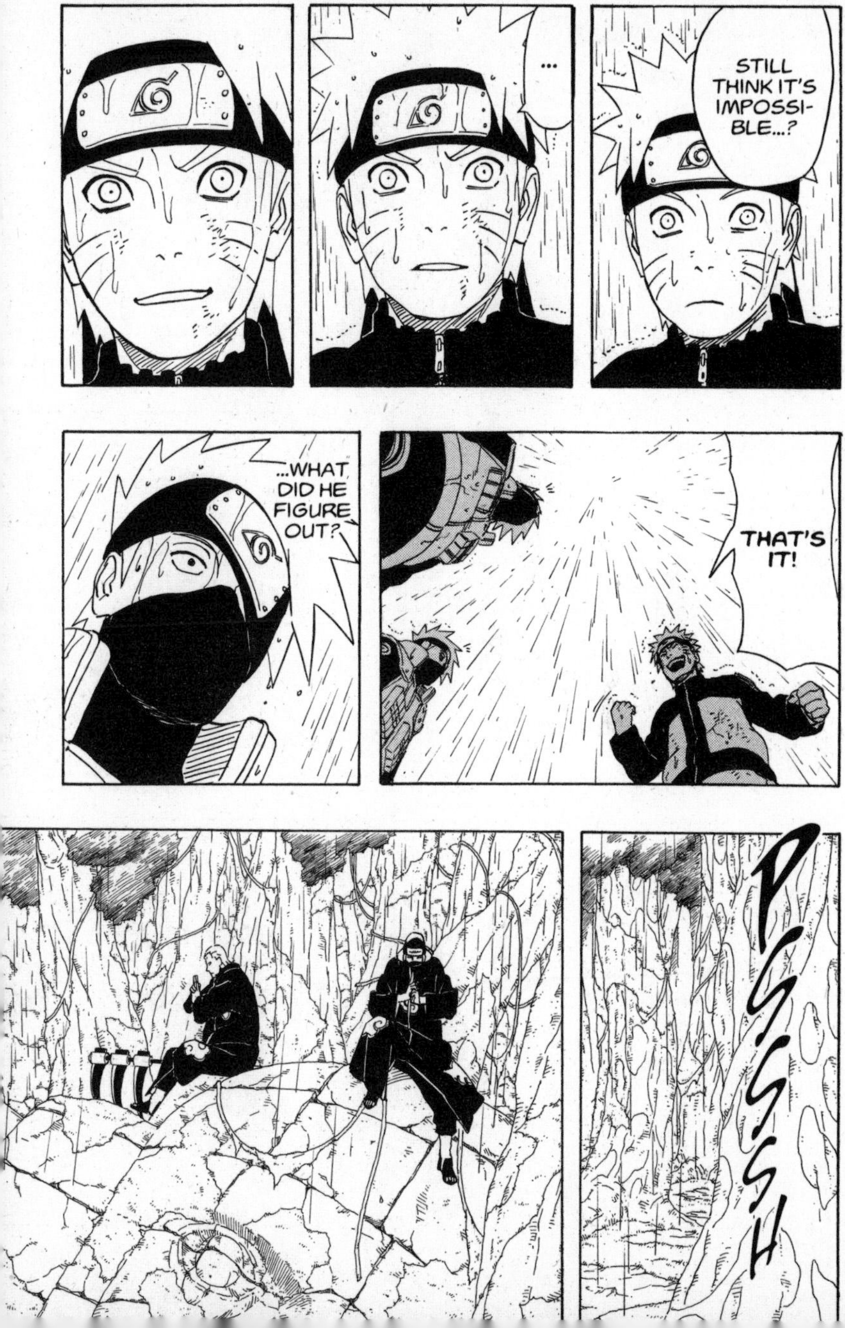
STILL THINK IT'S IMPOSSI-BLE...?
...
THAT'S IT!
...WHAT DID HE FIGURE OUT?
PSSSH

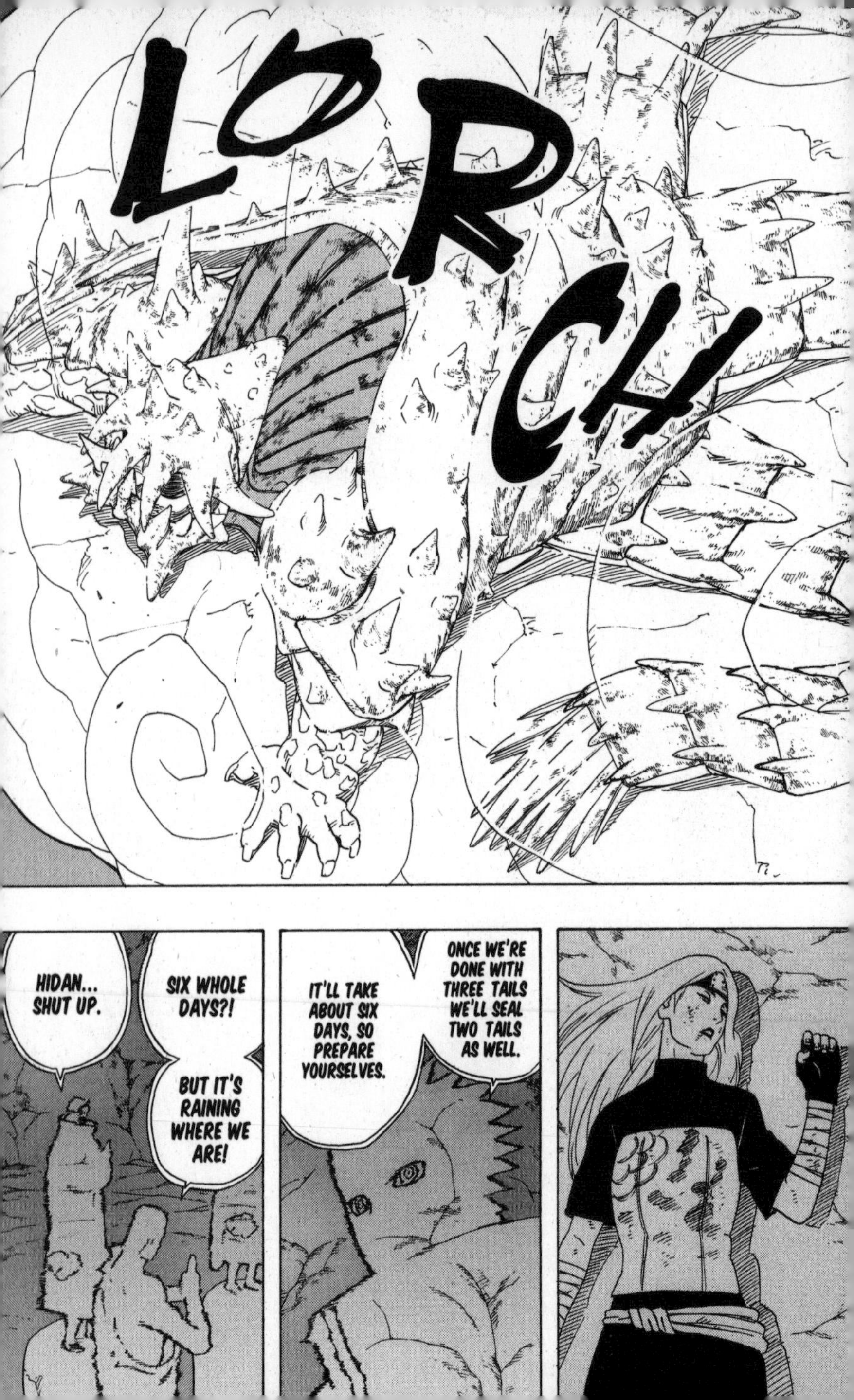
LORCH
ONCE WE'RE DONE WITH THREE TAILS WE'LL SEAL TWO TAILS AS WELL.
IT'LL TAKE ABOUT SIX DAYS, SO PREPARE YOURSELVES.
SIX WHOLE DAYS?!
BUT IT'S RAINING WHERE WE ARE!
HIDAN... SHUT UP.

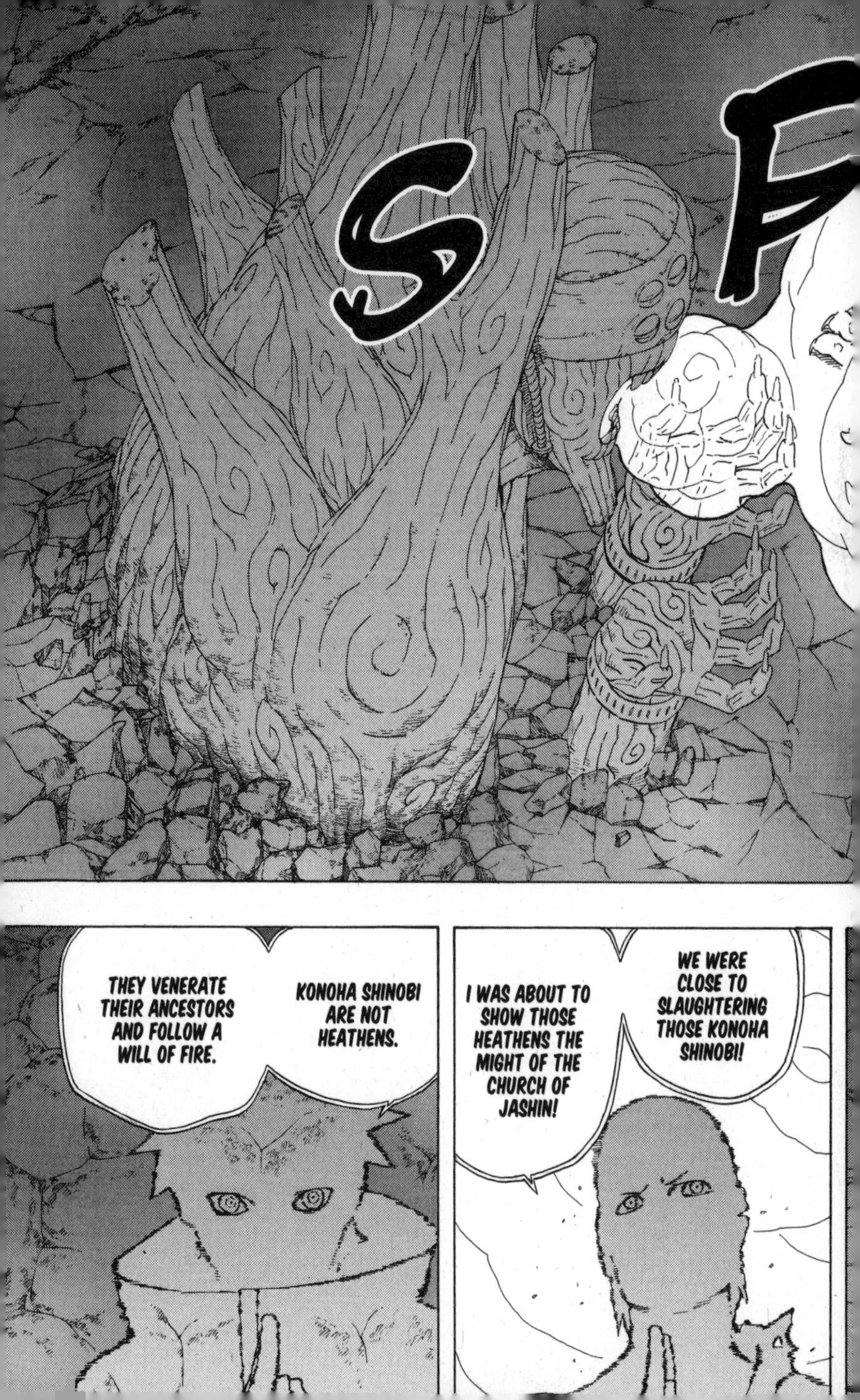
SF
WE WERE CLOSE TO SLAUGHTERING THOSE KONOHA SHINOBI!
I WAS ABOUT TO SHOW THOSE HEATHENS THE MIGHT OF THE CHURCH OF JASHIN!
KONOHA SHINOBI ARE NOT HEATHENS.
THEY VENERATE THEIR ANCESTORS AND FOLLOW A WILL OF FIRE.

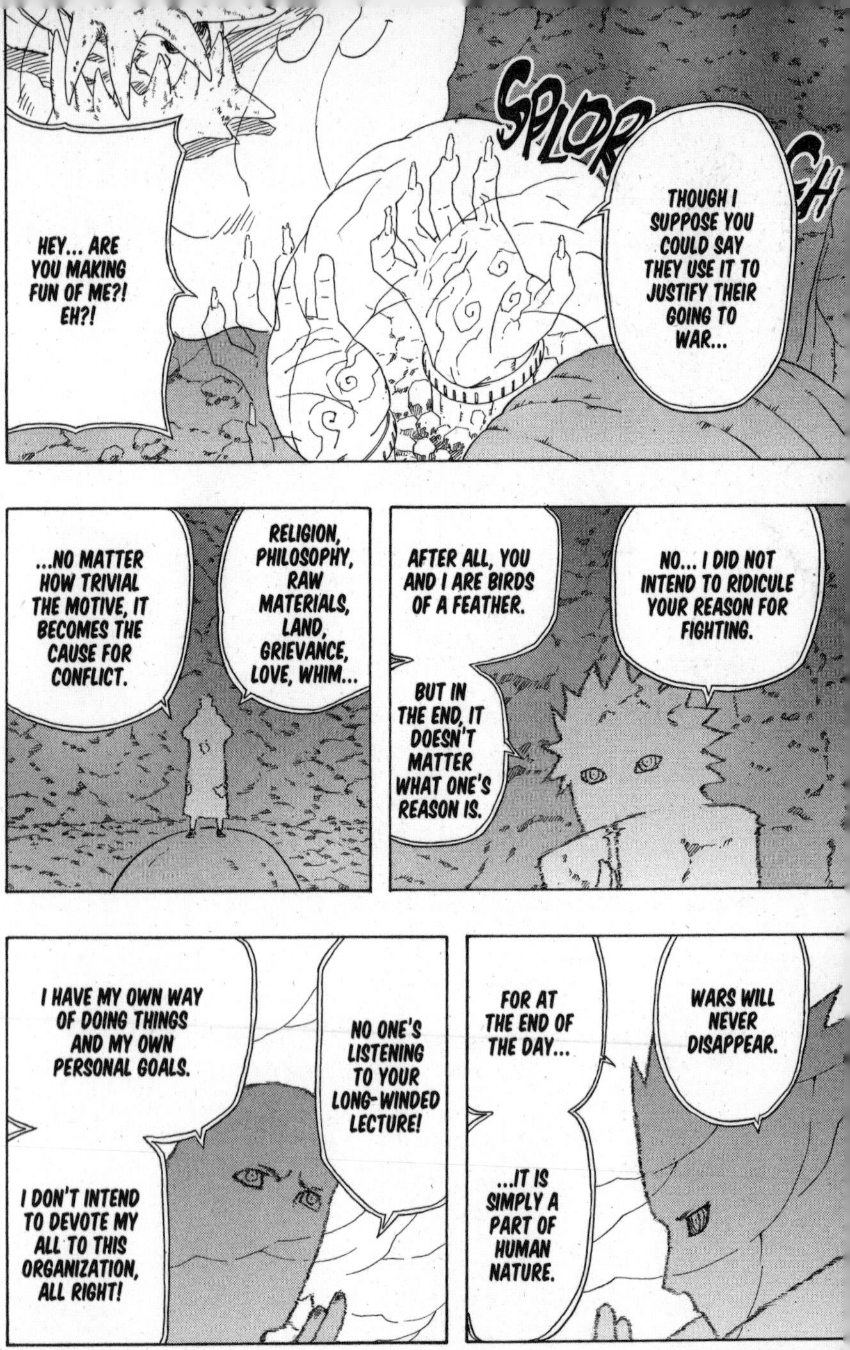
THOUGH I SUPPOSE YOU COULD SAY THEY USE IT TO JUSTIFY THEIR GOING TO WAR...
HEY... ARE YOU MAKING FUN OF ME?! EH?!
NO... I DID NOT INTEND TO RIDICULE YOUR REASON FOR FIGHTING.
AFTER ALL, YOU AND I ARE BIRDS OF A FEATHER.
BUT IN THE END, IT DOESN'T MATTER WHAT ONE'S REASON IS.
RELIGION, PHILOSOPHY, RAW MATERIALS, LAND, GRIEVANCE, LOVE, WHIM...
...NO MATTER HOW TRIVIAL THE MOTIVE, IT BECOMES THE CAUSE FOR CONFLICT.
WARS WILL NEVER DISAPPEAR.
FOR AT THE END OF THE DAY...
...IT IS SIMPLY A PART OF HUMAN NATURE.
NO ONE'S LISTENING TO YOUR LONG-WINDED LECTURE!
I HAVE MY OWN WAY OF DOING THINGS AND MY OWN PERSONAL GOALS.
I DON'T INTEND TO DEVOTE MY ALL TO THIS ORGANIZATION, ALL RIGHT!

READ THIS WAY

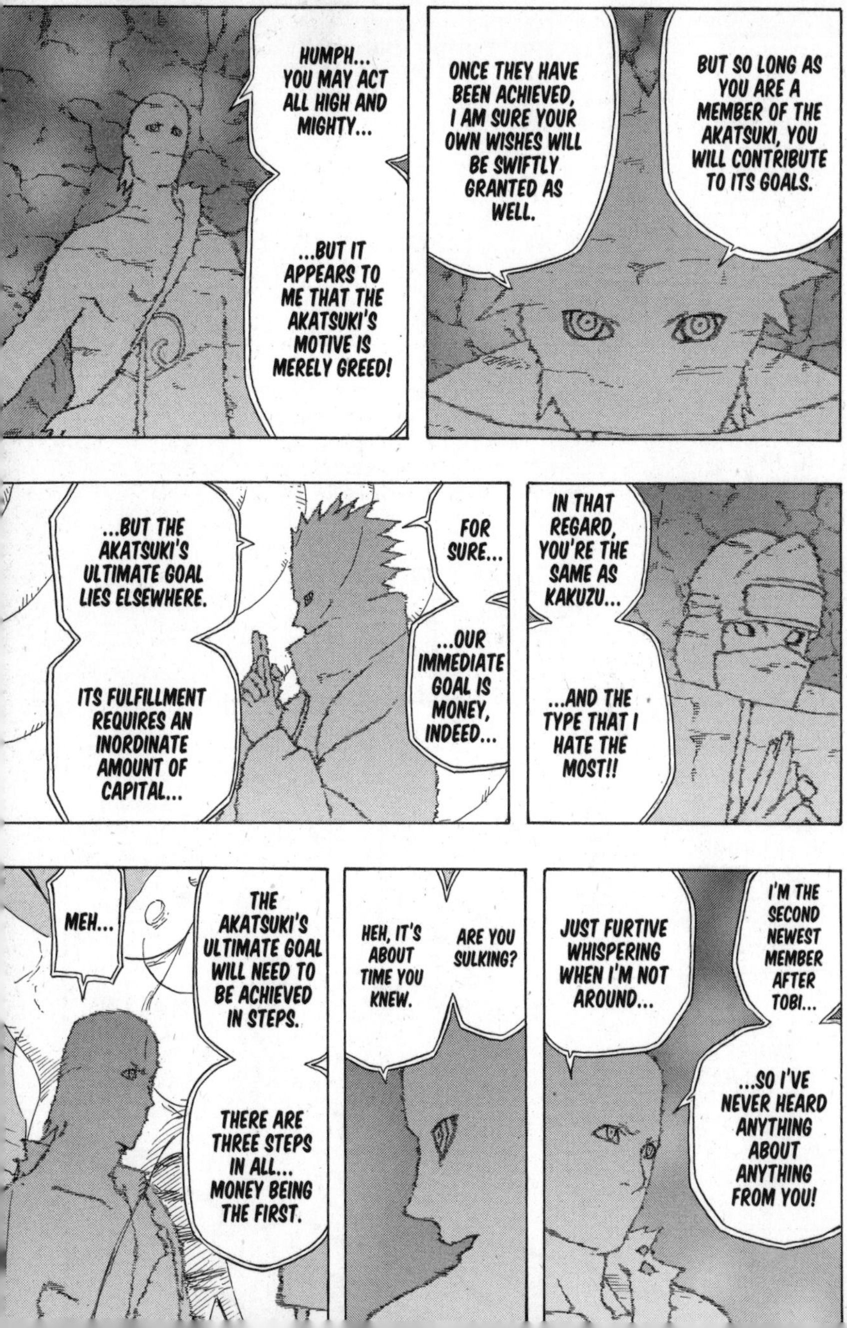
BUT SO LONG AS YOU ARE A MEMBER OF THE AKATSUKI, YOU WILL CONTRIBUTE TO ITS GOALS.
ONCE THEY HAVE BEEN ACHIEVED, I AM SURE YOUR OWN WISHES WILL BE SWIFTLY GRANTED AS WELL.
HUMPH... YOU MAY ACT ALL HIGH AND MIGHTY...
...BUT IT APPEARS TO ME THAT THE AKATSUKI'S MOTIVE IS MERELY GREED!
IN THAT REGARD, YOU'RE THE SAME AS KAKUZU...
...AND THE TYPE THAT I HATE THE MOST!!
FOR SURE...
...OUR IMMEDIATE GOAL IS MONEY, INDEED...
...BUT THE AKATSUKI'S ULTIMATE GOAL LIES ELSEWHERE.
ITS FULFILLMENT REQUIRES AN INORDINATE AMOUNT OF CAPITAL...
I'M THE SECOND NEWEST MEMBER AFTER TOBI...
JUST FURTIVE WHISPERING WHEN I'M NOT AROUND...
...SO I'VE NEVER HEARD ANYTHING ABOUT ANYTHING FROM YOU!
ARE YOU SULKING?
HEH, IT'S ABOUT TIME YOU KNEW.
THE AKATSUKI'S ULTIMATE GOAL WILL NEED TO BE ACHIEVED IN STEPS.
MEH...
THERE ARE THREE STEPS IN ALL... MONEY BEING THE FIRST.

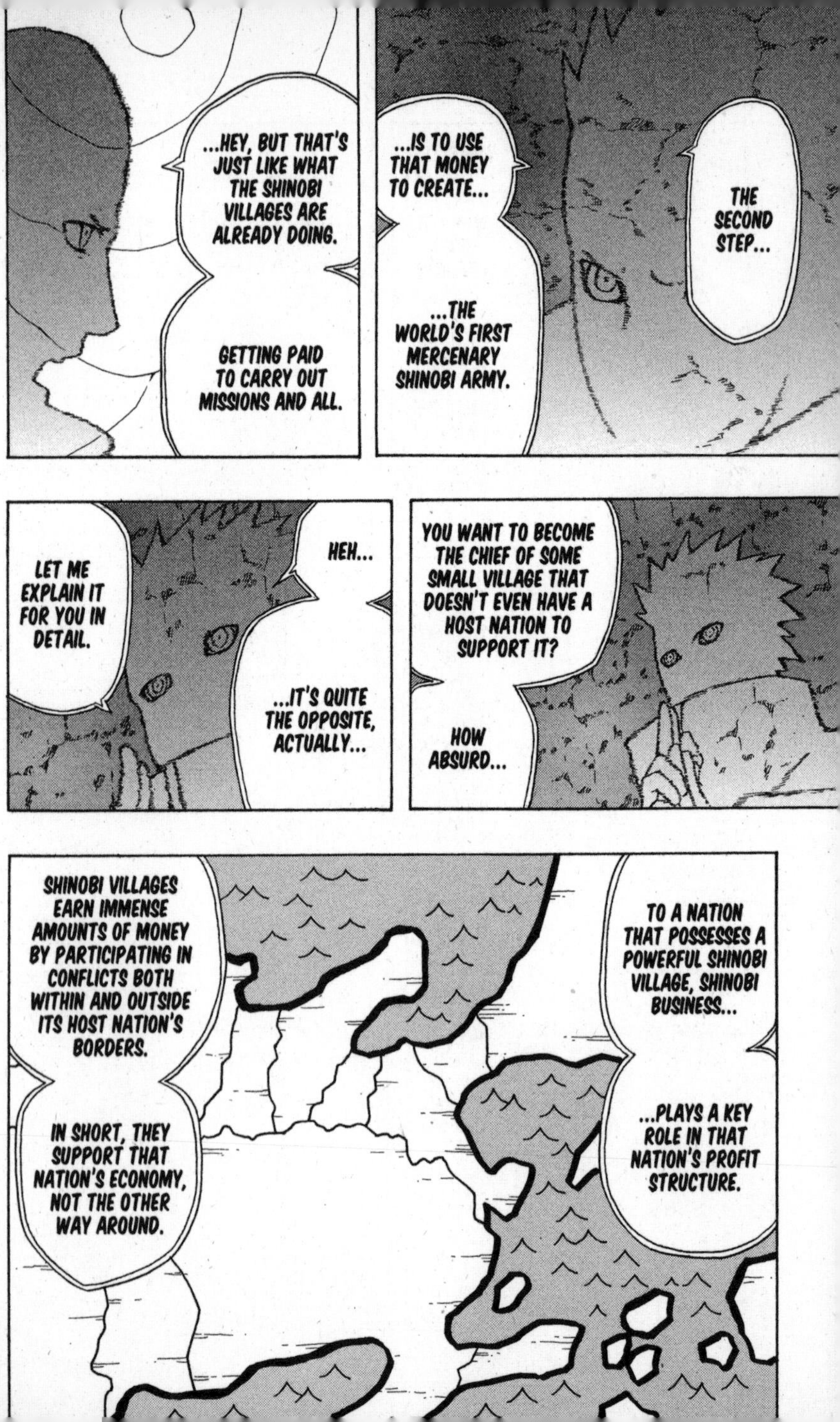
THE SECOND STEP...
...IS TO USE THAT MONEY TO CREATE...
...THE WORLD'S FIRST MERCENARY SHINOBI ARMY.
...HEY, BUT THAT'S JUST LIKE WHAT THE SHINOBI VILLAGES ARE ALREADY DOING.
GETTING PAID TO CARRY OUT MISSIONS AND ALL.
YOU WANT TO BECOME THE CHIEF OF SOME SMALL VILLAGE THAT DOESN'T EVEN HAVE A HOST NATION TO SUPPORT IT?
HOW ABSURD...
HEH...
...IT'S QUITE THE OPPOSITE, ACTUALLY...
LET ME EXPLAIN IT FOR YOU IN DETAIL.
TO A NATION THAT POSSESSES A POWERFUL SHINOBI VILLAGE, SHINOBI BUSINESS...
...PLAYS A KEY ROLE IN THAT NATION'S PROFIT STRUCTURE.
SHINOBI VILLAGES EARN IMMENSE AMOUNTS OF MONEY BY PARTICIPATING IN CONFLICTS BOTH WITHIN AND OUTSIDE ITS HOST NATION'S BORDERS.
IN SHORT, THEY SUPPORT THAT NATION'S ECONOMY, NOT THE OTHER WAY AROUND.

READ THIS WAY

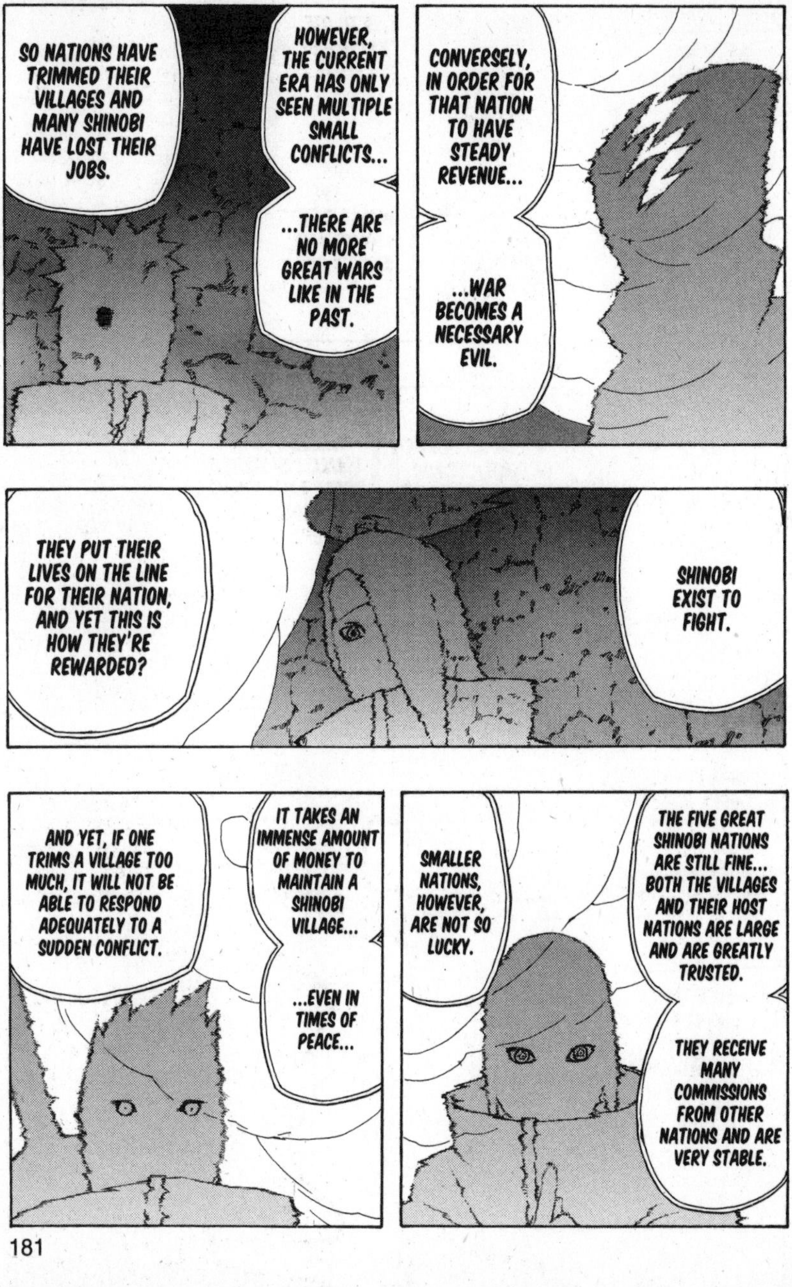
CONVERSELY, IN ORDER FOR THAT NATION TO HAVE STEADY REVENUE...
...WAR BECOMES A NECESSARY EVIL.
HOWEVER, THE CURRENT ERA HAS ONLY SEEN MULTIPLE SMALL CONFLICTS...
...THERE ARE NO MORE GREAT WARS LIKE IN THE PAST.
SO NATIONS HAVE TRIMMED THEIR VILLAGES AND MANY SHINOBI HAVE LOST THEIR JOBS.
SHINOBI EXIST TO FIGHT.
THEY PUT THEIR LIVES ON THE LINE FOR THEIR NATION, AND YET THIS IS HOW THEY'RE REWARDED?
THE FIVE GREAT SHINOBI NATIONS ARE STILL FINE... BOTH THE VILLAGES AND THEIR HOST NATIONS ARE LARGE AND ARE GREATLY TRUSTED.
THEY RECEIVE MANY COMMISSIONS FROM OTHER NATIONS AND ARE VERY STABLE.
SMALLER NATIONS, HOWEVER, ARE NOT SO LUCKY.
IT TAKES AN IMMENSE AMOUNT OF MONEY TO MAINTAIN A SHINOBI VILLAGE...
...EVEN IN TIMES OF PEACE...
AND YET, IF ONE TRIMS A VILLAGE TOO MUCH, IT WILL NOT BE ABLE TO RESPOND ADEQUATELY TO A SUDDEN CONFLICT.

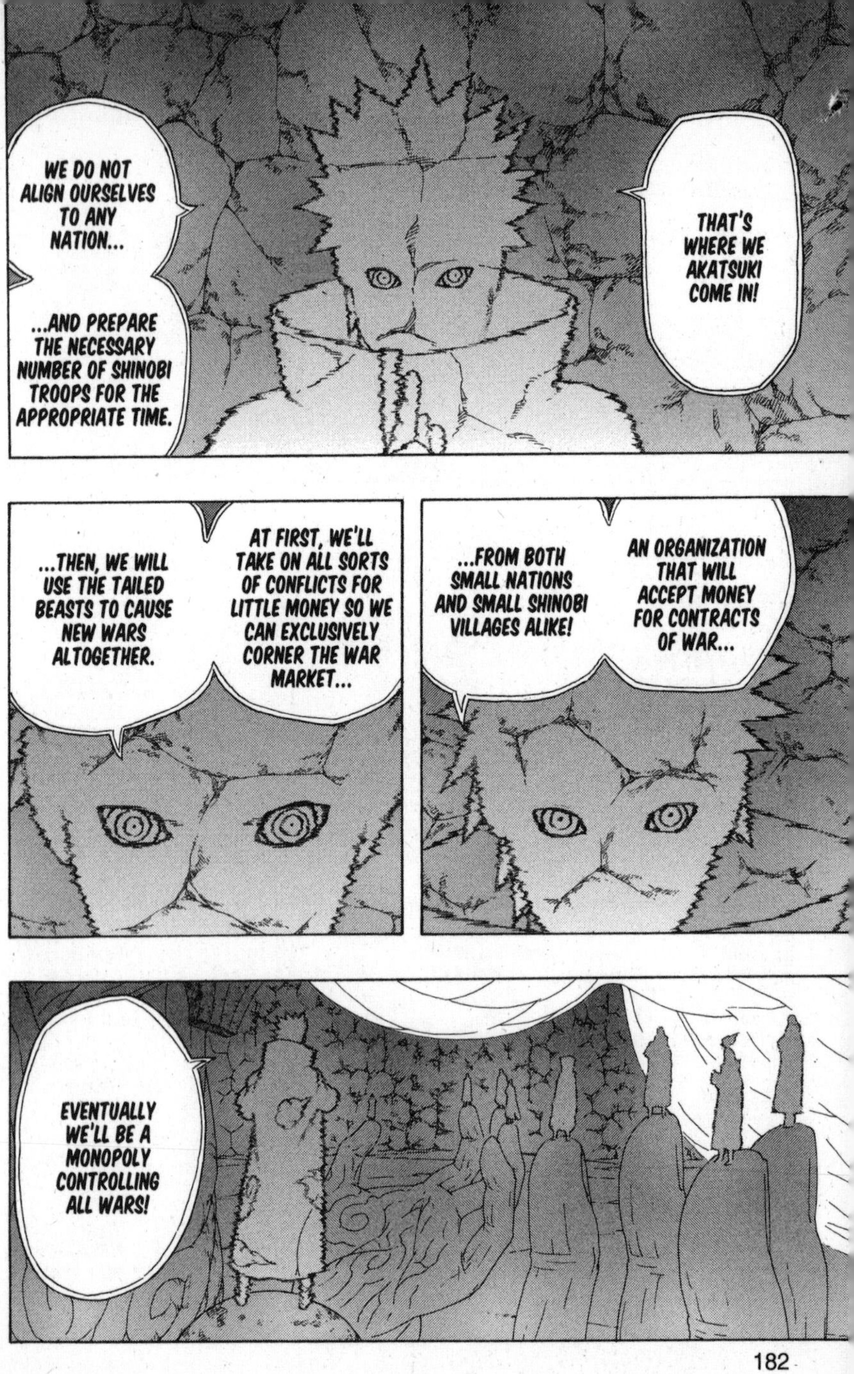
THAT'S WHERE WE AKATSUKI COME IN!
WE DO NOT ALIGN OURSELVES TO ANY NATION...
...AND PREPARE THE NECESSARY NUMBER OF SHINOBI TROOPS FOR THE APPROPRIATE TIME.
AN ORGANIZATION THAT WILL ACCEPT MONEY FOR CONTRACTS OF WAR...
...FROM BOTH SMALL NATIONS AND SMALL SHINOBI VILLAGES ALIKE!
AT FIRST, WE'LL TAKE ON ALL SORTS OF CONFLICTS FOR LITTLE MONEY SO WE CAN EXCLUSIVELY CORNER THE WAR MARKET...
...THEN, WE WILL USE THE TAILED BEASTS TO CAUSE NEW WARS ALTOGETHER.
EVENTUALLY WE'LL BE A MONOPOLY CONTROLLING ALL WARS!

READ THIS WAY

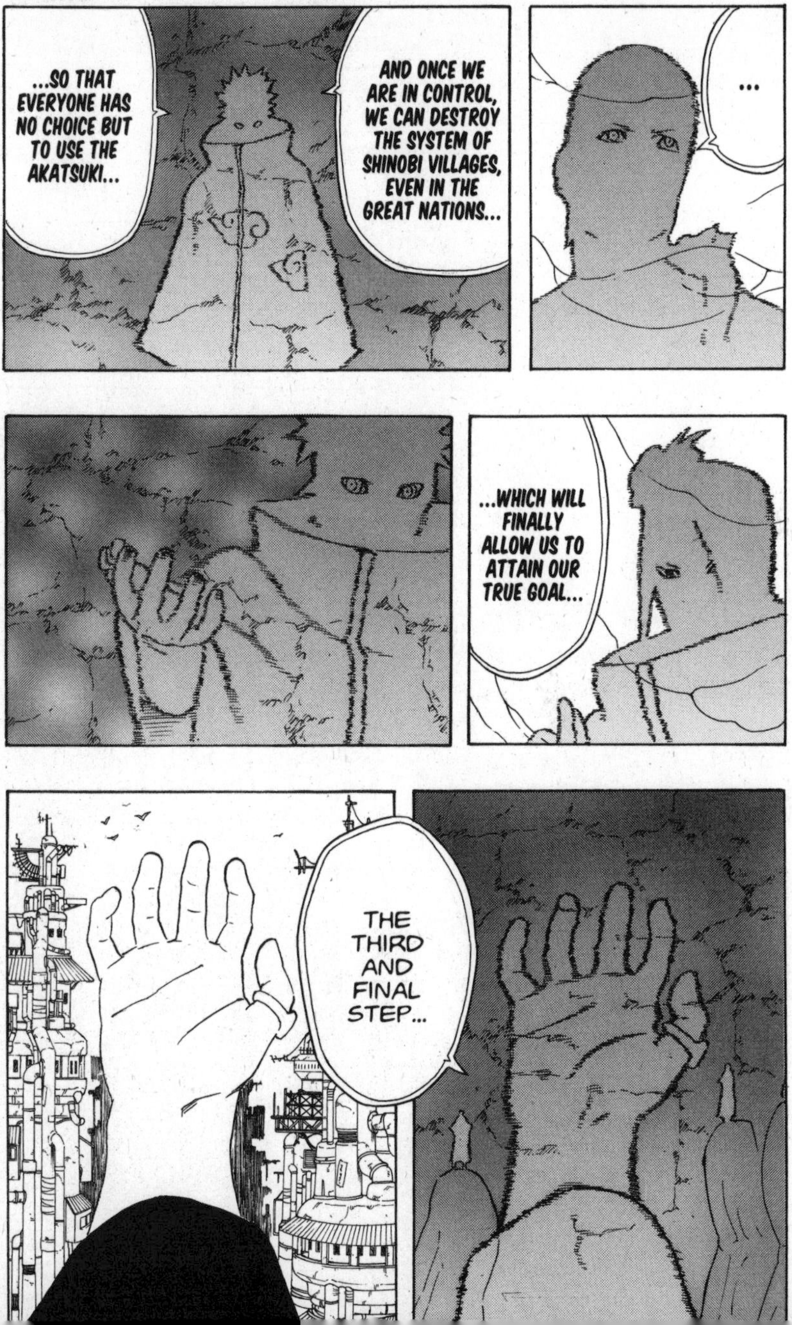
...
...SO THAT EVERYONE HAS NO CHOICE BUT TO USE THE AKATSUKI...
AND ONCE WE ARE IN CONTROL, WE CAN DESTROY THE SYSTEM OF SHINOBI VILLAGES, EVEN IN THE GREAT NATIONS...
...WHICH WILL FINALLY ALLOW US TO ATTAIN OUR TRUE GOAL...
THE THIRD AND FINAL STEP...

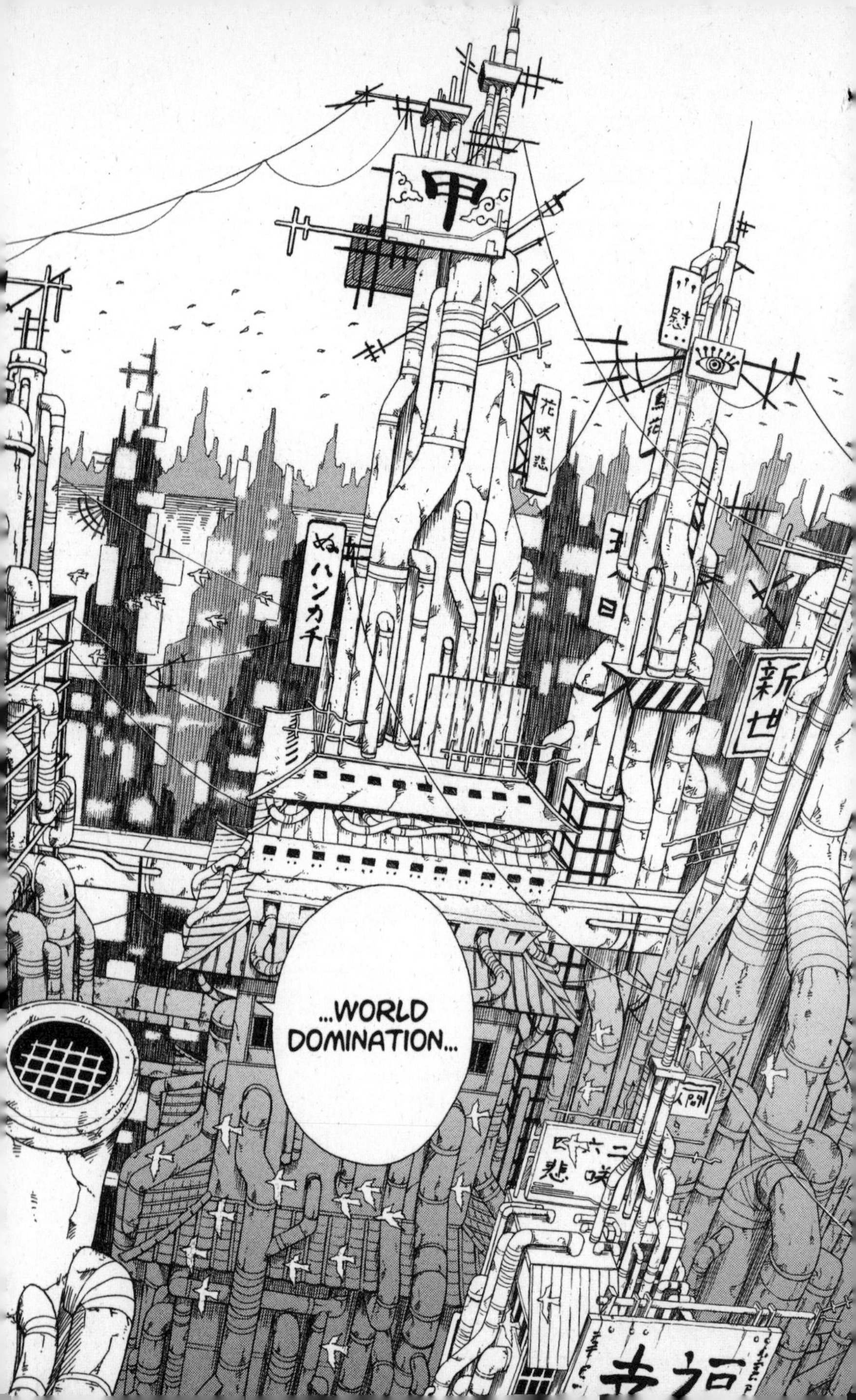
甲
新世
花咲悲
ぬハンカチ
...WORLD DOMINATION...

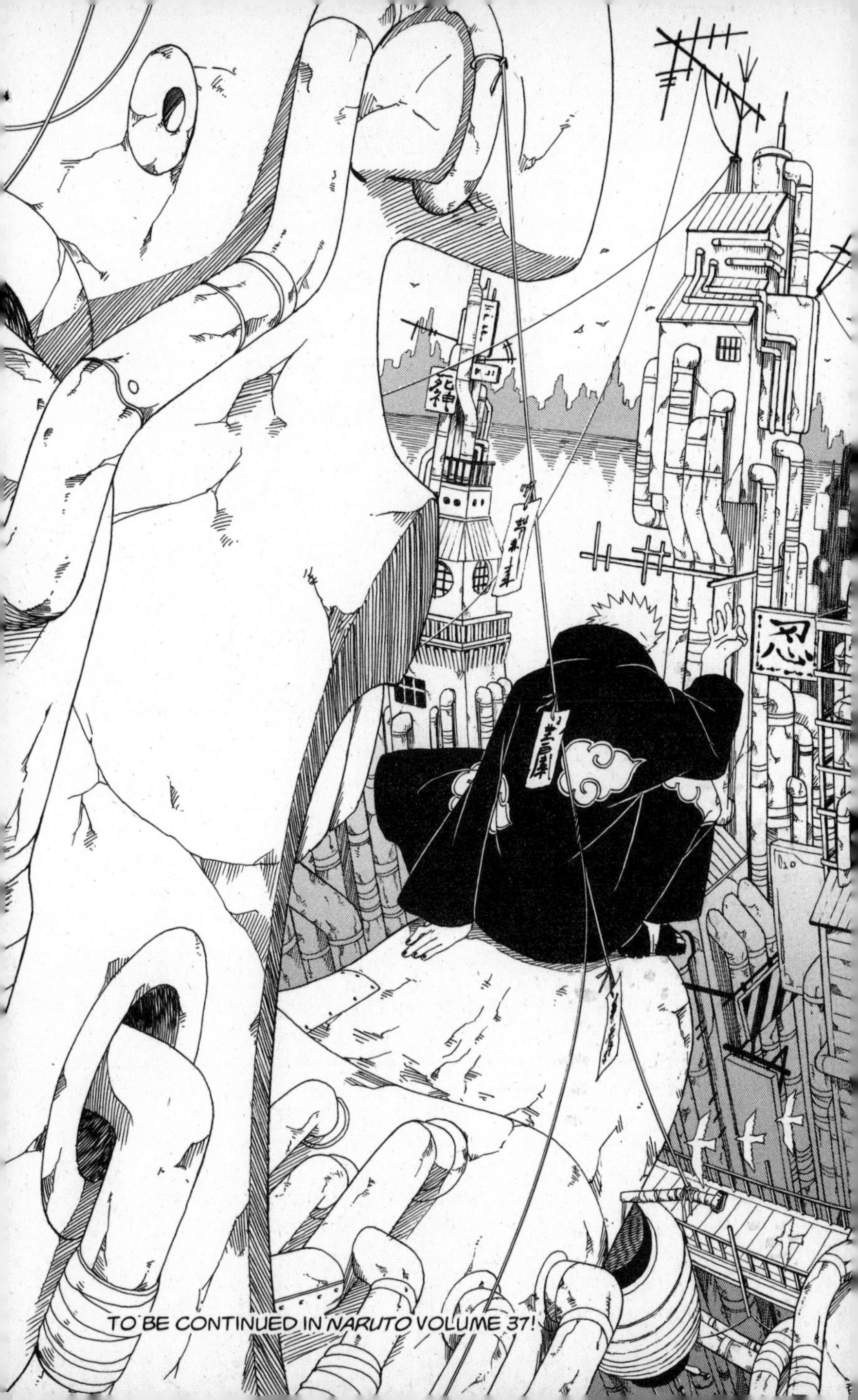
死神
忍
TO BE CONTINUED IN *NARUTO* VOLUME 37!

IN THE NEXT VOLUME...

SHIKAMARU'S BATTLE

Shikamaru's team is out for revenge against their mentor's murderers. Tsunade tries to stop them, but Kakashi wants to help! As the divide among the ninja grows, the mysterious Akatsuki organization continues their brutal attack on the tailed spirits, the Biju, and the young ninja who host them, including Naruto! He's older and stronger, but has Naruto trained enough?!

AVAILABLE NOW!

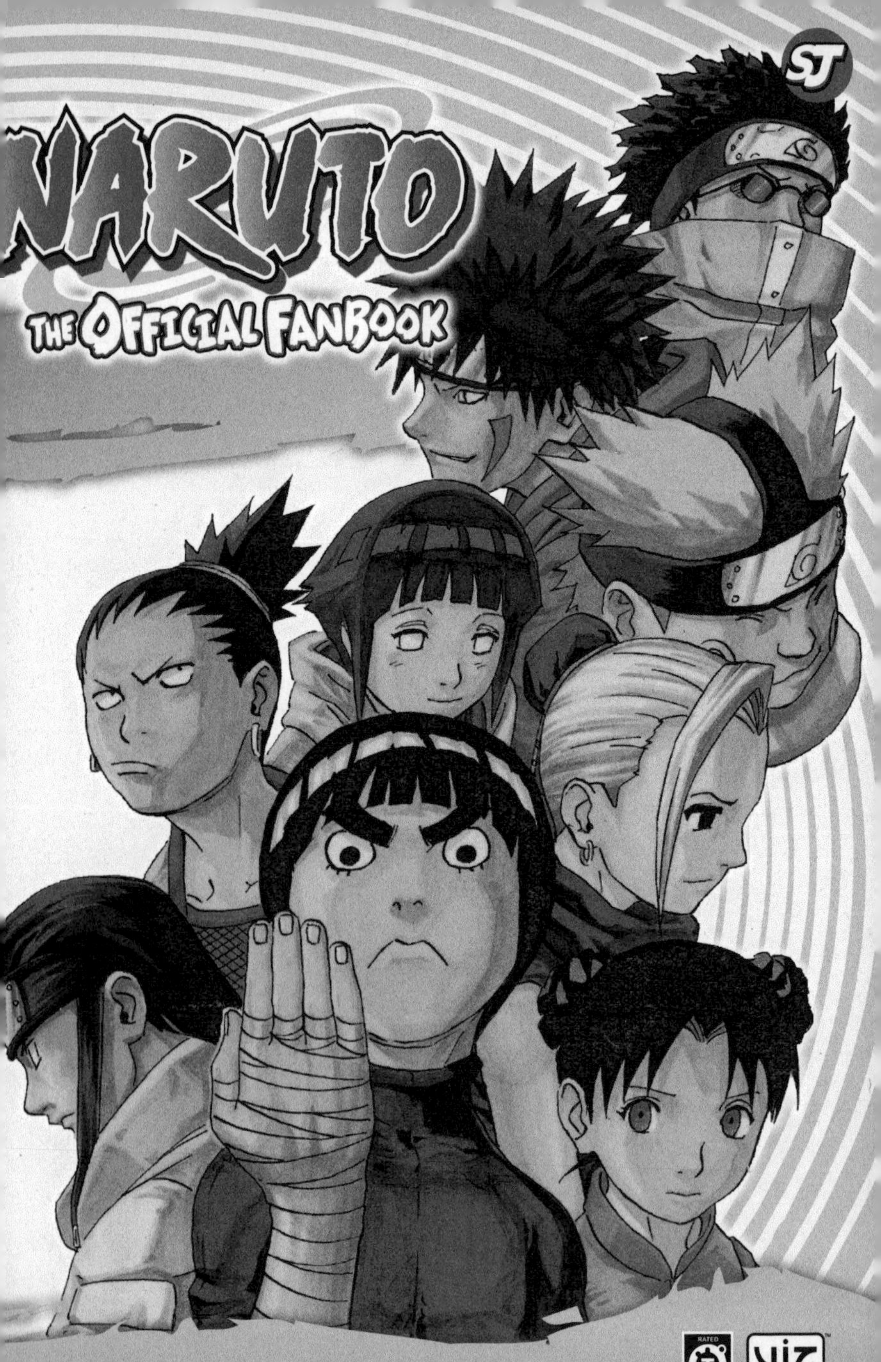
SJ
NARUTO
THE OFFICIAL FANBOOK
RATED T FOR TEEN
ratings.viz.com
VIZ media
www.viz.com

Tell us what you think about SHONEN JUMP manga!

Our survey is now available online.
Go to: www.SHONENJUMP.com/mangasurvey

Help us make our product offering better!

THE REAL ACTION STARTS IN...

SHONEN JUMP
THE WORLD'S MOST POPULAR MANGA
www.shonenjump.com

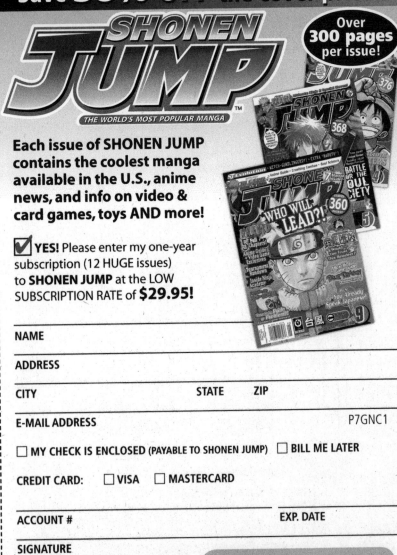